D1563906

Tacitus
in Renaissance Political Thought

Kenneth C. Schellhase

Tacitus
in Renaissance Political Thought

The University of Chicago Press
Chicago and London

The University of Chicago Press, Chicago 60637
The University of Chicago Press, Ltd., London

Printed in the United States of America
81 80 79 78 77 76   987654321

KENNETH C. SCHELLHASE is Associate Professor of History at Northern Michigan University.

Library of Congress Cataloging in Publication Data

Schellhase, Kenneth C
Tacitus in Renaissance political thought.

Bibliography: p.
Includes index.
1. Political science—History—Europe. 2. Renaissance. 3. Tacitus, Cornelius—Influence. I. Title.
JA84.E9S3 1976   320.5′092′4   75-36399
ISBN 0-226-73700-4

This book is for

Nancy and Ernest
Eric & Ellie

—for the life, the goal, the desire:
but mostly for the love

Contents

Preface ix

Introduction 3

1 Tacitus in the Political Thought of Fifteenth-Century Italian Humanists 17

2 Tacitus in Reformation Political Thought 31

3 Tacitus in the Political Thought of Sixteenth-Century German Historiographers 50

4 Tacitus in Italian Political Thought of the Early Sixteenth Century 66

5 Tacitus in the Development of ''Reason of State'' 101

6 Tacitus and the End of Renaissance Political Thought 127

7 The Legacy of the Renaissance Political Use of Tacitus 150

Notes 173

Selected Bibliography 235

Index of Names 249

Index of Ancient and Renaissance Citations and Quotations 258

Index of Subjects 266

Preface

Cornelius Tacitus, one of the greatest Roman historians, was about sixty-one years old when he died around A.D. 117. A few years earlier he had been the proconsul of Asia. He had achieved this prize office, after the usual *cursus honorum,* through the favor of emperors from Vespasian to Trajan. His interest in politics was the chief preoccupation of his life. Yet he could detach himself enough to look critically at the political history of his own time and of the time shortly before his birth—when emperors first began to control the Roman state. On the first period he wrote the *Historiae;* then, on the second period, he wrote the *Annales.* And even his much smaller works—the *Dialogus de oratoribus,* on the merits of rhetoricians before and after imperial times; the *Agricola,* on the military career of his father-in-law; and the *Germania,* on the customs of German tribes—are saturated with his political interest. These legacies—the political history of his century and the characteristically succinct style in which he wrote it—are the bases for his immortality.

Tacitus is usually left to the scholars in the mid-twentieth century, for historians no longer use him as a model, and prose writers no longer imitate his style. Political philosophers prefer Raymond Aron, Hobbes, or, at the earliest, Machiavelli, as sources of inspiration or information, and political activists are far too preoccupied with Mao Tse-tung and William F. Buckley, Jr., to worry about the antics of Tiberius and Domitian.

But, four centuries ago, scholars, lawyers, and politicians not only used Tacitus as a guide to the formation of political theory but did so with actual political application in mind. It is precisely an affinity between philosophy and action, thought and practice, that characterized the Renaissance political use of him.

The importance of Tacitus in Renaissance political thought has been recognized by a number of students of the period. One of the first was Felice Ramorino, in *Cornelio Tacito nella storia della cultura* (Milan:

Hoepli, 1898), who gathered much evidence to support his thesis of a general intellectual tradition of Tacitus in European thought; however, he gave too much attention to pre-Renaissance times and provided really little of political value. Twenty years later Paul Joachimsen, in "Tacitus im deutschen Humanismus" (*Neue Jahrbücher für das klassische Altertum* 27 [1911]: 696–717), attempting a more precise study, answered the "when" and "what" of his problem with much documentation but somehow avoided the "how" of the man, the text, and the political circumstance—ideas seem to have an influence all by themselves. Shortly thereafter, Hans Heinrich Louis Max Tiedemann, in *Tacitus und das Nationalbewusstsein der deutschen Humanisten, Ende des 15. und Anfang des 16. Jahrhunderts* (dissertation, Berlin, 1913), did a similar study—except that the patriotic tinge is a little more obvious. In 1921, Giuseppe Toffanin published his *Machiavelli e il "Tacitismo," la "politica storica" al tempo della Controriforma* (Padua: A. Draghi). He demonstrated the confusion that grew in persons' minds in the late sixteenth century between Tacitus and Machiavelli; and, in proving his thesis, he opened to view much Renaissance Tacitan literature for the first time. Still, he confuses his readers by imprecise definition; for example, he calls Tacitus a Machiavellian and Machiavelli an anti-Tacitan Tacitist. Toffanin, like his predecessors, ignored the *context* demanded by the more recent understanding of what intellectual history ought to be.

Mary F. Tenney, in "Tacitus in the Politics of Early Stuart England" (*Classical Journal* 37 [December, 1941]: 151–63), was the first to introduce a better method. Improving on her dissertation—which, written ten years before, was little more than a grab bag of quotations—she now gave a more meaningful context for the uses of Tacitus within the main trends of politics. However, she did not look much beyond specific instances to the larger political issues, nor did she feel compelled to arrange her material in chronological order.

Arnaldo Momigliano, on the other hand, in "The First Political Commentary on Tacitus" (*Journal of Roman Studies* 37 [1947]: 91–101; reprinted in *Contributo alla storia degli studi classici* [Rome: Edizioni di Storia e Letteratura, no. 47, 1955], pp. 38–59), surpassed all earlier attempts to understand the relevancy of Tacitus at a certain moment in the Renaissance. Despite its limited scope, it is an example of Momigliano's brilliant methodology, which combines acute philological analysis with cautious chronological investigation and a keen political understanding of the background of the commentary's composition.

One year later, Giorgio Spini published a valuable synthesis about "I trattatisti dell'arte storica nella Controriforma italiana" (pp. 109–36 in *Contributi alla storia del Concilio di Trento e della Controriforma,* Florence: Vallecchi, 1948). His central theme is that the rivalry between the pro-Livian or the anti-Tacitan writers of *ars historiae* and historians, on the one hand, and those who looked to Tacitus as a model, on the other, was deeply embedded in the actual political conflicts of the late-sixteenth and early-seventeenth centuries.

Then, in 1955, Hans Baron first published his famous *Crisis of the Early Italian Renaissance* (Princeton University Press; 2d rev. ed., 1966). Baron shows Bruni's dynamic application of Tacitus to political reality and the tradition of this application for about the next thirty years; he demonstrates the close unity between political developments and political theory and propaganda.

However, the excellent methodology of these last three scholars was not emulated by Jürgen von Stackelberg in his *Tacitus in der Romania: Studien zur literarischen Rezeption des Tacitus in Italien und Frankreich* (Tübingen: Max Niemeyer, 1960). He compiled a handbook rather than composed a thematic synthesis of his subject. Thus he does not provide a comprehensive thesis, but he does give mounds of facts and piles of quotations, which have facilitated my own work. Much less valuable is Reinhard Häussler's *Tacitus und das historische Bewusstsein* (Heidelberg: Karl Winter, 1965). Häussler makes Toffanin seem concrete by comparison. Men of all ages and places, five or ten at a time, are mentioned in the same breath as having been influenced in the same way by Tacitus. Fortunately, however, Else-Lilly Etter in *Tacitus in der Geistesgeschichte des 16. und 17. Jahrhunderts* (Basel: Helbing & Lichtenhahn, 1966) avoids the extremes of Häussler's nebulosity and von Stackelberg's narrowness. With philological precision she analyzes the Tacitist commentaries of the period from 1580 to 1650 and, with a unifying thesis, attempts to delineate this literature along the lines of a Hapsburg monarchic Tacitus and a French antimonarchic Tacitus. However, while improving greatly over her recent German colleagues, she too fails to develop a really successful methodology; the quest for a "Geistesgeschichte" gets in the way and vies with her frequent awareness of actual historical contexts. The reader is left confused about real cause-and-effect relationships in her conception of intellectual history.

Some other recent writers have discussed the role of Tacitus within the context of other studies. Eric Cochrane, for instance, in his *Florence in the Forgotten Centuries, 1527–1800: A History of Florence and the Florentines in the Age of the Grand Dukes* (University of Chicago

Press, 1973), dedicates several pages to Scipione Ammirato, the late-sixteenth-century Florentine historian and political thinker, who adapted Tacitus to his own very immediate political circumstances. A few others have considered one or two specific moments in particular places. Thus, Edwin B. Benjamin, in "Bacon and Tacitus" (*Classical Philology* 60 [April, 1965]: 102–10), attempts to show certain Tacitan influences on Bacon's stylistic, philosophical, and political characteristics. In effect, however, he reveals less about Bacon than he does about Bacon's England experiencing a kind of backwash of Tacitan developments from the Continent. His brief account is vitiated by vague associations and probable influences, which he could have made more factually concrete with Tenney's study—which he totally ignores. Three other scholars, finally, have considered the political ideology of "Tacitism" in seventeenth-century Spain: E. Tierno-Galván, in *El Tacitismo en las doctrinas politicas del siglo de oro español* (in *Anales de la Universidad de Murcia,* Curso 1947/48, pp. 895–975), was heavily influenced by Toffanin; Arnaldo Momigliano, in "Il 'Tacito Español' di B. Alamos de Barrientos e gli 'Aphorismos' di B. Arias Montano" (in *Contributo alla storia degli studi classici,* pp. 61–66, cited above), who here also shows his brilliant approach; and, Francisco Sanmarti-Boncompte, in *Tacito en España* (Barcelona, 1951), who admits (p. 28) that his countrymen incorporated themselves only late into the Tacitan movement, with their first translated and partial edition appearing in 1613 and the first commentary on Tacitus, by Baltasar Alamos de Barrientos, in 1614. Thus, Tacitus' political context in Spain has almost nothing to do with the Renaissance.

Still, the role of Tacitus in many other countries of Europe is still largely unknown—for example, in Scandinavia and in eastern Europe, though a few leads are noted by Peter Burke in his survey of "Tacitism" (in *Tacitus,* ed. T. A. Dorey [London: Routledge & Kegan Paul, 1969], pp. 149–71). Besides, almost everyone since Toffanin has concentrated on the role of Tacitus within the Tacit*ism* of the 1580s to the 1680s. Moreover, several of the studies mentioned follow methodological presuppositions that are no longer wholly acceptable. The context of the particular man, the text of Tacitus, and the Renaissance political reality were usually not considered as a synthetic whole. Finally, no one has yet attempted to show the relationship between one moment in the Renaissance tradition of Tacitus and the next and, thus, to provide a unified assessment of the phenomenon, within a unified context of history, from the beginning to the end.

This study is intended as a contribution to just such a synthesis. It is limited, first of all, to political thought, though it finds support from areas such as ethics, historiography, rhetoric, and law. Second, it is confined to certain geographic areas: to Italy, Germany, France, and, to a lesser extent, England; it was in these places that the main developments of Tacitan political thought took place in the Renaissance. Third, it is restricted to the chronological extremes imposed by the definition of the subject: essentially, it is a study of Tacitus in the age of Renaissance humanism. Specifically, for the political *use* of Tacitus, the bounds extend from 1403, with Leonardo Bruni, the great Florentine humanist, to 1613, with Triano Boccalini, the famous Italian patriot.

Still, within this period the various moments are continuous and connected. For example, Jean Bodin, the great political thinker, writing in France about 1565, knew very well what Francesco Patrizi, the famous Paduan philosopher, did or did not do with Tacitus around 1560. For another instance, Bodin used the same critical edition of Tacitus—prepared in 1513 by Andrea Alciato, the influential Milanese legal scholar—as had Beatus Rhenanus, a German historian and philologian working about thirty years earlier. Moreover, this study attempts to show not only a tradition of ideas but also the context of these ideas as expressed by certain individuals, experiencing life in their own way. Each lived in the course of particular political events; each usually read Tacitus with very personal biases, ideals, and misconceptions; and each influenced his contemporaries and other generations in diverse ways. The political use of Tacitus in the Renaissance was as alive and real as the users themselves.

I wish to express my gratitude to Eric Cochrane, Professor of History at the University of Chicago, for reading the manuscript, pointing out its weaknesses, and offering me encouragement; to George Javor, philologist and Professor of Foreign Languages at Northern Michigan University, for giving me valuable advice for my translations into English; and to Dorothy E. Johnson, dearest friend and best school teacher anywhere, for typing and listening.

Tacitus
in Renaissance Political Thought

Introduction

Tacitus survived the Middle Ages only precariously and in mutilated form. Over half of his work had been lost, and the rest was preserved in single manuscripts only. Other ancient writers, on the other hand, like Cicero, Virgil, Livy, and Caesar, flourished in more healthy manuscript traditions.[1] Recognizing this contrast, some Renaissance humanists believed that the sad fate of Tacitus was not merely the result of blind and capricious fortune. It seemed to many that Tacitus had been intentionally neglected. Montaigne, for example, was

> certain that in those early times when our religion began to gain authority with the laws, zeal armed many believers against every sort of pagan books, thus causing men of letters to suffer an extraordinary loss. I consider that this excess did more harm to letters than all the bonfires of the barbarians. Of this Cornelius Tacitus is a good witness: for although the Emperor [Claudius] Tacitus, his kinsman, had by express ordinances populated all the libraries in the world with his works, nevertheless not one single complete copy was able to escape the careful search of those who wanted to abolish them because of five or six insignificant sentences contrary to our [religious] belief.[2]

Others, such as the Saxon humanist Albert Krantz (along with many Germans of the early Reformation), saw an Italian-papal conspiracy to conceal Tacitus: "Let them give back to us the entire History of Tacitus which they have hidden away, let them return Pliny's twenty books on Germany."[3] But, unlike Krantz, Montaigne at least had some historical basis for his opinion. Tertullian, the early Christian polemicist, considered Tacitus "that most loquacious of liars" (for saying that Jews worshiped a god with an ass's head), and Orosius, the historian friend of Saint Augustine, had even harsher things to say: Tacitus was a liar, a flatterer, a fool, a sloppy historian, and a hateful man.[4]

Despite Tertullian and Orosius, who hated just about everything pagan, most early Christians agreed with Saint Augustine that the good in pagan literature could be taken with profit, as Moses had taken gold from the Egyptians. Thus the popularity of Tacitus was increased rather than diminished exactly because of the information he provided about the early Christians and Jews. The passages about the monstrosities that Nero performed on the early martyrs and, especially, those on the heroic struggle of the Jews against Titus, the destroyer of Jerusalem, were, in fact, about the only passages that interested the early Fathers. Saint Jerome, in his *Commentarii in Zachariam,* related the story about Jerusalem and, with complete indifference, merely footnoted his remarks in referring to Josephus and Tacitus as his sources (remarking, of Tacitus, that he "wrote about the lives of the caesars from Augustus until the death of Domitian").[5] About the same time, Sulpicius Severus, the historian, used Tacitus on the Jews in a similarly casual way; two of his quotations are extremely valuable, coming as they do from the lost part of the *Historiae*. Without even mentioning his source in his *Historiae sacrae,* he told of Nero's gruesome lawn parties and other atrocities against the Christians, using quotations and verbal imitations from Tacitus.[6] In Severus, as in Saint Jerome, there are no vituperative epithets for the author whom Tertullian and Orosius went out of their way to malign. Nor, on the other hand, did they praise him.

There was only one early Christian writer who admired Tacitus. Apollinaris Sidonius, of the highest Roman aristocracy in Gaul, flourished around 430. His poems and letters show a depth of religious fervor as pure as the classical language in which it is expressed. Though he considered himself a disciple of Pliny the Younger for his own epistolary style, he thought of Tacitus as the master of historical narrative—Tacitus, "whom by reason of his fertile genius no tongue must tacitly ignore."[7] Sidonius' knowledge of Tacitus must have been fairly thorough, at least enough for picking just the right quotation (from *Historiae* v. 26) to serve as a thematic springboard in a letter to his friend Polemius, praetorian prefect of Gaul: just because Polemius now enjoyed high office, it did not mean that he should forget about writing to his old friends.[8] Sidonius' enthusiastic attitude toward Tacitus is in sharp contrast to the indifference of Sulpicius Severus and Saint Jerome; but all three are a far cry from the bigoted narrow-mindedness of Tertullian and Orosius. In general, Christians were not averse to taking pagan gold.

Tacitus was not suppressed; he was forgotten. A century after Sidonius, Cassiodorus, the famous preserver of ancient literature, vaguely referred to Tacitus with "as Cornelius wrote,"[9] and by the time of Jordanes (c. 551) he was merely "a writer of annals."[10] The former used the *Germania* on the fact that amber was found on the shores of the Baltic Sea. The latter used the *Agricola* on the description of Britain. After Jordanes there are only four certain uses of Tacitus for over 800 years—up to the time of the first manuscript discovery in the fourteenth century. These occur in the *Annales Fuldenses* for the year 852 (on the name of the Weser River—Visurgis—from *Annales* ii. 9–17); in Rudolf of Fulda's *Translatio Sancti Alexandri,* of the mid-ninth century (on the description of the Saxon race, from *Germania* iv, ix, x, and xi); in the twelfth-century *Vita Sancti Severi* of Peter the Deacon (which takes many sentences from the *Agricola*); and in Bishop Paulinus Venetus' *Mappa mundi,* written in the 1330s (in which there is bold plagiarization from *Annales* xii through xv on the environs of the see of Pozzuoli [ancient Puteoli] and on the Campanian regions in general). These references are certain; but scholars are still in doubt about hints of Tacitus in Meginhard, Einhard, Widukind, Adam of Bremen, the anonymous author of the *Vita Henrici IV,* Guibert of Nogent, William of Malmesbury, John of Salisbury, Peter of Blois, Otto of Freising, and others.[11] Most of these doubtful traces of Tacitus are based on meager verbal parallels, which are probably accidental. Even if all of them were accepted as certain indications of Tacitus, they do not indicate that he was popular; had he been, he would have been copied more often, and the manuscripts would have been more widely disseminated. Indeed, his name does not even occur in medieval library catalogues, and the medieval literary glossaries contain only a few mentions of him.[12] In France, moreover, there is no trace of Tacitus at all. In Germany Tacitus was revived during the Carolingian Renaissance only—two of the manuscripts later discovered were written in Germany during the ninth century. In Italy Tacitus survived in a single copy. Even Petrarch, eager to become acquainted with so many of the ancients, remained ignorant of it. He learned nothing of the discovery made by Boccaccio, his intimate friend and admirer.

Boccaccio had already discovered *Annales* xi–xvi and the *Historiae* before 1371, probably in 1362.[13] The manuscript, arriving in Italy about 1050 from Germany,[14] is in Beneventan "Lombardic" minuscule of the eleventh century and is known as the Mediceus II (Medicean-Laurentian, LXVIII. *2*). Boccaccio's discovery of this literary treasure, amid the dust of the library at Monte Cassino, was accidental.[15] Like Petrarch, though without as much enthusiasm, he generally endeavored to search out the lost texts of the ancient writers. But there is no evidence that he went to Monte Cassino in 1362 with any particular author in mind. He had twice before visited Naples, about fifty miles from the revered monastery, once between 1328 and 1340 and once again in 1348. But in the '30s and '40s Petrarch's wonderful finds (especially the *Letters* of Cicero, 1345) had probably not yet sufficiently inspired him to go running around the Campania to a lot of old monasteries filled with monks he generally disliked. Though a treasure would have been worth a hundred-mile trip, the library at Monte Cassino was in such a dilapidated condition that news of its contents never stirred any dust within the walls, let alone any enthusiasm outside them. And Boccaccio probably never read Paulinus Venetus' *Mappa mundi;* for he had read Paulinus' earlier work, the *Satirica historia* (in which some scholars have wrongly placed the Tacitus uses),[16] and only ridiculed it.[17] Even if he had read the *Mappa mundi*, he would not have received any clues of Tacitus, for Paulinus had plagiarized heavily without mentioning his source. In all, Boccaccio was ignorant of Tacitus before 1362. But in that year, when finishing *De claris mulieribus,* he definitely used Tacitus.[18] Onto the very end of this work he tacked those sections about the Roman women Agrippina, Epicharis, Pompeia Paulina, Poppaea Sabina, and Triaria assimilated from his new knowledge of Tacitus' *Annales* xii–xvi and *Historiae* ii and iii. Just one of many comparisons of the texts makes this imitation clear:

> Obtulit ingenium *Anicetus* libertus, *classi apud Misenum praefectus* et *pueritiae* Neronis educator . . . ; *navem posse*. . . . [Tacitus *Annales* xiv. 3.][19]

> . . . ab *Aniceto prefecto classis apud Misenum,* olim a *pueritia* nutritore suo, ostensum est *navim posse* fragilem. . . . [Boccaccio, "Agrippina," xc.][20]

On leaving Naples the same year, Boccaccio probably left his manuscript with Niccolò di Montefalcone, abbot of San Stefano in Calabria; for, nine years later (January 1371), again at Naples and preparing to depart for Florence, he wrote the abbot asking for the return of only a "quaternus" (a quire) of Tacitus: "I asked you at least that you send me that quire which you took away from Cornelius Tacitus so that you will not make my work [*laborem meum*] in vain and add greater deformity to the book."[21] It is impossible to say whether Boccaccio left this quire with the abbot in 1362 and brought the rest with him to Florence or whether, leaving Naples in 1371, he was asking for the quire still loaned out, the rest having been returned to him during this latter visit. The problem is all the more complicated if ''laborem meum'' implies either a copy which he had labored to write, or the original, which he had discovered after so much effort and difficulty. In any case, Boccaccio must have had either the manuscript or a copy with him when, back in Florence, he wrote the *Genealogiae deorum* (beginning in 1373); for his account of the founding of the cult of Venus at Paphos (iii. 23) is based on *Historiae* ii. 3. In his next major work, the *Commento sopra la Commedia* (xiii and xvi) he used Tacitus also: on the death of Lucian, on the heroism of Epicharis during the conspiracy of Piso, and on the death of Seneca. All are based on the *Annales*—xv. 70, xv. 57, and xv. 63–64. The *Commento* was written before October 1373.

From this date on, it is very unclear what happened to the manuscript or how it came to Florence. Perhaps Boccaccio had brought it with him. Some scholars assert that it was Zanobi da Strada, the jurist and poet laureate, who discovered it and brought it there.[22] They suppose that since Zanobi was the vicar of Bishop Acciaiuoli, Paulinus Venetus' successor in the see of Pozzuoli, and since he stayed at Monte Cassino from 1355 to 1357, it was he who discovered the Mediceus II and took it to Florence with him. But these are arguments from silence. There is no evidence for Zanobi's knowledge of Tacitus; nor, if he had carried the manuscript to Florence, did any Florentine know of it before 1373, except Boccaccio. Even after Boccaccio's return to Florence in 1363 no one else learned of the new author. And they could have gotten no hints from *De claris mulieribus,* completed the year before in Naples; for Boccaccio, like Paulinus before him, had closely imitated Tacitus without mentioning him. Only in Boccaccio's other two works in which he used Tacitus (1373) is there any acknowledgment of the new author. Here he was explicitly given his due in ''secondochè Cornelio Tacito scrive'' and similar phrases.[23] These ''footnotes'' were almost certainly based on Boccaccio's reading of the actual Mediceus II archetype, taken from Monte Cassino in 1362. Only in the 1420s are there again traces of it.

Whatever the fate of the archetype may have been after Boccaccio's death in 1375, a few humanists read copies—perhaps even the original—during the next fifty years. Besides the anonymous Tuscan translator (about 1382) of the few excerpts from *Annales* xiv. 53–56, there are only five men who read and employed Tacitus: Benvenuto Rambaldi of Imola, Domenico Bandino of Arezzo, Coluccio Salutati, Leonardo Bruni, and Sicco Polentone. The individual circumstances of each use, as well as the reasons for the slow rise in Tacitus' popularity, will receive a detailed explanation in chapter 1. But the last-mentioned, Sicco Polentone, a humanist of Arezzo, is important here because he might have had the Mediceus II in his possession. About 1420 he wrote the *Scriptores illustres linguae latinae* and used *Annales* xi. 14 on the origin of the alphabet. He also described the codex of Tacitus that he saw:

> I certainly dare not affirm the exact number of his books. Indeed, I saw the fragments of an eleventh book and the others successively to the twenty-first, in which he elegantly and fully related the life of Claudius and [of those] who were emperors after him down to Vespasian.[24]

Polentone counted twenty-one books, because in the Mediceus II the *Historiae* i–v follow immediately upon the *Annales* xi–xvi. Perhaps he saw the original. But it might have been only a copy.

If Polentone spoke of the original manuscript, he had probably seen it in Florence; for by 1427 it was definitely in the hands of two famous Florentines, Niccolò Niccoli and Poggio Bracciolini. Both were almost fanatically enthusiastic searchers for ancient texts and were intensely jealous of rival circles of manuscript hunters. Such competition bore fruit, and both men are responsible for having found and preserved much of classical literature. Though Poggio was more famous for his great discoveries, Niccoli boasted a vast collection of the ancient authors, owning more than 800 manuscripts at his death. Tacitus—the original Mediceus II—was one of them; he acquired it as early as 1427. But rather than brag of his treasure, he concealed it. In this year he sent it to Poggio on condition that his friend keep it absolutely secret!

> When Cornelius Tacitus arrives [writes Poggio], I will keep it a secret. Indeed, I know all that gossip, and from what place it arises and through whom, and who will lay claim to it. You may be sure that I will not breathe a word.[25]

However, Poggio was not trying to keep secret something that had already been read and used by a half-dozen writers since Boccaccio, one of them being Leonardo Bruni, the great Florentine humanist and statesman, who by now had used Tacitus for political propaganda (see chapter 1). Obviously, Poggio was referring to the actual manuscript and not its contents; he spoke of "one who will lay claim to it." Anyone really wanting to know what Tacitus wrote could have availed himself of a copy. Poggio himself mentioned two copies a month later, when he wrote back to Niccoli to complain that the manuscript he had been sent was almost illegible:

> You have sent me a book of Seneca and Cornelius Tacitus, for which I thank you; but it is in Lombardic letters and for the most part faded and unclear. If I had known this, I could have spared you the trouble. Once when I was at your place I read one in ancient letters. I don't know if it belonged to Coluccio [Salutati] or to someone else. I wish to have that one or another that can be read. For it will be difficult to procure a scribe who can correctly read this codex. Therefore take care that I may have another, if it can be done; you will certainly be able to do so, if you care to take the trouble.[26]

The faded manuscript in Lombardic letters was probably the Mediceus II; the one in "ancient" letters was probably a copy in the new humanist script for which Salutati, among others, was noted. Whether Poggio held in secrecy the manuscript he could not read or sent it back to Niccoli is unknown; in any case, one or the other kept it secret. Only after Niccoli's death (1437) does it again turn up. Poggio, however, despite his strenuous complaints, was again disappointed by Niccoli. About eight months after his first letter he informed Niccoli: "I have given Bartholomaeo de Bardiis [manager of the Roman branch of the Medici bank] the *Decade* of Livy and the Cornelius Tacitus, so that he can send it to you; in your Cornelius there are lacking many pages in various places."[27] How frustrating for poor Poggio! But at least he got to read some Tacitus descendant from the Mediceus II. He had also heard of more Tacitus up in Germany; and though he tried with great effort to acquire it, he failed completely.

He sought the "minor works" (*Agricola, Germania, Dialogus de oratoribus*), the second of the three great Tacitus discoveries. A part of the manuscript, the Codex Aesinus, was found in the private library of Count Balleani at Iesi near Ancona in 1902. It contains only a few leaves of the *Agricola* from the ninth-century Hersfeld manuscript of the complete "minor works," brought to Rome probably by Enoch of Ascoli in 1455.[28] Enoch was a grammarian, a poet, and a tutor to some of the most prominent Florentine families, including the Medici. These were his professions. His passionate vocation, however, was searching for texts of the ancients. It is for this reason that he came to the notice of Pope Nicholas V, himself very much in love with ancient literature and a spendthrift on manuscripts and ornately bound books. To assuage his thirst for antiquity, the pope sent Enoch on a manuscript hunt to the east. On Enoch's return in 1451 he was immediately sent off on a similar mission to Scandinavia, Denmark, and Germany. In 1455 he returned, bearing great gifts for his patron, only to find that Nicholas had died. Among his treasures from the north was a Tacitus manuscript of the "minor works," which he had most probably taken from the monastery at Hersfeld. He shared his great discovery with his friends, one of whom was Pier Candido Decembrio, the eminent scholar and humanist of Milan. Decembrio wrote a lengthy description of Enoch's manuscript which matches exactly with the *Agricola* leaves of the Codex Aesinus. The text was soon acquired by Eneo Silvio Piccolomini, cardinal of Siena, one-time chief secretary to the Emperor Frederick III and soon to become Pope Pius II (1458). But with Eneo Silvio began a wholly new story about the revival of Tacitus (see chapter 2). The works were mentioned by Poggio as early as 1427 in the very same letter in which he promised to keep the Mediceus II a secret:

> About the Cornelius Tacitus which is in Germany, I hear nothing. I expect an answer from that monk. Nicholas of [Cusa] Treves has not yet returned there. I have heard nothing further about the books. Yesterday, when I questioned him regarding this matter, he said he had nothing certain. I have given up my concern for the books that are not here, and I turn my attention to those that are here: for I hear nothing but fables.[29]

"For I hear nothing but fables." After almost two years of avid expectation—from the time, that is, when Poggio first heard of "some works of Cornelius Tacitus unknown to us"[30]—he had become quite disgusted with waiting. He had apparently agreed to further a cause at the curia in Rome for a monk of Hersfeld (probably a certain Heinrich von Grebenstein). The "fee" was to be some specified volumes of the classics, containing, among others, some works of Tacitus still "ignota." The monk made two trips to Rome to make sure that Poggio was on his toes in pursuing his cause, but Tacitus was never part of his baggage. Poggio probably tried to enlist Nicholas of Cusa to help pry open the monk's hand. All to no avail. Perhaps the monk was holding out for a better deal from another clique of jealous manuscript hunters, non-Florentines, made up of Antonio Panormita and Giovanni Lamola in Bologna, together with Guarino, the great educator, in Verona.[31] It is hard to say. At any rate, Poggio's friend, Niccoli, soon tried a more direct method to achieve their end. He tried to have someone go and get the manuscript. In 1431 Niccoli heard that Cardinal Giuliano Cesarini, the dynamic trouble-shooter for Pope Martin V, was going to Germany.

For him, and for another cardinal going to France, he wrote out a list of volumes they should watch out for and bring back. In Niccoli's "inventory" are listed each of the "minor works," each with beginning sentences—information which von Grebenstein had probably sent to Poggio.[32] However, Niccoli, like Poggio and all the others, never succeeded. The "minor works" again drop from history for about twenty-eight years until, finally, they are certainly in Rome after Enoch's return in 1455.

There is some doubt whether Enoch really brought these works to Rome in this year. Clarence W. Mendell,[33] one of the greatest Tacitus scholars of this century, argues that Enoch did not bring the *Agricola* to Italy because it was already there, at Monte Cassino, when Peter the Deacon quoted from it in the twelfth century.[34] Also, he raises serious doubts about Enoch's having brought the *Germania* and the *Dialogus,* though in the end he concludes that he did. Mendell argues that

> we must believe that there were three sources of manuscripts of the Minor Works in Italy in the fifteenth century: the Monte Cassino *Agricola,* Enoch's *Dialogus* and *Germania* and the manuscript which Decembrio saw containing all three items. All the evidence goes to show that the ultimate source of all three was the same, probably the Benedictine monastery of Fulda.[35]

In the opinion of Remigio Sabbadini, however,[36] one of the greatest recent specialists on the revival of classical literature in the Renaissance, Enoch brought all three works to Rome, Decembrio described Enoch's manuscript, and the Iesi manuscript is a part of the Hersfeldensis that matches Decembrio's description[37]—which is exactly where Mendell differs. In conclusion, Sabbadini decided that

> the eight leaves of the Hersfeld codex contain the nucleus of the middle of the *Agricola* which have been very recently found at Iesi . . . and described by Decembrio . . . , [and] we may therefore conclude that Enoch brought back with him the Hersfeld archetype.[38]

Three years later Eneo Silvio was to use the *Germania* in a quarrel with Martin Mayer, chancellor of Mainz, over papal taxation. The first use of the "minor works," unlike the Mediceus II, was, therefore, political; and, as will be shown, it was ultimately a major cause of German antagonism against "papist" Italy in the early Reformation.

This dynamic effect of the *Germania* in Germany was directly responsible for the first political use by a German of the third major

Tacitus revival, *Annales* i–vi, within ten years after it had come to light. The manuscript, the Mediceus I (Medicean-Laurentian, LXVIII. 1) is of the mid-ninth century and written in near-Lombardic letters, and it was taken from the monastery of Corvey in 1509 by Angelo Arcimbaldo, special agent of Cardinal Giovanni de' Medici in a manuscript probe in northern Europe. It remained almost unknown until 1515, when Giovanni, now Pope Leo X, commissioned the philosopher and philologist Philippus Beroaldus to publish it in the first *opera omnia* of Tacitus. In the late autumn of this year, Ulrich von Hutten, the militant reforming humanist and warrior, arrived in Italy for another visit. He was already afire with an idealized conception of the Germans, kindled by his reading of the *Germania*. Now, while in Italy, and before 1517, he read about the great German hero Arminius, annihilator of Varus and his three legions, in the first two books of the *Annales*. In 1519 he wrote a dialogue called *Arminius,* which created such patriotic enthusiasm among Germans that the "Arminius cult" (see chapter 3) lasted for decades thereafter and contributed much to the Protestant German hatred of Catholic Italy.

But the first to make any political use of the new discovery was not Hutten but, four years before him, Machiavelli. He used a passage for a very crucial argument in the *Discourses on Livy* (see chapter 4). But Machiavelli may have known of the existence of the Mediceus I as early as six years before writing the *Discourses*. Any time after 1509 he may have seen the letter of Cardinal Francesco Soderini, brother of the Piero who was the life-president of the Florentine Republic, to Marcello Virgilio, secretary of Florence and colleague of Machiavelli in the government. It is in this letter that Cardinal Soderini described the new manuscript which Angelo Arcimbaldo had just brought to Rome "ex Germania." To please Virgilio, Soderini described what Tacitus said about the Florentines in *Annales* i. 79:

> You will see that our men, called Florentines over fifteen hundred years ago, were held in honor before the Roman people: since there was recently brought to us from Germany a codex of great antiquity, of parchment, written down in letters not very far from the Lombardic, whose author is inscribed as P. [Publius] Cornelius. It is condensed into five books,[39] from the decease of the divine Augustus to the death of Tiberius, and embraces the deeds of the Roman people both at home and abroad. All these—the name of the author, and the gravity of the style, and the order of narration—are such that we judge it to be the work of Cornelius Tacitus. But

> whoever the author may be, the book is old and nearly venerable. In it it is said that the Florentines were listened to. Their wishes were complied with by the Senate, that the Clanis not be diverted into the Arno. I have included the words of the author in this letter so that you will glory with us in the antiquity of our country. [The passage from *Annales* i. 79 follows.][40]

This letter could easily have come to the notice of Machiavelli, Virgilio's colleague in the chancellory until 1512. Besides, as Paolo Giovio, the great Venetian historian, later remarked, Virgilio was accustomed to loaning texts to Machiavelli.[41] It is impossible to tell whether Machiavelli got to see it. At any rate, he did see, and quickly made use of, the new texts, after they were first published in the Beroaldus edition of Tacitus' complete works in 1515.

Even before the first partial editions, that is, before 1470, Tacitus had been gradually disseminated throughout Europe in manuscripts. Even in 1427, when Poggio and Niccoli were hoarding the Mediceus II archetype in secrecy, many had already read it or possessed copies. After Niccoli's death in 1437, when the archetype probably passed to the library at San Marco (made into a public library by Cosimo de' Medici in 1441),[42] others soon acquired copies. The small groups of humanists who had used or had at least read Tacitus before 1440 were almost all Florentines, and it was their popularization of Tacitus which soon encouraged their friends and enemies in other cities to become interested in the new author. One great incentive here was the political emphasis that Leonardo Bruni, the most famous of early quattrocento humanists, placed on a passage from the *Historiae*. It became a pivot for his philosophy of civic humanism. Inspired by Bruni, Francesco Barbaro, statesman and scholar, advanced civic humanism in Venice; and it is most likely that in this connection he came to possess a copy of Tacitus before 1440. His friend, a certain Gottardo de Sarzana, borrowed the copy and had to apologize for keeping it so long.[43] By 1453 Barbaro had again loaned out his copy to Cardinal Bessarion, the great diplomat and bibliophile, so that the cardinal could have a copy of it made for himself.[44] Pier Candido Decembrio also probably read Tacitus, as a direct outcome of his debate with Poggio and Bruni over civic humanism, long before he made his own copy in 1461—a copy which somehow ended up at Wolfenbüttel in Germany.[45] Perhaps Decembrio had copied it from the one owned by Giovanni Corvini of Arezzo, who was part of the humanist circle of Milan. Angelo Decembrio, Candido's brother, humanist, and secretary to the king of Naples, also had a

Tacitus and recommended it to others.[46] Angelo was in the circle of Guarino of Verona at Ferrara; and Guarino, along with Pier Candido, was a strong opponent of Florentine and Venetian civic humanism and debated Tacitus' political value with Poggio. Though without connection with the debate on civic humanism, there were others who owned (or at least read) copies of Mediceus II in the '40s: in Florence, Leon Battista Alberti, the famous architect; in Naples, Lorenzo Valla, the great historian and philologian; in Rome, Flavio Biondo, the first historian of the Middle Ages. By 1470 the number of Italian readers had increased further because the texts of Tacitus had multiplied in Italy, and, by that time, there were also three copies in England and two in Germany.

It is little wonder that, with this gradually increasing dissemination of the text of the Mediceus II, there was such keen interest in acquiring the "minor works" after 1425. As late as 1455 no one had succeeded in getting them until Enoch brought them from Hersfeld. Even then no more than three or four people saw the manuscript before 1470. A handful of copies were probably made; but, in general, almost no one knew of these works before they were first published, in 1470 and 1476.[47] The Mediceus I, similarly, was almost unheard of until published in the 1515 edition of Beroaldus. Only in the age of printing did Tacitus become widely known.

In fact, before the first decade of the seventeenth century there were about sixty main publications in whole or in part of the works of Tacitus.[48] The noteworthy editions in this publishing tradition are, first, Vindelinus de Spira's first edition of everything available except the *Agricola* (Venice, 1470). Vindelinus was the first to set up a printing press in Venice. But he was a better typesetter than a philologian, for he probably could not figure out the especially mutilated manuscript of the *Agricola* and so decided not to include it in his collection. Second, Franciscus Puteolanus' edition of the *Agricola* (which he believed the Venetian printer had faultily produced; see chapter 1), along with some writings of Pliny the Younger and Petronius (Milan: Antonius Zarotus, 1476).[49] Puteolanus could do what Vindelinus could not, both because of his superior humanistic talent in textual analysis and, of equal importance, because of his ability to collate Vindelinus' manuscript with others—including, perhaps, even the Hersfeld *Agricola* or a copy of it by his countryman, Decembrio.[50] Third, Puteolanus' edition of the whole corpus of Tacitus then available (Milan, 1475–80). Fourth, Beroaldus' *Opera Omnia* (Rome, 1515). The addition of *Annales* i–vi must have promised large returns for the edition, for Leo X forbade anyone else to publish the works of Tacitus for ten years. Fifth, Andrea Alciato's complete editions, despite the papal ban (Milan, 1517; Basel, 1519; Venice, 1535 and 1554—three versions in all). In fact, Alciato's edition replaced that of Beroaldus as the popular text. Sixth, Beatus Rhenanus' two versions, in many editions (Basel, 1533; Frankfurt, 1542; Lyons, 1542; Basel, 1544; etc.). Rhenanus went far beyond the few philological improvements made by Alciato and established the best text (especially of the *Germania*) for some decades. Of special fame was Rhenanus' 1542 edition, published by Sebastian Gryphius, containing the prefaces and notes of Rhenanus himself and those of Beroaldus, Alciato, and Aemilio Ferretti. It is known as the "Gryphius," after the name of the publisher. Lastly, Justus Lipsius, "Sospitator Taciti," established the text from which all modern texts derive through his seven versions, each with frequent reprintings (Antwerp, 1574, 1581, 1585; Louvain, 1588; Antwerp, 1589, 1600, 1607). Lipsius was the first scholar firmly to distinguish the *Historiae* from the *Annales* and to determine six books for the first part of the latter work rather than five. Lipsius made hundreds of corrections, only a few of which have been rejected to this day. Thus, as the sixteenth century wore on, readers had a better and better text at their disposal.

Those who could not easily read Latin had many good translations to choose from.[51] In Italy there was already an anonymous translation of the *Historiae* and the *Annales* (Venice, 1544)—the first in Italian since the anonymous Tuscan translation of a few excerpts from *Annales* xiv in 1382. The first complete Italian rendition was by Giorgio Dati (Florence and Venice, 1563, with reprints in 1582, 1589, 1598, and 1607). The *Agricola,* alone, was done by Giovanni Maria Manelli (London, 1585). The first book of the *Annales,* alone, appeared in 1596, and the complete works in 1600 (both Florence), both done by Bernardo Davanzati. The latter earned Davanzati the title "Tacito Fiorentino" and became a little classic of Italian literature. It was widely employed for seventeenth-century Italian commentaries on Tacitus. In France, too, there were many translations: *Annales* i–vi by Etienne de la Planche (about 1548); the *Agricola* by Ange Cappel (1572 or 1574); the *Germania* by Blaise de Vigenère (1575); the same by a certain Guillomet (1580—though it had existed in manuscript since 1551); the complete works—except *Annales* i–vi, borrowed from la Planche's translation—by Claude Fauchet (1582). The last was reprinted in 1584, 1594, 1609, and 1612. In Germany, Johann Eberlin von Günzburg did the first German translation of the *Germania* in 1526.[52] Jacobus Micyllus followed with his 1535 edition of all the works. In England, Sir

Henry Savile did the *Historiae* and the *Agricola* (1591; reprinted in 1598 and 1614), and Richard Grenewey did the *Germania* and the *Annales* (1598), which were published along with Savile's work. The English were the last, with the exception of the Spanish, to translate Tacitus. In Spain there were no translations until those of Manuel Sueyro (1613) and Alamos de Barrientos (1614). Thus, by the beginning of the seventeenth century, Tacitus was readily available in many vernacular as well as Latin editions. However, by then he was already beginning to be shelved as a guide to potential action and as a stimulant to new ideas.

In political thought, especially, his works were no longer as applicable as they had been throughout the Renaissance. From the time of Petrarch until late in the sixteenth century all texts recovered from antiquity were appreciated for the practical guides they offered the reader. Speaking more persuasively, writing in pleasing style, painting pictures, planning and erecting buildings, living happily and with better morals, creating more just and realistic legal systems, commanding armies, running a state more efficiently—these *arts* and others the humanists learned through the classics. They detested the scholastics more for their ineffectual philosophizing than for their immorality. Few things were more odious to them than a learned man in an ivory tower. At first, men like Petrarch experienced some pain from their ambivalent aspirations, which wavered between the active life and the contemplative life. Petrarch's conscience bothered him very much, and he felt compelled to thrash out his problem with Saint Augustine on the top of Mount Ventoux (1336). Later, when he learned, through the letters to Atticus (1345), of Cicero's political and financial dealings, he was so shocked that he castigated Cicero for ever having left the sweet *otium* of his villa for the active life in Rome. Bruni, however, had no such conflict. For him the good citizen must become wise through study so as to act wisely in politics; and this political activity would afford so much experience and practical knowledge that studies would become more pleasurable and meaningful. It was Bruni who translated Aristotle's *Politics* and *Ethics,* and from these works he taught his fellow citizens that wealth through trade and manufacturing was not really ill-gotten gain from usurious practices but was instead the prerequisite for a liberal education and a magnanimous nature. It was Bruni also who read Tacitus' *Historiae* and taught his fellow Florentines that genius thrives well in a republic but is snuffed out under a tyrannous regime. That fascinating story begins in 1403.

1 Tacitus in the Political Thought of Fifteenth-Century Italian Humanists

In 1402 the Florentines were struggling desperately to keep their independence.[1] Since 1390 Giangaleazzo Visconti, duke of Milan and "the Messiah" of Italy,[2] had forced or intimidated almost every Italian city north of Rome to accept his tyranny, his Pax Italiae. Militarily the Florentines were no match for Giangaleazzo. Politically they had suffered an appalling loss of prestige. They had sent emissaries to Venice who were unable to convince the Venetians to join them in the defense of civic liberty. They had not been able to hinder the Sienese from admitting the soldiers of Milan or the Pisans from officially recognizing the duke as their lord. They now feared the inevitable and began to despair. With the fall of Bologna, their only loyal ally, the end seemed imminent. Weak in arms and weak in influence, they fell prey to ideological lethargy as well. Invigorating political ideas, civic ideals based on historical interpretations of the role of city-state liberty, were smothered beneath a cloud of fear and anxiety. Then, suddenly, Giangaleazzo died of the plague on 3 September. They awoke as from a nightmare. In the summer of 1403 (or 1404) Leonardo Bruni was one of the first to realize the great import of his city's recent escape from tyranny. He caught a spark of inspiration for a new historical basis of Florence's survival in liberty. It came from almost the very first words of Tacitus' *Historiae:*

> Of the former period, the 820 years dating from the founding of the city, many authors have treated; and while they had to record the transactions of the Roman people, they wrote with equal eloquence and freedom. After the conflict at Actium, and when it became essential to peace, that all power should be centered in one man, these great intellects passed away. Then too the truthfulness of history was impaired in many ways; at first, through men's ignorance of public affairs, which were now wholly strange to them, then, through their passion for flattery, or, on the other hand, their hatred of their masters.[3]

Specifically, great historians flourished in republican freedom and perished under imperial tyranny. Tacitus provided Bruni with grounds for exalting republican Florence, for praising the city which had allowed so many great men to thrive in liberty and had resisted the man who would destroy that liberty. He wrote the *Laudatio Florentinae urbis,* in which, mindful of the threat of Giangaleazzo a year or two before, he paraphrased Tacitus on what happened when Rome passed from Republic to Empire: "after the republic had been subjected to the power of one man, those brilliant minds vanished, as Cornelius [Tacitus] says."[4] With these words Tacitus was born into Renaissance political thought. Politically, Tacitus was now an offspring of Bruni's love of Florence in her struggle for freedom.

Bruni's judgment of the Roman Empire was "something new—and something which until Bruni's day had been unimaginable—not only as an expression of humanistic and civic sentiment, but also because it rested on a new source of information."[5] Thus Hans Baron sees Bruni's interpretation of the newly discovered Tacitus manuscript as the cornerstone of his argument for the origin of civic humanism.[6] The interpretation was new. Baron points out that Bruni selected "one possible facet of Tacitus' views, one which in Tacitus' eyes reflected only a secondary effect of the coming monarchy" and that Tacitus "referred exclusively to the course of Roman historiography," while "to Bruni, the 'vanishing of brilliant minds' became a general historical verdict on the effects of imperial government."[7] But Bruni's interpretation was not merely new, it was revolutionary.

Bruni's statement was an ideological act of secession from the late Roman and medieval political theory of the universal imperium. Down to Bruni's time the idea of a single imperial government was everywhere accepted. Scripture, the writings of the Church Fathers, tradition, law, and history all sanctioned the belief in one God as ruler over all things and one emperor, who, under God, governed all nonspiritual matters on this earth. The conflicts between *sacerdotium* and *imperium,* between pope and emperor, between Guelph and Ghibelline, were not the inevitable clashes of a dualistic system; instead they reflected differences of opinion over the workings of a monistic temporal government. Were certain matters of a spiritual nature or of a civil nature? Did the emperor receive authority directly from God or indirectly through the mediation of the pope? Papalists and imperialists were divided on these questions, but there was no division over the general principle of a single imperium, willed by God, for this world. Even

Aegidius Colonna (arch-defender of papal involvement in worldly affairs) and Dante (ferociously dedicated in support of imperial powers) were essentially in agreement on this principle. Boniface VIII was almost universally hated because he seemed to have usurped the imperial position. In Italy, the arena of the papal-imperial struggle, traditionally pro-papalist cities such as Genoa, Venice, and Florence were as proud as the pro-imperial ones in tracing their origins back to foundations by Julius Caesar. Florentines, in particular,[8] felt no shame in being descendants of the founder of imperial Rome, at once the destroyer of the Republic of Rome. Neither papalist nor imperialist was horrified when Dante placed Brutus in the deepest pit of hell; no one was shocked that an assassin of his legitimate prince should thus be punished most terribly. The sin of Brutus was as hideous as that of Judas. But God's will prevailed, and the Empire was firmly established under Augustus, in whose reign Christ chose to enter the world. This general view was not challenged. Even Petrarch, who, in his *Africa* (1338–39), painted the Republic in its brightest colors and the Empire in its darkest, never came to the conclusion that just because of the Empire per se, just because of the rule of one man, there came about an inevitable decay of virtue, liberty, and culture. In the *De gestis Caesaris,* which he wrote late in life, there is hardly a trace of the republican sentiments expressed in the *Africa*. The point of view in Petrarch has become once again the traditional one. But in a few decades Bruni was to completely negate it. And, to a large extent, it was Tacitus who helped him to do it. The change was thus very abrupt.

To be sure, Bruni had no example to follow for any political use of Tacitus—let alone a prorepublican one. Between Petrarch and Bruni there were four ardently republican humanists. All were close friends, and all were familiar with certain manuscripts of Tacitus which one of them, Boccaccio, discovered. Boccaccio's uses of Tacitus were all purely literary, without even a hint of any political overtones. The second was Benvenuto Rambaldi da Imola, who wrote the *Commentum super Dantem Allegherii* between 1379 and 1383. In it he employed Tacitus twice (though perhaps indirectly, from Boccaccio's works)[9] and for literary purposes only (on Cleopatra's sex life and on the death of Seneca).[10] The third was Domenico Bandino of Arezzo, the grammarian and encyclopedist, who used Tacitus in several places in his *Fons memorabilium universi,* a massive encyclopedia written between 1370 and, at the latest, 1403.[11] Imitating Boccaccio, he wrote on some famous women—Agrippina, Messalina, Poppaea, and the goddess

Venus—and he took most of his information on them from the new manuscripts provided by his friend Boccaccio. But in the section called "De viris claris virtute aut vitio," he went one step further and used Tacitus for his accounts of some famous men—Lucan, Mela, Nero, and Piso.[12] Moreover, in this section of the *Fons* (written between 1392 and 1395), he goes further than merely using Tacitus as a source; he comes out with a clear eulogy of the author: "A most eloquent orator and historian, as is attested by his histories, which I have read with great pleasure."[13] The fourth of the republican humanists, Coluccio Salutati, the chancellor of the Florentine Republic, took somewhat longer to get hold of the manuscripts. In February 1392, writing to Juan Fernandez de Heredia, the sage Aragonese diplomat and scholar, Salutati bewailed the loss of much ancient eloquence:

> but in a curious way the histories have perished, for the loss of which I am heartbroken: where are the annals of Ennius, of Quadrigarius, of Gnaeus Gellius, of Q. Claudius, of L. Piso, or of Fabius? . . . where is Cornelius Nepos, where is Tacitus, where is Tranquillus . . . where are an infinite number of others?[14]

But when he did finally see at least Tacitus, around 1395, his impression was much less favorable:

> For what should I say about Cornelius Tacitus? Although a very learned man, he wasn't able to equal those closest [to Cicero]. But he was even way behind Livy—whom he proposed to follow—not only in historical series but in imitation of eloquence.[15]

Still, he obviously read Tacitus, and it was probably through him that Bruni became interested in the new author.

Thus Tacitus was already established as an ancient author to be considered seriously during the years immediately preceding Bruni's coming to maturity as a writer. But he had been considered by the first readers almost wholly for literary and stylistic purposes. They had no incentive for using the new text politically (instead of Cicero and Aristotle, for example), and their desire to use the new text developed only very slowly. Hence it was Bruni who first came to see the importance of Tacitus as a source of political and historical ideas. And he did so partially with the help of two developments in Florentine culture, one in the area of historiography, the other in the domain of law.

In historiography, first of all, Bruni was guided by the growing belief that it was not Caesar who had founded Florence, but Sulla, and that the city was thus of republican origin—a view he himself was eventually to sustain in his *Laudatio* and his *Histories of the Florentine People*. Throughout the trecento, Florentines held the medieval belief that their city was founded after Caesar had pursued Catiline's army to Fiesole and other surrounding hills. Dante in his *Inferno* (xv), Giovanni Villani in his *Cronica* (i. 38–39), and Filippo Villani in his *De origine civitatis Florentiae* (1381–82) all related the traditional story. But even as Filippo Villani wrote, there was at least one who had doubts. Rambaldi, utilizing the new philological methods developed by Petrarch, asked in his *Commentum* how Caesar had enough time during the conspiracy of Catiline to go running around founding so many cities. After offering some detailed criticism on this point, Rambaldi, confused, abandoned the problem about the foundation of Florence and admitted "when, how, by whom, I confess I know not."[16] But by 1403 Salutati provided an answer. From his careful philological research, based mainly on Sallust's *Bellum Catilinae* and Cicero's second oration against Catiline (both known throughout the Middle Ages), he decided that Florence was founded by veterans of Sulla.[17] Bruni argued the same thesis, though not as well, in his *Laudatio*.[18]

The second development was legal; it was based, in general, on the growth of sanctions for tyrannicide and, in particular, on the legal justification for Caesar's assassination. Throughout the fourteenth century most commentators on Dante touched on the question of the rightness or wrongness of Caesar's assassins. They all condemned Cassius and Brutus. Rambaldi shared this view and, following the conclusion of Petrarch (almost with the very words from *De gestis Caesaris*), decided that Caesar suffered "a most undeserved death, which seemed to have displeased God and men";[19] he also, again following Petrarch, had to admit that his thorough study of the sources showed that "both [contestant parties] strove for power, both were ungrateful to their patria."[20] But where Petrarch resolved his historical conclusion of equal ingratitude with his belief that Caesar's death was nevertheless displeasing to God, Rambaldi was unable to reconcile the one with the other. As with the problem of Florence's origin, he could not make up his mind. He sent his *Commentum* to Salutati in 1383 and, as with the first problem, Salutati was sure where his friend was not. Seventeen years later Salutati stated his conclusions in his famous *De tyranno* (written in 1400; published in February 1401). Though the work deals with Caesar, Salutati probably had Giangaleazzo in mind: the problems of legitimacy involved with the murder of his uncle Bernabò in 1385; the legality of his title of duke, presented by the Emperor Wenceslaus in 1394; the emperor's deposition for having granted it; the acceptance by the

Milanese of the duke as their rightful lord, etc. After affirming that a *true* tyrant could be legally dispatched by a group, or even by an individual executing the will of the people, he concluded that Caesar was not a tyrant, for he did not lack a legitimate claim or title (*defectu tituli*) nor did he have a despotic nature (*superbia*). Therefore, "those murderers of Caesar did not kill a tyrant but the father of his country, the most clement and legitimate prince of the whole world."[21] By implication, in contrast with Caesar, Giangaleazzo would not have gotten off so well had he been assassinated.[22] But on Caesar, Salutati sided with Dante. Bruni did not agree.

In the *Dialogus I,* written in mid-1401, two or three years before the *Laudatio,* Bruni exonerated Brutus and Cassius by considering their deed most patriotic.[23] Bruni was a revolutionary in two ways: both in accepting Salutati's argument for Florence's foundation by Sulla and in rejecting Salutati's condemnation of the assassins of Caesar. It is little wonder, then, that such a political avant-gardist should avidly clutch at Tacitus' hint that eveything declined when the Empire began. Although Bruni paraphrased a line from Tacitus specifically on historians, he did not have to read far to find similar statements of a wider bearing. Bruni's reading of Tacitus in the wake of the Florentine crisis was a catalyst which synthesized Bruni's two revolutionary attitudes. The result was the *Laudatio*. In it are four new elements: the proud realization that Florentines had withstood the onslaught of Giangaleazzo, the belief in the foundation of Florence by Sulla, the contention that rule by one man is tyranny, and the acceptance of Tacitus' views on the vanishing of great men. The *Laudatio* was dynamic in its influence. Its ideas created controversies, and Tacitus was at their center.

In 1436 Pier Candido Decembrio, the eminent humanist at the court of Filippo Maria Visconti in Milan, wrote a panegyric on Milan meant to counter Bruni's *Laudatio*. Tacitus' statement in *Historiae* i. 1 was the focal point of Decembrio's *Panegyricus*.[24] "You have almost forgotten," he addressed Bruni, "that Cicero, Livy, and especially Virgil, divine minds, flourished in the times of Caesar and Augustus. Therefore, where did those brilliant minds vanish, as Cornelius said?"[25] Another humanist courtier, Guarino da Verona at the d'Este principality of Ferrara, had asked the same question of Poggio the year before.[26] Poggio had answered Guarino so well that Bruni did not trouble himself now to refute Decembrio. Poggio had referred to Tacitus' statement in Bruni's *Laudatio* when he made his answer:[27]

> From the words of Seneca in which he states that brilliant minds had been born in the age of Cicero, but later had declined and deteriorated; and from the testimony of Tacitus who asserts that those brilliant minds disappeared after power had been concentrated in one hand; it is quite obvious how great a damage Roman letters suffered by the loss of liberty.[28]
>
> Virgil, Horace, Livy, and Seneca were born and bred while the Republic was in its vigor; for Livy was in his sixteenth year when Caesar was slain, Seneca (as he states himself) could still hear Cicero's speeches. Virgil was twenty-four when the battle of Pharsalus between Caesar and Pompey was waged; Horace was seventeen. Thus all the learned and eloquent men who lived later either were born in the days of liberty and nursed on that earlier eloquence, or they were born soon afterwards, while some seeds of that earlier eloquence still survived.[29]

These arguments, pivoting on Tacitus, had been asserted continuously, in many works by Bruni and by others, ever since the *Laudatio*.[30] With so much of Florence's prestige resting on a single statement in Tacitus, emphasizing and illustrating much of his sentiment, it is not difficult to see why Poggio had, in 1427, promised Niccoli to keep the manuscript archetype safely concealed. But perhaps Niccoli thought he was its own best keeper and never did send it to Poggio. In either case the archetype was kept in the utmost secrecy. Giangaleazzo had once sent hired killers to do away with Chancellor Salutati.[31] Perhaps agents of Filippo Maria would now not stop at stealing or destroying a manuscript; Poggio himself spoke of one "who will lay claim to it." There were some copies available, but these were not very good.[32] Indeed, Tacitus was extremely valuable to the Florentine humanists. No wonder Poggio was so anxious to get his hands on those of his works still "unknown to us," of which the monk at Hersfeld spoke. But Poggio never received these new works. If he had, he would certainly have buttressed his argument with Guarino with information about the decline of eloquence from the *Dialogus* and about the extinction of a great man under imperial despotism in the *Agricola*. But with the Tacitus that he had in 1435, Poggio ably defended the Florentine ideal from the attacks of Guarino and Decembrio (1436). And it was only after Niccoli's death in 1437 and Cosimo's foundation, in the monastery of San Marco, of the first public library of Florence in 1441—around the core of books that Niccoli bequeathed to the city—

that a half-dozen new writers used Tacitus. With one exception, none of them was Florentine. With no exceptions, none of them used Tacitus for political purposes. Times had changed since 1403, and especially since 1434.

When Cosimo de' Medici returned from exile in 1434, he quickly and quietly rose to a position of dominance; while preserving all the external forms of republican government, he achieved power principally by controlling the elections.[33] In 1440, the year before Tacitus' works probably were moved to the new library, Cosimo secured his rule by the Florentine victory over the forces of Filippo Maria at Anghiari (29 June). Milan was no longer a threat. In fact, Florence became a threat to Milan. Filippo Maria was so weakened after Anghiari that he finally decided to rely on the ambitious condottiere, Francesco Sforza, whom he allowed to marry his daughter in November 1441. Cosimo now began to back Francesco over the question of the Milanese succession. Though some Florentines grumbled at the political risk involved (the risk of alienating Venice) and complained about the heavy taxes the policy required, they could really do nothing about it. Nor would discontented citizens get any help from the exiles of Cosimo's regime, for they too had been soundly beaten at Anghiari. Florentines were beginning to accept the rule of one man. But even before Anghiari, Bruni, who was chancellor from 1427 until his death in 1444, had noticed the change. In his pamphlet *On the Politeia of the Florentines* (1439) he observes that the people now have the right to accept or reject laws, even though all decisions are made by a small ruling group.[34] Poggio, who years later became chancellor (1453) and remained in this office until his death in 1459, lived to see the end result of what Bruni had seen in transition only. In 1458 Cosimo wanted certain constitutional changes, and the vote of the people was to be taken on 11 August: "The partisans planted in the square will shout 'Yes! Yes!' and the common people will join in the cry according to custom"—so wrote an intimate of Cosimo *before* voting day; and, on 11 August, the people performed as directed.[35] Poggio's *Historia Fiorentina,* a narrative of Florentine wars from 1350 to 1445, is almost totally devoid of comment on internal affairs. It was safer that way. Florence had passed under the rule of one man.

The Florentines resigned themselves to the rule of Cosimo in the 1440s and '50s. Nevertheless, Bruni's ideas, based on what Tacitus said had happened when Rome passed under the rule of one man, had a deep and lasting influence, an influence which, however, would have no dynamic impact until the Soderini Republic and Machiavelli. But from Tacitus directly, the Florentines ceased to derive any new inspiration. They almost forgot about Tacitus altogether. Anyone interested could have gotten hold of a copy—many were in use by 1450; and if anyone wanted to see the archetype itself, he had only to go down to the new library—it was right there: the seventh book in the fifth bank. But with one exception (Leon Battista Alberti—see below) there is no evidence that any Florentine ever bothered.

Elsewhere in Italy, however, Tacitus was just at this moment beginning to attract considerable attention. This interest, however, was inspired by very different reasons from those that had prevailed in Florence; for until the late fifteenth century in Germany and the early sixteenth century in Italy no one used Tacitus again for political ends. Until then, from the demise of the political interest in Tacitus inspired by Bruni, Tacitus was employed in two ways only: for the study of classical antiquities and for historiography.

Interest in Tacitus as a source of information on Roman antiquities is evident in two writers, both of whom sought information on Roman buildings: Leon Battista Alberti, the famous Florentine scientist, and Flavio Biondo, the great historian and antiquarian. In Alberti's *De architectura* (1451 or 1452) there are five places where Tacitus provided examples for some of Alberti's principles: that mausoleums should be modest but durable (ii. 2), that certain stones had a fireproof quality (ii. 9), that Jerusalem's angular walls were difficult to storm (iv. 3), that Nero's wide streets were hot and unhealthy (iv. 5), that the vacant space left next to city walls should be large (viii. 6).[36] Such information was very practical for Alberti's purposes, and his work served as a guide for the new buildings of Renaissance Rome and other cities. Alberti had little time for political problems. Biondo,[37] on the other hand, despite a stormy political career, was never inspired to use Tacitus for political purposes. Exiled from his native Forlì in 1422 and secretary of many temporal princes and five popes, he made enemies and friends among the rulers of his day. With Pope Eugenius IV Biondo was especially intimate; and Bruni, realizing this fact, chose Biondo to be his agent in recommending his new Latin translation of Aristotle's *Politics* to Eugenius (1437). But despite their close ties during the very time of Poggio's dispute with Guarino and Decembrio's attack on Bruni over Tacitus, Biondo did not become involved. Instead, he devoted himself increasingly to scholarship: *Roma instaurata* (1440–46), *Italia illustrata* (1448–53), the *Decades de inclinatione Romani imperii* (the first medieval history, 1440–53), and the *Roma triumphans* (1456–60). The *Roma instaurata,* like the others except the *Decades,* is a work of antiquarian research. More particularly, it was an attempt to describe the sites and architectural remains of ancient Rome with reference to contemporary locations. For at least a dozen pieces of information he quoted or at least referred to Tacitus; these related to the great fire in the reign of Nero, the obelisk which stood in the gardens of Lircus, the original city which Romulus built, the theater of Pompey, etc.[38] In the *Roma triumphans,* an encyclopedia of facts and definitions on every conceivable facet of Roman life and institutions—all bearing, very indirectly, on the Roman triumph—he again used Tacitus merely as a source of data. The same is true for the *Italia illustrata,* a geographical-archeological survey and biographical dictionary. Despite the practical aims of these works as a whole—resistance to the Turk, glorification of ancient virtue in comparison to the modern religious eminence of Rome, patriotic exhortation to popes to repair and maintain ancient edifices—neither Tacitus nor any classical author is used with direct political intention. "In all the welter of factional history Biondo's work has, in fact, a kind of detachment which is both rare and salutary"[39]—as Denys Hay, one of Biondo's most recent scholars, has it. Thus, in neither Alberti nor Biondo was Tacitus of any political value; and perhaps, given the nature of their works, none should be expected.

The field of historiography, on the other hand, might seem to have offered better opportunities for the conveyance of political ideas based on Tacitus. But here, too, the search is vain. In fact, Tacitus was hardly ever used by historians for any purpose whatsoever. Sicco Polentone, the famous Greek professor at Florence, used Tacitus, it is true, in his *Scriptores illustres linguae latinae* (1447) on the life of Seneca; but it is a rare use of Tacitus at this time. The basis for the general neglect of Tacitus was that his style was considered atrocious; that is, it was un-Ciceronian. History was part of rhetoric. This is not to say that it was deceitful panegyric (though, contrary to its true aim, it often degenerated to this) or truth distorted for moral purposes. On the contrary, rhetorical history was the truth told beautifully:

> The humanist rhetoric of history did not visualize history as a method, as a system, or as a body of facts which could become tools for theoretical analysis. It visualized history rather as *historiae,* as fact given form and life through eloquence, and as moral

> types made concrete in order to fulfill its purposes—*docere, movere,* and *delectare*.[40]

Thus Hanna H. Gray, one of the best authorities on Renaissance historiography, summarized her studies on the fifteenth-century *artes historiae*. To teach, to persuade to moral activity, to please: these were the three stars or ideals of fifteenth-century historiography, and Ciceronian eloquence was seen as the *primum mobile*. From the time that Salutati first read him and found his style displeasing, Tacitus' popularity was generally held in check because he was un-Ciceronian.[41] Moreover, Lorenzo Valla, the philologian at the court of Alfonso of Aragon, contributed to this disregard for Tacitus by his establishment of Ciceronian style as Latinity at its best. His greatest work, the *Elegantiae linguae latinae,* was motivated by a concern to establish correct usage, based on a thorough study of the ancient authors. Those of the Ciceronian age seemed most pure to him. The book had a tremendous reception, so much so that in the following century the Ciceronians became the leaders of a tyrannous cult. But Valla himself was not so dogmatic. Though he thought Livy was the most eloquent historian, he did not hesitate to use Tacitus as authority for many of his own usages, and it is in this connection alone that Tacitus has a place in Valla's historical writings. In his *Recriminations against Fazio* (begun in 1445) he fell back on Tacitus at least five times to defend certain grammatical usages in his *De rebus a Ferdinando Aragoniae Rege gestis* (1445–46), a history of Alfonso's father. In one place only did he refer to Tacitus to support a fact (that a deputation came to Nero's senate from Puteoli) rather than a fine point of grammar;[42] in another place Tacitus is named along with Livy, Sallust, and Trogus as a historian who manifestly committed errors.[43] But to Bartolomeo Fazio, the vituperative critic of Valla's history, the occasional unorthodoxies of style were not of prime importance. What really bothered him was Valla's historical realism—his descriptions of a queen trembling in fear, a king nodding off to sleep during diplomatic negotiations. Such presentations of human weaknesses, and especially those of royalty, seemed to destroy the *moral* purpose of history. When Fazio got around to writing his own history, that of his patron, King Alfonso, it was nothing but a panegyric. Though fifteenth-century historiography did not always degenerate to Fazio's level, Valla's experiment in stark realism and his "extreme" liberty of style were not imitated. The realism of Tacitus was appreciated just as little, and Valla's own *Elegantiae* was largely instrumental in causing a general lack of enthusiasm for Tacitus' style. How could such an un-Ciceronian manner of speech teach, move, and delight? Tacitus' popularity did not increase even when the first printed editions appeared; he was read more often,[44] to be sure, but liked just as little.

Around 1476, Franciscus Puteolanus, the editor of the second edition of Tacitus' works, tried to convey some of his own enthusiasm for his author among prospective buyers. Speaking about the *Agricola,* he pronounced it a work "which so affects me, delights me, and holds my interest that I have read nothing with equal pleasure."[45] Readers probably did not agree with him. A little later, in another preface (written before 1480), he again spoke of the *Agricola,* but now with some regret over the "many sleepless nights and the most intent study" expended on his work.[46] Then (somewhat like Petrarch expressing his anger at the scholastics for making a mess of Aristotle) he finds someone to blame for his jumbled Tacitus:

> Indeed, the Venetian printers have trodden upon and disfigured this divine work and have not only contaminated the majesty of Cornelian eloquence, but scarcely any sense can now be conjectured. Let the learned judge what I have accomplished—but only after they have collated copies.[47]

Perhaps Puteolanus was helped by the manuscript of the Hersfeld *Agricola;*[48] if not, both he and the Venetian printer, Vindelinus, might justly have blamed some medieval copyist. However, he did not have to make any excuses for the works which had come to him less mutilated. To be sure, Tacitus' style almost charmed him:

> In my opinion, he easily surpasses all in this skill; so thick is the content that the number of words almost equals the number of ideas. So keen and forceful with words is he that you do not know whether the subject matter is elucidated by the language or the words by the ideas. In speeches (and indeed I dare to disclose what I feel) he comes even before Livy, and he imitates Sallust's incisive terseness more than Livy's fullness . . . ; he will always teach with an ingenious variety and will delight with immense pleasure.[49]

"And indeed I dare to disclose what I feel."

To be sure, Puteolanus was going against the grain of the taste of his time. The historians might have approved of Puteolanus' praise of Tacitus' experience, honesty, and diligence; but the style was simply unpalatable to them, and it remained so for the next several decades. In the dialogue *Actius* (1499),[50] Giovanni Pontano, the famous Neapolitan humanist, has his speaker Altilius (*pro historia*) sum up his opinions on classical models for historiography; in them Tacitus was not highly rated:

> What, I implore you, is so opposed to history as falsehood, when history is said to be the mistress of life? We have required as much elegance as possible especially on this account, that this kind of writing is itself destitute of very many other merits and virtues. And thus what it lacks in refinement and other great merits is at least counterbalanced by elegance . . . ; for although both Tacitus and Curtius are abundantly equipped with their own merits and virtues, nevertheless the whole glory of Latin history is thought to rest with two men who had different styles, Livy and Sallust. In addition, the injustice of time has taken Trogus completely from us, and Curtius and Tacitus appear to us as maimed images, so that one must surmise and conjecture rather than deliver any completely absolute and certain judgment about them.[51]

Exactly contrary to Puteolanus' bold assertion, Pontano did not think Livy and Sallust inferior to Tacitus. In fact, he ignored Tacitus almost entirely. In five dialogues, including the *Actius,* Tacitus is cited in only three other places, twice on grammatical points and once on the fact that Tacitus wrote on the origin of the Jews.[52] The *Actius* was based on actual discussions about poetry, literature, and history held in 1495 at Pontano's academy in a garden at the foot of Mount Vesuvius. Bernardo Rucellai, Florentine statesman, diplomat, and humanist, attended the meetings in this year and, in a letter to a friend about them, came to similar conclusions about Tacitus: "He is far from pristine dignity and grace."[53] Because of these sentiments, Tacitus was generally ignored in fifteenth-century historiography; and even when he is used in historical works, he is never the subject of any political interest.

This entire situation was soon to change quite drastically. Even as Rucellai conversed with Pontano and his other friends at the foot of Mount Vesuvius, a storm swept down on Italy from over the Alps: Charles VIII, king of France, and his armies. Italy was suddenly dragged into the maelstrom of European politics. Just as suddenly, Italian statesmen and historians were forced to think differently about the role of politics and history. Machiavelli and Guicciardini are the best representatives of the new way of thinking, and it is only with them that Tacitus came to prominence as a historian and political thinker. This story about Tacitus' new practicality in political thought does not end until early in the seventeenth century and will be considered in later chapters. However, at about the time that this development began in Italy, Tacitus' popularity was reaching a high point in Germany.

Tacitus' *Germania* was well known in Germany by 1500. In it many German humanists were beginning to see a new ideal for German greatness of culture, prowess in warfare, and moral superiority. Conrad Celtis, the German archhumanist, was the first to create this image out of the newly discovered text. His successors carried his enthusiastic example to such dynamic heights that the Reformation (although essentially spiritual in its cause) was politically successful in Germany largely because they used the *Germania* to stir up national patriotic aspirations—providing, at once, foundation for local movements of civic patriotism and structure for more concerted action in a common national ideology. One of these successors, Ulrich von Hutten, the great patriot and Reformer, reinforced the idealism acquired from the *Germania* with what he learned about Arminius, the slayer of three Roman legions in 9 A.D., in the newly discovered sections of the *Annales*. But by this time, around 1519 and after, the texts were creating a hurricane of passion among Hutten's compatriots. This had all begun about sixty years earlier, in 1458, when the Germans were first introduced to the *Germania* by Enea Silvio Piccolomini. Enea Silvio was the first to use the new text, which had been discovered only three years before. When he now wrote to Chancellor Martin Mayer of Mainz, he employed the *Germania* to buttress his argument that Mayer and other Germans should be grateful sons of the Church and readily pay their papal taxes. Piccolomini could never imagine the storm this use of Tacitus was to bring. He gave the Germans the *Germania,* and, in doing so, he ultimately helped lose half of Europe for the Catholic Church.

2 Tacitus in Reformation Political Thought

"The world is a haystack; everyone grabs what he can lay hands on," is a German proverb depicted in Hieronymus Bosch's *The Hay Wagon,* painted between 1485 and 1490.[1] The hay wagon, drawn by half-human monsters, leads a procession of the great ones of the world: prelates and princes, the pope and the Holy Roman emperor. Many throw themselves insanely at the wagon; many are crushed beneath its huge wheels. The wagon is being driven to hell. To Bosch, Europe of the late-fifteenth and early-sixteenth centuries was this hay wagon, just as to Sebastian Brant it was a *Narrenschiff* and to Erasmus it was *Stultitia*'s oration hall.

They had good reason to be skeptical about the world around them. Chaos reigned in the empire; war raged outside the empire. The Diet of Worms (1495) and the Diet of Augsburg (1500) only emphasized rather than alleviated the tension between the imperial government and the independent cities. The quarrels of the empire with Bohemia, Hungary, Poland, France, the Swiss cantons, and the Italian states frequently resulted in armed conflict. Many thought that the Turks were infernal angels of divine retribution, carrying out God's punishment for Germany's sinfulness and for the wickedness of the ecclesiastical hierarchy—of the pope in particular. Some, indeed, even thought of these events as a portent of the Last Days. Philip the Handsome, archduke of Austria, commissioned Bosch to paint *The Last Judgment* in 1504, and many believed in the astrologers' prophecies of the end of the world. Pessimism and fear of doom were the characteristics of the age; and, for Germans, the inept Frederick III had done little to brighten the murky situation of the empire.

With the accession of Maximilian I, the young German humanists might have anxiously sighed and said words similar to those of Tacitus when Trajan came to the throne: "Now, at last, our spirit is returning."[2] Maximilian, according to one observer, possessed "true joy in the prospering of the sciences and the arts."[3] He had become emperor in 1493 and soon recognized Conrad Celtis, poet (presented with the poet's laurel by Emperor Frederick III in 1487), playwright, and philosopher, as an invaluable source of power for his own patriotic idealism. Celtis was a burning patriot, and he dedicated to Maximilian his *Germania generalis,* which was published with Tacitus' *Germania* in 1500.[4] In gratitude, Maximilian granted Celtis the charter which established the Poets College at the University of Vienna in 1501. Celtis was the first humanist to lecture on Tacitus in a German university, and Tacitus was at the core of Celtis' patriotism.

It was Celtis who first made Tacitus generally popular among the Germans. Inspired by the *Germania,* he in turn inspired German patriots for generations to come by passing on to them all the wealth of the Golden Age which he had discovered. In the empire's darkest hours, Johannes Aventinus, Ulrich von Hutten, and Beatus Rhenanus were the principal heirs of Celtis' patriotic hope that Germany could achieve unity and regain her ancient glory. Indeed, in unity lay the basis of German military power; and that truth was one they could back up with the authority of Tacitus: "Fortune can give no greater boon than discord among our foes" (*Germania* xxxiii). Celtis became the greatest foe of German discord, and he found in the *Germania* the golden sword with which to lead his brothers onward.

It is difficult to say just when Celtis first learned of the *Germania*. It was introduced to the Germans from Italy. First, it came through Enea Silvio Piccolomini, who in 1458 defended the papacy against charges of cupidity made by Martin Mayer, the chancellor of Mainz. Mayer had written Enea Silvio around 31 August 1457 to congratulate him on his recent elevation to the office of cardinal;[5] but one thing bothered him—the fact that Enea Silvio had received the scarlet hat at a time when the papacy was so corrupt. The present pope, Calixtus III, so Mayer thought, had not only ignored the settlements of the Council of Constance and the Council of Basel but was refusing to honor the contracts made by his predecessor, Nicholas V. The papacy believed it could trample all over the Germans. The Holy See was contriving a thousand ingenious and subtle methods for extorting gold from the Germans, as though from barbarians.[6] The Germans, who had once conquered the Roman Empire, were now reduced to poverty and made handmaidens and tribute-payers. But the princes of Germany were now beginning to wake up ("quasi ex somno excitati").[7] Again he said that it was a shame that Enea Silvio had been raised so high when the papacy was so low. To counter these charges, the cardinal wrote a tractate-letter, in which, as part of his defense, he cited the *Germania*. He contrasted ancient Germans with contemporary Germans and argued that only when the barbarians had become subjected to Rome and to the papacy did they rise to their present condition of civilization:

> Cornelius Tacitus, who lived in Hadrian's times, writes even more ferocious things about Germany. Indeed, the life of your ancestors in that time was scarcely different from that of beasts. Indeed, most of them were shepherds, inhabitants of forests and groves. Aristotle is the authority that such kind of life is inert and lazy. Among them there were no fortified cities nor towns surrounded with a wall. There were no castles built on the high mountains, no temples erected from cut stones were seen. They lacked the delight of gardens and villas; they cultivated no orchards, no farms, no beautiful valleys, no vineyards. Rivers gave abundant refreshment. Lakes and pools were at hand for baths and also if nature provided warm waters. Silver was rare among them, and gold was even more rare; the use of pearls was unknown. There was no ostentation of gems, no vestments of purple or of silk. Not yet were mineral mines searched out. Not yet did thirst of gold push wretched men into the viscera of the earth. These things ought to be praised and extolled above our own ways. But, in this manner of living there was no knowledge of letters, no discipline of the laws, no study of the fine arts. Even the religion was stupid and barbarous, fosterer of idols and, in fact, tottering with illusions of demons—so that it ought not be doubted that human enemies were often sacrificed among them [*Germania* ix] to obtain favorable omens. Robberies were praised. Everything was foul; everything was abominable, harsh, barbarous, and, to use the proper words, savage and brutal.[8]

The tractate-letter was not published in Leipzig until 1496, when it appeared under the title *De ritu, situ, moribus et condicione Germaniae descriptio*. Its effect on German humanists was immediate. "With this, there fell among them, wholly unexpected, a beam of light upon the early history of the Germans," as Hans Tiedemann, one of the first investigators of the phenomenon, put it.[9]

Though the publication of Enea Silvio's letter may have been "wholly unexpected," it had in fact been preceded, twenty-five years earlier, by Giovanni Antonio Campano's speech to the citizens of Regensburg in 1471.[10] Campano, court poet of Pius II and later a historian, reminded the Germans of the great and noble deeds of their ancient fathers, and his speech was calculated to ignite their spirits to take a strong offensive against the Turks. But since he really didn't think the

Germans would understand it, he had it published at least for Italian readers.[11] It was widely read, too, and Campano unwittingly encouraged its diffusion in Germany by letters to his friends in Italy, especially to Cardinal Giacomo Piccolomini Ammanati, papal secretary and humanist, in which he revealed: "I despise not only the customs, but even the very name of Germany."[12] Such letters were circulated widely shortly after they were written, and they provoked a number of angry responses.[13] Celtis was only twelve years old at the date of the speech and the letters, and any "angry responses" from him could have been made, to be sure, only after 1497, the year in which the letters were published. The actual text of the *Germania,* moreover, must have been known to Celtis five years before the letters were published (and four years before Enea Silvio's *De ritu, situ, . . .*) since he used it for his famous oration at Ingolstadt in 1492; and it is probable that Celtis had the text, in manuscript or printed form, five or even ten years earlier. It was not, however, Enea Silvio's tractate-letter or Campano's speech and letters (which stirred up only a momentary furor) but Celtis' *Oratio* that drew contemporary interest to the *Germania,* nineteen years after it had become available in Germany.[14] The first recension of the *Germania* was in the *editio princeps,* or *Spirensis,* of the German printer Vindelinus de Spira in Venice in 1470. Vindelinus' recension was then reprinted, with slight modification, in Bologna in 1472,[15] in Milan in 1475, and in Venice in 1476, 1481, and 1497. Two editions then appeared in Germany, both following the recension of the *Germania* established by Frederick Creussner in Nuremberg in 1473; and a third appeared in Rome the following year. The third recension was that of Celtis himself, published in Vienna in 1500.[16] Hence, there were plenty of texts; but the texts themselves provoked no special interest until Celtis pointed to their importance by his *Oratio;* indeed, it was only after the *Oratio* that Enea Silvio's letter and Campano's vituperative letters were seized upon as "hot" enough to publish.[17] Moreover, even Celtis' interest was aroused only after he had become involved in patriotic quarrels. After all, he could easily have seen the Italian editions of *Germania* even if he had missed the German ones. But only in 1487, when he broke off his friendship with Marcus Sabellicus, the historian of Venice and librarian of Saint Mark's, for disparaging the titles of German princes and calling them barbarians,[18] is there any sign of his having a knowledge of the text; and it was only thereafter that he struck up a friendship with Philippus Beroaldus, the Venetian philologian, who was congenial to German humanists and who was very interested in Tacitus.

By 1492, then, when he finally took up his position at the University of Ingolstadt,[19] the polemical context was clear. The *Oratio* supported the imperial policy of Maximilian; it railed against the abuse of papal and episcopal authority for worldly ends; and it exhorted the Germans to restore military honor and the imperium:

> O free and powerful people, O noble and valiant race, plainly worthy of the Roman Empire, our famous harbor is held by the Sarmatian [Pole], and the gateway of our ocean by the Dacian [Dane]! In the east also powerful peoples live in slavery, the Marcomanni, the Quadi, the Bastarnae, and the Peucini, who all live as it were separated from the body of our Germany.[20]

Tacitus turned out to be eminently serviceable for such ends; hence, the names "Marcomanni," "Quadi," "Bastarnae," and "Peucini" are taken from no other source than *Germania* xlii and xlvi. Had Celtis been speaking in the language of his audience, he would have referred instead to the Bohemians, the Moravians, the Slovaks, and the Silesians. Though Celtis had come to despise these peoples on his journeys, he realized their value to the empire; and forcing somewhat their names at least permitted him to demonstrate that they were Germans and should therefore submit to imperial rule. He had in mind particularly the Bohemians, and indeed he was soon to be embroiled in an argument with the Slavic humanist Augustinus Moravus.[21] Celtis argued that Mannus, son of the "earthborn god, Tuisco" (*Germania* ii), had conquered the enemy Boii, a Gallic tribe; the remnants of the Boii were combined with their conquerors, but their basically German nationality survived through the Boe-manni (or Bohemians); this name, associated again with the conqueror Mannus, corresponded, so Celtis thought, with the Marcomanni also. To be sure, Tacitus, in *Germania* xxviii, said that "the name Boiemum still survives, marking the old tradition of the place, though the population has been changed"; and this very territory, "from which the Boii were driven in a former age [by the Marcomanni], was won by valor" (*Germania* xlii).

If Maximilian, still archduke of Austria at the time of the *Oratio,* had difficulty in maintaining suzerainty over Bohemia, he was to find even more difficulty in reestablishing it over Lombardy. But to Celtis the policy was already clear—the policy, that is, which Maximilian would in fact adopt as soon as he succeeded to the imperial throne and which would carry him across the Alps shortly afterward, in 1495. "Let us be ashamed, noble gentlemen," Celtis continued,

> that certain modern historians (who, publishing new *Decades,* boast that they have equaled the ancient Roman Empire) should speak of our most famous leaders merely as "the barbarians" . . . ; such has been the power of that long-standing and irreconcilable hatred between us that [would], . . . in view of the hostile spirit on both sides, inevitably have led to mutual slaughter, had not prudent Nature separated us by the Alps and by rocks towering to the stars. [*Oratio,* sentence 37.][22]

Celtis, it seems, was getting even with Sabellicus, who had divided his *Historiae rerum Venetarum ab urbe condita* into *decades* on the model of Livy. Celtis, attacking his newly made enemy, used poetic figures on the model of Tacitus. In *Germania* i the first sentence states that

> Germany is separated from the Galli, the Rhaeti, and Pannonii, by the rivers Rhine and Danube; mountain ranges, or the fear which each feels for the other, divide it from the Sarmatae and the Daci.[23]

Despite the Alps, Celtis declaimed,

> Assume, O men of Germany, that ancient spirit of yours, with which you so often terrified the Romans, and turn your eyes to the frontiers of Germany, collect together her torn and broken territories. [*Oratio,* sentence 41.]

Was Celtis thinking of Tacitus?

> In the space of this long epoch many losses have been sustained on both sides . . . ; Germans, by routing or making prisoners of Carbo, Cassius, Scaurus Aurelius [etc.] . . . deprived the Roman people of five consular armies, and they robbed even a Caesar of Varus and his three legions. [*Germania* xxxvii.]

Perhaps referring more specifically to Tacitus, Celtis explained that the Greeks and the Romans have written about Germany,

> and though it seems rough and wild, I imagine, in comparison with their own climate, they have expressed our customs, our emotional makeup, and our spirits as graphically as a painter might delineate our bodies. [*Oratio,* sentence 31.]

Surely, the reference to Tacitus, Celtis' "graphic painter," is unmistakable:

> Who would leave Asia, or Africa, or Italy for Germany, with its wild country, its inclement skies, its sullen manners and aspect, unless indeed it were his home? [*Germania* ii.]

Besides, neither Caesar, Pliny, nor Strabo was as graphic. Only Tacitus had depicted German mores so thoroughly, both the virtues and the vices. But, after all, German vices were only Italian imports, or so Celtis believed.

> To such an extent are we corrupted by Italian sensuality and by fierce cruelty in exacting filthy lucre, that it would have been far more holy and reverent for us to practice that rude and rustic life of old, living within the bounds of self-control. [*Oratio,* sentence 66.]

For Tacitus, too, the vices of Germans were often imported. Tacitus described the Germans before contact with the Romans:

> Of lending money on interest and increasing it by compound interest they know nothing—a more effectual safeguard than if it were prohibited. [*Germania* xxvi.]

> You may see among them vessels of silver, which have been presented to their envoys and chieftains, held as cheap as those of clay. [*Germania* v.]

But, after contact with the Romans: "We have now taught them to accept money also" (*Germania* xv).[24]

These and other parallels certainly suggest that Celtis had Tacitus in mind. Though the *Oratio* nowhere contains a mention of Tacitus, it is obvious that Celtis' theme of the contrast between contemporary Germans, corrupted and weak, with those of the Golden Age was the principal purpose behind his use of the text. Celtis' use of the text was the same as Enea Silvio's—with one difference: for Celtis the Germans were corrupted, not civilized, after contact with Rome and the papacy. The theme is even more evident in three other works by Celtis: *Germania generalis* (including the text of *Germania*) (Vienna, 1500); *Quattuor libri amorum secundum quattuor latera Germania* (*Liber amorum*) (Nuremberg, 1502)—a description of the four corners of Germany, symbolized by Celtis' four loves: Hasilina the Pole,[25] Elsula of Nuremberg, Ursula of Mainz, and Barbara of Lübeck; and *De origine, situ, moribus et institutis Norimbergae libellus* (*Norimberga*) (Nuremberg, 1502)—a description of Nuremberg, with a hymn to its patron saint, Saint Sebaldus, and illustrations in woodcut by Dürer.

Though these works had been fermenting long in Celtis' mind, their appearance between 1500 and 1502 is itself an important event, considering the close ties between Celtis and Maximilian and considering the condition of the empire in these years. The *Germania generalis* was dedicated to Maximilian; and in 1500 Maximilian was in narrow straits. On 10 April (the very day that Ludovico il Moro, tyrant of Milan and regent for Gian Galeazzo Sforza, fell into the hands of the French) Maximilian opened the imperial Diet of Augsburg. Hopelessly opposed by the diet, he was powerless to hinder the truce concluded with France, which, in effect, gave Milan to Louis XII. This opposition to Maximilian on the part of the diet was the immediate result of the drastic blow sustained by the imperial power through the defeat at Dornach (24 July 1499) and the subsequent Treaty of Basel (22 September 1499)—events which made up "a long chain of serious external failures, for which, in some respects, the burden fell wholly on the person of the emperor himself and his indiscreet politics," according to Rudolf Buchner, Maximilian's most recent biographer.[26] The establishment of the Reichsregiment seemed to deprive the emperor of almost all his power. The Diet of Nuremberg of 1501 posed nothing less than a threat of revolutionary reforms. Faced with the dissolution of his remaining power, Maximilian resorted to an appeal for the revival of the chivalrous and adventurous spirit of the princes; German unity and glory, he believed, could be achieved by fighting the Turks and the French, not by wrangling over constitutional reform—not by parliamentary debates but by blood and iron! In the light of these events and Maximilian's invocation of the ancient German spirit, the *Liber amorum* of 1502 and the *Norimberga* of 1502 were calls to action. All three works were Celtis' poetic exhortation to seek a solution of the problems of the empire; they were a legion of hexameters charging forth from the Golden Age to stir the breasts of modern Germans.

Celtis had ample precedent for his purpose of writing history to inspire action in emulation of the deeds and ideals of the Golden Age. It was a Renaissance tradition that had begun with Leonardo Bruni. In his preface to the *Histories of the Florentine People* Bruni had stated that "there is no doubt that historical information is most useful, particularly to whoever rules or governs," and he had hoped "that the citizens, in reading of the worthy things done by those in the past, [would] be encouraged to do likewise." The same purpose is evident throughout Celtis' historical works; and it is possible that he felt himself a part of the humanist tradition he had learned to appreciate in Italy. Scholarship, at any rate, served primarily a rhetorical purpose; and Celtis saw to it that the lessons he drew from the past were enhanced by vivid imagery. Like Bruni, Celtis was inspired in large part by Tacitus:

> They have chests as mighty as the limbs of their bodies, and generous nature endowed them with milky necks which carry their white bodies with these huge arms and legs. Their hair is reddish gold, and their eyes blaze with golden splendor. Their limbs hold the proper stature in just the right proportion.[27]

Thus the Germans were associated with the mythological heroes and demigods of Greece and Rome. Celtis also knew that such beautiful creatures were native to the German soil, that they were a race pure in itself:

> The race, unconquered, remains the most famous in the whole world. . . . Indigenous, no other race is more primordial. The womb of Demogorgon spread open and scattered the race widely, where, under the winds of the air, it was created, all together at the same moment.[28]

Thus the ancient Germans, begotten by heaven, were free from pollution of foreign blood.[29] They were also free of alien vices, especially greed: "No one knew interest and usury in that time, since sustenance was gained wholly from the sod of the fatherland."[30] So pure, so naturally moral, so close to the earth were the ancient Germans that they even had their equine oracles: "There were also many herds of horses which were reared at the public expense and never were contaminated by mortal use."[31]

Indeed, in what seemed the eventide of the German empire, Celtis reminded Maximilian of how brilliantly golden was the dawn. The emperor, Celtis, and the scores of German humanists whom Celtis had loosely organized in his Rhenish and Danubian *sodalities* all knew that the night must come; but they hoped it would be short and that, with the new day, the Emperor Frederick Barbarossa, slumbering on the Kyffhäuser, would come to restore the Germans to their ancient glory. The young humanists were even hoping that Barbarossa would infuse his spirit into Maximilian. But when would the spirit awaken? Could things become any worse than they were? The emperor riding alongside the pope, directly behind Bosch's hay wagon, could very well be taken for Maximilian himself.[32] Doom, damnation, seemed inevitable. Celtis, after reading Tacitus, at least made a reversal of direction seem possible: the hay wagon might not go to hell after all.

Celtis died in 1508. Had he lived a little longer, he would have recognized Ulrich von Hutten as a personification of his ideal German. The archhumanist had been dead three years when the sickly and impoverished Hutten rode into Vienna with the horse, the clothes, and the money that had recently been given him by the charitable Thurzo, bishop of Olmütz. He was poor because his father had disowned him for wanting to become a poet and not a monk, and he was sickly because he had worn himself to exhaustion traveling around northern Germany in search of the classics and the classicists. His fortunes, however, were soon to change. He soon met the leaders of German humanism, Crotus Rubianus, Joachim Vadianus, Peter Eberbach, Eobanus Hessius, and Mutianus Rufus; and after a short stay in Vienna, he was off to continue his education in Italy.

He had scarcely touched Italian soil (January 1513) when his friends in Vienna published a poem to Emperor Maximilian which Hutten had written in the midst of his fatiguing travel in Germany. The poem, ''Ad Caesarem Maximilianum ut bellum in Venetos coeptum prosequatur,''[33] was an important turning point in his career; from minor personal and literary pursuits, he now turned to the affairs of his country. Maximilian's plans to march on Rome to be crowned in 1508 had been frustrated by the Venetians, who had blocked his military advance at Padua. The poem served as an antidote to discouragement. It advised the emperor not only to conquer Venice but to go on to conquer the Turks and, finally, the whole world. He had then (1511) added a long poem calculated to shame the emperor into action. The aim is obvious from its title: ''Quod Germania nec virtutibus nec ducibus ab primoribus degeneraverit'' (''That Germany may have degenerated from the foremost nobles in neither virtues nor leaders'').[34] So also is the source, for it is clear that Hutten had read Tacitus' *Germania*. His image of the ancient Germans (just like the modern ones, he fervently hoped) was, in substance, taken directly from the *Germania:*[35]

> We got rid of silver, too, and we did without noble gold; we chose gems instead. And where once it was said that no terrain was more infertile, it now produces all kinds of vineyards, beautiful saffron, superb clothing, sheep, and cattle.[36] We discovered certain arts, so glorious that no age will sufficiently praise them.[37]

About the silver and the gold, Tacitus, in *Germania* v, had said the same thing.[38] The ''gems'' refer to the amber, or *glaesum,* mentioned in *Germania* xlv, for which the natives were surprised to be paid, since they had considered it useless. The ancient Germans were rich in things which Roman greed had made valuable; but both the ancient and the modern Germans were rich in the things which were truly wealth, the fruits of nature.[39] By nature, too, they were endowed with a genius for invention, from the simple tools of the ancients to the great invention of printing. In all, Hutten thought it obvious that the Germans were superior to any other people and that their emperor was superior to all other sovereigns: "Christ has the heavens; below them Caesar rules everything. He regards no lord except the lord of heaven."[40]

This is just a mild example of the praise that Hutten expressed for his emperor in the following poetic work, *Ad Caesarem Maximilianum . . . epigrammata* (1513).[41] In a collection of 151 epigrams the emperor is praised in direct proportion to the most violent invective against the Venetians, the French, and the pope. Toward the end, he lashes out against the bellicosity of the helmeted Julius II and bewails the rape of Germany by the ruse of indulgences. Why must the emperor stand for this? he asked. Tuisco and Mannus would never have tolerated Maximilian's situation. They would have relied on themselves. Maximilian should expect no help from the ancient heroes to solve his problems. True, he should emulate them; but the action must come from himself:

> Why, O Germany, do you marvel at your kings of old? Why do you recall the ancient leaders in these times? Do not seek Gambrivus and all the sons of Tuisco, courageous hearts that were seen under the god Mannus, eagerness in arms from Hermiones and the sons of Ingevon, the chiefs of the Cimbri and the Teutonic race. And if you look for people who can make you glorious, both at home and abroad, seek neither Ariovistus nor fierce Arminius. Believe me, Charles—as great as he was—is needlessly recalled to the present age.[42]

Hutten's heroes were almost all taken from the *Germania*. But rather than just daydreaming over his edition of Tacitus, Hutten (if not Maximilian) was doing something about Germany's plight. Just a few months earlier, Hutten had been recovering from a diseased leg in Pavia when the city was besieged and taken by the Swiss imperial troops. The soldiers believed him to be a French agent, and Hutten had to pay everything he owned to keep from being taken prisoner. The destitute youth had gone to Bologna, where he managed to survive for a time; then, out of necessity as well as patriotism, he joined the imperial army. It was while he was in the army that he wrote the *Epigrammata*.

Toward the end of 1513 Hutten was back in Germany. Some months later (March 1514), the Margrave Albert of Brandenburg was elected archbishop of Magdeburg, administrator of Halberstadt, and archbishop of Mainz. Eitelwolf von Stein, Hutten's earliest patron, had already been attracted to Albert. Stein, who was attempting to revive letters at the University of Mainz (founded in 1477), provided Hutten the chance he needed by asking him to write a panegyric on the occasion of Albert's solemn entry into Mainz in November of that year. The panegyric, *In laudem reverendissimi Alberthi Archiepiscopi Moguntini . . . panegyricus,*[43] is full of imagery from the *Germania* (especially from chaps. ii, viii, ix, xv, xvii, and xxxvii) on the German gods, heroes, and warring peoples. The passages on the moral purity of the Germans, first used by Celtis, are frequently alluded to also. The Germans are exhorted to live up to their ancient traditions.

Albert was very pleased. He gave Hutten 200 golden gulden and promised him a position as soon as he had finished his legal studies in Italy—studies which Hutten had grudgingly undertaken (short of becoming a monk) to win back his father's good will. In the autumn of 1515 Hutten was again on his way to Italy, and in the spring of 1516 he was in Rome, where, he noted, "you may even buy the privilege of sinning in the future."[44] About the same time, Maximilian advanced into Lombardy and, making a fool of himself—again—retreated to Germany. While the French snickered, the Romans made fun of him; he was represented riding on a crab, with the motto: "We are proceeding toward Latium" ("Tendimus in Latinam"). While Hutten's sword was engaged in brawling with Frenchmen in the streets of Rome, his pen was just as busy defending his emperor's honor. He was especially enthusiastic in his *amor patriae* at this time, probably because it was during this stay in Italy that he first read of the greatest German hero, Arminius, slayer of Varus and his three legions, in the new section of the *Annales* just published by Beroaldus. True, he had heard of Arminius before, from other Roman historians;[45] but now he had a detailed delineation of his hero. Hutten associated Arminius with himself. As Hajo Holborn, Hutten's best and most recent biographer, explains: "Here he found the ideal of the man of politics after his own heart, possessed of valor, manliness, and will-power which yielded not to obstacles because grounded not on the fluctuations of circumstances but on constancy of purpose."[46]

For the present, however, he must have been too busy to exploit this new source in political propaganda, for it was only at the end of 1519, or early in 1520, that he wrote his famous dialogue *Arminius*. For the time being, he turned out shorter works aimed at urgent political circumstances. In rapid succession (during 1516) appeared his *Marcus, De piscatura Venetorum,* and the *Epistola ad Maximilianum Caesarem Italiae fictitia.*[47] These were all intended to conceal the blush which, he imagined, lay on his emperor's cheeks after the recent Venetian fiasco. They added greatly to the notoriety he already enjoyed from his *Phalarismus,* directed against the powerful Duke Ulrich of Württemberg, who had murdered Hutten's cousin,[48] and from his major contribution to the infamous *Epistolae obscurorum virorum,* directed against the Cologne theologians. Hutten was fighting many battles on many fronts, and his mouth and pen were as free as his sword. Hated at Bologna for his outspoken views, he went to Ferrara. From there he went to Venice, where he was protected by some humanist friends. From Venice he went back to Bologna; then, after hiding out for a few days, he returned to Germany, in June 1517.

One month later, on 12 July, Hutten was crowned with the laurel wreath of the poet by Emperor Maximilian. His poetry and patriotism were further rewarded when Archbishop Albert gave him a high position in his court. Aside from a diplomatic mission to France and a tour of the Saxon dioceses with his prince, Hutten had ample opportunity for literary work. Of note are his *Ad principes Germanos ut bellum Turcis inferant exhortatoria* (written in response to Selim I's magnificent victories in Syria and Egypt)[49] and *Febris I.*[50] Hutten had intended to read the *Exhortatoria* at the Diet of Augsburg in the summer of 1518, but Conrad Peutinger and other humanist friends dissuaded him from delivering or publishing it for fear that its assaults on Rome would bring him into danger; perhaps they thought it best to remain disassociated from the attacks Martin Luther was making, up in Wittenberg. But, certainly, they feared for Hutten because Cardinal Cajetan, the papal legate, had come to the diet to ask the Germans for money to fight the Turks. They were concerned lest Hutten, assailing the great prelate to his face, would become marked as a hot-headed sower of discord and, at the same time, would embarrass Archbishop Albert, who certainly wished no one in his service to state German grievances quite so forcefully. Though unable to speak, Hutten nonetheless became disgusted with Cajetan's supercilious manners; more basically, he hated Cajetan merely because he was a papal legate, a devious Italian come to extort money from the innocent Germans. Restraining himself for a few months, Hutten finally published the *Exhortatoria* against the advice of his friends in December (?) 1518. Two months later, in February 1519, he followed up with an attack on Cajetan himself in *Febris I.*[51] The theme of this poem is that the cardinal has come to Germany ostensibly to win money for the Turkish campaign but, in reality, wants money for the fat Pope Leo X and his pampered curial minions.

Hutten took no notice of Cajetan's talks with Luther at Augsburg

(7–20 October 1518); but after the turn of the year he gradually became an outspoken supporter of Luther, particularly after he met with Franz von Sickingen, an unscrupulous robber baron and fervent follower of Luther, in January 1520. Hutten's new attitude was put forth in the five dialogues that appeared in April 1520; and again, especially in the famous *Inspicientes* (*The Observers*),[52] the patriotic fervor and the antipapal grievances both lean heavily on the *Germania*.

The observers are Apollo and his son Phaethon, who have stopped their chariot at high noon above Augsburg to rest. Cardinal Cajetan complains about the heat, and here Hutten begins a most hilarious invective.[53] Tacitus' *Germania* supplied much of its fuel. After speaking of the way the Germans are getting wiser to the tricks of the Italian papacy, the discussion turns to the Italian charge that the Germans are barbarians. Apollo and Phaethon then review the customs and mores of the Germans, and one by one the usual accusations against them are battered down. Drinking, first of all, is disposed of:

> SOL: Indeed, I do not just say this, [but] in truth, fact itself shows that they accomplish many things better than any other sober people and dispose of affairs more prudently. For they follow that proverb that is well known among them: "counsel from dawn, conviviality from sunset"—for they imbibe nourishment until late in the night and from dawn they remain without having eaten and consider the state and important matters.[54]

Next, the question of marital fidelity:

> SOL: And they do not hold [wives] in common but exhibit their faith in this matter: hardly anywhere where the modesty of women is guarded is it more unimpaired than here, where it is neglected and placed in danger. Indeed, adulteries are nowhere more rare; nowhere is matrimony cherished more religiously and held in sanctity.[55]

The discussion then turns to German self-sufficiency and simplicity:

> SOL: Listen. From the beginning there were no cities in Germany, nor were the houses contiguous—indeed, each and every house was apart.[56]
>
> PHAETHON: I know.
>
> SOL: Nor at that time did merchants approach them who imported stuff from another land. They used all things produced among them and only these things.

They clothed themselves in the pelts of wild beasts. In food as well, they used only those things which the soil of the fatherland produced. External things were everywhere unknown. No peddlers defrauded anyone in that time. There was rigid probity everywhere, and everyone adhered to it. Nobody had seen any money, nor did they have silver and gold.[57]

PHAETHON: This was the best time of Germany.

A little later Sol describes the inherent energy and restlessness of the ancient Germans:

> He [the ancient German] was especially eager for military glory; a despiser of money, he exercised himself in hunting, and, impatient of tranquillity, he had a hatred of quietude.[58]

When Hutten wrote these words, Maximilian had already died. He probably wrote them when he was hopeful of the new emperor, Charles V. Maximilian had proved inept and had too much opposition, but Charles, heir to half of Europe, would be able to carry out the aims Hutten envisioned. Perhaps Charles would prove to be the new Arminius. Probably with such a parallel in mind, Hutten wrote his famous dialogue *Arminius* late in 1519 or early in 1520.[59] He wrote it in the polemical context of theological and political issues being brought into sharper focus between the Leipzig Debates and Luther's excommunication. During this time, other Reformers began stepping up their output of violent pamphlets and counterpamphlets, usually illustrated with scurrilous woodcuts. Even John Froben, the respected Basel printer, was not above using blatant propaganda for selling books that really did not need any. An example is the frontispiece he added to the second edition of Erasmus' New Testament (1519). It shows Arminius, conqueror of Varus, commanding his Roman victim, a viper, to "finally desist from hissing" ("Tandem vipera sibilare desiste"). Hutten, no doubt seeing from this woodcut that his own ideas on the German hero were very timely, then wrote his dialogue. It was at once the first fruit of his reading of the new Tacitus discovery and the first political use of the text by a German.[60] Though he certainly read of Arminius with great excitement, he either did not read too carefully or, more probably, he suppressed what did not fit in with the idyllic picture he had already concocted on the basis of the *Germania*. Hutten conceived of Arminius not as he actually appeared in the *Annales* (chiefly in books i and ii) but as he might have appeared in the *Germania*. And, what is worse, he attributes to Germans in general any good qualities which Tacitus saw in Arminius in particular. Tacitus showed Arminius in a good light (especially in *Annales* ii. 88),[61] but Hutten magnifies Tacitus' praise into a sweeping glorification of the Germans in general—which Tacitus himself certainly did not do. In fact, the Germans of the *Germania* and the Germans of the *Annales* are very different in some respects.[62] In the *Germania* German bravery is emphasized; the *Annales* show the Germans brave only when desperate. In the *Germania* the Germans fight with good organization and with discipline, and they bravely fight for liberty; in the *Annales,* on the other hand, their fighting is wild, is for plunder, and is cowardly, for they are victorious only when the Romans are at a great disadvantage. In the *Germania* the leaders are chosen from the bravest warriors, and their followers are bound to them by affection, pride, and loyalty (the famous *comitatus*); in the *Annales* there is not much about the leaders, but it is clear that their position is due only to chance or to the fact that the people happened to like their daring counsels. Even a comparison of the treatment of particular tribes in the two works, for example the Chatti and the Chauci, shows a contrast as obvious as day and night. In short, Hutten remembered what he liked and forgot the rest. One of Tacitus' phrases in the *Annales* (ii. 88) especially impressed him; in this passage Tacitus speaks of Arminius as, "without doubt, the liberator of Germany" ("liberator haud dubie Germaniae"). Thus, Arminius, father of his country—"Brutus Germanicus," in Hutten's words—is molded by Hutten into the ideal of that *Germania* which both he and Celtis created.

The *Arminius* is modeled after Lucian's *Dialogi mortuorum*—the twelfth dialogue in particular. It involves a *Totengespräch* between Alexander the Great, Scipio Africanus, and Hannibal before the throne of Minos. In Lucian their places of honor are in that order; but in Hutten Arminius comes before Minos to argue his own priority. While Arminius is presenting his case, Mercury brings in a witness to aid him—none other than Tacitus himself. Tacitus relates the history (here, with great embellishment) of the death of Arminius (*Annales* ii. 88). Before Arminius follows up with his own account of his glorious deeds, Minos pronounces Tacitus a most trustworthy witness:

> For he was especially honest, and there was no one who had written a history more sincerely and with less affectation than he. Indeed, he even saw Germany and described the customs of its people; and he was extremely curious about the deeds done there.[63]

The popularity of the work (published first in 1529) was tremendous and is no doubt the principal cause of the astounding development of interest in Tacitus—especially in the *Germania*—in sixteenth- and seventeenth-century Germany. From 1500 to 1649 there were twenty-six separate editions of the *Germania* (not counting collections of all the works) published in Europe. Twenty-one of them were published in German-speaking areas.[64]

So great was the impression made by the *Arminius* that historians now speak of an "Arminius cult" in Reformation Germany. Arminius became associated with national political liberty among some of the Reformers and humanists. Even his Roman name soon became irritating to them. They changed it to Herman the German. At first the change was probably made without conscious ideological motivation. Johannes Aventinus, the famous historian, merely translated the name along with the whole of an earlier work he did originally in Latin. This translation was done between 1522 and his death in 1534; a more exact date for the inception of "Herman the German" cannot easily be determined.[65] But perhaps it was Martin Luther, and not Aventinus, who was the first to use the new name. If so, Luther, for one, certainly knew what he was doing and was proud of it:

> For we find that our old Germans gave their princes and lords unusually fine names. . . . *Herman,* which the Latins have corrupted into Arminius, means "a man of the army," one who is strong in war and battle, who can rescue and lead his own people, and risk his life in doing it.[66]

Luther wrote this, in a commentary on Psalm 82, in 1530. Andreas Althamer, the author of a 300-page commentary on the *Germania* (first published in 1529; second edition in 1536),[67] and Philipp Melanchthon, who also wrote a commentary on the work (1538),[68] thereafter began to use the German name also. However, the Latin form continued, too. This fact is shown by George Spalatin, the counselor of Frederick the Wise of Saxony and a friend of Luther, who published a history of Arminius' deeds in German: *Von dem thewern Deudschen Fürsten Arminio* (Wittenberg, 1535); inspiration for the work came when Spalatin, on a trip with Duke Johann Friedrich of Saxony, decided to look for the actual site of Varus' defeat. But whatever his name, these authors and others saw the ancient warrior as the symbol of German freedom. By the 1530s, however, the polemics had already begun to wane. Arminius became more and more a historical figure and less and less an ideal for immediate political inspiration. The geographer-historians like Aventinus succeeded the political propagandists like Hutten. Before the mid-1530s, however, the ideal of Arminius was still very vibrant and influential. Hutten tried to imitate the ideal of Arminius, and he never rested in the cause of German freedom.

If only the Germans were like their ancient fathers, they would not be in such a disastrous condition: this was the theme that Hutten expressed through almost his entire literary career, until his death in 1523. His pen was devoted to the fatherland, and so was his sword. Hutten was the patriotic idealism of Celtis put into dynamic action. Though he failed to inspire Maximilian and Charles V to take any real action on behalf of the fatherland—the former did not because he could not, the latter, because he was unwilling—Hutten himself never failed to act on his idealism to the day of his death. From the time when he had fought off, singlehanded, five French soldiers who had derided Maximilian in the streets of Rome in 1516, to the time when he threatened Jakob von Hochstraten—the chief object of Hutten's enmity in the *Epistolae obscurorum virorum*—with physical violence on the road from Brussels in 1520,[69] the young Hutten was a man of action as well as words. In 1522 he would have joined Sickingen in his war against Trier; but Sickingen, mindful of Hutten's precarious health, advised him to hide from their many enemies in his castle at the Eberberg. There was nothing of the slacker in Hutten.

Nor would he let his friends rest in the cause of German liberty. In 1519 he had written to his Erfurt associates, Eobanus Hessius and Peter Eberbach, exhorting them not to hold back in expressing their love of liberty. When, late in life, he discovered that even his beloved Erasmus was not prepared to give his all for Germany, he became disappointed to the point of hating him. Hutten had first met Erasmus at Mainz in 1514 when the latter was going to Basel on his way back from England. When Erasmus was en route to England again in 1515, Hutten spoke with him at Frankfurt am Main. On both occasions they had got along well; both had agreed on the basic program of humanistic reform of church, state, and culture. Erasmus had only warned his young friend not to be so impetuous; changes would need time, and one could effect more by being patient with the enemies of reform than by causing them to hate their helpers. By 1519 Erasmus was warning Hutten, in letters, to restrain his fiery pen. But Hutten, outlawed almost everywhere by the end of 1522, fled the empire and made his way toward Basel; he stopped off at Schlettstadt to visit a friend, Beatus Rhenanus, the great Tacitus scholar and philologian. He told Rhenanus that when he got to Basel he was going to plant new courage in Erasmus, who was just not doing his part. When Hutten reached Basel, the misunderstanding quickly developed into an absolute break. Hutten denounced Erasmus in his *Expostulatio,* and Erasmus retorted with his *Spongia Erasmi adversus aspergines Hutteni*. The details of their dispute are many, but the essence of it is explicit in Hutten's chief accusation: "O disgraceful spectacle! Erasmus has submitted to the Pope."[70]

In fact, of course, Erasmus never submitted to the pope, and he was equally unwilling to submit to Luther. Hutten couldn't understand such moderation. To Hutten, moderation was weakness. No, the Germans had been moderate, and thus weak, for too long. Protestantism, and the political program it necessitated, became the creed of the German patriot. Luther himself was advising the princes to "consider whether the Germans are quite such simpletons as not to grasp or understand the Roman game."[71] In fact, some years later, Luther explained that there was, in the German soul, a real simplicity, a dignified simplicity, which had kept the Germans strong and wise and which now enabled them to see through the duplicity and insidious disguises of the papal church:

> No virtue has been praised so highly in us Germans and, I believe, has elevated us to such a height and kept us there, as the fact that men have considered us to be faithful, truthful, and trustworthy people who have let yes be yes and no be no, as many histories and books will testify.[72]

The allusion to the Tacitan ideologists is unmistakable; and they, along with Luther, were now saying no. They no longer wanted to be called "barbarian." Indeed, the Germans were no longer barbarians: Enea Silvio had been right! But when he had first used the *Germania* to convince the Germans to pay the pope his due, he could never have imagined that he was giving them a text to help them cut themselves completely from the pope. Celtis would have marveled at the enlarged scope and drastic practical results which were effected when the patriotic ideal he had discovered in Tacitus was commingled with the blood of an ardent religious idealist and soldier, as it was in the heart of Hutten. But what of the German patriot who became an Erasmian moderate in religion? Johannes Aventinus was just such a German patriot.

3 Tacitus in the Political Thought of Sixteenth-Century German Historiographers

To Johannes Aventinus, Celtis bequeathed his vision of the German past as to a son. The first entry in Aventinus' *Haus-Kalendar,* a journal he kept for the years 1499–1531, clearly points to the source of the young Bavarian patriot's inspiration: "I am Johannes Aventinus. Conrad Celtis is my teacher."[1] Two years earlier, in 1497, when Celtis had opened the Poets College at the University of Vienna, they lived *contubernalis,* in the classic manner. After three years of living so intimately with his master, Aventinus was indelibly marked as "Celtis' man." From Celtis' colleagues at the college, and later from the humanistic professors at Cracow (1501–2) and at Paris (1503–4), Aventinus acquired skills for the humanist's career; but from Celtis himself he learned how to use what he had learned. Aventinus became a historian. He studied all the classics, but Tacitus became—for him, as for Celtis—his special interest.

Aventinus read Tacitus even more thoroughly than Celtis had. Also like Celtis, he had a vivid poetic imagination, and in some senses he was more of a poet than Celtis: his feeling was so much stronger, his vision of the German past so much more certain, his patriotism so much more ardent. What he lacked was Celtis' excellent technical skills. In short, he was a poetic spirit with little poetic ability. Like Celtis, too, he borrowed his poetic material from Tacitus; but in Aventinus there was not the well-ordered and refined assimilation of the *Germania* that we find in Celtis' *Liber amorum* and *Norimberga*. Instead, the *Germania* is carelessly scattered through Aventinus' tedious, repetitive, and tangled writings (some unfinished, some never revised beyond the first draft). He was more a compiler than a writer. His writings were as disorganized as his spirit. However, the disorganization was not entirely a fault of his character, for, unlike Celtis, Aventinus was directly involved in the government. His confusion, his disunity of purpose, his frustrated ambitions, were merely a reflection of the political situation in Germany and, more particularly, in Bavaria.

Machiavelli clearly recognized that Germany's weakness arose from political wrangling;[2] and it was only about five months after Machiavelli had returned to Florence from his diplomatic mission to Germany, at the end of 1508, that Aventinus received his post in the Bavarian government. He won his position as *praeceptor* to Duke Wilhelm's younger brothers, Ludwig and Ernst, after he had sent congratulatory verses to Wilhelm's father, Duke Albrecht the Wise of Bavaria, who had just unified the two Bavarias. Shortly after Aventinus assumed his office, Duke Albrecht died and left a situation in which his three young sons almost brought his state to disunity once again. The crisis of the succession was itself a serious matter, but it was made all the worse because it aggravated the conflict between the government and the estates. The disputes between the brothers were settled by the wise influence which Chancellor Leonhard von Eck exerted over the eldest son, Duke Wilhelm, but the trouble with the estates was not so quickly overcome. Aventinus was expected to support Eck and the shaky new government against them. Eck could not have found a more loyal assistant for himself or a more sincere and devoted tutor for the two younger princes.

Aventinus' loyalties were not, however, limited to the compass of one state. He sincerely sympathized with the aging Maximilian, who was then beset with grave tribulations. In 1507, one year before Celtis' death, the emperor's situation was already drastic. Aventinus wrote, in the words of Pliny, that "much depends on the time in which any virtue occurs. A case in point is that best of emperors, Valentinian—if only he had had the chance to use better counselors, [things would have turned out better]. So, too, the virtue of Maximilian occurred in an unfavorable age."[3] The comparison between the Rome of the fourth century, on the point of disintegration, and the present Holy Roman Empire is explicit. Maximilian had just been severely weakened at the Diet of Constance. Nine years later, with the Treaty of Brussels (December 1516), Maximilian lost Milan to the French and Verona to the Venetians. Action was what was needed, but the old emperor had only memories—memories that became dreams, and dreams that became myths. A few months after the Treaty of Brussels, Maximilian published his fable of *The Dangers and Adventures of the Famous Hero and Knight Sir Teuerdank,* an allegorical poem describing his chivalrous courtship of Mary of Burgundy. But, after all, Maximilian only dreamed the songs the German humanists were chanting. Aventinus' poem "Imperatori Maximiliano Caesari Augusto" was just one of the many the emperor so frequently received from his learned subjects. Aventinus "salutes a god with a lyrical song.''[4] He would keep to himself his thoughts on the parallel between Maximilian and Valentinian.

But even if Maximilian was too troubled and too busy to pay the piper, Aventinus' patriotism was rewarded at home, in Bavaria, with the title ''Historiographer to the Dukes,'' together with a generous stipend and a commission to write a history of Bavaria. Aventinus intended to produce ''a better book than the scraps put together by the stupid, inexperienced, foolish scribblers who nowadays undertake to write chronicles,''[5] but his designs were too large, his ambitions larger than his judgment, and his patriotism stronger than his ability. Trying to outdo all predecessors, he failed, and he eventually begat the *Annales ducum Boioriae,* a 1,200-page monster, and the 1,600-page *Bayerische Chronik,* its freakish twin: the Gog and Magog of German historiography. The *Annales,* and especially the *Chronik,* ''suffer from a fatal dissolution of focus,'' as Gerald Strauss, Aventinus' recent biographer, puts it.[6] These works were as disorganized as Aventinus' methods and intentions in writing them. He wished to produce something like Celtis' *Norimberga;* but he also wished to produce a work that would surpass the achievements of his mentor, a work like the *Germania illustrata,* which Celtis always envisioned but never wrote. Aventinus wanted humanistic, exhortatory propaganda in a work which he thought should be objective, complete, and descriptive. After two years of arduous research and of tramping around to visit over eighty German cities, he sat down to write the *Annales* in 1519; but by 1522, after publishing an *Epitome* of the work in order to gain publicity and to encourage his patrons, he suddenly stopped writing and, with intense spirit, began on his German version of the same work. Perhaps he thought that few readers would be inspired to political action by plowing through the more than a thousand pages of gnarled Latin he had already written. A German version would not only be easier to read but would be available to a greater number of his compatriots. He would also make it more explicit in its relation to contemporary events. Thus, though he wrote the *Annales* as history, he wrote the *Chronik* as propaganda—all 1,600 pages of it; but both were highly idealistic and, at times, fantastic.

Like Celtis and Hutten, Aventinus conjured his vision of ancient German history from carefully selected passages of Tacitus' *Germania* and the *Annales,* i.e., those which put the Germans in a favorable light. He somehow blinded himself, as they had before him, to the passages that told of the drunkenness, laziness, and generally primitive condition of his ancestors. It was certainly not because of these negative passages that Aventinus praised the author of the *Germania:*

> In the time of the Emperor Trajan, Cornelius Tacitus wrote about the customs, morals, situation, and ancient origin of the Germans. His successor became a Roman emperor. No one among the ancient Romans, at least among those whose books we still have, has written more about us.[7]

Throughout the *Annales,* and especially the *Chronik,* there are frequent little eulogies of the great Tacitus. In Aventinus' mind, Tacitus ranked with the greatest men who had ever lived—with Cato, Caesar, Augustus, Charlemagne, and Ludwig the Bavarian. That Tacitus and Cato did not exactly fit with the other names in the list did not disturb Aventinus. Lacking the warrior leader in his own age, he found his heroes in past ages. He loved Tacitus principally because Tacitus made it seem that all the ancient Germans were heroes:

> But—as Tacitus and Pliny the Younger themselves have written—the Germans killed, struck down, blotted out, and captured huge numbers of people, great armies, and all kinds of good fighters. As a result, the Romans not only worried that they would lose the ancient boundaries of the Roman Empire, but, in fact, they did lose them.[8]

They sound more like butchers than heroes! But the graphic verbs were meant to thrill the work's avid readers.

Aventinus knew that such heroism was the clear result of the generally noble and virtuous life of the ancient Germans. His use of Tacitus allowed him to go into much detail on several aspects of ancient German virtue. The chapter headings and subheadings in book 1 of the *Chronik* were planned to provide an easy manual for the interested patriot: "On the Service of God: How King Tuisco Determined It,"[9] "On Marriage and the Raising of Children,"[10] "On the Landscape, On Wrongdoers and the Sentence of the Law,"[11] "On Inheritance,"[12] etc. These, and the chapters on German heroism, were the ones to which his fellow Germans would turn. With respect to both the arts of war and the arts of peace—namely, the maintenance of justice—the Germans could look back on ancient practice with pride. In a chapter titled "How One Should Punish Evil and Reward Good," Aventinus writes:

> He [Tuisco] ordered and arranged that the priests and ministers should proceed against the lawbreakers. By them they were seized, bound, tied firmly, and beaten with rods. But not as though for punishment or through the power of the prince, but rather as if it came about from the special command and will of almighty God, who called these priests his "myrmidons" and "heralds."[13]

This description was Aventinus' expanded commentary on his earlier statement in the *Annales:*

> *Sacerdotibus quidem* dumtaxat *animadvertere, vincire, verberare permisit, non quasi in poenam* aut *ducis iussu, sed velut deo imperante*. [Italics mine.][14]

He did not acknowledge his source for this statement, but it happens to be *Germania* vii:

> Ceterum neque *animadvertere* neque *vincire,* ne *verberare quidem* nisi *sacerdotibus permissum, non quasi in poenam nec ducis iussu, sed velut deo imperante,* quem adesse bellantibus credunt. [Italics mine.]

In writing of the bravery and simplicity of the ancient Germans, Aventinus was an inspired patriot. In writing of the religion of the ancient Germans, he was not a Lutheran but a Christian humanist, not a rebel against the Church, but—like Erasmus—a critic of it. His *Chronik,* therefore, was what Gerald Strauss calls "a confession of faith";[15] it was Aventinus' answer to the confessional crisis of the early years of the Reformation. In the *Chronik* as well as in his other works there is no doubt as to Aventinus' religious orthodoxy—as there is no doubt of that of Erasmus. But there was some suspicion of his orthodoxy because of his previous connections with Lefèvre d'Etaples, the famous Aristotelian syncretist and follower of Giovanni Pico della Mirandola, in his schooldays at Paris (1503–4); but Lefèvre's teaching was not so inebriating in its effect on Aventinus as to bring him into open revolt and heresy. Since Lefèvre was suspected of heterodoxy (especially between 1519 and 1522), so was Aventinus. Besides, his white-hot criticism of the abuses of the Church easily convinced heretic-hunters that he had gone over to Luther. But their suspicions were unfounded. Aventinus was a Catholic. In fact, Aventinus did not wish to do more than point out some of the abuses in the Church; and, after reading the *Germania,* he saw the abuses more clearly. Under the rubric "On the Service of God: How King Tuisco Determined It," he wrote:

> From the first he arranged the service of God thus: he never built any churches or altars; he consecrated some tree, some glen or forest, and forbade anyone ever to cut there. To these places the people came to pray, to practice spiritual things, and to offer their devotion and service to God under the clouds and the open sky. He considered it as true, and so proclaimed it to the people, that God,

> who truly lives in heaven, is immortal and is so great that men should not shut Him up in stone and walls, in buildings and piles of stones, set together by mortal hand.[16]

This was Aventinus' more homespun way of saying what he had said in the *Annales:*

> *Caeterum lucos et nemora,* in quibus res divina rite perpetraretur, *consecravit. Arbitrabatur caeleste* numen pro *magnitudine* sua *nec parietibus cohiberi nec in ullam humani oris* vultusque fluxaeque rei *speciem adsimulari* debere. [Italics mine.][17]

With support from *Germania* x, xi, xxxix, xl, and xliii, the main source for Aventinus' information on ancient German religion was *Germania* ix:

> *Ceterum nec cohibere parietibus* deos *neque in ullam humani oris speciem adsimulare* ex *magnitudine caelestium arbitrantur: lucos ac nemora consecrant* deorumque nominibus appellant secretum illud, quod sola reverentia vident. [Italics mine.]

In taking over his language directly from Tacitus, Aventinus did little more than change Tacitus' plural verbs (pertaining to the Germans, and usually to Germans of particular tribes only) to singular forms to accord with his myth that Tuisco was a type of Lycurgus.

The expression of such things in 1519 (Aventinus was then working on book i of the *Annales*) and in 1522 (while working on book i of the *Chronik*) did not yet get Aventinus into trouble with the authorities. In Saxony the Lutheran Reform was already raging, but in Bavaria it had raised scarcely any enthusiasm at all. The rulers of Bavaria themselves were not sure which way was politically most expedient for them. But by 1526 Duke Wilhelm realized that the papal side offered the greater political advantages, and he began to hunt down all possible sources of heretical, and hence disloyal, sentiment. Even Aventinus was suspected. In this same year Aventinus finished the *Annales,* which he had taken up again after writing the *Chronik*. He presented the work to the duke; but the duke thought it safe to leave the book to rot on a shelf in the archives, and there it remained until it was finally published in 1554 by Hieronymus Ziegler, a theologian at the University of Ingolstadt. Ziegler's edition was completely expurgated: just as Duke Wilhelm's successor, Albrecht V, wanted it to be. However, so strong were Duke Wilhelm's suspicions that, by the autumn of 1528, Aventinus was placed under arrest for heresy. Though he was released almost immediately, he realized he could no longer think freely under this lord.

He left his dominions and took up permanent residence in Regensburg, an imperial free city; but even here he did not feel able to speak his real mind. True, he continued to write; but he published almost nothing.

The works Aventinus wrote were not published in his lifetime. Most of the works he promised to write he never got around to—like the *Chronicle of All Germany*. He failed where Celtis had failed: his plans for a *Germania illustrata* remained merely grandiose plans. One little book only, the *Ursachen des Türkenkrieges,*[18] can be called a completed work (and not merely *finished,* like the *Annales* and the *Chronik*). But it too was published only much later, in 1563. However, unlike any of his other works, the *Ursachen* did have some slight effect in arousing his contemporaries to action or at least in convincing them that action was necessary and possible.[19] Aventinus wrote the little book in 1526 and began to send copies of it around to prominent persons. He revised it in 1529, just when the Turks were besieging Vienna, the *Sedes Imperii* itself. He profoundly realized, as never before, that given the apathy, strife, moral decrepitude, and internal hatred among his fellow Germans—and among Christians in general—they would be unable to take practical action against the Turk unless they first took moral action within their own hearts. God was punishing the Germans because of their sinful division and hatred:

> God is just and a mighty Lord over the world, and a kindly father to us all. Therefore, the enormous misery which exists in the world must needs be caused by equally enormous evil and sin among men.[20]

The *Ursachen* was more a sermon than a political and military exhortation. Aventinus believed that religious bigotry was the principal cause of the Germans' corruption, weakness, and sinfulness, and he was equally harsh with both sides in the religious controversy. His words are so violent they can almost be heard. He scalded the Catholics on one page:

> But among those who oppose Luther, corruption and treachery are the rule. . . . They listen to none but bloodthirsty, ignorant, niggardly, arrogant, whoring priests. . . . Their ambition is to be feared, not loved. Who would not rather belong to a band of heretics than to such bloodthirsty Christians?[21]

And on the next page he lashed the Lutherans:

> However, I do not really want to make excuses for those who call themselves evangelical. Day and night they have their noses in the

> German Bible and think they can find all the answers there. . . . God will deal with them more severely than with the orthodox. For a servant who knows the will of his Lord and observes it not is guiltier than one who is ignorant of the Lord's will. It will go with the Lutherans as with the Jews: their study of Scripture will make them blind.[22]

But it was for the Catholic "heretic-hunters" that Aventinus (remembering his own arrest by them) reserved his most searing words:

> Where are our brave heretic-hunters now? Are there not enough unbelievers in the land? Against harmless books and defenseless folk they fight like lions. But when it comes to Turks, they scatter like rabbits.[23]

A few detachments of Turks from the siege of Vienna had reached even as far as Regensburg, where Aventinus was rewriting the *Ursachen*. He did not know how far they would come in subsequent invasions. He wondered who would be able to lead the Germans. Poor Maximilian had died with a heart full of pain, a head full of troubles. Charles V? Charles, even aside from the Turks, had a difficult time keeping the empire together—in regulating its quarrelsome rulers and in fighting his own wars. No, there was no one to save the Germans.

Aventinus knew the situation was desperate. In fact, it was so hopeless that the *Ursachen,* because of its furious denunciation of religious abuses as the ultimate cause of the Turks' success, had to be surreptitiously passed around, as pornography is passed today. Aventinus the patriot failed. And the ideal he had derived from Tacitus' *Germania* failed with him. Aventinus the patriot had become Aventinus the penitent. By 1529, shortly after the siege of Vienna, when he was writing the preface to the third book of the *Chronik,* he had come to realize that God, and not the Tacitan ideal, was the salvation of the Germans:

> We have lived in this country of ours for about a thousand years now, undisturbed and peaceful. But if the Turk comes much closer, and if we do not take this to heart and let it be a warning to us, I fear that we may have to leave our homeland and return to the grim forests across the Danube from where we came. I hope to God that I am wrong. I shall gladly hear myself called a liar. But God alone turns the wheel of fortune. As he spins it, so things come out.[24]

These are the words of a man who believes action to be impossible. The sentiment has no roots in Celtis or in Hutten.

All the fighting spirit he had imbibed from the example of Celtis and

Hutten was gone. But Aventinus was only one of many. The change in his attitude is part of a general trend. There were many beneficiaries of the vision which Celtis had discovered in the *Germania* about the Golden Age of the Germans. Though none were as energetic in the practical pursuit of this ideal as Hutten, there were others whose Tacitan inspiration is reflected, as with Aventinus at first, in works immediately connected with the political events of the time. Among the first to follow Celtis was Jakob Wimpfeling, the Alsatian patriot. His *Epitoma rerum Germanicarum usque ad nostra tempora* (Strassburg, 1505) might be considered the first comprehensive history of Germany; but, as Gerald Strauss puts it, "given the political purpose of his writings, Wimpfeling could have no real interest in description for its own sake."[25] Description was constantly subordinated to his practical political interests.[26] Another follower was the Swabian patriot, Franciscus Irenicus, who became a Lutheran minister shortly after finishing his *Exegesis Germaniae* (Nuremberg, 1518). In the words of Gerald Strauss, "it is a stormy, unrestrained, impulsive confession of his faith in the excellence and honorable antiquity of his country."[27] In Irenicus, as in Hutten, reforming religious enthusiasm and patriotic idealism are inextricably united with scholarship. This union is obvious, too, in another heir of Celtis, Andreas Althamer, a Swabian Catholic priest who became a Lutheran theologian after 1525. He published his *Scholia in Cornelium Tacitum* in 1529 (Nuremberg) and again, in a greatly expanded version, in 1536. He has already been noted, along with Spalatin, Melanchthon, and Luther, as an early member of the "Arminius cult." Sebastian Franck's *Germaniae chronicon* (Frankfurt a.M., 1538) is still another great example of German history written for religious and political polemics. Thus, late into the '30s, the tradition originally inspired by Celtis still had active adherents. Tacitus still exhorted German humanists to practical involvement in political matters.

But already a change is noticeable. Franck's extreme sentiments, for example, perturbed even Melanchthon; he called the work "a book of libels rather than a history."[28] With the growing success of the Reformation, the polemics began to wane. The Protestants made great gains after Melanchthon presented his *Confession* at the Diet of Augsburg in 1530, after the organization of the Schmalkaldic League in 1531, and especially after the religious peace concluded at Nuremberg in 1532. But this was only the beginning. In the judgment of G. R. Elton, the well-known Reformation scholar, "in the years 1532–36, Lutheranism once again seemed to carry all before it.''[29] During the '30s, Lutheranism solidified the Reform, and the foes of Protestantism in general were held at bay. In this newfound breathing space German historians turned from their preoccupation with political arguments to other objectives. They became avidly involved in scientifically describing the history and geography of their land. The *interpretation* of history in the light of present events succumbed to the *description* of geographical history for its own sake. Or, if there was any interpretation at all, it was now no longer political but ethical and—at worst—confessional. Aventinus was a historian who ended up by trying to be both a scientific describer and a moralist. Others were usually less dynamic, in that they devoted themselves almost entirely to their descriptive endeavors. Most famous among them was Sebastian Münster, who wrote his *Cosmographia* from 1526 to 1544 (published at Basel in 1544). Münster's aim was to gain precise information for a geographical-historical description of all Germany. Like Aventinus, he tried to succeed where Celtis had failed. For his project he tried to enlist the help of scholars all over Germany; they were to describe their own regions minutely and send the information to him to be organized. True, he found space for the expression of some religious sentiments, but they are almost totally confined to the prefaces and introductions and do not intrude into the text.[30] Though his motive was ''to bring honor to our country and place its beauties in the clear light of day,''[31] the aim of the first clause is forgotten beneath the excessively detailed descriptions of bridges, roads, mountains, towns, forests, and rivers of the second. The aim of writing objective topographical history, more or less freed from the popularizing ambitions of the early humanists, was not new with Münster, however. Around 1513 Sebastian Brant wrote his *Beschreibung etlicher Gelegenheit Teutscheslands,* which is unusual among the work of Alsatian historians at the time in that its patriotism is well under control; as Gerald Strauss puts it, ''the purpose of his description is to describe.''[32] Willibald Pirckheimer, a jurist of Nuremberg, also wrote unpolemical descriptive history in his *Germaniae ex variis scriptoribus perbrevis explicatio* (Nuremberg, 1530). The same applies to Johannes Bohemus' *Omnium gentium mores, leges et ritus* (Augsburg, 1520). All of them were heirs of Celtis' project for a *Germania illustrata;* but none of them was his follower in the political motivation and enthusiasm behind the project itself. What is new with Münster is that the tradition passed from Celtis to Wimpfeling, Irenicus, and the others is now wholly abandoned for the one which began with Brant. In short, humanist political activism is absorbed and forgotten in passive and merely descriptive scholarship. The difference, that is, between Celtis and Münster.

The career of Aventinus is a clear demonstration of this transition. Aventinus became aware of the impossibility of political activity, and he therefore passed on no political idealism to the German historiographers. Aventinus and other humanists forsook their vocation, and, in the void, Münster set the tone of German historiography for the rest of the century. Between his *Cosmographia* (1544) and Matthias Quad's *Enchiridion cosmographicum* (Cologne, 1599)—a miniature cosmography and a handbook on how to write them—German historians did not write to exhort anyone to do anything. True, most of them were interested in the religious development of their times, and many of them could see none but confessional links in cause-and-effect relationships; but their interest never moved them to advise their readers to revolt against a prince or to attack a neighboring state because of differences in belief. It is true also that most of them contrasted the Book of Genesis and the *Germania* with the tumult and crassness of their own age; but from these contrasts they meant to inspire no activity in their readers. Instead, they would merely sigh and reflect on the time "when the world was still golden and men kept faith."[33] The principal aims of these historians were to thrill their readers with accounts of strange wonders in the world, accompanied usually with detailed woodcuts, and to amuse them with descriptions of various places, peoples, and fascinating customs. They almost entirely avoided political questions. Gerald Strauss, in the conclusion of his book, sums it up thus:

> A lack of depth and intellectual sophistication will be only too obvious to a reader who comes to these authors from the literature of the Italian renaissance. Political analysis, for example, is hardly to be found. The form for their works presented German writers with innumerable opportunities to study and compare the constitutions, the governments of their territories and cities. Describe them they did; that was part of their task. But they were not tempted to organize their comments into statements of political theory.[34]

Though Tacitus was neglected in this general demise of political thought, he continued to be the basic text for all German historiography. In fact, the purely historiographical interest in him pushed out the political. The development of geographical history from Münster to Quad represents only one aspect of the retreat of Tacitus into the realm of pure scholarship. Another aspect is the philological-historical. In Germany it began with Beatus Rhenanus, the greatest philologian before Justus Lipsius. In 1525 Aventinus asked Rhenanus to help him in his researches by traveling around Germany to rummage through libraries.[35] Though Rhenanus was impressed by the reasons behind the request, he never did pack his bags. He was too busy with his philological investigations. Besides, he did help Aventinus in his own way: he helped him to coordinate ancient and modern German place-names. Why should Rhenanus waste his time running all over Germany when he could find out so much in the comfort of his own study?

If the idealistic tradition of *Germania* became anemic with Aventinus, it all but wasted away with Rhenanus. Nothing shows more clearly how inactive this tradition had become than the passive existence of Rhenanus himself:[36]

> After reading or writing at home he was accustomed to take a walk in the gardens of his villa. He ate lunch at the tenth hour and supper at the sixth, . . . His house was closed to any libidinous and immodest things; he admitted no revelry. He rarely gave dinners, and only for the best people.[37]

Such were the last eighteen years of his life at Schlettstadt. The town itself was not sleepy, backward, or without brilliant examples of the active life. Wimpfeling, one of the hottest reforming firebrands and energetic patriots of Germany, had lived the last thirteen years of his life there, and he wrote some of his finest propaganda in Schlettstadt. He died in 1528, one year before Rhenanus arrived. No, it was not the place but Rhenanus himself. And his sixteen years before that, at Basel, were pretty much the same. He married only in the last few years of his life, he refused a position with Charles V, and he was disturbed only now and then by the religious and political upheavals in Germany. He heard what was happening through his many correspondents; but his studies were, after all, too pressing for him to be stirred to any activity. He required tranquillity: "Great was the solitude of his home."[38] How else could he have produced such an enormous amount of philological work?

Between 1505 and 1540 he published over sixty-five texts of the classical authors. He is famous for his editions of Velleius Paterculus, Prudentius, Origen, Seneca, Tertullian, Pliny the Elder, and especially Tacitus (1519, 1533, 1544).[39] In the *Germania* alone he successfully restored the text in over fifty dubious passages. After Rhenanus nothing of constructive criticism was done on the *Germania,* or on Tacitus as a whole, until the first edition of Justus Lipsius in 1574. His philological studies certainly dominated his time and attention, but it would be wrong to assume that they obliterated all other interests.

Even in the edition of Tacitus of 1533 (prepared in 1532) there are a few places in the notes[40] where Rhenanus used selections from the *Germania* as springboards for his own political and, especially, ethical views. For example, in commenting on *Germania* xiv, in which Tacitus speaks of the German youths who in times of peace sought war in other nations, Rhenanus added: "And indeed how often do we see it happen today that German mercenaries are observed in opposing ranks in armies on both sides?"[41] Aside from attending the Diet of Augsburg (1530), Rhenanus learned of the sad condition of his fellow Germans through his many correspondents and the few visitors to his quiet home. From them he learned of the advances of the Turks. He expressed his fears by way of a small digression in commenting on a phrase in *Germania* xxxiv. Tacitus' comment that there are certain German tribes not too well known in history led Rhenanus to mention the expansion of certain peoples in the past—the Alemanni, the Saxons, the Romans—who were once obscure if not entirely unknown; and,

> till now, there is for us the example of the Turks, of whom nobody had a more obscure and uncertain a beginning: if only, perish the thought, I may compare with this most ferocious enemy of ours—with whom we have recently taken up a just and pious war—our nation, deserving the best on account of its Christian piety. And let this turn out well and happy under the auspices and leadership of Augustus Charles and Caesar Ferdinand.[42]

But despite Rhenanus' hesitant hopes in the prowess of the Christian armies, Ferdinand in fact achieved peace with Suleiman (1533) only by buying it with tribute. Just three years later, when Suleiman had settled his Persian problems, Francis I of France signed a formal alliance with Suleiman against Charles V. Indeed, all Christendom seemed to be breaking to pieces. But it was so especially in Germany: peasants against princes, Catholics against Protestants, and Protestants against each other. Like Aventinus (in the end), Rhenanus thought the solution to his country's ills lay in a return to the good old morality. Using Tacitus' declaration that "no one laughs at vice there; no one calls seduction, suffered or wrought, the spirit of the age" (*Germania* xix),[43] Rhenanus, playing on the words "the spirit of the age" ("saeculum vocatur"), became splendidly eloquent in showing the Germans how immoral they had become since the times of their ancient fathers:

> How much more pure were the heathens than we are! For how few today do not laugh at vice, and how few do not cover it up with enormous offenses! Such is the spirit of the age. If anyone condemns the man who commits adultery or who abuses girls, immediately he hears that such is the spirit of the age. If a good man reprehends that most evil habit of drinking, soon there will be somebody present to excuse it because such is the spirit of the age today. If anyone condemns the custom by which young men thoughtlessly join mercenary armies to learn any art of crime, it is soon said to him, that such is the spirit of the age. If anyone is surprised that the priesthood is insatiable in procuring benefices, he hears, that such is the spirit of the age. If anyone deprecates the excessive inherent human interest in acquiring wealth, illicit gain, and iniquitous contracts, it is alleged—as if oblivious to them—that such is the spirit of the age now. In short, we mitigate all errors, wickedness, and crimes: such is the spirit of the age. Therefore, since we are dissimilar to our forefathers, we laugh at vice and we are indulgent with ourselves; and, corrupting and corrupted, while we are defrauding and cheating others, we throw off our faults onto the times.[44]

These views on the basis of Germany's ills are as night to day when contrasted with those of Celtis and his early followers. Rhenanus saw his countrymen suffering from their self-wrought hypocrisy and sin; Celtis, Hutten, and the young Aventinus saw Italian lust and papal deceit and greed as the sources of evil. To them the Germans were innocent and noble. To Rhenanus they were sinful and depraved. His predecessors advised patriotism and military might as the solution. Rhenanus recommended penitence and moral reform. In Hutten's time, a humanist like Heinrich Bebel (1472–1516), the poet of Tübingen, pointed to the same passage cited from *Germania* xix to show that the Germans were *still* not barbarians and that their morals were *still* just as high.[45] Rhenanus' commentary on the passage argues decline and degeneration. Like the older Aventinus, Rhenanus interpreted the world about him in predominantly ethical, not political, terms.

When Rhenanus did think in political terms, it was usually in the context of being a German; but, unlike his predecessors, his pan-European interests were far stronger. More in effect than by intention, he belonged to that group of humanists, headed by Erasmus, who supported the movement of reform in both its religious and its political aspects. But their support went only up to the point where Christian society in its whole unified context could still be maintained. Rhenanus saw the consequences of confessional disunity, which were unknown to Celtis and ignored by Hutten. Unlike them, Rhenanus was a European first, a German second; and, as a result, he believed himself a better German precisely because he regarded the unity of Christian Europe as more important. Faced with the theological confusion caused by Luther, the excesses of the Anabaptists, the Peasants' War, the Sack of Rome, and the steady advances of the Turks, he came to forget political and theological issues entirely in the hope of reaching a settlement on common ethical grounds. This was certainly his attitude when he thought about politics; but his political thoughts were none too frequent. He came to his position more because of his character than because of any seriously thought-out ideological program. Unlike Erasmus, he never expressed himself in propaganda. Rhenanus busied his mind with his philology. He was a type who demanded peace and quiet in order to study his old manuscripts. Erasmus could write in a printer's shop, handing each page to the printer as he finished it. Rhenanus had to work in the solitude of his home, surrounded by his more than 200 books. At Basel his life had not been much different. But when Johannes Oecolampadius, the fervent evangelical reformer, won the confessional struggle in 1529 and proceeded to suppress the Catholics, both Erasmus and Rhenanus left. In the last seven years of his life Erasmus continued to fight for the peace of Christian society; in the last eighteen years of his, Rhenanus did nothing but correct classical manuscripts.

His editions of Tacitus filled much of this time. In his notes on Tacitus, comments of a political nature are rare and, when they do occur, are usually of a quiescent and passive nature. For example, in the *Rerum Germanicarum libri tres* (1531)—which consists of notes on Tacitus (preceding those of his 1533 edition) and is one of his few original works—he commented on *Germania* vii in this way:

> The peoples of ancient Germany lived in the greatest liberty. Do not think, however, that liberty led to anarchy. They took kings on the basis of their nobility and leaders on grounds of their valor, as Tacitus writes.[46]

He was careful to specify that the ancient German liberty did not imply anarchy, and in writing this admonition he thought of the excesses of his age. Indeed, so terrible were the times that it was better to talk softly, avoid too much concourse with people, stay at home to correct the classics, and keep out of trouble. In the preface to his 1533 edition, he advised his readers to study Tacitus to learn

> how one man has suffered an undeserved death bravely; what another man, summoned to the law maliciously, said or did; how one ought to proceed cautiously with those who, by a nod alone, are able to destroy; how one ought to place one's trust only with circumspection—these and other similar instances do much to instruct the mind of the reader with examples of prudence.[47]

With Rhenanus, Tacitus ceased to provide incentives for political action; he became, rather, a teacher of prudence, quiet, and retirement.

But the German scholars ignored Rhenanus' commendation of even these passive virtues to be gained from reading Tacitus. They were already too immersed in the details of writing their geographical histories to notice the novel political attitude which he hinted at in his edition of Tacitus. They were in fact already too prudent, quiet, and retired in political matters to be much aroused by a statement so close to their very own attitudes. They accepted the statements about prudence without question. Using Rhenanus' excellent text as just one more historical source, they missed the significance of the conclusions he arrived at in his preface. Rhenanus was in fact prophetic of a view which was to become common and explicit among Germans only much later. Only with the introduction of Italian *ragion di stato* at the end of the century did the Germans find a theoretical basis for what in fact had long been their attitude. Only with Arnold Clapmarius, a professor of law at the University of Altdorf and a correspondent of Scipione Ammirato, the famous Florentine political thinker, were the Germans introduced to *ragion di stato*. Through Clapmarius' *De arcanis rerum publicarum libri vi* (1605) they certainly learned one aspect of it: to cringe before the absolute will of the prince. A vital part of Clapmarius' view came from Tacitus.[48] Rhenanus, in an indirect manner, presages it. But Rhenanus himself would probably never have arrived at his own vague expression of resignation in politics had he not read it in the preface to Andrea Alciato's 1517 edition of the *Annotationes in Cornelium Tacitum* (Milan; 2d ed., Basel, 1519).[49] With Alciato, the famous legal scholar, a new chapter of Tacitus in the political thought of the Renaissance begins. And, together with Machiavelli and Guicciardini, the foundations of Tacitus as the great teacher of *ragion di stato* are first laid.

4 Tacitus in Italian Political Thought of the Early Sixteenth Century

By 1494 the Florentine tradition of the political application of Tacitus, first begun by Bruni, had been considerably attenuated during the period of Medici supremacy. In the latter half of the quattrocento, after the deaths of Bruni and Poggio, its principal exponents, this tradition was almost forgotten beneath the long years of peace and security. Only after the expulsion of the Medici, in the wake of the new crisis brought on by the French invasions, was the potential there for someone to revive it in all its antimonarchical significance. Niccolò Machiavelli realized this potential.[1] He was to find Tacitus as useful for the defense of the republic as Bruni had found him. But it was by no means inevitable that he should do so.

In fact, during the years of Machiavelli's most ardent activity in behalf of the Soderini Republic, it is very doubtful that he ever used Tacitus at all. And, if he did, it was in a context quite unrelated to his immediate political situation. While on his mission to Emperor Maximilian in 1508, he was supposedly inspired by Tacitus' *Germania* to praise the simplicity of German culture in opposition to the complexity and struggle of Italian political life. At least some scholars believe they see this interpretation in Machiavelli's three German *relazioni:* the *Rapporto delle cose della Magna* (17 June 1508), the *Discorso sopra le cose della Magna e sopra l'Imperatore* (1509), and the *Ritratto delle cose della Magna* (after April 1512). In the first of these especially, Pasquale Villari, author of the monumental *Niccolò Machiavelli e i suoi tempi,* believed he saw an encomium to the noble German savage, uncorrupted by the ways of Latin civilization, free, frugal, etc.[2] And, most recently, Daniel Waley, an economist and political scientist, likewise discerns a connection between Tacitus' *Germania* and Machiavelli. This supposedly lies in Machiavelli's association of primitive frugality with military prowess in contemporary Germans. Although Waley backs away from a complete acceptance of Villari's thesis, he nonetheless concludes, in the end, that there is "probably" an "unconscious" and "indirect" link.[3] This erroneous viewpoint has been demolished by Sergio Bertelli and Gennaro Sasso, two of the most acute modern critics; they have made it clear that Machiavelli does not praise German frugality and liberty, but, on the contrary, condemns these characteristics.[4] Villari and his followers[5] have apparently missed this sentence in the *Rapporto:* ". . . and in this [land] they enjoy their rough and free life, and they do not want to go to war unless you pay them exorbitantly, and even that is not enough unless the community commands them."[6] Besides, in all three works there is not a scrap of evidence for any debt to Tacitus. Indeed, only in the *Ritratto* is there a single cross-reference to an ancient author on the Germans, and that is to Ceasar's *De bello Gallico* and not to Tacitus.[7] In general, Machiavelli's earliest works are void of any Tacitus.

Only when Machiavelli came to write the *Prince* (between August and December 1513) did he use Tacitus.[8] There are two places. The first use is certain and is in chapter xiii, "Of Auxiliary, Mixed, and Native Troops." He concludes his argument by stating that

> no prince is secure without his own troops, on the contrary he is entirely dependent on fortune, having no trustworthy means of defense in time of trouble. It has always been held and proclaimed by wise men "that nothing is so infirm or unstable as the fame attached to a power not based on its own strength" ["quod nihil sit tam infirmum aut instabile quam fama potentiae non sua vi nixa"].[9]

He seems to have forgotten his source and is quoting Tacitus not too exactly from memory. The line comes from the *Annales* xiii. 19 and is in reference to Agrippina's suddenly becoming estranged from almost everyone she knew when it was known that Nero was suspicious of her political activities: "Of all things human the most precarious and transitory is a reputation for power which has no strong support of its own." ("Nihil rerum mortalium tam instabile ac fluxum est quam fama potentiae non sua vi nixae"). The second use—and it is very doubtful—is in chapter xvii, "Of Cruelty and Clemency, and Whether It Is Better to Be Loved or Feared."[10] In weighing this problem, Machiavelli condemns princes who attempt to gain love by lavish bestowal of benefits; for, in return, men give mere promises of support:

> And the prince who has relied solely on their words, without making other preparations, is ruined; for the friendship which is gained by purchase and not through grandeur and nobility of spirit is bought but not secured, and at a pinch is not to be expended in your service.

There is no direct quotation, and there is no mention of Tacitus, but Machiavelli may have been using *Historiae* iii. 86, where Tacitus criticizes Vitellius for his unwise liberality:

> Believing that friendship may be retained by munificent gifts rather than by consistency of character, he deserved more of it than he secured.

The identical order of the ideas (in the lines on friendship) and (unlike the reference in *Prince* xiii) the parallelism of the contexts seem to remove any doubt about this connection. But a reading of the lines in the original languages shows that the similarities are slight and so renews uncertainty:

> [Machiavelli:] perché le *amicizie* che si acquistono col prezzo e non con grandezza e nobilità d'animo, si *meritano,* ma elle non si *hanno,* . . . [Italics mine.]

> [Tacitus:] *Amicitias* dum magnitudine munerum, non constantia morum contineri putat, *meruit* magis quam *habuit*. [Italics mine.]

To deny the relationship would be rash; to admit it could be foolish. It must remain a doubtful case. But even admitting it to be a definite use of Tacitus, this use, along with the first, shows that Machiavelli was still unconscious of the antimonarchical Tacitus of Bruni. On the contrary, Tacitus provided Machiavelli with excellent advice for a prince.

In this context he used Tacitus with a practical and immediate effect in mind. Machiavelli saw the return to Florence of monarchical rule after the eighteen years of that republic which he had defended with his every thought and action. On 1 September 1512 the Medici had returned to Florence under the leadership of Giuliano de' Medici, the youngest son of Lorenzo the Magnificent. And, just as in the days of his father, the prince now ruled behind the façade of the republican constitution, with the addition (one year later) of the very same innovations which his father had used to secure his tyranny: the Council of the Seventy and the Council of the Hundred. However, the bluff was even less convincing now and perhaps really unnecessary, for the Spanish soldiers remained in the city to patrol the streets and to guard the entrances to public buildings. But even Giuliano was not autocratic enough to please the real Medici ruler of Florence, Pope Leo X. In May 1515, the pope had him replaced by Lorenzo, the son of the Piero who was ousted in 1494. Lorenzo was arrogant and unapproachable; he even wore Spanish dress to emphasize his distance from the citizens. It was to this ruler that

Machiavelli, hoping to gain employment, dedicated his *Prince* (1516). Three years after its composition, Machiavelli observed that the same political situation had recurred. In 1513, after the disastrous defeat of the French by the Swiss at the Battle of Novara (June), Machiavelli had believed the moment right for Giuliano to free Italy from the "barbarian." And now, after the victory of the French over the Swiss at Marignano (September 1515), he saw the same opportunities for Lorenzo: one prince must establish a strong rule in Central Italy so as to temporarily unite Italians for the expulsion of the foreigner. After Lorenzo's bold conquest of the duchy of Urbino in March 1516, Machiavelli's expectations must have reached ecstatic heights—here perhaps was a new Cesare Borgia. But Lorenzo remained satisfied with Urbino and the consolidation of his rulership over Florence. If he ever in fact received the *Prince,* he certainly never gave heed to it. The words of Tacitus and the other ancient writers buttressing Machiavelli's theses fell on deaf ears. Lorenzo, the new monarch, cared to learn nothing from Machiavelli: a glaring name on the Medici blacklist of republican unreliables.

Frustrated over his neglected advice and miserable in his unemployment, Machiavelli found some consolation in discussions with his new friends of the Oricellari Gardens. Under the stimulation of the learned circle of humanists who met there, Machiavelli pursued the writing of his *Discourses* during 1516 and 1517. The host of the Orti Oricellari, Cosimino Rucellai, probably influenced him to expand his work from a mere commentary on Livy (begun in September 1515) into a general handbook on politics founded on a historical basis.[11] This being his intention, it is easy to imagine how enthusiastically Machiavelli and his friends must have welcomed the new Tacitus discoveries just published by Beroaldus. Their discussions about these new texts must have contributed greatly to Machiavelli's deeper understanding of Tacitus. Perhaps someone mentioned what he remembered about Tacitus from Bruni's *Laudatio*. At any rate, in the *Discourses* Machiavelli has taken up the tradition of Bruni's use of Tacitus: the criticism of monarchy.

Indeed, Machiavelli's first use of Tacitus in this work centers on the same particular theme as Bruni's: when the Republic of Rome passed beneath the rule of one man, brilliant minds vanished. In Machiavelli the parallel idea is argued in book i, chapter 10 of the *Discourses* and was written in 1516.[12] But more in line with the opening words of Tacitus' *Historiae,* Machiavelli, unlike Bruni, specifically pointed to the decline of historians with the advent of Caesar's Empire:

> Nor let any one be deceived by the glory of that Caesar who has been so much celebrated by writers; for those who praised him were corrupted by his fortune, and frightened by the long duration of the empire that was maintained under his name, and which did not permit writers to speak of him with freedom.

Machiavelli was probably unaware that he directly contradicted his statements on Caesar's liberality in chapter xvi of the *Prince,* where he said that if Caesar "had not moderated his expenses, he would have destroyed that empire." Machiavelli's disappointment over Lorenzo was probably responsible for his change of interpretation; but Tacitus' condemnation of one-man rule was probably of equal influence. When Lorenzo failed to fulfill the monarch's destiny which Machiavelli had envisioned, the latter no longer saw much value in this form of government. Along with Tacitus, and along with Bruni, Machiavelli completely condemned the greatest monarchy of all time, the Roman Empire. But here Machiavelli discovered a historical problem which Bruni had missed: Titus and the Five Good Emperors. In a general condemnation of the empire, Machiavelli certainly saw something incongruous when he considered these emperors:

> During the period of the good Emperors he [a prince who should read of the empire] will see that golden age when every one could hold and defend whatever opinion he pleased [after Tacitus in *Historiae* i. 1: "rara temporum felicitate ubi sentire quae velis et quae sentias dicere licet]; in fine, he will see the triumph of the world, the prince surrounded with reverence and glory, and beloved by his people, who are happy in their security.[13]

His solution was to make the good emperors an exception because they (aside from Titus) had ascended to the throne by adoption and not by inheritance.[14] The picture he then gave of the empire under those emperors who had ascended by inheritance is truly dire:

> If now he will but glance at the times under the other Emperors, he will behold the atrocities of war, discords and sedition, cruelty in peace as in war, many princes massacred, many civil and foreign wars, Italy afflicted and overwhelmed by fresh misfortunes, and her cities ravaged and ruined; he will see Rome in ashes, the Capitol pulled down by her own citizens, the ancient temples desolate, all religious rites and ceremonies corrupted, and the city full of adultery; he will behold the sea covered with ships full of flying exiles, and the shores stained with blood. He will see innumerable

cruelties in Rome, and nobility, riches and honor, and above all virtue, accounted capital crimes. He will see informers rewarded, servants corrupted against their masters, the freedmen arrayed against their patrons, and those who were without enemies betrayed and oppressed by their friends.

The language is dynamic. It happens to be a paraphrase of the second chapter of book i of the *Historiae* of Tacitus:[15]

> I am entering on the history of a period rich in disasters, frightful in its wars, torn by civil strife, and even in peace full of horrors. Four emperors perished by the sword. There were three civil wars; there were more with foreign enemies; there were often wars that had both characters at once. . . . Now too Italy was prostrated by disasters either entirely novel, or that recurred only after a long succession of ages; cities in Campania's richest plains were swallowed up and overwhelmed [Pompeii, etc.]; Rome was wasted by conflagrations, its oldest temples consumed, and the Capitol itself fired by the hands of citizens. Sacred rites were profaned; there was profligacy in the highest ranks; the sea was crowded with exiles, and its rocks polluted with bloody deeds. In the capital there were yet worse horrors. Nobility, wealth, the refusal or the acceptance of office, were grounds for accusation, and virtue ensured destruction. The rewards of the informers were no less odious than their crimes; for while some seized on consulships and priestly offices, as their share of the spoil, others on procuratorships, and posts of more confidential authority, they robbed and ruined in every direction amid universal hatred and terror. Slaves were bribed to turn against their masters, and freedmen to betray their patrons; and those who had not an enemy were destroyed by friends.

The *Historiae* was written on the period A.D. 69–96. For Machiavelli the work (or at least its first and second chapters) became a universal condemnation—aside from the exceptions noted—of the period from Caesar to Maximinius, if not of the whole Roman Empire. Though Machiavelli did not acknowledge his source, it was, without doubt, a source he regarded as severely critical of monarchy. Throughout the *Discourses*—by no means only a prorepublican and antimonarchical manual—Tacitus, unlike other ancient authors, is used for one purpose only: the condemnation of monarchy.

The only exception to this rule occurs in *Discourses* ii. 26: an exception because Machiavelli neutrally offered his warnings to bad generals of *both* monarchies and republics. He argued that "Contempt and Insults Engender Hatred against Those Who Indulge in Them, without Being of Any Advantage to Them." Without mention of the author, he quoted Tacitus in Latin at the very end of the chapter, and Tacitus' words are the source of its title:

> so dangerous did the Romans esteem it to treat men with contempt, or to reproach them with any previous disgrace, because nothing is more irritating and calculated to excite greater indignation than such reproaches, whether founded upon truth or not; "for harsh sarcasms, even if they have but the least truth in them, leave their bitterness rankling in the memory" ["nam facetiae asperae, quando nimium ex vero traxere, acrem sui memoriam relinquunt"].

The quotation, slightly altered, comes from the *Annales* xv. 68 and pertains to Nero's hatred and fear of the consul Vestinus:

> saepe asperis facetiis inlusus [i.e., Nero was, by Vestinus], quae ubi multum ex vero traxere, acrem sui memoriam relinquunt.

The context is different, for Tacitus refers to a prince and his subject and Machiavelli to generals and their armies and, to a lesser extent, to chiefs of republics and their citizens, as well as to people of besieged cities. The very fact that Tacitus' statement is not confined to monarchs and their generals makes it a unique case in the *Discourses*. The statement is so generally sound that Machiavelli had no intention of using it only in an antimonarchical context—and this is true even though Tiberius Gracchus, the famous tribune, is Machiavelli's shining example of a wise general, one who does not need Tacitus' admonition. But in all other uses of Tacitus, throughout the *Discourses,* Machiavelli's antimonarchical aim is clear.

Tacitus' famous "golden sentence" (Machiavelli's own term for it) in *Discourses* iii. 6 seems to argue against this assertion—but only if one has not read the chapter too carefully. It is quite long (twenty-five pages) and treats the subject "Of Conspiracies." An understanding of Machiavelli's context for Tacitus' words is very important:

> It seems to me proper now [having explained, in the last chapter, how princes lose their thrones] to treat of conspiracies, being a matter of so much danger both to princes and subjects; for history teaches us that many more princes have lost their lives and their states by conspiracies than by open war. But few can venture to make open war upon their sovereign, whilst everyone may engage in conspiracies against him. On the other hand, subjects cannot undertake more perilous and foolhardy enterprises than conspir-

> acies, which are in every respect most difficult and dangerous; and thence it is that, though so often attempted, yet they so rarely attain the desired object. And therefore, so that princes may learn to guard against such dangers, and that subjects may less rashly engage in them, and learn rather to live contentedly under such a government as Fate may have assigned to them, I shall treat the subject at length, and endeavor not to omit any point that may be useful to one or the other. And certainly that is a golden sentence of Cornelius Tacitus, where he says "that men should honor the past and obey the present; and whilst they should desire good princes, they should bear with those they have, such as they are";—*and surely whoever acts otherwise will generally involve himself and his country* [*patria*] *in ruin.*
>
> In entering upon the subject, then, we must consider first against whom conspiracies are formed; and it will be found generally that *they are made against the country* [*patria*] *or against the prince.* [Italics mine.][16]

The "golden sentence" is in Italian and is a free translation of the opinions of Marcellus Eprius, Nero's prosecutor in treason trials, as expressed in the *Historiae* iv. 8. There is not an exact parallel in context because Marcellus does not directly apply these words to conspiracies. Machiavelli has generalized the statement into "*men* should..." whereas Tacitus has Marcellus express his own sentiments only:

> I may regard with admiration an earlier period, but I acquiesce in the present; and, while I pray for good emperors, I can endure whomsoever we may have.[17]

With regard to the related passages, von Stackelberg emphasizes two verbal problems. The first, he admits, is unimportant: Tacitus says "to admire" (*mirari*) and Machiavelli says "to honor" (*onorare*); but he regards the second as having almost mastodonic significance:

> However, to accept rulers, of whatever kind, *as they are*, and to bear with rulers, regardless of the manner in which *they have become such* (si sieno fatti), is indeed not the same thing. The little word "si" in Machiavelli's rendition of the Tacitus passage deflects the sentence to a more decisive rendering: Tacitus' "golden sentence" thus becomes a Machiavellian principle. If a man like Cesare Borgia is energetic and clever enough to rise up to leadership, then one should—according to Machiavelli's use of Tacitus—accept him as a ruler. Machiavelli's yearning for an end to the political disorder of Italy expresses itself here—and not perhaps a basic conservatism.[18]

Two points of criticism must be raised against these arguments. First, Tacitus does not say "regardless of the manner in which they have become such"; *qualiscumque* does not mean this but rather "of whatever kind" or "any whatever." In translating from the Latin, an appositional "such as they are" may or may not be added without changing the meaning. Thus, when von Stackelberg brings up another possibility for the translation of Machiavelli's "*si* sieno fatti," he does so without good grounds, for he assumes that Machiavelli did not know his Latin well enough to understand the meaning of "qualiscumque" in his golden sentence. The responsibility for any deflection of meaning must rest with von Stackelberg. Second, the argument about Cesare Borgia has absolutely no basis in fact in light of *Discourses* iii. 6 as a whole. Later in the chapter Machiavelli argues that a prince who has achieved his position *through any means* is a tyrant who has subjected his country to servitude, who deserves to have conspiracies formed against him, and who must either abandon his position or eventually be killed. Despite such proof, von Stackelberg explicitly states that Machiavelli's use of Tacitus here sanctions *illegitimate* rulers.[19] The "golden sentence" must be read in its own context and not in that of the *Prince*.

Despite first impressions, the "golden sentence" gives Machiavelli no sanction for tyranny: neither tyranny (in the case of principalities) when a legitimate ruler becomes cruel, nor tyranny (in the case of republics or *patriae*) when any man attains illegitimate rule. In the first instance, conspiracies against cruel princes, there are four reasons why this statement is true. To begin with, Machiavelli does not condemn conspiracies outright; he gives his advice only that subjects may *less rashly* engage in them because they are so very dangerous and so rarely succeed. Second, in wishing to teach princes how to guard against conspiracies, he makes it clear (after a few sentences in the second paragraph) that the most important basis for their genesis is "his being hated by the mass of people." Throughout the rest of the chapter he advises the prince not to do this or that evil thing.[20] In short, if the prince is a good prince, he need not fear conspiracies. Third, though it is too dangerous and too difficult for the mass of subjects to attempt conspiracy, the great men in the state have a chance to succeed. No others,

> unless they are madmen, can engage in conspiracies; for men of low condition, who are not intimate with the prince, have no chance of success, not having necessary conveniences for the

> execution of their plots. . . . And therefore those who know themselves to be weak avoid them, . . . and when they have cause for hating a prince, they content themselves with cursing and vilifying him, and wait until some one more powerful and of higher position than themselves shall avenge them.[21]

However, he adds that, if a low person did try, he would be praised for his brave intentions. Finally, despite the fact that Machiavelli promises to consider both sides of the question, he almost forgets to give the advice that may be useful to the prince. There are only two short instances where he remembers. The first, ten lines tucked away in the middle of the chapter,[22] contains a magnificently poignant critique of the prince who could use the advice: the prince who, because he has a guilty conscience, will think everyone is talking about him. Because of this, he may chance to overhear something which may bring about his discovery of the conspiracy! The second, the last two pages of the chapter, is prefaced by the warning that there is really no way for the prince to escape his just deserts:

> There is, then, no greater misfortune for a prince than that a conspiracy should be formed against him; for it either causes his death, or it dishonors him. If the conspiracy succeeds, he dies; if it be discovered, and he punishes the conspirators with death, it will always be believed that it was an invention of the prince to satisfy his cruelty and avarice with the blood and possessions of those whom he had put to death.

The whole chapter shows that such belief among the people will bring on new conspiracies. Unless a prince is a very good prince, there is no hope for him. In all, it is impossible to see the quotation from Tacitus as a sanction for tyranny. But Mario Bonfantini, the well-known editor of Machiavelli's works, implies just the opposite, because he believes that Machiavelli was himself frightened of a tyrant and used Tacitus' sentence to protect himself: "out of motives of prudence, in order not to become enemies with the princes of his time, and especially the Medici."[23] In truth, however, Tacitus merely provided Machiavelli's readers with an exhortation to caution in planning conspiracies against princes. Besides, there are three places where Machiavelli (without mention of his source) takes material on the conspiracy of Piso against the dreaded Nero from no other historian than Tacitus. His purpose is to point out the errors in Piso's unsuccessful plans and to point out what

Piso should have done instead.[24] Tacitus, it seems, was of eminently positive value for Machiavelli's purpose: the assassination of all but good princes.

But it does not follow that Tacitus served Machiavelli with arguments for supporting even a good prince. On the contrary, he used Tacitus here as a critic of monarchy. Machiavelli always considered even the best monarchy inferior to a good republic. Even his praise of the Five Good Emperors in *Discourses* i. 10 needs the qualification at the end of *Discourses* iii. 5. He extols Timoleon of Corinth and Aratus of Sicyon, "whom their people constrained to reign to the end of their lives, though they often wished to retire to private life." His enthusiasm for these kings, who were retained in their positions *by the people,* and for the Five Good Emperors, who were *adopted* and not hereditary, shows his real sentiment: to Machiavelli a good prince was little different from a president of a republic. If the prince in *Discourses* iii. 6 were to do everything he was supposed to do in order to avoid conspiracy, he would have to become like Timoleon or Aratus. But it is really unnecessary to belabor the point; the shortest chapter of the *Discourses* (i. 20) removes all doubt:

> After Rome had expelled her kings she was no longer exposed to the dangers which we have spoken of above, as resulting from a succession of feeble or wicked kings; for the sovereign authority was vested in the Consuls, who obtained the authority not by inheritance, or fraud, or violent ambition, but by the free suffrages of the people, and were generally most excellent men. Rome, having the benefit of the virtue and good fortune of these men from time to time, was thus enabled to attain her utmost grandeur in no greater length of time than she had existed under the rule of kings. For if, as has been seen, two successive good and valorous princes are sufficient to conquer the world, as was the case with Philip of Macedon and Alexander the Great, a republic should be able to do still more, having the power to elect not only two successions, but an infinite number of most competent and virtuous rulers one after the other; and this system of electing a succession of virtuous men should ever be the established practice of every republic.

These sentiments must be considered in analyzing the use of Tacitus in *Discourses* iii. 6. When Machiavelli comes to speak of conspiracies formed against republics or *patriae*[25] as distinguished from those against princes and sovereigns, he prefaces the whole section with the caution that

> this is understood to apply to a republic that is already partially corrupted; for in one not yet tainted by corruption such thoughts [of conspiracy] *could never enter the mind of any citizen.* [Italics mine.][26]

It is in this sense, on republics, that Machiavelli quoted Tacitus. In order to remove any ambiguity—for the quotation from Tacitus does speak of *princes*—Machiavelli added the little tail to the paragraph: "and surely whoever acts otherwise will generally involve himself and his country [*patria*] in ruin."[27] The terms *patria* and *principe* are technical and do not vary throughout the chapter: he defines his problem in the first sentence of the second paragraph as concerning conspiracies "contro alla patria o contro ad uno principe," and in the whole chapter there is never a confusion of terms. Thus, the tail sentence to the first paragraph proves more clearly what Machiavelli thought of the quotation from Tacitus: in a good republic, one still uncorrupted, men should not desire to set up dictatorships; they should honor past tradition.

No wonder Machiavelli called the sentence golden: it says so quickly what he, on the two themes he treats, needed twenty-five pages to explain. In short, if one is so unfortunate to live under a bad prince (and what prince to Machiavelli can really be good?), then one must be cautious in planning and executing conspiracies. On the other hand, if one is so blessed as to live in a good republic, one would be foolish and evil to think of conspiracy—"for such thoughts could never enter the mind of any citizen."

Another use of Tacitus as a critic of monarchy occurs in *Discourses* i. 29, and it is by no means as problematical as the preceding instance. It is on the theme of "Which of the Two Is Most Ungrateful, a People or a Prince?" Ingratitude springs from either avarice or fear. The example involves a victorious and glorious general who is wronged:

> And yet there are many princes who commit this wrong, for which fact Tacitus assigns the reason in the following sentence [quoting *Historiae* iv. 3 in Latin]: "Men are more ready to repay an injury than a benefit, because gratitude is a burden and revenge a pleasure."[28]

Machiavelli explicitly states that he is here speaking of ingratitude out of avarice, not out of fear. The point is driven home at the very end of the chapter:

> In concluding, then, this discourse, I say that, as the vice of ingratitude is usually the consequence of either avarice or fear, it will

> be seen *that the peoples never fall into this error from avarice,* and that fear also makes them less liable to it than princes, inasmuch as they have less reason for fear, as we shall show further on. [Italics mine.]

The meaning is obvious: only princes are ungrateful out of avarice, and Tacitus explains why.

But not nearly so obvious is the remaining use of Tacitus in the *Discourses*. Like those already analyzed, it is a criticism of monarchy; and it, too, shows Machiavelli's strong antimonarchical sentiments. The references are in chapter 19 of book iii: "Whether Gentle or Rigorous Measures Are Preferable in Governing the Multitude." As noted in the Introduction, it is the first political use of the newly discovered Mediceus I, which was first published by Beroaldus in 1515. Machiavelli's use of Tacitus here is so full of problems that von Stackelberg, in his recent study of Tacitus in Renaissance literature, has denied the relationship altogether.[29] But the problems are not really so insurmountable, despite their difficulties. The first of these is that Machiavelli, in utilizing *Annales* iii. 55, takes great liberties with the quotation. The second is that Tacitus said exactly the opposite from what Machiavelli quoted. Both points are obvious in the following citations:

> [After speaking of two generals of the Roman Republic, Titus Quintius and Appius Claudius, the former humane and victorious, the latter cruel and a failure] whence it would seem that a multitude is more easily governed by humanity and gentleness than by haughtiness and cruelty. Nevertheless, Cornelius Tacitus (followed in this respect by many other writers) holds the opposite opinion, and says: "To govern the multitude, severity is worth more than gentleness" ["In multitudine regenda *plus poena quam obsequium valet*"]. [Italics mine.][30]

But Tacitus, in trying to explain how, in Vespasian's reign, the aristocratic families curbed their excessive lust of luxury, says just the opposite:

> Henceforth a respectful feeling toward the prince and a love of emulation proved more efficacious than legal penalties or terrors [*Obsequium* inde in principem et aemulandi amor *validior quam poena* ex legibus et metus]. [Italics mine.][31]

The third problem follows from the first two. If Machiavelli was so unsure of his source, it is surprising that he was so specific in naming

Tacitus three more times here in the course of reconciling his own opinion with the ancient author. In fact, the whole chapter (along with an elucidation of its points in the next four)[32] is concerned with this reconciliation. It may be considered the first political commentary on Tacitus.[33] The three places are as follows. First, and immediately after the quotation given above:

> In attempting to reconcile these two opposite opinions, we must consider whether the people to be governed are your equals or your subjects. *If they are your equals, then you cannot entirely depend upon rigorous measures, nor upon that severity which Tacitus recommends.* And as the people of Rome divided the sovereignty with the nobles, any one who had temporarily become chief of the state could not rule them with harshness and cruelty. [Italics mine.]

He then refers to the opening theme of the chapter by speaking of the success of humane Roman generals. Next, he returns to his reconciliation with Tacitus:

> *But he who has to command subjects, such as Tacitus speaks of,* should employ severity rather than gentleness, lest these subjects should become insolent, and trample his authority under foot, because of too great indulgence. This severity, however, should be employed with moderation, so as to avoid making yourself odious, for no *prince* is ever benefited by making himself hated. [Italics mine.]

Then, concluding his theme:

> Thus, Quintius was more entitled to praise than Appius; *and the judgment of Tacitus can be approved only when confined within just limits,* and not applied in the manner of Appius. [Italics mine.]

A few chapters later, in *Discourses* iii. 22, he clarifies this last point: the controlled and just severity of Manlius Torquatus, the famous Roman general, is all right because it brings a corrupted republic "back to her first principles, and to her ancient virtue."

It is odd to observe Machiavelli so intent, in *Discourses* iii. 19, on a reconciliation with an author whom he misquotes so badly. But he is not contradicting himself. First of all, the parallelism of the passages is clear. Unlike the doubtful case of *Prince* xiii and *Historiae* iii. 86, where the differences—despite some slight similarities—between the Latin and the Italian create suspicions, the parallel sentences here are identical in three or four key words. Moreover, the contextual connection not only shows that Machiavelli had *Annales* iii. 55 in mind; it also helps to explain his misreading of the passage. In Tacitus, for chapter 55 and the three preceding ones, the subject is the attempts of the emperors to end the viciously luxurious and wasteful expenses of the decadent nobles. The chapters are full of expressions like "the requisite energy and severity," and "severe and harsh remedies,"[34] and these expressions refer to what an emperor, particularly Tiberius, should do to crush licentiousness and effect a return to old-time sobriety. The subject ends a few lines after the quotation which Machiavelli mistakenly abused. This is the place where Tacitus suddenly throws in the statement that, with Vespasian, harsh measures were *un*necessary. One can easily imagine the busy Machiavelli scribbling his notes as he swiftly read the section and reading this about-face in the narrative with his mind still in the pattern that Tacitus had been creating for four chapters: harsh remedies and the good old morals as opposed to obsequiousness and laxness on the part of the emperors and a continuation of the same rotten habits among the nobles. Perhaps, too, Machiavelli misheard one of his friends reading the chapters from Tacitus as he sat in the Orti Oricellari. However he made the error, the context of *Annales* iii. 52–55 explains how easy it was for him to do so. Machiavelli interpreted Tacitus correctly; he only chose the wrong sentence (though one that obviously sums up Tacitus' discussion) to express it.

Machiavelli is not arguing with Tacitus here. He is arguing about whether Tacitus' advice is good if "the people to be governed are your equals *or* your subjects."[35] If they are your *equals*, then Tacitus' advice is not valid. But if they are your subjects, "such as Tacitus speaks of," then one should employ severity. But here, the *prince* should apply Tacitus' teaching only "within just limits"—which is to say that he should not be "naturally cruel," like Appius, and thereby, it is implied, bring conspiracy and ruin upon himself. In short, if it is a monarchy—or a corrupted republic, which, to Machiavelli, deserves the curse of monarchy—where everyone is rotten to the core with lust for luxury and pleasure, then harshness is proper. But in a republic it is wrong. Thus, in this instance also, as in all the other places in the *Discourses,* Machiavelli interpreted and used Tacitus as a critic of monarchy. In summary, then, Tacitus supports monarchy in the *Prince* and condemns it in the *Discourses;* and, regardless of the fact that the *Discourses* are not prorepublican only, it is apparent that Machiavelli, when he came to write them, was reasserting the Tacitus of Bruni and his followers.[36] In both works, moreover, the use of Tacitus was meant to have a practical effect in curing the real political ills of Florence and of Italy.

However, when Machiavelli again used Tacitus, it was without any political efficacy in mind; instead, Tacitus supplied him with a historical fact only. It occurs in book ii, chapter 2, of the *History of Florence*. It is difficult to say when it was included during the history's composition (late 1520 to 1525). Reference is made to *Annales* i. 79—though in this case von Stackelberg argues that it came from Tacitus only indirectly[37]—for the strictly historiographical purpose of tracing the origin of the name "Florence":

> . . . Pliny in that passage explains where the Florentines were located, not what they were called, and that reading "Fluentini" must be corrupt, because Frontinus and Cornelius Tacitus, who wrote close to the time of Pliny, give the names of Florence and the Florentines. Already in Tiberius' time they were ruled in the manner of other Italian cities, and Cornelius says that Florentine ambassadors came to the Emperor to ask that the water from the swamps of Chiana should not empty upon their land. Nor is it reasonable that this city at the same time should have two names. I believe, then, that she was always called Florence, whatever the reason for that name.[38]

A similar strict attention to the event itself and to the avoidance of politically relevant personal comment is characteristic of the whole *History of Florence*. Indeed, a drastic change is obvious from the *Art of War* (1519–20), the *Life of Castruccio Castracani* (1520), and the *Discourses on Florentine Affairs* (1520). These works, along with the *Prince* and the *Discourses*, had offered a practical program for remedying the political maladies of Florence. The *History*, on the contrary, concentrates very heavily on non-Florentine affairs (what he criticizes Bruni for doing), and continues only as far as the death of Lorenzo the Magnificent in 1492. This date is a natural conclusion to the failure of the republic. Perhaps, too, he did not proceed beyond this date because he would not have had free rein to speak his mind on contemporary and immediate politics. Even his views on historical political situations had to be hidden. Donato Giannotti, a political theorist of the now disbanded Rucellai circle, reports what his friend Machiavelli told him about the problems in writing such a work: Machiavelli had to be cautious; he described actions truthfully but avoided a discussion of causes (for example, the means and tricks of Cosimo the Elder in taking over the government); and, in speeches at least, he tried to disguise his own criticisms.[39]

To be sure, Machiavelli had sound foundations for his caution. Cardinal Giulio de' Medici had replaced Lorenzo as direct ruler of Florence after the latter's death in May 1519. If Giulio was less ostentatious in his princely manners, or if they were blurred by his ecclesiastical pomp, he was all the more wily and more successful than Lorenzo in keeping Florentines controlled. Part of his scheme was to play the Magnifico in patronizing the intellectuals, thereby keeping them busy and holding a watch over their activities. It was for this reason, as well as through the intercession of some friends, that Machiavelli was commissioned to write the *History*. Besides, it was better to throw him a sop such as this than to allow him to acquire a political job. Machiavelli was considered meddlesome if not actually dangerous. When war broke out again in August 1521, and when the plots were hatched against Giulio in the next year—coinciding with the advance upon Siena of the army of Cardinal Francesco Soderini, brother of the former chancellor—Machiavelli was seen as an instigator of revolution in the city. Though nothing could be proved, it was believed by the government that his republican writings had incited the plotters, many of them former members of the Rucellai circle. At any rate, he managed to retain his commission. When Giulio went away to become Pope Clement VII in 1523, he installed the repulsive and despised Medici bastards, Ippolito and Alessandro, as rulers of Florence under the tutelage of the cardinal of Cortona, a mere provincial. It was against the background of these depressing developments, then, that Machiavelli wrote his *History*. The work reflects his utter despair that his plans for the reform of Florence and the salvation of Italy could ever be realized.

The advice of Tacitus and all the other ancient writers now became almost useless to the depresed and disappointed Machiavelli. Without a practical political goal, and without an active political life in pursuit of that goal, the classics spoke to a soul partially deaf. Earlier, when opportunity had still presented itself, he had absorbed immediately into a practical political context whatever he read. His chief mentors were then Livy, Plutarch, and especially Polybius. By Tacitus too (though he was far less influential than the others) Machiavelli was enthusiastically inspired to criticize the political problems of his time. Livy and Polybius, however, thrilled him more. It is wrong to overemphasize the importance of Tacitus on Machiavelli's thought, for Machiavelli saw him mostly in a negative manner, that is, as a *critic* of degenerate republics and their offspring, monarchies. Livy and Plutarch by contrast provided him with knowledge of states and statesmen of a golden age, and Polybius taught him how the politics of this golden age really worked.

Nevertheless, certain scholars harbor an *idée-fixe* of a massive and dominant influence of Tacitus on the thought of Machiavelli. Chief among these is Giuseppe Toffanin, author of *Machiavelli e il "Tacitismo."*[40] Toffanin's style is very unclear, but it appears that, in his view, Tacitus was a Machiavellian and that Machiavelli was a Tacitan. Their temperaments were the same, and their political experiences, of corrupted republics passing under the principate, had great affinities. True, Machiavelli was influenced to a certain extent by his reading of Tacitus, but what really mattered was "the influence of the one upon the other so very dynamically, but so very unconsciously, in a mystery of spiritual assimilations."[41] Whatever this means, it explains nothing. Then, on the fringe between historical scholarship and fantasy, comes Giuseppe Prezzolini and his book *Machiavelli Anticristo,* heavily influenced by Toffanin.[42] While speaking of Machiavelli's style, Prezzolini says:

> One time Machiavelli cites Tacitus (*Discourses* iii. 19) and instead of writing "quando dice" writes "quando *ait.*" I would like to know what a critic of sweet little words would say. It seems probable that Machiavelli restrained his admiration for Tacitus (for he is cited by name only twice by him [?]), so that, not being able to manifest his admiration otherwise, he may have used the Latin word, as though Tacitus was unable to *dire* simply, like any mortal (like Dante, for example, *Letters,* 10 December 1513), and as though the effect of pronouncing a sentence only with an *ait* signified something more majestic, more solemn, and perhaps more brief (one syllable) than in Italian.[43]

Next, on a quite different level of scholarship, are scholars, like Pasquale Villari, who have attempted to see the *Germania* behind Machiavelli's reports on Germany. But this error has already been referred to. Finally, there are those who seek Machiavelli's important concept of Fate or Fortuna in the writings of Tacitus. Among them are L. J. Walker, C. Marchesi, and P. Beguin.[44] But Gennaro Sasso, one of the finest experts in tracing the genesis of Machiavelli's ideas, rightly doubts that so rich and varied a tradition as that of Fortuna can be traced from his subject directly and solely back to Tacitus. He recognizes a clear classical derivation for Machiavelli's concept (in *Discourses* ii. 29 at least) but considers it common to many diverse traditions.[45]

Machiavelli's concept of Fortuna is the key to understanding his trust in the applicability of classical learning—or, for that matter, any human endeavor at all—to the control of political reality. Though it is impossible to follow the particular intellectual tradition behind Machiavelli's Fortuna, it may be possible to define his original contribution to it. But perhaps he destroyed the traditional concept altogether. This, at least, is the view of Sasso, who has given the best explanation yet, namely, that Fortuna was, for Machiavelli,

> not a transcendental divinity but the consequence of a limitation of human nature; and therefore it can always be brought back to that human root—which is its own very condition. Machiavelli had proposed, therefore, to comprehend the real boundaries of a historical situation, to clarify for his own thought an agonizing and tragic reality.[46]

Yet, within this reality, human action was possible, despite the power of Fortuna. The famous chapter of the *Prince* (chap. xxv) bears out these statements. If human nature was imprisoned within the walls of its own history, it was also free within this domain, behind these walls. Fortuna, "an impetuous river," could penetrate these walls, these "dykes and banks"; but, when she came, a human being with intelligence and *virtù* could exploit her. Thus, political action was possible. If Fortuna were outside history, if she were a transcendent power, politics would be impossible because history itself would be denied. There would be no rules, no pattern, no independent area in which human nature could act. To Machiavelli the classics were guides to human nature in dealing with Fortuna. His trust in the applicability of ancient experience was still strong before 1521. But when he wrote the *History of Florence* he was no longer so sure. Between the Tacitus of the *History* and the Tacitus of the *Prince* and the *Discourses* there is a vast gulf of interpretation. It is bridged only by the unique experiences and personality of the individual man as he struggled to understand and control his political environment.

In the same general conditions which the French generated in Italy with the invasions of 1494, another man might read Tacitus with entirely different eyes. Another man might have a different attitude toward Fortuna or a different feeling about his ability to affect political reality. Such a man was Andrea Alciato of Milan, one of the greatest legal scholars of all time, whose influence upon the history of Tacitus in Renaissance political thought was to be as great as Machiavelli's.[47] And, as with Machiavelli, his contribution to that thought was the result of a unique combination of experience, thought, and personality. Alciato was only two years old when the French descended upon Italy. Since the countryside of Milan was disturbed by war, he spent most of his youth in the city, where he began his early education. He was precocious, and he plunged energetically into the study of the classics and history while still a boy. At the age of fourteen he wrote the *Collectanea* and the *Rerum patriae libri*. The one is a collection and interpretation of Milanese inscriptions; the other is a short history of his city, which he never completed beyond the succession of Emperor Valentinian. Alciato's work, remarkable for one so young, was due in large part to the historical-philological emphasis of his renowned teacher (from 1504 to 1506), Aulo Giano Parrhasius, professor of eloquence at the palatine school. Parrhasius' scholarly methods were in the tradition of Lorenzo Valla, Agnolo Politano, and Pomponeo Leto. Had Alciato remained with him longer, his specifically historical and philological interests might have led to greater works. But in 1508 Alciato was sent to the University of Pavia and then to the University of Bologna (1511–14) to study law. Nevertheless, Parrhasius' influence had its effect: Alciato's approach to law remained historical. While he was at Pavia and Bologna, however, Alciato's own juridical orientation was encouraged to some extent by Guillaume Budé's *Annotationes in Pandectas* (1503), which was really the first sign of the new humanistic jurisprudence in Europe.[48] In 1513 Alciato wrote his own *Annotationes in tres posteriores codicis libros* (published in 1518). He completed it in just fiteen days;[49] but it contains the fruit of years of profound study of ancient literature, and it reveals the first sign of the new philological and historical interpretation of Roman public law in Italy.

Already in this work Tacitus was one of Alciato's important sources. But Alciato must have developed a special interest in Tacitus, for in 1517 he published his first really great and influential work, the *Annotationes in Cornelium Tacitum* (Milan), along with all of Tacitus' works—and this despite the edict of Pope Leo X against the publication of any edition of Tacitus for ten years following that of Beroaldus (1515). In 1519 it was published again (Basel) with minor changes, and twice more, in 1535 and 1554 (both Venice)—the last edition thus appearing four years after the author's death. Though the critical editions of Beatus Rhenanus had by then taken first place in popularity, Alciato's achievement brought him lasting fame: he had shown lawyers that law could be learned through a study of history. His edition was praised as late as 1561. In that year François Baudouin, the great legal authority, wrote his *De institutione historiae universae et eius cum iurisprudentia coniunctione* ΠΡΟΛΕΓΟΜΕΝΩΝ *libri ii,* and in it he praised the work of Alciato and his follower, Aemilio Ferretti:[50] with pleasure he recommended Tacitus for the study of law: "And I admit that two very noble interpreters of the law in our time, Andrea Alciato and Aemilio Ferretti, have done a great deal of work in emending and explicating the *Annales* of Tacitus."[51]

The *Annotationes in Cornelium Tacitum* are, aside from some purely grammatical, geographical, and chronological items, concerned mainly with the clarification of points of law. He was the first to use Tacitus in this way, and in his later legal works he constantly quoted and cited Tacitus to explain various questions of ancient Roman law, to provide information on the lives of the emperors, and to illustrate the history of the epoch in general. But Alciato used Tacitus principally, as he used other ancient authors, as a mine of facts on particular matters of legal interest: the condition of slaves, the salaries of the magistrates, various types of franchises, and so forth. Through Alciato, Tacitus suddenly became a primary historical authority for the study of Roman law.

Though Baudouin was to find Tacitus and Livy of equal importance for the study of law,[52] Alciato himself, in all his works combined, used Tacitus second only to Cicero, while Livy is in fifth place. Indeed, it is Alciato's attitude toward Tacitus as compared to Livy that made the *Annotationes* such a great landmark in the history of classical scholarship. To Alciato, Livy was very inferior when set against Tacitus. And he said so without any of the hesitation and apologies of Puteolanus, whom, over the last forty years, everyone had pretty much ignored. Alciato now declared his position in the three-page preface to the *Annotationes,*[53] which was as damaging to the old-fashioned beliefs as the very method of the *Annotationes* themselves. Moreover, this preface marks the beginning of a new era in the use of Tacitus in Renaissance political thought.

Alciato begins his preface with a general encomium to history, in which he brings up the fact that philosophers and not historians were chased out of ancient Rome. He then takes up the question of veracity versus elegance in historiographical composition. He brands as sophists those who argue that "the reality of truth proceeds from very elegant words." One by one Herodotus ("prince of sophists"), Diodorus Siculus, Philinus, and Aristides are proscribed as belonging to this category. In fact, all the Greek historians are dishonest.[54] Historical truth resides with the Romans, "where, with a more polished style, there is coupled greater instruction.'' And, among Roman historians, Tacitus is best. Livy's language contains too much of the ''Paduan,'' Sallust uses antiquarian words, Caesar's work is too brief, Quintus Curtius' style is just plain bad. But Livy receives the most severe attacks: a reader's stomach may find Livy's milky richness distasteful, but it is never satiated with Tacitus. With Livy the reader is ''oppressed with long and tedious narrations,'' but Tacitus lets his mind continue to think. Livy (and Sallust) have merely been known longer, but Tacitus has more dignity. True, both Livy and Tacitus (along with other historians) relate of wars, seditions, and conspiracies, and such accounts do little to promote good morals:

> but among the others you may not come upon the equal [of Tacitus] when he relates the statements of the senators, when he describes certain mighty spirits at the very brink of death, when he declares the principles of history, when he tells of the various impulses of princes and of the necessary arts in time of peace. But Livy becomes shabby [*sordescet*] before us, compared to Tacitus, when the latter lays down for us, in the example of famous men, many precepts for our instruction: how crimes are turned upon the heads of their perpetrators, how much fame we ought to seek from steadfastness and fortitude of soul, how we ought to behave cautiously with evil princes, how it is fitting to proceed modestly with everyone.[55]

Livy, it is implied, may be all right for those who live in well-ordered republics; but Tacitus is best for those who live under evil princes and in troubled states. Alciato, caught up in the tumult of war, revolution, and military rule which followed upon the French invasions of 1494, obviously felt strong affinity with the unfortunate and cautious men whom Tacitus described. Tacitus is the best teacher for ages of trouble and unrest. It is this view which so impressed Rhenanus—who expressed it in almost the very same words—when he read Alciato's preface.[56]

Alciato derived his interpretation from the *works* of Tacitus; he was not thinking of the *man*. In other words, Tacitus' value for Alciato was based on *what* Tacitus wrote, not on *when* he wrote.[57] Puteolanus, the first editor of Tacitus (1475–80) had emphasized the man when he mentioned that Tacitus wrote ''with both eloquence and liberty'' and that his honesty in writing history brought him to the highest honors under the Flavian emperors.[58] But Beroaldus, the editor of the first complete edition (1515), had confused the works and the man; even his imagery reveals his confusion:

> And, to be sure, it seems to me that Cornelius not so much lost his renown [*caput*] through so many ages, but had hid it of his own accord. He found that the cowardice of the times was so great, and that the contempt for literature was so strong, that he considered it not worthwhile to see anyone or even to be seen.[59]

Beroaldus, not realizing that Tacitus wrote all his works in the happy days of Nerva and Trajan, implies that Tacitus was crushed beneath an evil age.[60] Alciato did not commit the same error; he was careful to base his conclusions on the dire times of which Tacitus wrote. And his observations, unlike those of Beroaldus, were not merely historically important; instead, he saw political significance: he applied Tacitus to the conditions in Italy after 1494—to war, conspiracy, revolution, despotic command. Among them, Tacitus provided Alciato with advice on how to live: Be prudent, and do not get involved.

Alciato didn't even wish to involve himself in the practice of law after receiving his degree in 1514. Relatively safe in Milan from the armies ravaging the territory outside, he certainly could have begun his practice. But, disliking such activity, he devoted himself wholly to legal scholarship. His attitude in these years, from 1514 to 1518, reflected itself in the preface to the *Annotationes*. Obviously, Tacitus seemed to provide some sanction, or at least some comfort, for his own mode of life. So deeply did he take Tacitus to heart that he no longer wished to get involved, even with Tacitus, in a political context. Beyond the comments in his preface, he never again expressed similar statements on the value of reading the author. Instead, Alciato's further uses of Tacitus are all strictly historical and, more specifically, are devoted to expounding niceties of law. Whether the Tacitus of the preface of 1517 was originally the cause or the effect of his attitude of taciturn prudence toward the political world, the attitude, at least, remained with him till his death in 1550.

Alciato was simply not interested in politics and political questions. From 1518 to 1522 he enjoyed the quiet of an academic environment at Avignon until forced to leave by the plague. He returned to Milan (1522–27), where the French army wiped out his villa and everything in it—including all his books—in November 1523. He fought in the Battle of Pavia (24 February 1525). He had soldiers quartered in his house on the return of Francesco Sforza II (1529). But through all of it he continued to grind out one more magnificent philological legal study after another. In his whole life the only "politics" which he vigorously pursued were academic; perhaps they helped to distract him from the real political world outside the universities. He changed universities every three or four years on the grounds that his colleagues hated him, his pay was not enough, his privileges were too small, his students tortured him, and other such reasons. He no sooner arrived at one school than he entered into complex and tiresome negotiations to find a job elsewhere. So taken up was he with these business dealings, his teaching, and his studies that it is small wonder he had neither time nor interest for becoming involved in what princes were saying and doing. By 1533 something snapped in him, and his work for the last seventeen years of his life was sparse and immensely inferior to that of his earlier years.[61] Perhaps, after all, he had not been successful in avoiding the effects of the ugly world about him, even though he had remained circumspect in refusing to say or do anything about it. But in an *Oration* delivered in Ferrara, on taking up his new position there in 1543, he abandoned his prudence slightly for one moment.[62] He explained that his frequent changes of university had been forced on him by the wars and the orders of princes. He said he had always sought a tranquil place for his studies but that he had been tossed about like a chip of wood on the waves. In "the orders of princes" he was referring to his harassment by the rulers of Milan (first Ludovico II and then the Spanish governors, Alphonso d'Avalos and Ferrante Gonzaga), who insisted that he teach at Pavia, Milan's university, and nowhere else. Ludovico II, desiring that such a famous scholar teach at his "home university," simply commanded Alciato, as a subject of Milan, to return. This order was backed with threats of a fine and a confiscation of property. It was first issued in 1532, and, after Ludovico's death in 1535, the succeeding rulers refused to rescind it. In 1546, still at Ferrara, Alciato heard that peace had been concluded between Charles V and Francis I; his first fear was that he would now have to return to Pavia because the rulers now had time to force him. Despite his protests, the pope and the Emperor Charles made him go back.

This struggle not to teach at Pavia is just one example of many to prove that Alciato, one of the most famous scholars of his day, was not completely divorced from contact with rulers. On the contrary. But being involved with politicians and being involved with politics and political thought are not the same thing. Alciato had relations with Jacopo Sadoleto, the famous reforming bishop of Carpentras. But he was not inspired by Sadoleto to become interested in the political problems of his day. Indeed, he asked the great ecclesiastic only for letters of recommendation to prospective employers; and, in 1529, Sadoleto soothed the ruffled tempers of the magistrates of Avignon after Alciato skipped town, without a word, to take up a better position at the University of Bourges.[63] Similarly, Francis I, king of France, served Alciato in 1533 merely by forcing the officials of Bourges to pay Alciato his salary. Also, Alciato reacted to Ludovico II, duke of Milan—who instigated all of his troubles over returning to Pavia—by going only so far as to write a nasty epigram, but only after the duke had died. In fact, Alciato had some contact with almost every political leader and political thinker in Europe, but such contact had singularly slight effects upon his thought and activity. Even his correspondence with Erasmus centered mostly around his attempts to have Erasmus destroy the autograph of the *Contra vitam monasticam* which he had sent him. He had written this work during the same period in which he wrote his politically minded preface to Tacitus (in 1514–18), and it shows a lively interest in contemporary social and religious problems. Alciato always regretted the work and tried to convince Erasmus that it was only a foolish endeavor of his youth. In general, it is difficult to discover any real breach in the program of noninvolvement which he first laid down for himself in the preface to his notes on Tacitus.

There are perhaps a few exceptions—at least in political thought—which may help to reveal Alciato's general political leanings in the broadest terms. They are contained in the *Emblemata,* epigrams, descriptive of figures or devices,[64] which first appeared in 1531[65] and were augmented by items in later years (1534, 1546, 1551). The work is a collection of enigmatic verses, each with an accompanying emblem. Politically speaking, a few of them are general moralistic statements on princely virtues and vices; but these are similar to the medieval "mirror-of-princes" genre. True, in two of them he expresses praise for the victories of Charles V's raising of the Turkish siege of Vienna and for his defeat of Barbarossa, the famous pirate, at Tunis;[66] but such *emblemata,* of general European significance and of little polemical content, were "safe" in their extremely general involvement. Another *emblema* proves this point: "Foedera Italorum" ("Alliances of the Italians"), with the picture of a lute, probably represents Alciato's desire for harmony among powers in Italy. It appeared first in his 1531 edition. But by 1534, having had second thoughts on possible particular applications his readers might see in it, he changed its rubric to "Foedera" alone.[67] But these three *emblemata,* themselves rare in their greater immediacy than all the others, are so general as to preclude any discovery of the author's attitude toward any really debatable issue. Even his broadest views as to the relative worth of monarchic and republican forms of government are difficult to determine. However, there is one emblem (the first one in the 1546 edition) which shows an extreme detestation of at least the Republic of Rome. The picture is of a huge coin set against the landscape. On it is inscribed "Of the Name of Marcus Brutus." These verses follow:

THE REPUBLIC LIBERATED

The destruction of Caesar: as if this were
the regaining of liberty!
Rather, for the Brutish leaders,
it was but a matter of this coin.
Short swords in the front ranks—though hover-
ing over: the slave's skullcap of liberty,
Which, the slaves, when emancipated, put on.[68]

The utter contempt of Alciato's sentiment, compacted into ingeniously turgid lines, cannot really be translated. Alciato, let it be noted, never taught for a republic. Perhaps here, behind the mask of difficult, enigmatic verse, he expressed what he dared not declare more openly elsewhere. If so, it is in line with his general attitude of caution in political matters.

So slight was Alciato's political involvement that the statements in the preface to his *Annotationes* on Tacitus were truly his guidelines: "to behave cautiously with evil princes" and "to proceed modestly with everyone." These comments, as well as the others there, were Alciato's original contribution to Tacitus' influence upon Renaissance political thought. Equally original and equally influential[69] were Alciato's setting-up of Tacitus as an authoritative source for the study of law and his systematic argument that Tacitus' style was better than Livy's, if not superior to all other Roman historians'. In these latter two contributions, Alciato's views were unopposed in his own time by any other important user of Tacitus. In the first, however, he stood in direct contrast to Machiavelli.

The difference between Machiavelli's and Alciato's political uses of Tacitus is enormous. Both had practical efficacy in mind, but Machiavelli's purpose was to change politics for the better, while Alciato's was to bear up under any political situation, no matter how bad it was. The biggest reason for this difference was, as noted, their entirely disparate personalities. In most general terms, Machiavelli's attitudes toward life evolved during the peace and security of Lorenzo the Magnificent's control over Florence; he was twenty-five when the French invasion forced him to reevaluate his life in relation to new and momentous political circumstances. Turbulence and crisis could not be assumed as a matter of course: the normal struggle of republican factions was one thing, riot and revolution were another. In short, Machiavelli had an earlier political orientation, which the French invasions shattered. He had some standard with which to actively resist the new and disturbing circumstances. Alciato, on the other hand, was a child of two in 1494. He grew up amid tumult and crisis and, for his whole life, seldom knew anything different in his own experience. Misery could be taken for granted, and stoical forbearance under it could become a usual mode of thought. The effects of war upon a developing character can be very influential. Though there is no automatic relationship between security and optimism and tumult and despair—and indeed, the connections are easily reversible—such elements can be quite important when combined with others. Among these—and, like the effects of the French invasions, they are of only the most general influence—is the fact that Machiavelli was educated in a republic and Alciato under a principate. In Florence, the tradition of civic humanism still inspired educated citizens to take part in political decisions and to hold political office in order to carry them out in practice. The Medici bosses were wise to keep at least the semblance of the republican constitution. The masses still acted as if they really had a part in decision-making, even though they didn't know any better. The educated, like Machiavelli, could influence politics at least a little and could hope for the day when the Medici control would be broken and the constitution returned to its pure expression in fact. In Milan, on the other hand, subjects had no fantasies about controlling political decisions. Government was the work of the prince only. The prince had no colleagues, only ministers. An educated man like Alciato could never hope to participate actively in government. Thus, in times of crisis and trouble, Alciato could only wait for his prince to do something about it. In the meantime, he would keep his mouth shut and study his books.

Their ages at the time of the French invasions and the forms of government under which they were respectively educated obviously had some influence on the formation of their characters. But of greatest importance are those myriad elements of an individual spirit which no psychology has ever explained—and probably never can. Only their aggregate expression can be described. Machiavelli enjoyed doing everything:[70] raising a family, pursuing love affairs, gambling in the taverns, fighting in battles. He gloried in activity. But Alciato just didn't want to get involved: he remained without a family, shunned legal practice, avoided women.[71] He gloried in repose. Machiavelli enjoyed political activity most of all: organizing armies, administering public offices,[72] going on diplomatic missions. Alciato was satisfied with scholarly quiet. He suppressed and always regretted his *Contra vitam monasticam,* remained inert with respect to political questions, despite his friendship with great political leaders, and was content to work out the texts of the law without regard for what later use was made of them. Indeed, it took Thomas More to complain in his *Utopia* that thieves and murderers were the products of society and were hanged by the law courts without true justice. This problem never entered Alciato's mind. Machiavelli always felt bad when he could do nothing practical. Alciato grieved when too much to do kept him from his studies. Machiavelli traveled with an enthusiastic interest in people and places. Alciato traveled only when he fled universities. Machiavelli was fascinated by people. Alciato was fascinated by books. Machiavelli and Alciato both studied the classics seriously: the one to change people, the other to change lawbooks. Both were historians: the one to gain experience, the other to gain knowledge. Both read Tacitus: the one to resist, the other to resign. Indeed, there are two distinct lives behind their uses of Tacitus.

Alciato knew Tacitus, and the classics in general, better than Machiavelli could have dreamed of knowing them; yet, despite this knowledge, he almost entirely avoided applying it in the spheres of ethics, religion, and politics. Alciato was more exactly a philologist than a humanist. Only once did he use Tacitus in a political context, and from that he learned never to apply Tacitus in a similar context again. From Tacitus he learned only resignation at best and obsequiousness at worst. He stands in glaring contrast to Machiavelli, the civil humanist. In Machiavelli there was that inextricable connection between study and activity. What he learned in books, he applied; and what he did helped him to better understand his books. From Tacitus, Machiavelli gave practical advice to the prince and to the republic. Only once did he use Tacitus for a merely historical fact. But in that case Machiavelli's disappointment with his own political program has nothing in common with the resignation of Alciato, who, after all, never had a political program. And it is precisely in this difference from Machiavelli that Alciato's use of Tacitus was to be so fecund in its influence. If one keeps in mind that Machiavelli's principal author was Livy and not Tacitus, then one will not find it surprising that men who despaired of affecting their political environment found Alciato's Tacitus more appealing than Machiavelli's Livy or, for that matter, Machiavelli's Tacitus. Among Germans, Alciato's Tacitus had its first direct impression on Beatus Rhenanus, but his motives were detached from Italian political events. Among Italians, Alciato's Tacitus had its first dynamic influence on Francesco Guicciardini, Italy's greatest historian.

Guicciardini,[73] who was himself to discover a new political use for Tacitus, did not take up Alciato's interpretation without first having developed a potential for it: before Guicciardini had experienced certain events inextricably tied together with Florentine and Italian political developments, Alciato's advice to read Tacitus for stoical consolation would have fallen on unreceptive ears. Indeed, until the early 1520s all Guicciardini's works were like Machiavelli's: they show a keen involvement with contemporary politics, and all contain programs and recommendations for political reform. For example, the *Storie fiorentine dal 1378 al 1509* (1508–9) is not so much a history as a commentary on the political situation under the Soderini regime. Subsequent works, such as the *Discorso del modo di ordinare il governo popolare* (1512), the famous *Discorso di Logrogno* (completed 27 August 1512), the *Discorso di assicurare lo stato alla casa de' Medici* (1516), and many others, all continued to advocate his ideas for political reform; and this consisted basically in his "middle link," namely, a small aristocratic senate which would protect the Florentine constitution from the tyranny of the mob, on the one hand, and the tyranny of monarchy, on the other. But already in the *Dialogo del reggimento di Firenze* (1521–25) a change is noticeable: a change not only in his ideas on reform but also in his belief in the possibility of effecting it. Though the *Dialogo* does not do away with the "middle link," something else is added. Now the subject of tyranny is irrelevant; what is important above all is the rule of law. A government should be "rationally efficient" in its protection of the security of the individual through law. In short, Guicciardini now sees the government from the view of the ruler, and his key terms are "efficiency," "security," and, above all, "rule of law." However, Guicciardini seriously wondered whether his program could ever be achieved in fact. Perhaps it was impossible because of the internal conflict within the city, the political situation outside the city, and, after all, the old age of the city itself. The best one could do was to wait, and, even then, the chances were slim.

They appeared slimmer still after 1526 and 1527. These are the years of Guicciardini's crisis in political thought. The failure of the League of Cognac, of which he was the chief engineer, and the resulting sack of Rome, brought him to the realization that, despite his long years of political service to Florence and the Medici popes, he had reaped nothing but defeat and ingratitude. Out of favor with Clement VII and despised by the new popular regime of Niccolò Capponi in Florence, he retired to his villa to brood over his troubles. The results were the *Consolatoria,* the *Oratio accusatoria,* and the *Oratio defensoria* (all written in the autumn of 1527). Even these attempts at a rational explanation did not altogether lift the heavy feelings of failure from his breast. In 1528 he again returned to his *Ricordi*[74] and now threw the blame for his condition on Fortuna:

> Some men attribute everything to prudence and virtue and try to ignore fortune. But even they cannot deny that it is a great stroke of luck to be around at a time when your virtues and the things you do best are highly valued. We see from experience that the same virtues are rated higher at one time and lower at another; the same act will be pleasing at one time, displeasing at another. [B-52.][75]

In his earlier works he had seen Fortuna as Machiavelli basically had: as the maiden who comes into any situation with flying forelocks, which the man of *virtù* and intelligence can grab. Now, in these later works, men must submit before her or be dragged. The woman whom Machiavelli beat was now doing the beating—or at least the dragging:

> How wisely it was said "*Ducunt volentes fata, nolentes trahunt.*" There are so many daily proofs of it, that, so far as I am concerned, truer words were never spoken. [B-80.]

Guicciardini, it is clear, was beginning to accept his fate. Guicciardini was beginning to accept tyranny, too. It is mainly in this connection that he used Tacitus politically:

> If you want to know the thoughts of tyrants, read Cornelius Tacitus, where he cites the last conversations of Augustus with Tiberius. [B-78.][76]

> If you read him well, you will see that the same Cornelius Tacitus also teaches very admirably how those who live under tyrants should conduct themselves. [B-79.]

> No one will be surprised at the servile spirit of our citizens when he

> reads in Cornelius Tacitus how the Romans, who ruled the world and lived in such glory, served so basely under the emperors that Tiberius, a tyrannical and proud man, was disgusted by their worthlessness. [B-101.][77]

The first and second of these *ricordi* might refer to his experiences under the Medici; the third, perhaps, to the demagogic tyranny (in Guicciardini's opinion) of the Soderini and Capponi regimes.[78] The third was not carried over into the next collection of *Ricordi,* written in 1530–32—hence, after the return of the Medici in 1530—probably because he saw it as no longer relevant. But then, besides retaining the first almost unchanged (C-13), he added a completely new idea to the second so as to keep up with developments:

> Cornelius Tacitus teaches those who live under tyrants how to live and act prudently; just as he teaches tyrants ways to secure their tyranny. [C-18.]

The last clause marks the beginning of a new age of Tacitus in Renaissance political thought (see chapter 5); it also seems almost like the logical conclusion to the ideas first uttered by Alciato.

Perhaps Guicciardini was influenced by Alciato's preface. If there is, indeed, a connection here, it took place only after 1526 and 1527, the years of Guicciardini's crisis in political thought. In fact, Guicciardini's first use of Tacitus came at a very critical moment in the political developments of those years. It occurs in a letter of 23 October 1526, containing advice to be read by Pope Clement VII. Guicciardini expresses his doubts that the accord between Francis I and Charles V (now that the latter has occupied Milan) will last. He tries to give what counsel he can, even though the situation is so unpredictable. Some policy must be formed, for "otherwise [Charles] will simply prevail over everybody, not through superior forces but, as Cornelius Tacitus has it, '*by the fatal cowardliness of everyone*' [fatali omnium ignavia]."[79] This use of Tacitus reflects Guicciardini's clinging hope in the possibility of rational politics. A calculation of superior force means nothing if there is a rational policy to meet and oppose it. The events of 1526 and 1527 were to remove even this shred of hope and show him, instead, that despite plans—despite his League—Fortuna or fate had made cowards of everyone.[80] And, as cowards, there was nothing for them to do but accept the dictum of fate: the tyranny of Spain over Italy, the tyranny of Capponi, and the tyranny of the Medici in Florence. In the retirement of his villa, Guicciardini then learned to live under tyranny: he was learning (in Alciato's words) to proceed modestly with everyone. Guicciardini's second use of Tacitus reflects this attitude; it is in the *Oratio accusatoria:*

> Read in Cornelius Tacitus, a very grave writer, that Augustus, until the very day that he died—until the point that he exhaled the spirit—even though the body and soul had already been consumed through age and infirmity—left it to be remembered by Tiberius, his successor, that there were those in whom he ought not to confide.[81]

Guicciardini's next uses of Tacitus (aside from one purely historiographical use regarding the name "Florence" in the *Cose Fiorentine*, an unfinished history which he began at this time)[82] are those of the *Ricordi*. In them Tacitus no longer merely teaches that fate can make cowards of everyone and no longer merely advises extreme caution with other men; he now shows how to live under tyranny as well. Thus, Guicciardini's growing despair is illustrated through his uses of Tacitus. This author must have had a very deep effect on him.[83] Except for one mention of Aristotle, one of Livy, and a quotation from Seneca, Tacitus is the only classical author cited in the whole of the *Ricordi*,[84] and he is cited not just once but five times, and only with the highest regard, never with specific references, and always concerning tyrants. Except for the phrase about Tacitus teaching the tyrants themselves, all have to do with bearing up under evil rulers. It is likely that Guicciardini had just recently read the preface to Alciato's edition, the most popular of the day, which his own experiences now made extremely meaningful to him.

Of course, Guicciardini could possibly have come to Alciato's conclusions independently. But Guicciardini himself was not one to pore over the classics; his vague and sometimes confused citations of Tacitus alone prove that. Even when he had the time, after his retirement to his villa in 1527, he was not one to find much satisfaction in the classics. True, when he needed some historical information, he would look it up. He may even have read many of the ancients to acquire historical knowledge in general. But throughout his historical and political works a classical quotation or even the mention of an ancient author is rare. They are almost nonexistent in his letters. Thus, outside his appreciation for a neat phrase or two—which he used here or there in his writings and letters—he really did not value his reading of them for anything personally meaningful. In this characteristic he stands in bold contrast to his associate, Machiavelli. But the contrast is even greater when it is a question of the applicability of the classics to contemporary politics. To Machiavelli, classical experience and his own experience were hardly distinguishable. But Guicciardini saw a deep cleavage between the two:

> How wrong it is to cite the Romans at every turn. For any comparison to be valid, it would be necessary to have a city with conditions like theirs, and then to govern it according to their example. In the case of a city with different qualities, the comparison is as much out of order as it would be to expect a jackass to race like a horse. [C-110.]

These sentiments were probably aimed at Machiavelli and, more specifically, at Machiavelli's Livy. But if Guicciardini regarded Livy and all other classical authors as completely inapplicable to the political world, it is strange that he made so strong an exception of Tacitus. Guicciardini's use of Tacitus in the *Ricordi* reminds one of a scholastic's use of Aristotle in laying down authoritative rules: "If you want to know . . ."; "Cornelius Tacitus teaches . . ."; "You will see that . . .," etc. This manner of using a classical author is strikingly opposed to his general attitude, so aptly expressed in another *ricordo*:

> It is a great error to speak of the things of this world absolutely and indiscriminately and to deal with them, as it were, by the book. In nearly all things one must make distinctions and exceptions because of differences in their circumstances. These circumstances are not covered by one and the same rule. Nor can these distinctions and exceptions be found written in books. They must be taught by discretion. [C-6.]

Despite the inner contradiction, Tacitus taught Guicciardini *discrezione*.

It was discretion which had enabled him to survive four revolutions of Florentine government, two Medici popes, and the ruin of Italy, climaxed by his own disastrous War of the League of Cognac. And it was discretion too (ironically bearing upon Tacitus' teaching tyrants how to secure their rule—as in *ricordo* C-18) which now let him work for Clement VII in preparing Florence for the tyranny of Duke Alessandro. Though Guicciardini had abandoned all hope in the possibility of imposing intelligence upon political affairs, he now suddenly thought that that possibility had reappeared and that, with Alessandro as figurehead, good, intelligent, well-born people like himself could once again direct the affairs of state. He responded well to Alessandro's appeal to him as the man "I have always held in the place of a father."[85] Guicciardini's role with Alessandro has been well summarized by Eric Cochrane, the most recent writer on the subject:

> He therefore became a sort of guardian, or "vice-duke" to Alessandro, drafting a defense brief for him at Naples in 1535, putting up with the diplomatic blunders he occasionally committed on his own, and chiding him for riding around Florence, ill-dressed and unprotected, with Lorenzaccio slouched behind him on the same horse.[86]

On this last point Alessandro left Guicciardini's advice unheeded. In the wee hours of 8 January 1537 Lorenzaccio stabbed him to death. Guicciardini was now left without a chance to work in politics. The new young duke, Cosimo I, had no need of his services. Now Guicciardini became merely one of Cosimo's "magnificent counselors." Without any activity the title didn't mean much at all. Now, in absolute despair, he returned to the retirement of his villa. Fortuna seemed all the more omnipotent and brutal now. He again began to contemplate her marvelous mechanisms, under which, he felt, he and all of Italy had been crushed. Even discretion seemed useless. He lost all energy to resist her.

It was no longer possible to do anything practical in politics. Fortuna made it impossible. If the theme of overbearing fortune became prevalent in the *Ricordi* of 1528, and if it became almost excessive in those of 1530–32, it now became paralytic in its effects on Guicciardini after 1536 (until his death in 1540). He dedicated himself completely to writing his masterpiece, his *History of Italy;* and it is a document of despair. He wished to show "from countless examples how unstable are human affairs—like a sea driven by the winds."[87] While he gathered his examples, Cosimo I gave Florence security, efficiency, and the rule of law: all the things Guicciardini had wanted in his *Dialogo del reggimento di Firenze* fifteen years earlier. In achieving the rule of law (upon which the other two depended), Duke Cosimo was aided by his chief legal advisor, Lelio Torelli of Fano, a follower and friend of Alciato. Cosimo tried very hard to get Alciato himself,[88] but Alciato, recently dragged back to teach at Pavia, was a tired old man who (finally) was disgusted with changing universities. Besides, even if he had wanted to come, he probably would not have been able. He had to remain where he was; he had to obey his prince. Aside from the

Venetians, few in Italy were without princes these days. And, for a long time to come, no one would use Tacitus, as Machiavelli once had, to encourage activity for republican liberty.

5 Tacitus in the Development of "Reason of State"

For a long time after Machiavelli, no one used Tacitus for the defense of republican liberty. And, for some time after Guicciardini, no one used Tacitus for any political purpose whatsoever. The only exception is Beatus Rhenanus, and he did so for the last time just one year after Guicciardini finished the *Ricordi,* in his 1533 edition of the works of Tacitus. Indeed, Tacitus passed out of the realm of political thought for the next thirty-three years or so in every part of Europe—even in Germany and Italy, where he had played so important a role until 1533. Thereafter, there is a vacuum. Indeed, the *Ricordi* could not have influenced anyone until after they were first published in 1576—which, clearly, is outside this period of political neglect of Tacitus. True, all the previous "Tacitan" material was readily available in print: Bruni's *Laudatio,* Celtis' many works, Hutten's dialogues, and Machiavelli's *Prince* (since 1532) and *Discourses* (since 1531). However, these works apparently led no one to look back into Tacitus, one of their important sources, for further inspiration.

Just because Tacitus passed momentarily out of the domain of politics, however, does not mean that he was forgotten. Philologians like Aldo Manuzio (1534), Andreas Althamer (1529 and 1534), and Iudochus Willichius (1551) continued to produce new editions of his works. At the same time, the text of Rhenanus, which had surpassed even Alciato's in reliability, continued to be read. No one, however, seems to have bothered with the political implications in the prefaces, either when these were published singly or—as in the famous "Gryphius" edition of Alciato, Rhenanus, Ferretti, and Beroaldus, of Lyons, 1542 (reprinted in 1551 and 1559)—when they were published together. Indeed, no one seems to have been incited even by the notes, which at the time were considered as important as the prefaces. Other philologians read Tacitus also—for instance, Francesco Benci, Latino Latini, and Paolo Manuzio; but much as they admired him, they never concerned themselves with the political implications of what they read and commented on. The translators, such few of them as there still were, said nothing about politics either—for instance, Jacobus Micyllus (1535), Etienne de la Planche (about 1548), and Giorgio Dati (1563).[1]

Many of the younger generation, to be sure, were now getting used to Tacitus' Latin syntax at an early age. But if they followed the advice of the great mentors of the age, Erasmus and, even more, Juan Luis Vives, they would have read Tacitus mainly for his warnings against evil and his exhortations to do good—not for how to govern a state.[2] Vives, tutor to Catherine of Aragon, also used Tacitus' speeches, as examples of elegant oratory, and his individual sentences, as examples of grammatical structure.[3] It was this latter application which impressed the grammarians, who were interested solely in the language. For example, Thomas Linacre, the English humanist educator and friend of Erasmus, demonstrated grammatical usage with at least fifteen sentences from Tacitus in his *Grammar* (1524).[4] But of greater influence was Erasmus' addition of over a score of sentences from Tacitus to his second edition of *De copia verborum* (1535), which had contained not one in the edition of 1511.[5] Both works reinsured Tacitus' popularity as a good writer, which dated at least from Baldassare Castiglione's *Book of the Courtier* (1528), where he defends the style of Tacitus and Silius Italicus as just as correct as Cicero's and Virgil's.[6] And, a little later, Thomas Elyot, author of *The Boke Named the Gouvernour* (1531), recommended the reading of Tacitus for his historical accounts and the orations they contained.[7] In other words, Tacitus came to be regarded as a master of style in spite of, and at times because of, his sharp departure from Ciceronian norms.

This great increase in Tacitus' stylistic popularity was true for most of western Europe—except for Spain, where Tacitus remained unknown until the 1580s.[8] It was not because the Spanish had any particular dislike for Tacitus. They simply ignored him, along with many of the other ancient authors, because of their minimal interest in the mainstream of developments in Renaissance humanism. Elsewhere, however, Alciato's praise of Tacitus' eloquence had, by the 1520s and '30s, become effective—much more effective, indeed, than his observations on Tacitus' political sagacity, to which no one any longer paid attention.

The legal scholars also failed to find a political use for Tacitus, but it is among them that Tacitus achieved his greatest popularity in these years. Indeed, they found him absolutely indispensable for their work after Alciato had pointed the way. As Guillaume Budé and Ulrich

Zasius had done earlier, so now Jacques Cujas, Aemilio Ferretti, and many other jurists all over Europe turned to Tacitus as a chief source for their studies of Roman law. By the requirements of the *mos gallicus,* they considered Tacitus among the most valuable historical texts. It is not surprising, therefore, that the most active study of Tacitus in these years took place among French scholars and among the Italian émigrés who had settled in France, as Arnaldo Momigliano has pointed out;[9] for France was the center of humanist jurisprudence—the *mos gallicus.*

The historiographers, finally, also neglected to apply Tacitus for political ends. This is true despite their increasing use of Tacitus as a historical source in these years, at least in Germany and England. In Germany, as has been shown, the geographer-historians constantly studied and wrote about the *Germania* and the sections about the Germans in the *Annales.* In England, historians were now beginning to mine the *Agricola* with similar intensity.[10] The first really modern historian of England, Polydore Vergil of Urbino,[11] was the first in England to employ it as a historical source there in his *Anglica historia.* Written over the preceding three decades, it first appeared at Basel in 1534. Vergil's history soon exerted a powerful influence on other English historians, even though they hated the author because he denied the veracity of the Arthur legend, because he remained a "papist" all his life (and went back to Italy to die in 1555), and, last but not least, because he wrote in an un-Ciceronian style. Vergil wrote in the tradition begun by Biondo, a tradition which placed accuracy over ornament. But the public still largely favored Ciceronian elegance in historical writing, and it held Livy to be the best model. Despite Vives and Erasmus, Linacre and Elyot, other highly respected teachers remained unmoved in their Ciceronian and Livian preferences and simply ignored Tacitus: John Cheke and Walter Haddon, tutors to King Edward VI, never knew Tacitus or, at least, never admitted it;[12] and, Roger Ascham, tutor to Queen Elizabeth, bothered with Tacitus on only two occasions, and then to cite him for historical trivia;[13] finally, all other authors in Elyot's genre, until 1607, do not mention Tacitus even once, and they never quote him.[14] For these reasons neither Tacitus nor Vergil provoked much enthusiasm, despite the great use English historians made of the information they provided.

Most readers in England preferred British-bred historians, who looked more sympathetically on their primitive past.[15] One of them, Hector Boece, a Scots professor of philosophy at Paris and, later, divinity lecturer at Aberdeen, published his entertaining and romanticized

Scotorum historiae a prima gentis origine in 1527 (Paris).[16] In it, mainly for its early sections, he relied heavily on Tacitus' *Agricola* and books xii and xiv of the *Annales;* in some cases, from the latter, he copied speeches. However, Boece's work and his reliance on Tacitus stirred little interest until translated into Scots by a certain John Bellenden in 1536. Boece's work now quickly overshadowed Vergil's in popularity, despite the appearance of revised and expanded editions of the latter in 1546 and 1555. Its fame remained intact at least until 1577, after which its reputation became even more secure when it was incorporated in *The Chronicles of England, Scotland, and Ireland.* This compilation was the work of Raphael Holinshed, a historian, and William Harrison, a topographer and translator. Holinshed, relying usually on Vergil, wrote most of the part on England; and, instead of bothering much to interpret Tacitus on his own, he simply translated, in a running commentary, the whole of Tacitus' *Agricola.*[17] Harrison, besides helping his friend with the England section, translated Boece's work into English and tried to improve it, without much merit, with secondhand and erroneous citations from Tacitus. About ten years later, William Camden,[18] after whom the famous historical society is named, in his *The Britannia: A Chronological Description of the Flourishing Kingdoms of England, Scotland, and Ireland* (1586) followed Holinshed's example: he simply lifted, without attribution, the whole of *Agricola* xvii–xl. Still, he was the first English historian to take the trouble to look into the *Germania* to see what Tacitus had said there about non-British barbarians; he looked, but was never inspired to make comparisons and contrasts. Camden (like Harrison, Holinshed, and Boece) marks the rule: British historiographers of the sixteenth century looked to Tacitus for information and to Vergil for incentive—mechanically with the first, begrudgingly with the second—to satisfy a narrow ethnic interest. In all, if the *Agricola* and the *Germania* had not gratified a certain national vanity, it is unlikely that Tacitus would have been used much by historians in either England or Germany.

This motive was wanting in France and Italy, and there the historians almost totally ignored Tacitus. At most they used him for only a fact or two, as the need arose. In France, indeed, historiography was largely annexed by the jurists, who used Tacitus, not as a source for history in general, but solely for the study of Roman law. The title alone of François Baudouin's *De institutione historiae universae . . . cum iurisprudentia coniunctione* (1561) is a case in point. In Italy, history remained an autonomous discipline; but here Tacitus was even more neglected—although few historians would have agreed with Ortensio Lando, monk and medic, that he told too many lies.[19] Closer to the real reason was that few of them would have agreed with Benedetto Varchi, Duke Cosimo I's historiographer, for his choice of Tacitus and Polybius as stylistic guides for his *Storia fiorentina* (begun in 1546). Indeed, the fact is that history was kept free of Tacitan influence by the power of the Ciceronians.[20] They included not only the consciously Ciceronian writers on history, like Cardinal Pietro Bembo and Paolo Giovio, but also the rhetoricians, who from the '40s on began to take over the task of writing the rules of historiography. One of these rhetoricians, Sperone Speroni, a professor at Padua, took the first step in establishing historiographical orthodoxy as early as 1542; and his work was continued thereafter by his colleague Francesco Robortello, in his *De historia facultate* of 1548, and by Dionigi Atanagi da Cagli, in his *Ragionamento della eccelentia et perfezione de la istoria* (1559). According to the rhetoricians, the authorities for the rules of historical writing were Cicero, Aristotle, and Lucian; and the historian who came closest to fulfilling the rules was not Tacitus but Livy.

The Ciceronian theorists read Tacitus, to be sure, but they could not accept his style, and they forced what little they took from him into a completely un-Tacitan framework. Typical in this respect is the famous philologian and Italian Protestant, Caelio Secondo Curione. Despite Curione's deep commitment to Protestant theology, he was unable to accept the frequent Protestant condemnation of Cicero and Aristotle as pagan idols. Neither, to be sure, was one of the greatest Protestant theologians, Melanchthon. But Curione went beyond Melanchthon and continued to worship the idols. Speaking of Cicero, he proclaimed:

> By the good gods, what a man! The greatest orator of all, living and dead and yet to come. And that, indeed, means the greatest philosopher and teacher of law, the ruler of all arts—so has he, and Quintilian, taught us to understand the conception of the orator.[21]

Even among his fellow Zwinglians at Basel, where he wrote these lines in 1548, he ardently emulated his model. To Markus Kutter, Curione's most recent biographer, this dedication to Cicero was incompatible with his confessional commitments. But Curione was no Saint Jerome, and this incompatibility never bothered him. He produced one edition of the classics after another, including many of Cicero's writings, without ever fearing a *non es christianus, sed. . . .* Of Tacitus he published only one work, and that, significantly, was the neo-Ciceronian *Dialogus de oratoribus*—which he included merely as an appendix to the text of Cicero's *Brutus* and his commentary on it.

When he occasionally does speak of Tacitus, therefore, Curione never gives the slightest hint of departing from Ciceronian orthodoxy. His comments are expressed in a letter to Basil Amerbach, printer and printer's son, who had asked him for a list of recommended historians and a method for reading them.[22] This was in 1554; and Curione's answer was published seven years after his death, in 1576, under the title *De historia legenda sententia*. Curione includes Caesar, Velleius Paterculus, and Sallust in his list. But he also includes Tacitus, whom he praises for his perspicacity and judgment. Tacitus, he says, "was most diligent in explaining motives [in consiliis explicandis] and most penetrating in enquiring into causes; no one has seen more acutely or described the arts of princes and those around them."[23] The line about the princes is not new. Alciato had said much the same thing long before: "He tells us of the impulses of princes." Curione's statements are merely an elaboration on Alciato's recommendations taken out of context and divorced from both legal and political practicality. But Curione sets the idea of Tacitus' penetrating judgment of princes into the Ciceronians' construct of reading history as the *magistra vitae*—as a way of learning prudence, of developing individual moral qualities, and of acquiring experience in rhetoric. He dumped Tacitus along with the other historians when he advised Amerbach on the manner of reading them: first, read the history in the way it was originally composed; second, study it from many points of view. That is, study it in the skeleton of events as annals; in its descriptions; in the measure of its good and bad exemplary events; in the examples of political forms, religions, and wars; and, finally, in the especially foolish and especially wise utterances of the great models of rulers.[24] The result was a work which Giorgio Spini, the most authoritative student of the writings of these Ciceronians, declares to be "of small intellectual value."[25]

It could have been unfortunate for Guicciardini's *History of Italy* that Curione was the first to publish a Latin translation of it in 1566. In the preface[26] he begged the readers not to castigate him, the mere translator, if Guicciardini sometimes offends them by negative statements on their rulers and lands; after all, it was the historian's job to bestow praise and allot blame. He also asked them to forgive his necessary use of unclassical language in many instances. But here Curione's study of Guicciardini betrays cracks in his Ciceronian wall. He questions the utility of forcing every expression into classical forms, since the very differences between the stylistic standards set by Sabellicus, Bembo, and Giovio—all Ciceronians—left him so confused that he no longer knew what to believe. Indeed, he, and the other Ciceronians less honest than himself, might have condemned the *History of Italy* to darkest oblivion along with other non-Ciceronian (or non-Livian) histories—as they did Vergil's *Anglica historia*. Or else they might have "refined" it, as Pius II had done in his *Epitome* of Biondo's *Decades*. But in 1560, the year before the *History of Italy* first came to light, something happened which was to ensure its survival in its original form.

In that year Francesco Patrizi, professor of philosophy at the University of Padua, published his *Dieci dialoghi della historia*.[27] It was the first of the *ars historiae* manuals to attack the Ciceronian dogma, and it eventually secured a victory for Tacitus over Livy. That the *Dialoghi* were written by a Paduan professor is itself important, because the university was the citadel of the Ciceronians, and the work reflects discussions carried on with them about the methodology and purpose of history. It considers the definition of history, its end, its kinds, its utility, and its methodological problems concerning "actor, occasion, time, place, mode of acting, and instruments."[28] It maintains the primacy of truth over beauty in historiographical composition. It distinguishes the poet, who makes much from nothing, from the orator, who adds to what is imperfect and subtracts from what is perfect; and it distinguishes from both the historian, who gives equal to what is equal. The historian must recount no more and no less than the truth; he must limit the use of words to whatever is necessary to make the matter clear.[29]

The most crucial confrontation occurs in the Tenth Dialogue, where one speaker reverts to the authority of Cicero. But the principal interlocutor maintains his point.[30] He insists that a long digression could have been avoided if the other speakers had not forgotten the first law of history which they had already laid down for themselves: the law, that is, which obliges the historian above all to tell what really happened—*res veras narrare*.[31] Only if history is true can it really be useful "for the governing of this republic and the conserving of its peace."[32] By "this republic" Patrizi refers to his own country, Venice. The historians best for Venice, it turns out, are the republican historians—Livy, Thucydides, Sallust, and Polybius.[33]

About Polybius, Peter Burke, who has studied the revival of classical historians in the Renaissance, is mistaken. According to Burke, Patrizi "argued that Polybius is not a historian but a philosopher, because it is philosophy which deals with causes, and history only deals with effects."[34] Only the distinction between philosophy and history is Patrizi's, not Burke's consignment of Polybius to the former. In fact, it is this very problem over Polybius which brought Patrizi to state his second law of history:

> The second law, therefore, which is prescribed for the historian, convicts not only Polybius, but, indeed, others who do likewise. Indeed, while they describe events in detail, they remain within the limits of the historian; but where they probe into the causes and the reasons of things, they enter into the duty of the philosopher.[35]

In short, Patrizi does not deny that Polybius is a historian because of the philosophical elements. On the contrary, he says that Polybius (and other historians) usually remains within the limits of history and that the reader should disregard those elements in his work which go beyond the limits. And, as with the other three historians of republics, Polybius, too, is politically valuable for Patrizi. Polybius was a great man, with many distinctions "and with so many useful arguments for the civic way of life."[36]

Besides these four historians there is another whom Patrizi praises and from whom he draws political utility: Plutarch. As if to remove any doubt as to his reasons for calling Plutarch most wise,[37] Patrizi had earlier made an important distinction. Historians who write about one man can write about either the "princeps absolutus" (who is lord of the army and the laws, with or without right), or the "princeps reipublicae" (who administers the army and the laws with the consent of the people only); or, these historians can write about those who serve either one. Thinking about Plutarch's *Lives,* Patrizi says that the author wrote about both kinds of princes and ministers and about exiles as well.[38] Alone, it is true, such comments do not reveal Patrizi's own political interest in Plutarch. But, twenty pages later, Patrizi proves that all historians (writing either about one man or many, private men or public figures, etc.) must write not for himself but for society: "Indeed, he is no historian who does not write with the purpose that he may publish."[39] Thus, Plutarch can be useful for Venetian society for his *Lives* of republican statesmen but not for those of princes. Only the historians of republics are adequate guides. Hence, Tacitus did not even enter Patrizi's mind,[40] for a historian of emperors had nothing to teach to the citizens of a republic.

Venice enjoyed a rare form of government in the mid-sixteenth century, when most states were rapidly being transformed into bureaucratic, authoritarian monarchies; but this does not mean that Patrizi's view of history was necessarily restricted to republics. On the contrary, one had only to substitute the word "monarch" for the word "republic" whenever the question of the utility of history arose, and to replace one ancient model with another, more appropriate one—like Tacitus, for instance. So, at any rate, thought Jean Bodin, perhaps the most learned of Renaissance political theorists. And with Bodin, the thirty-three-year moratorium on the use of Tacitus for political thought was suddenly broken. Bodin thought he recognized a fault in Patrizi—and in Machiavelli, Thomas More, and two others[41]—for not speaking of Tacitus:

> They say much, gravely and copiously, about cultivating morals, remedying peoples, educating the prince, and establishing laws; but they speak only lightly on the state; and on those things which Aristotle calls the σοφίσματα [devices] or κρύφια [secrets] of princes, and which Tacitus calls the secrets of state, they do not even touch at all.[42]

So, to make up for Patrizi's lack of concern about such matters, Bodin wrote his own treatise in 1565 and published it in 1566. It was called the *Methodus ad facilem historiarum cognitionem*.

Only in its understanding of the scope of history is Bodin's *Methodus* similar to Patrizi's *Dialoghi*. To Patrizi, Bodin is indebted for his emphasis on the historian's duty *res veras narrare* and for his further prescriptions that these *res* include events both human and natural and that the "human" include economic, financial, judicial, and social as well as political events. But there is utter disparity in the political aspects of both works. Bodin's is a political treatise grounded in history; Patrizi's is a historiographical treatise with a political aim brought in merely to complete the definition of history by explaining its utility. The contrast is apparent even in the explicit intentions expressed at the beginning of each work. For Bodin:

> Indeed, in history *the best part of universal law* lies hidden; and what is of great weight and importance for *the best appraisal of legislation*—the custom of the peoples, and the beginnings, growth, conditions, changes, and decline of all states—is obtained from it. *The chief subject matter of this Method consists of these facts*, since no rewards of history are more ample than those usually gathered about the governmental forms of states. I have written

> more on this topic [over half the work] than on the other topics because few have treated the problem, so vital to comprehend, and those few only superficially. [Italics mine.][43]

For Patrizi, however—dissenting from Alphonso Bidernutio, who seems to argue the views of the Paduan Francesco Robortello, Patrizi's one-time Ciceronian professor:

> To the first, I hardly know what to say, except that one cannot find out what the qualities of history are before one knows what it is.

Then, dissenting from the Neapolitan Giovanni Pontano, the Ciceronian author of the *Actius:*

> Pontano teaches what history should consist of and what its purpose should be—but he does not show what it is; and yet that was our first objective.[44]

After another thirty pages Patrizi is still being begged to tell what history *is*. Problems follow upon problems, and the definition of history slowly evolves. But Bodin's aim is different: his work is a study of politics in history. He seeks to discover principles of government for the creation of necessary laws. He wants to find agreement between political philosophers and historians—to ground political philosophy in history and, at the same time, history in political philosophy:

> It seemed to me useful, for this *Method* which I am planning, to study the disputations of the philosophers and historians about the state and to compare the empires of our ancestors with our own. When all have been duly noted, the general history of principalities may be more plainly understood. *We shall carry away from the discussion this benefit, that we may easily understand what laws are needed* in a monarchy, and likewise what are necessary in a popular and in an aristocratic state (for of these laws there are as many varieties as of the government).[45] [Italics mine.]

For Bodin, the study of history is thus the study of government, and the study of government is the study of law. But history is still the starting point; and since history is contained in the writings of the historians, it is essential that the historians be evaluated according to the accuracy with which they record the facts. This is why Bodin finds Tacitus to be superior to all others. This is why Bodin finds that Tacitus' honesty, lack of bias, purity and gravity of style, careful use of documents, skill in narrative, and critical acumen provide such a reliable account.[46] Moreover, his experience in the ''intimate halls of princes''[47] enables him to reveal of ''what kind was the cognizance and jurisdiction of princes.''[48] Tacitus was an authority on his subject, in other words. ''If we seek the legal and senatorial arts . . . there is nowhere a richer harvest.''[49] ''Nor is there any historian after the battle of Actium who has treated more fully the military or legal system.''[50] In fact, ''Why say more? Certainly no historian seems more useful to the magistrate and the judge.''[51] Tacitus has still another advantage—precisely the one that Patrizi thought was a disadvantage: monarchy is the most excellent form of government, and Tacitus is the most useful ancient historian for illustrating the principles upon which monarchies operate. Finally, he provides the most important source for the practice as well as the principles of politics.

Bodin's reevaluation of Tacitus constitutes one of the most significant moments in the history of Tacitus in Renaissance political thought. Enlarged and refined by others, it was eventually to lead to ''reason of state.''

Bodin did not arrive at these judgments without the help of predecessors. Alciato was of some assistance, but Bodin reacted explicitly to only one specific aspect of Alciato's interpretation of Tacitus. He overlooked Alciato's recommendation of quietude and resignation in dealing with princes (that idea is completely absent in Bodin's Tacitus). What he noticed was Alciato's encomium of Tacitus' style. But here it is surprising that he both recognizes and denies his debt to Alciato in the very same breath:

> But the reproach of certain men distresses and disturbs me, which would need refutation less if their authority were not so great. For Alciato, in a letter he wrote to Giovio, dared to call that clearly divine history ''thickets of thorns'' [senticeta]. It is true that it is usually considered rough by those who prefer the lighter trivialities of the grammarians to the most serious narratives of those who have spent their entire lives in public affairs. Still, I do not see why Alciato despises so great a man; he is the very one who should appreciate [his] eloquence. Perhaps it is because Decius [Alciato's professor], removing him from the list of jurisconsults, called him a Ciceronian [for having sought and praised eloquence in Tacitus]. And similar is Jerome, who, as he himself writes, was beaten with straps before the tribunal of Christ because he was a Ciceronian and not a Christian. But, joking aside, this one [Jerome] suffered straps, and that one [Alciato] insult, without deserving them.[52]

''He is the very one who should appreciate [his] eloquence.'' This statement indicates that Bodin was thinking of Alciato's preface. Bodin knew that Alciato had loved Tacitus' style. Besides, as the parallel to Jerome shows, Bodin thought Philipp Decius' attack on Alciato unjustified.[53] Moreover, Bodin admits he is joking about the ridiculous implication that Alciato praised Tacitus only to win back the favor of his professor, who had acted like Jerome's Christ. Alciato was not a Ciceronian in Bodin's eyes. Still, Bodin casts doubt on the sincerity of Alciato's preface by making capital out of a probably spurious statement invented by the Ciceronian historian Paolo Giovio.[54] Even if Alciato had written such a letter to Giovio, Bodin himself should have been more cautious in giving credence to one whom he had just ridiculed at length for utterly fallacious historical writing.[55]

Bodin apparently wants to show himself superior to the old triumvir of humanist jurisprudence. He wants to show that he, and not Alciato, recognizes the real value of Tacitus' style. Moreover, in another passage he exclaims that Alciato was disturbed over what was, in his opinion, an unproblematic point of law. In still another he accuses Alciato of stupidly making a philological error in his interpretation of Plautus and Catullus.[56] In truth, however, Bodin owed more to Alciato than he could have (or cared to have) realized: the method of studying the classics to learn Roman law; the recognition of Tacitus as the best source for this study; and the adoption of Tacitus' purity and gravity of speech, undistorted by Ciceronian ornament, as a model for conveying the knowledge of the law. For all three points the line goes back directly to Alciato.

On the other hand, Bodin had some real basis for lording it over the old master, and this explains his supercilious failure to acknowledge his real debt to him. Bodin's purpose and scope in studying the law were, after all, certainly not the same as Alciato's. Bodin went beyond Alciato in two important respects. He said that law is universal and that it is to be learned through experience as well as through books. Therefore, a jurist should study the laws of all nations, not just those of ancient Rome; and he should move out of the musty cubicles of universities and into the law courts. One ignorant of the work of the magistrate and the judge could not properly interpret the ancient authors on law. Only a jurist with experience could make effective in civic reality what he had learned in books.

Bodin did not possess these ideas *ex ventre*.[57] His ideas developed out of his own life and experience. As late as 1560 (his thirtieth year) he was still a follower of the Alciato-Budé school. As a student at the University of Toulouse he learned its methodology, and as a lecturer there (as a private teacher only) he taught it. He remained in Toulouse from 1550 to 1560, except for two years around 1552. It is then that he may have been in Geneva. And it may have been his stay in Geneva that stimulated his liking for the city, his knowledge of its constitution, and his high regard for Calvin. His concept of a universal law may indeed have been inspired by Calvin's legalistic theology, with its all-prevailing divine law; at least he always remained tolerant of Calvinism thereafter, even though he never abandoned the Catholic Church. He also learned that a particular religion is not esesntial to the well-being of civic life. Religious conflict, he now observed, was at the point of bringing disaster upon Toulouse and, indeed, upon all of France. The best way to escape it was through a study of the humanities, coupled with a study of law.

These are the views which Bodin expressed in his *Oratio de instituenda in republica juventute* before the senate and people of Toulouse in 1559. Most of the professors and the small bourgeoisie of Toulouse, who were furiously pro-Catholic, were alienated by these views, but they did not drive him into the arms of the nobles of Languedoc and Navarre, who formed the avant-garde of the Protestant party. The principal effect of the *Oratio* was to bar him both from a chair at the university and from a seat in the *parlement* of Toulouse. He therefore gave up hope of entering the faculty of law. In 1560 he went to Paris; and there, with the help of old friends, he became an *avocat* of the *parlement* of Paris.

Bodin's service as an *avocat* forced a crisis in his legal philosophy. In Paris, humanist jurisprudence had not been well received, and indeed Roman civil law itself had been received only as an adjunct and auxiliary to common law. Bodin's observation of the consummate practical skill of the Parisian lawyers, evidently superior to the professors' when it came to dealing with concrete cases, led him to this conclusion: a true jurisconsult was one who drafted necessary laws and laws which had a definite application in given instances. Professors, on the other hand, were depending solely on the authority of grammar and historical knowledge. It was on this matter that Bodin broke with Jacques Cujas, perhaps the most famous professor of humanistic jurisprudence of the day. Roman law, Bodin felt, was just not sufficient to prevent the rapid deterioration of political order in France. The professors studied their books only, and they studied only the books of Roman law. What was needed was experience—experience grounded in the law courts and in the administration of the government. However, Bodin did not completely abandon the old methods; indeed, he kept them but wedded them to a still more ancient tradition, that of the Bartolus school, which emphasized *application* from the lawbooks. He maintained the humanistic method of cleaning out the errors of the post-glossator Bartolists, but he took the Bartolists' tradition of applied law. The correct law must be discovered and then applied. When Bodin came to write his *Methodus,* he elaborated these ideas; and he coupled them with the argument that the best form of state is monarchy and that the best laws are those which maintain the sovereignty of the monarch.

If experience enabled a jurist better to understand history, experience enabled a historian better to write it. And the most appropriate kind of experience was that which involved the ways of princes and *arcana imperii.* For these reasons Tacitus was Bodin's best ancient historian—better than Suetonius, Plutarch, Thucydides, and all the others; for the same reasons, his best modern historian was Guicciardini, "that very father of history."[58] Guicciardini "sprinkled grave judgments everywhere appropriately, like salt."[59] "He was a diligent investigator of things, places and persons and, indeed, of plans and deeds."[60] He was endowed "with the highest wisdom, erudition, integrity, and experience of practical affairs."[61] In all, he "brought into the clearest light many plans of many men, no matter how secretive."[62] Bodin had read the *History of Italy* only within the past five years; and it may have been as much Guicciardini who led him to reevaluate Tacitus as it was his reevaluation of Tacitus that made him appreciate the similar qualities in Guicciardini.

If, like Curione, Bodin had written the *Methodus* simply as a handbook on reading history, this parallel between Tacitus and Guicciardini would have remained sterile. And if, like Patrizi, he had fallen back into a treasure hunt for *exempla,*[63] it would have remained inert. On the contrary: to Bodin, the two historians provided storehouses of accurate observations on princes and well-informed exposures of the secrets of state.

To be sure, Guicciardini was not the only modern historian whom Bodin admired. He also had much in common with Machiavelli. They used history in the same way because they both wrote political treatises based on their historical knowledge. Machiavelli was able to "rightly give a decision [concerning] . . . the secrets of princes and the life of the palace."[64] He "also wrote many things about government—the first, I think, for about 1,200 years after barbarism had overwhelmed everything. [His sayings] are on the lips of everyone."[65] But Machiavelli had many defects as well. First of all, his experience, as opposed to his book learning, was limited. Second, he was full of contradictions. For example, in one breath he said that men cannot be extremely wicked and, in the next, that the Italians, Spanish, and French are the wickedest of all races.[66] Consequently, he completely misunderstood the functions of the French chancellor and the French king.[67] Worst of all, he vehemently approved the absurd opinion of Polybius that the sovereignty of the state was partly in the people, partly in the senate, and partly in the consuls.[68] He even misconstrued the constitution of his own city.[69] The history of Florence from 1215 on is a dire account of the atrocities of the mob and the quarrels of the optimates. For example, in 1494: ''the plebs roamed about, hither and thither, like a flock without a shepherd, fearing the designs of both men and wild beasts''—as Machiavelli himself reported, Bodin is careful to add.[70] Thus, when summarizing his criticism of popular government, Bodin manages to malign all three of Machiavelli's most well-known works within a few pages:

> About the popular kind [of government] I should think nothing ought to be written if it were not supported by the opinions of many men. N. Machiavelli, for example, is persuaded by arguments and reasons that it is the most excellent. But on this matter I think he ought to be believed less, especially since he overturns the foundations of his own argument; for, in the *Institution of the Prince,* at the very beginning, he posited two forms of government only: monarchy and republic. The same author, in his book on Livy, affirms the Republic of Venice to be the best of all; but he regards it as popular, for in book iii he wrote that the popular forms of government have always been more laudable—against the approved opinion of philosophers and historians and of all great men.[71]

> And I do not know why Machiavelli, the man of Florence, should praise popular government so much, since from his own history it is clear that, of all states, none was more unfortunate than Florence in the period when it was democratic.[72]

How could anyone be so blind? Bodin's condemnation of Machiavelli's ignorance, lack of insight, naïveté, and illogical thinking, all seem to follow from the charge of inexperience:

> But there is no doubt that he would have written more truly and better if to the writings of ancient philosophers and historians he had coupled experience.[73]

Obviously, or else he would have seen the truth contained in his historians. Bodin's views on Livy and Polybius, Machiavelli's most important historians, certainly stand in bold contrast. To be sure, Machiavelli turns out to be inferior to his two principal ancient models. Livy, after all, used documents in support of his statements, he varied his style admirably, he included much detail (even too much of it!), and, most important, he could rightly speak on civil affairs.[74] Indeed, Bodin took nearly all the material for his diatribe on the Roman plebs right out of Livy.[75] Polybius, similarly, was intelligent, serious, sparse in bestowing praise, honest, and accurate. He was also a wise legislator, a good general, and a critical observer of men and places.[76] Yet both shared with Machiavelli an incorrect judgment of political institutions.[77] They could help him find the laws of only bad politics, not good politics. They revealed only states that were foul with the domination of the vulgar mob and rank with the quarrels of the corrupt politicians. Despite their republican sympathies and ideologies, these writers showed only that republics are miserable forms of government and that a political science based on them is erroneous. None of the three, therefore, could contribute anything constructive to the understanding of modern politics.

It was to Tacitus, therefore, that Bodin turned for what he could not find in other historians. Through Tacitus he could observe, almost with his own eyes, the workings of the Roman monarchy, and he could thus penetrate to the principles behind all monarchies. He would not be confused by any nonsense about the mixed state or republic. And he could recognize clearly that, in great affairs, all power must rest entirely with one man.[78]

This was the main argument of the *Methodus*. It was also the main argument of his next work, *De la République,* first published in 1576.[79] In the meantime, Bodin's erudition had expanded enormously, and Tacitus and Guicciardini become lost among the many scores of authorities cited. Still, it was Tacitus' lessons about political philosophy that led to his conclusion; and Tacitus' lessons had been reinforced still further by his own experiences.

Less than a year or two after beginning his work as an *avocat* for the *parlement* of Paris, the most active center for the suppression of heresy in France, Bodin signed the formulary of June 1562 against the enemies of the Catholic Church in France. Other lawyers and magistrates—for example, Jean Bautru des Matras, Bodin's colleague in Paris—refused to sign it. But Bodin did not hesitate. "States are not established for the sake of liberty," he said, "but for the sake of living well."[80] He granted that liberty was very desirable—but only so far as living well was assured by good order. Similarly, he believed that religious liberty was desirable (aside from the question of the truth of any religion itself)—provided it did not result in civil discord. When religious dissent broke out into armed conflict, it was treason and should be treated as such.

Most people—whether Frenchmen or foreigners, Catholics or Protestants—could see no difference between a heretic and a traitor; and, with a few notable exceptions, they regarded politics and religion as inseparable. What seems occasionally to be religious toleration was usually just political expediency. The principle of "cuius regio, eius religio" was not a religious but a practical political formulation. Moreover, it had a catch. It made no judgment about what prince with what religion was the *right* prince with that religion. When people could not agree on who should be their prince, they usually sought a solution in war.

A case in point is the Low Countries after 1568. The Protestants favored William of Orange, and the Catholics upheld Margaret of Parma. Twenty thousand Spanish soldiers, under the duke of Alba, came to help crush the Protestants. Less than a year before hostilities began in the North, Justus Lipsius, soon to become the greatest of all Tacitus scholars, had gone to Rome as a secretary to Antoine Perrenot, bishop of Granvella, adviser to Margaret of Parma and one of the emperor's emissaries sent to congratulate Pius V on his election.[81] Lipsius had just written a masterpiece of Ciceronian prose in his *Variae lectiones,* which he dedicated to Granvella.[82] But in Rome he came into contact with Latino Latini, Francesco Benci, Paolo Manuzio, and especially with Marc Antoine Muret, perhaps the finest classicist of the late Renaissance; and it was through them that he first learned to appreciate the un-Ciceronian style of Tacitus. His enthusiasm was apparently unbounded, for so hard did he study during his two years in Rome that on his return to Louvain at the age of twenty-two, late in 1569, he abandoned himself momentarily to wine and women. He was soon back at work, however, thanks in part to the meagerness of the estate his father left him in 1565. But not soon enough! Fleeing the fires of an adulterous affair,[83] he left his troubled homeland and decided to go and present himself to Emperor Maximilian II in Vienna. He saw the emperor but left without a job. On his way home he heard that his modest estate had been confiscated. He halted in Leipzig for a while. There, Joachim Camerarius, the famous scholar and friend of Melanchthon, told him a position was open at the University of Jena. Lipsius grabbed it. In 1572 he was ready to teach his first course. By this time he knew his Tacitus pretty well; and it was on Tacitus that he decided to teach his course.

The inauguration lecture he gave (not published until 1607) is one of the most dynamic applications of Tacitus to politics in the Renaissance.[84]

Lipsius begins the *Oratio* by explaining how, through the period of his travels, he has come to see the truth of true religion. He is thankful now to be freed from his prior papal superstition. He laments the chaos reigning in his homeland. He grieves over its invasion by the Spanish. He is shocked especially by the cruelty of the duke of Alba, that "sanguinolentus tyrannus."[85] But he hopes that the good prince of Orange will bring liberation. He then turns to attack the dreaded Inquisitors, who, "just like hunting hounds, probe into everyone's homes, conversations, and doorways."[86] But now, he adds, he is safe in a land with good religion and a good prince. Finally, he comes to the point:

> I shall satisfy your expectations: there is nothing more useful to me or to you, and there is nothing more suited to afflicted states in such disasters, than that I should set forth for you publicly from this spot and interpret the *Annales* of Cornelius Tacitus, that most accurate writer.[87]

Compared to Tacitus, Livy is sweet nothingness:

> What is Livy able to offer which pertains to the state and to our mores except wars, armies, and seditions of the tribunes? I confess him pleasing to the ears, but I desire pleasure of the ears combined with utility for the soul.[88]

Nor is Sallust much better, when compared to Tacitus: he is very faithful to the truth, and his polished style is always pleasing to discriminating ears; but his descriptions of wars and armies are of no great interest. Tacitus far outshines him:

> And indeed, Tacitus certainly has pure Latinity in diction; yet, to certain people it may seem rough and difficult. Moreover, he is brief in narrations, acute in explicating causes, and he is a fair judge—about which I can verily say this: Tacitus can please no one unless of distinguished taste. He marvelously delights the attentive reader as much as he skips and bypasses the nonattentive and indifferent.[89]

Moreover, what he says is very pertinent to the issues of the present age:

> Truly, how very many things in him are pertinent to civil matters, to social upheavals, and to jurisprudence; and in the picture of a similar tyrant, how many examples for our times? Well then, for instance Tiberius: deceitful, steeped in continual murders, drenched

> in the blood of innocent citizens—is that not a distinct image of that bloodied and frenzied tyrant, the duke of Alba?[90]

Lipsius then goes through a list of the public crimes and private enormities ("the clandestine and wicked lusts") of both Tiberius and Claudius. Finally, he returns to the Inquisitors:

> How prudent Tacitus was about those things, and how apt for our time with its heretics going around burning books! Indeed, he wrote that when a certain man wrote something too freely about Cassius and Brutus, he was condemned by Tiberius, and his writings were confiscated by the aediles and burned.[91]

He ends by saying that the students can learn much from his course by his illustrations of Tacitus' text with contemporary coins, monuments, and inscriptions.

All this sounds as if Lipsius were using Tacitus as a means of promoting concrete political action. True, he had some things to say about Tacitus and politics; but actual political activity was another matter. That, after all, is what Bodin was doing just then in France, where he had embarked on a career of public service. But Lipsius had no such end in mind. His references to the duke of Alba were mere bombast. What he took from Tacitus was a program, not for action in society, but for protecting himself as an individual in an age of evil princes. What he wanted was "utility for the soul."[92] In this he echoes, not Bodin, but Alciato. He may in fact have known Alciato's preface. Many of his lines seem to be almost paraphrases of it, but he could have borrowed from many other sources just as easily. Comments in Bodin's *Methodus* (the second edition had just appeared), in Rhenanus' preface and notes, in Machiavelli's *Discorsi,* in Aventinus, in Baudouin, in Hutten, or in others—all could have inspired the various elements in the *Oratio*. What is important is that Tacitus again had become the chief source for instruction in political wisdom, whether for a man as a subject or for a man as a citizen. And Lipsius reinforced what he had said by publishing a new edition of Tacitus in 1574.

Others soon took up Bodin's and Lipsius' incentive for the mining of Tacitus for political instruction. This was especially true in France. In 1573, for example, the well-known legal philosopher, François Hotman, wrote the *Franco-Gallia*—a pamphlet which argued that the earliest Gallic monarchs (being little more then figureheads) had once been dependent on the tribal nobles; Tacitus was one of his important authorities.[93] In 1579, Claude Fauchet, a translator of the classics, argued against Hotman in his *Antiquitez gauloises et françoises:* "that which Tacitus says about the Germans seems to be the true portrait of our first French kings"[94]—implying that they had more authority than Hotman cared to admit. When Fauchet got around to publishing a translation of the first six books of the *Annales* in 1582, he added a note: "It is not always necessary that the prince give reason publicly for his actions."[95] Another translator, Blaise de Vigenère, published a French version of Caesar's *Gallic Wars* in 1576, and he attached a translation of Petilius Cerialis' speech to the rebellious Gallic tribes from Tacitus' *Historiae* (iv. 73–74). In 1576 also the *Discours sur la servitude volontaire,* written some thirty years earlier by Montaigne's young friend Etienne de la Boétie, came to light. It is an attempt to answer the question of how the Romans lost their freedom under the emperors, and naturally Tacitus is one of its sources. It had no immediate reference to the political circumstances of the time in which it was written,[96] but the readers of Hotman and Fauchet who came upon it in the 1570s must certainly have been aware of what by then had become obvious parallels between Rome in the first century and France in the late sixteenth.

In Italy, similarly, the *Avvedimenti civili* of Gianfrancesco Lottini (d. 1572) appeared posthumously in 1574. Lottini had been the private secretary of Duke Cosimo I in Florence and of Paul III and his two successors in Rome. He had kept track of his experiences in a collection of over 550 maxims, very much like Guicciardini's *Ricordi* (first published in 1576), which, of course, Lottini could not have read. Thirteen of them were more or less influenced by his reading of Tacitus, even though Tacitus is mentioned only twice by name; and having been prepared by Machiavelli, Alciato, Lipsius, and Bodin, his readers would have had no difficulty in catching the references. Indeed, Bodin's *Methodus* went through its third and fourth editions in 1576 and 1579; and the *République,* loaded with references to Tacitus, came out in a new edition almost every year after its first appearance in 1576. Readers could now check the accuracy of his citations and quotations against much more accurate texts—namely, those of Lipsius, which were republished with further refinements and emendations in 1576. And they all began avidly to search through the texts for guidance in the theory and art of politics.

Needless to say, what each of them found was often very different from what others found. According to Bodin, Tacitus provided an ideal constitution and showed how monarchies ought to work as well as how one particular monarchy actually did work. According to Lipsius, Tacitus showed individual subjects what evil monarchy or tyranny was in order to enable them to escape the consequences. Then in 1576—the same year in which Guicciardini's *Ricordi* came to light[97]—still another interpretation became available. According to Guicciardini, Tacitus had spoken not to subjects or to political philosophers but (especially in *ricordo* C-18) to monarchs themselves; and he had produced what was essentially a handbook for tyrants. That suddenly gave Tacitus a role that previously had not been recognized. What Guicciardini suggested in only one of his verses (though implying it in others), Marc Antoine Muret expanded four years later in a lecture to one of his packed classes in Rome. Not only, he said, could Tacitus teach rulers; in fact he actually had taught one of them, namely, Paul III:

> Paul III, Pontifex Maximus, than whom our age has seen no old man more wise, wore out his Tacitus by reading him so frequently; and there was no profane writer whom he read more willingly.[98]

For one who before had busied himself only with philological problems in Tacitus, this was a very political-minded discovery. And he had more to offer on the same idea:

> Cosimo de' Medici, who was the first Duke of Etruria, a man born to rule, who taught us that what is generally considered luck consists of planning and prudence, held the books of Tacitus in special regard; and he most avidly enjoyed reading them.[99]

Besides,

> even today there are many princes, or many of those whom princes use whenever they consider the highest matters in counsel, who read this same author very diligently; and they hold him almost as a kind of master of prudence.[100]

This was a new view of Tacitus; but Muret went no further with it. *Princes,* he said, not tyrants, are the ones who profit from reading Tacitus. (To be sure, a view different from Guicciardini's emphasis.) For example, the Emperor Tacitus, the historian's kinsman, was one of those "who, not led by the inane sound of words but by the goodness and gravity of the judgments, have always held Tacitus in special honor."[101] It is because of this moral utility that the Emperor Tacitus gloried in studying Tacitus. Unlike Lipsius, in fact, Muret could find no modern example of a tyrant:

> Although, thanks be to God, our age has no Tiberiuses, Caligulas, or Neros, it is good to know that, even under them, good and prudent men were able to live, and to know in what way and to what

> extent they were able to bear up under their vices and were able to dissemble. . . .[102]

There may be some bad princes, to be sure; but reading Tacitus is a good way both for the subjects to learn how to put up with them and for princes to overcome their defects:

> There are often many things in princes which a good man is not able to praise, which he is able to conceal and pass over in silence. Those who know not how to shut their eyes to them both create danger to themselves and generally make those princes worse. Indeed, there are many princes who, believing their vices escape notice, little by little get rid of them on their own accord because they fear they may be uncovered. And, while they are thought good, they become good.[103]

Muret was no republican despiser of princes;[104] they, after all, paid his salary. He found no difficulty, therefore, in accepting the theses of Bodin's *Methodus* in the rest of this oration and in the one given a year later, in November 1581. As a historian, Tacitus was wise, acute, honest, etc., and, most important, he was a skilled decipherer of secrets of state. As a stylist, Tacitus is grave, terse, and weighty; and Alciato was wrong (and here Muret forgets Bodin's vindication of Alciato) in calling his works "thorn patches." Admittedly, he is obscure—but this trait has the advantage of acting "as a veil, to exclude the view of the vulgar."[105] Finally, he cannot be blamed for despising Christians; after all, he was only being pious according to the principles of his own religion.

While Muret was saying these things, Carlo Pasquali, or Paschalius, a Piedmontese Christian Stoic who became a French diplomat and civil servant, published the first political commentary specifically dedicated to Tacitus.[106] He was the first to take up the suggestions in Machiavelli's *Discorsi;* and he did so in his *C. C. Taciti ab excessu divi Augusti Annalium libri quattuor priores, et in hos observationes* (Paris, 1581). Two examples are typical of his method and thought. On Germanicus' words in *Annales* i. 42—

> Neither wife nor son is dearer to me than my father and the state. But he will surely have the protection of his own majesty, the empire of Rome that of our other armies—

Paschalius comments,

> A great prince ought to take care not to have all his troops with him always assembled in the same place at the same time.[107]

And, on *Annales* i. 47, where Tacitus says,

> Notwithstanding these remonstrances, it was the inflexible purpose of Tiberius not to quit the headquarters of empire or to imperil himself and the state,

Paschalius remarks,

> The prince and the state are united by the same bond, so that nothing can happen to either one separately that does not pertain to both. Thus, it follows that the prince should think nothing useful to himself which does not benefit the state.[108]

Otherwise there is nothing really new about Paschalius' political interpretation of Tacitus. Momigliano, who knows this commentary better than anyone, appraised it as ''diluted and pedestrian Machiavellianism'' and ''Machiavelli reduced to mere prudence.''[109] If by ''Machiavellian'' Momigliano means looking at politics totally aside from any considerations but success, then Paschalius deserves his criticism. He failed to formulate principles of political action, for he lacked Machiavelli's acumen and breadth of historical vision. Moreover, he completely ignored the philosophical and religious implications of his own political precepts. Paschalius did not study a text as a source for experimental politics. Rather, he treated it as a mine for *sententiae*, with little regard for their eventual application; and he made no effort comparable to Machiavelli's to combine what he read in Tacitus with what he had learned from his own experience. This fact is all the more surprising given the realization that he dedicated the work to Duke Carlo Emmanuele I of Savoy, who was playing dangerous games between France and Spain, and that he knew the Savoyard court to be, in Momigliano's phrase, ''a nest of Machiavellians in action.''[110] Apparently he had learned nothing from his own career as a statesman and diplomat for Henry III and Guy de Pibrac, chancellor to Marguerite de Valois. Or at least he managed to insulate perfectly what he did from what he read. Books, for Paschalius, were one thing; real life was quite another.

The task of following Machiavelli's example, of putting Tacitus' Rome together with modern Europe and coming up with the general laws of politics, fell instead to another sometime follower of the House of Savoy: Giovanni Botero, one of the most influential political theorists of the late Renaissance.[111] Botero, moreover, came to conclusions that were strikingly similar to those of Machiavelli—even though he sought to do just the contrary. Politics, he discovered, could be justified only in terms of politics—however much political expediency might at times coincide with the prescriptions of morality. And he baptized this discovery with a name that was to enjoy a remarkable success for centuries afterward: "reason of state," or *Ragion di Stato,* which was the title of the work he published in 1589.

To be sure, the phrase itself had been used before—by Guicciardini, for example, in his *Dialogo del Reggimento di Firenze* (1521–22), where he recommended that all the Pisan prisoners be killed according to "ragione e uso degli stati." But Guicciardini did not use the phrase with the meaning which Botero gave to it.[112] Nor did the anonymous writer who mentioned "la prudenza politica o ragione di stato" around 1525.[113] Giovanni della Casa, the famous author of *Il Galateo,* came closer to the concept in 1547 in the oration he wrote to be presented before Charles V, *Concerning the Restitution of the City of Piacenza:*

> Some men blind with avarice and in their cupidity affirm that Your Majesty will never consent to give up Piacenza because what concerns the reason of the city does not correspond with the reason of states. I say that this rumor is not only not very Christian but is even less humane. . . . Vainly therefore do they affirm these things who make two reasons—the one unjust, false, dissolute, disposed to thievery, and to make evil; and to this they have put the name "reason of state" ["ragion di stato"].[114]

Apparently, the phrase was already coming into common parlance to indicate a higher jurisdiction, a higher ruling prerogative, to which subordinate powers were subject; for Della Casa is intent upon defining it according to usage, not upon coining a new term. Still, for the next forty-two years no one ever broached the subject again, in spite of the widespread admiration for Della Casa as a master of manners and of language. It was not until Botero that the term was finally endowed with a clear technical function in political philosophy.

Botero was born in Savoy and became a priest and then the friend and private secretary to Charles Borromeo, the reforming archbishop of Milan. His intimate understanding of Charles gave him a spiritual and sentimental attitude toward all of life. Nothing ever shook Botero from his religious orientation toward the world. Like Augustine, centuries before, he came to see an unavoidable connection between politics and evil. Man, necessarily political, is torn between intellect, which recognizes the normal ways of politics, and spirit, which is repulsed by them. This was Botero's realization, as it had been Machiavelli's long before. Botero worked it out in a way very different from Machiavelli's. In the age of the Counter-Reformation, he could not relegate religion to a completely separate category. In his first political work, *De regia sapientia* (written in 1580–82 and published in 1583), he had tried to show princes that the growth and maintenance of their states depended upon God. In the words of Luigi Firpo, one of the most authoritative students of Botero today, this work is "inspired by the rigor and the fervor of the Catholic restoration aroused through the example of Saint Charles Borromeo."[115] After Borromeo himself had approved it, Botero dedicated it to his prince, the same Carlo Emmanuele of Savoy to whom his countryman, Paschalius, had dedicated the *Observationes;* and Carlo Emmanuele rewarded him by sending him on a delicate diplomatic mission to Paris in 1585. In that same year Botero dedicated another work, his *De predicatione verbi Dei,* to Borromeo. It is pervaded with concern over God's providence and that force before which men are helpless, to which they give such names as fortune and fate. Indeed, it is an elaboration upon the *Del dispregio del mundo,* which he had written in 1583 and which is a masterpiece of refined asceticism. At the end of 1586 Botero followed Charles's twenty-two-year-old nephew, Federico Borromeo, who had just been made a cardinal, to Rome; and it was there, in the city that shared with Milan the honor of being the New Jerusalem of Counter-Reformation Catholicism, that he turned once again from religion to politics. He began to write his *Della Ragion di Stato.*[116]

Its opening words, in the dedication to Wolf Dietrich von Raitenau, archbishop of Salzburg, are famous. After many travels to the courts of princes in Italy and beyond the Alps,

> among the things that I have observed, I have been greatly astonished to find Reason of State a constant subject of discussion and to hear the opinions of Niccolò Machiavelli and Cornelius Tacitus frequently quoted: the former for his precepts relating to the rule and government of peoples, the latter for his lively description of the arts employed by the Emperor Tiberius in acquiring and retaining the imperial title in Rome.[117]

He is shocked to hear that such a "barbarous mode of government" has gained such wide acceptance.[118] Indeed, he has been so shocked that, "provoked by indignation or zeal, I have often been emboldened to write of the corruption fostered by these two men in the policy and counsel of princes."[119] The words "I have often been" are very significant, for the present-perfect tense indicates a rather recent discovery.

In 1582–83, when finishing the *De regia sapientia,* he had still not heard of Tacitus as a political thinker.[120] It must have been a little later that he became aware of Machiavelli and conscious of a connection between Machiavelli and Tacitus as guides to "ragion di stato."

Neither Meinecke nor Spini has attempted to give an explanation of why Tacitus should so suddenly have been endowed with this new role,[121] and the attempts of Toffanin, von Stackelberg, and Etter to find the answers have yielded only hints of apparent similarities.[122] Momigliano's suggestion is more concrete: Botero, while in Paris in 1585, may well have been introduced to Tacitus by none other than Carlo Paschalius.[123] But there is a still more probable explanation. First, Botero could easily have heard what Muret had been saying in his lectures delivered between November 1580 and the spring of 1582. Second, he could not have overlooked Bodin when he went to France; after all, he had studied the *Methodus* carefully and was soon to incorporate (none too successfully) Bodin's theories on climatic determinism, economics, and universal law into his *Ragion di Stato*. Third, he may easily have been impressed by the parallels between modern rulers and Tiberius which had been drawn by Lipsius (1572), Guicciardini (after 1576—republished 1585), and Muret.

Yet, Botero could actually have done without any of these direct sources of inspiration. After all, as he himself reports, Machiavelli's ideas were still widely known and discussed—in spite of the efforts of Innocent Gentillet to discredit them and of the Holy Office to destroy them.[124] The more literate of contemporary princes, moreover, were now reading and quoting Tacitus—which Botero also noticed. All he had to do was to put them together under the rubric *ragion di stato,* which he first systematically conceptualized. And, unlike all his more scholarly predecessors, he had only to transfer to Tacitus the moral opprobrium that was already beginning to fall upon Machiavelli.[125]

6 Tacitus and the End of Renaissance Political Thought

Botero's condemnation of Tacitus as one who proffered evil counsel to rulers was to become the predominant political interpretation of Tacitus in the next century. For the moment, however, it stood in direct opposition to all judgments made about him during the Renaissance. For instance, Guicciardini said that Tacitus, "a very grave writer," revealed neutrally, both to rulers and to subjects, techniques of tyranny and pathways of prudence; Bodin said that he provided guidelines for the most just laws possible; Lipsius said that he unmasked the schemes of tyrants and taught either how to foil them or at least to be saved from their consequences; Muret said that his judgments were good and grave and, indeed, that they had been accepted by decent and wise rulers from the Emperor Tacitus down to Paul III. No one had been hesitant to recommend Tacitus as a guide to practical politics, and no one had believed that he gave evil advice.

Moreover, even aside from politics, no one in the Renaissance thought that Tacitus spoke evilly about any subject whatsoever—with one exception: his statements about Christianity. But even here, Budé, the great jurist, stands pretty much alone in attacking Tacitus for anti-Christian sentiments. It was Budé who revived, in 1514, both Tertullian's charge that Tacitus was a liar and Orosius' that Tacitus was a worthless and bad man.[1] A year later, Erasmus (though probably unaware of Budé's view) admitted that Tacitus wrote against the Christians but said that he should be read despite this imperfection, which he shared with many other writers whom ignorant theologians would like to suppress.[2] Some fifty years later, however, Bodin again brought up the matter. Budé was definitely in Bodin's mind, for he defended Tacitus against him in a detailed argument.[3] In doing so, however, Bodin was simply displaying his own erudition; no actual polemics were involved since, from the time of Budé himself, no one had taken up his criticism of Tacitus on religious grounds.[4] In fact, it was Bodin's defense of Tacitus which seems to have popularized the view he had set out to destroy. Only then did Montaigne (between 1573 and 1580)[5] and Muret (1581)[6] feel compelled to exonerate Tacitus. In his *Essays* the former blamed the early Christians and their excessive zeal, which led them to suppress Tacitus' writings for five or six "insignificant sentences contrary to our belief." In speaking out on this question, Montaigne had no one (except himself) to answer to. Muret, on the other hand, needed his paychecks! Only after eight years of trying to convince two of his academic superiors, of the college of cardinals—Guglielmo Sirleto, head of the Bibliotheca Vaticana, and Francesco Alciato, nephew of Andrea, the jurist and teacher of Borromeo—that Tacitus was safe to lecture on did he publicly defend Tacitus for condemning Christians out of piety for his own religion. But only in these two cardinals is there any influence of Budé upon Botero's contemporaries. Botero himself, coming to Rome in 1586, either never heard of the problem or didn't care. At any rate, his writings before 1589 show no awareness of Tacitus the anti-Christian; and, at this time, he certainly never condemned Tacitus for this or any other reason. But with his *Ragion di Stato,* all that changed. For Botero had tied Tacitus to Machiavelli, and Machiavelli's name had become synonymous with wickedness. It now became indiscreet, if not actually dangerous, to hold the traditionally favorable opinion of Tacitus.

Yet the morally favorable judgment of Tacitus was by now almost two centuries old—too old, that is, to vanish instantaneously. Indeed, it had recently been reinforced by one of the most prestigious writers of the time—Montaigne.[7] Not only did Montaigne never think of Tacitus as an evil political counselor; on the contrary, he admired him not only as a political thinker but, even more, as a man. Still, Montaigne thought different things at different times, as Donald Frame has shown.[8] Before 1580—before his conversion from Stoicism, that is—Montaigne was mostly interested in Tacitus as a stylist, and he saw him as a political writer or a moralist usually through the eyes of Seneca.

To one who valued Plutarch's and Seneca's works so highly, the unassuming terseness and direct statement of Tacitus had much appeal.[9] In a very important essay, "The Education of Children" (*Essays* i. 26), he points to Aper, Tacitus' representative speaker for modern rhetoric as opposed to the ancient, in recommending a simple and pure style, free of the glitter of Ciceronian elegance. In "Presumption" (ii. 17), he further remarks that the falsifying appurtenances of and buttresses to eloquence, such as the voice, the robe, the physical stance, are not really essential and give only an appearance of ability to orators who may truly lack it. He then refers to another speaker in the *Dialogus*[10] to support still another point: that such things as constricting robes can actually weaken eloquence. Indeed, he found these arguments right in Tacitus' one "non-Tacitan" work, the neo-Ciceronian *Dialogus.* Yet he took much more than arguments from Tacitus; he may have discovered similarities between Tacitus' phraseology and that of Seneca,[11] which he had appreciated during his Stoic period, and he may well have read Alciato's and Bodin's evaluation even earlier, during his years of legal study in Toulouse. In any case he soon learned to appreciate Tacitus' style. In "The Grandeur of Rome" (ii. 24) he particularly commended the "marvelous touch" with which Tacitus wittily described the policy of the Roman emperors, "which employs kings as the instruments of servitude" ("ut haberet instrumenta servitutis et reges"—*Agricola* xiv).

Although Montaigne's appreciation for Tacitus' style may owe something to Alciato and Bodin, his *Essays* in this period show no interest in Tacitus for the law. It was very probably Bodin's *Methodus,* still going through many editions, that directed him to the statement in *Annales* xiv. 44 that all laws contain some injustice against individuals.[12] Still, he makes the quotation without Bodin's concrete and practical intentions. Indeed, he puts it in a completely different context, in the essay "We Experience Nothing of the Pure," where he is making a philosophical point, not a legal one (justice cannot exist without injustice).

For philosophy, not law, was his chief interest when he retired from active life in 1573. He wanted to meditate, to think, to study. The chaos of his own mind, and his preoccupation with some of the most basic problems of human existence, were intensified by the current wars of religion. For help, he turned to the classics. And to make sure that the help would be effective, he decided to write down what he learned. The Stoics impressed him the most: Cicero's various writings, Epictetus' *Enchiridion,* and Marcus Aurelius' *Meditations.* But in Plutarch's *Moral Essays* and especially in Seneca's *Letters to Lucilius* he discovered his principal guides. From Seneca he was stirred to a Stoical interest in Tacitus. He used Tacitus as a source for further information to illustrate theses he took from Seneca. His ideas came from Seneca, his examples from Tacitus. To be sure, his fascination with Seneca soon led him to the description of the great Stoic's death in Tacitus' *Annales* (xv. 60–65). It is not surprising to find the story in "Three Good Wives" (ii. 35), where it is set within the context of the suicide attempt of Paulina, Seneca's wife (whom Nero condemned to live, by ordering that her slashed wrists be treated and bandaged). In another essay, the ''Defense of Seneca and Plutarch'' (ii. 32), he declares that Tacitus was one who spoke very honorably of the excellent and virtuous life and death of Seneca.

Moreover, his later insertions of material from Tacitus into these pre-1580 *Essays* (i.e., books i and ii, inserted at a time when he had long given up his Stoicism—see below), clearly show—if nothing about Tacitus before 1580—that Montaigne recognized the way he had been thinking when he first wrote of Seneca's death. For in the 1588 edition of the *Essays* there are five new Stoical deaths, and in the posthumous 1595 edition there are five additional ones. All ten are grafted into the first two books; all ten are from Tacitus. One of these additions, in the ''Defense of Seneca and Plutarch,'' is on Epicharis' painful and glorious end, taken from *Annales* xv. 52. But more in line with his simple preoccupation with suicide are the three examples in ''Judging the Death of Others'' (ii. 13): Plautius Silvanus (*Annales* iv. 22), Ostorius Scapula the Younger (*Annales* xvi. 15), and Albucilla (*Annales* vi. 47–48)—whose attempt, however, failed. The worthiness of the individual was of no consequence to Montaigne: a wanton wench like Albucilla, a general of old Roman courage like Ostorius, and a man like Silvanus, on trial for having thrown his wife out the window—all, by taking their own lives when they thought it necessary, were equally ideal examples to him. In the ''Customs of the Isle of Cea'' (ii. 3) he says that ''history is chock-full of those who in a thousand ways have changed a painful life for death.'' Here, six of his examples come from Tacitus' *Annales:* Lucius Arruntius (vi. 48), who opened his veins; Gravius Silvanus (xv. 71), who fell by his own hand;[13] Statius Proximus (xv. 71), who almost certainly killed himself; Sextilia, wife of Mamercus Scaurus (vi. 29), who shared in her husband's suicide; Paxaea, wife of Pomponius Labeo (vi. 29), who, like him, opened her veins to bleed to death; and, finally, Cocceius Nerva (vi. 26), who, as Tacitus reports, ''adopted the resolution of dying.'' Indeed, Montaigne's quotation from Seneca, toward the beginning of the essay, sets the stage for Tacitus' bloody pageant:

> For death is everywhere. Gracious is this, God's plan:
> That though our life may be destroyed by any man,
> No one can take our death; a thousand roads lead there.[14]

However, when it is remembered that the ten scenes are later insertions, it is clear that Tacitus was of far less Stoical inspiration to Montaigne at the time when Montaigne was really a Stoic. Besides, Tacitus was never more than a source of examples for the philosophy which Montaigne learned in Seneca.

Moreover, Montaigne's use of Tacitus' account of Seneca's death had long been standard material for humanists. Boccaccio first made use of the section (along with the one on Epicharis) before 1373, in the *Commento sopra la Commedia;* Sicco Polentone, the professor so important in introducing Greek to the Florentines, vastly increased the section's accessibility in his *Scriptores illustres linguae latinae,* written in 1447; and Erasmus used the story for his edition of Seneca's works of 1515 (republished in 1529). In fact, just about everyone who published Seneca's works, commented on them, and wrote about their author used the information Tacitus provided. Calvin, Muret, and the many French Christian Stoics like Guillaume du Vair and Pierre Charron (both friends of Montaigne) used the section as a matter of course.

Yet Montaigne was not committed, as his Stoic friends were, to the use of Tacitus merely for illustration. For one thing, he was willing to consider all the ancient authors equally, and not just the Stoics, as aids in solving the personal and philosophic problems he had posed; and he deplored the loss of so many of them:

> It is certain that in those early times when our religion began to gain authority with the laws, zeal armed many believers against every sort of pagan books, thus causing men of letters to suffer an extraordinary loss. I consider that this excess did more harm to letters than all the bonfires of the barbarians. Of this Cornelius Tacitus is a good witness: for although the Emperor Tacitus, his kinsman, had by express ordinances populated all the libraries of the world with his works, nevertheless not one single complete copy was able to escape the careful search of those who wanted to abolish them because of five or six insignificant sentences contrary to our [religious] belief.

This plaint comes from the essay "On Liberty of Conscience" (ii. 19).[15] From the book burning and other excesses committed in the name of religion in his own day, Montaigne knew very well what he was talking about. For another thing, he was not in principle committed to a Stoic solution. And in the long "Apology for Raymond Sebond" (ii. 12), he gradually abandoned it. The "Apology," in fact, marks a crisis in his previously accepted philosophical principles. His Stoicism breaks down into Pyrrhonism. Indeed, as Frame suggests, "it is likely that most of the essay was written simply as an attack on human reason and presumption'' and was only later arranged as the ''Apology.''[16] Tacitus was not at the moment an agent in this transition. But ten years later Montaigne realized that he might have been, for he then used Tacitus (in the same breath with Augustine) to hit at the essence of the argument with a single stroke: ''It is more holy and reverent to believe in the works of the gods than to know them'' (''Sanctius est ac reverentius de actis deorum credere quam scire''—*Germania* xxxiv).[17]

By 1580 that statement had acquired no little actuality. Montaigne was always pained to see the extent to which his countrymen acted in total ignorance of Tacitus' wisdom in the passage from the *Germania*. For many years he observed Protestants and Catholics cutting each other's throats in France. He saw each side invoking God's sanction for its enormities. He had even made an attempt in 1572 or 1573 to reconcile the duke of Guise and Henry of Navarre. The attempt had failed, and he had turned instead to reconciling the conflicts within his own soul. But even in this limited area the solutions were unsatisfactory. He tried Stoicism but soon found it vain, presumptive, and unrealistic. His new solution then became Pyrrhonism. But at least some of his basic ideas had now been worked out.

Beginning in 1580 one more gradually emerged: human solidarity.[18] Before the fifth edition of the *Essays* in 1588 he would develop it. Four main experiences in these years were to cause the final change in his thinking: his trip to Italy, the success of his *Essays,* his two terms as mayor of Bordeaux (1581–85), and his struggle to survive the plague in the summer of 1586. ''The humanization of the humanist'' was now complete, according to Frame.[19] Montaigne now reread Tacitus in a new light. He says (in iii. 8) that he has discovered something in Tacitus ''il n'y a pas longtemps,'' and quotes a line from *Annales* iv. 18.[20] He would not have used the phrase ''not long ago'' if he had been thinking of his first reading of the *Annales,* about fifteen years earlier. Besides, he now read the *Historiae* for the first time, at the suggestion of a friend. The work impressed him immensely: it had been twenty years since he had last read a book at one sitting. Apparently, the new Montaigne saw much in Tacitus that he had never noticed before.[21]

Now Montaigne sees Tacitus not as a source book of Stoic suicides (despite the many additions he now makes to earlier *Essays* to illustrate Seneca's philosophy), not primarily as a stylist, and not as an example of the loss of classical literature. He now looks at Tacitus the man. He is intensely fascinated, first of all, with Tacitus' personality or, in other words, with Tacitus' judgment. Appropriately, he most fully describes his new Tacitus in the essay "On the Art of Judgment" (iii. 8).[22] He is explicit: "I have chiefly considered his judgment." Indeed, Tacitus' work "is rather a judgment of history than a recital of it." It has more precepts than accounts. It is full of *sententiae* on right and wrong. No other historian mingles, in a register of public events, so many moral considerations and personal viewpoints. In them Tacitus always pleads with reasons solid and vigorous. Tacitus erred, however, in giving so many sterile death scenes—even though he himself realized (*Annales* iv. 33) that the long string of beautiful deaths (*belles morts*) might anger or bore the reader. Tacitus colored his material, wrote with affectation, and allowed suspicions to blind him to actual evidence.[23] Although Tacitus was honest, upright, and generous, his judgment was, after all, "a little mean-spirited." Montaigne, in short, thinks Tacitus substandard in self-judgment. He feels that Tacitus should have been more honest and open with himself. He implies, in fact, that Tacitus should have made *essais* of his own judgment. He does not boast; he only wishes that Tacitus had tried as he was trying. This fact is clear from the way he ends the section and, at once, the essay: "That is what my memory of Tacitus offers me in gross, and rather uncertainly. All judgments in gross are loose and imperfect." By testing Tacitus' judgment, he was testing his own.

Second, Montaigne is intrigued with Tacitus as a man involved with politics. Although his statements on Tacitus as a teacher of political wisdom could all have come from Bodin, Lipsius, or, better, Muret—whose lectures he may have heard while in Rome from November 1580 to April 1581—their context is immediate and personal. Tacitus "is more suited to a disturbed and sick state, as ours is at present; you would often say that it is us he is describing and decrying" (*Essays* iii. 8). Tacitus' kind of history, which deals with good men in bad straits, is "by far the most useful," for public movements depend on fortune but private ones on ourselves. Alciato and Rhenanus had once said the same things, but neither had had any firsthand experience in politics. To be sure, the significance of these sentiments is peculiar to Montaigne precisely because he was careful to maintain this distinction between his actual public and private lives. "The mayor and Montaigne," he reveals (in "The Management of the Will," iii. 10). "have always been two—with a very clear separation." Even as mayor he had been able to remain detached, just when he was most busily engaged in the duties of his office. Montaigne, in short, figured out how to become active in the world without being eaten up by it. This is why he found Tacitus' personality so fascinating: here was a statesman and a political thinker who could nonetheless remain his own man, could be a detached observer, a critic of the very thing which most engaged him but which could not subdue or absorb him. Neither Tacitus nor Montaigne avoided political responsibility. Yet each could assume it only by maintaining a sharp dualism between it and his personal life. Each knew that there was a real difference between the state and all its laws—

> We have in France more laws than all the rest of the world together, and more than would be needed to rule all the worlds of Epicurus, "so that whereas once we suffered from vices, we now suffer from laws" [quoting from Tacitus, from the *Annales* iii. 25]. [*Essays* iii. 13]

—and the individual man who had to live under them. In Tacitus, Montaigne saw a parallel to himself as man and statesman. Each led two distinct lives.

These conclusions explain why Montaigne (in *Essays* iii. 8) was so shocked to discover in Tacitus "some fault of the heart," illustrated by his unwillingness to speak of himself and, when once he did, by his apology for doing so. Montaigne recites Tacitus' comments in *Annales* xi. 11, where he states that he had been *praetor* and *quindecimvir* in a certain year (88 A.D.) and then apologizes with: "a fact which I recall not in vanity, but because . . . ." Montaigne decides that

> this touch seems shabby [*bas de poil*] for a soul of his kind; . . . We must pass over these common rules of civility in favor of truth and liberty.

Tacitus, who had loaded his writings more with personal viewpoints than with accounts, had suddenly become embarrassed by the separation between Tacitus the man and Tacitus the statesman. He had to excuse himself to explain to the reader that he, the man, was not vain in mentioning his own political office. A man who really kept his two roles sharply distinct should not blush to speak openly of the political one if the subject matter demanded it. In all, Montaigne was shocked to find a flaw of character in the man with whom he felt so intimate. Still, it was an exception. In general, Montaigne found immense personal and political value in reading Tacitus—just at the time when Botero began to damn Tacitus for his wickedness and for his evil political counsel.

If Montaigne was one of the last to use Tacitus as a political guide, Justus Lipsius was one of the first to ignore Tacitus for that purpose.

Lipsius was the greatest Tacitus scholar, a giant of philological erudition.[24] It was mainly for his work on Tacitus, from the first monumental edition of 1574 onward, that contemporaries considered him one of the most learned men of the age. They called him one of the "Triumviri," along with Joseph Scaliger, the great Grecist and author of *De emendatione temporum,* and Isaac Casaubon, the great classicist and professor at Geneva. Today little is generally known of him as a person beyond the apocryphal anecdote about his reciting Tacitus with a dagger held to his breast. He suffers from the neglect of recent scholarship.[25] He is usually regarded only as a sixteenth-century quiz kid, but he himself is partially responsible for the image that has come down to us: that of a head full of facts and a heart apparently empty of desire. Lipsius' heart was in his studies, and his studies concerned the minutiae of an age long past.

What seems like his political involvement, in the Jena Oration on Tacitus in 1572, in which he compared the duke of Alba to the bloodthirsty Tiberius and all the rest, was insincere. True, after it he signed the articles of the Augsburg Confession, gave a speech against the papacy, and delivered a fine eulogy upon the death of his Protestant lord, the duke of Saxe-Weimar. But his colleagues, suspicious of his religious and political sincerity, made his life miserable.[26] To avoid trouble, Lipsius left Jena. He returned to Louvain, married a pious Catholic widow,[27] and received his doctorate in law from the university in 1576. But he soon became disgusted with the legal profession. He decided that its advocates were avaricious, opportunistic, and, worse, unlettered. In despair, he retreated to his Tacitus notes and busied himself in preparing the next, the second, edition (1581).

Compared to the Jena Oration of 1572, no greater contrast can be imagined. Lipsius (writing its preface in August, 1580) is quite explicit in revealing his apolitical, purely scholarly interest in editing Tacitus:

> I have confirmed some old corrections; I have added new ones. I have made these without going overboard, because certainly we critics already err enough on this side; and as once the text was suffering from flaws, it is now suffering from remedies. Here and there I have noted certain corrections of other authors, not because I was disposed to it, but because they fell beneath my hand. As certain flowers are born in a field spontaneously, so in these writings —notes of another genus. I have given all my enthusiasm to history and to mores whenever there was a need for it, but only then.[28]

Scholarship was an end in itself, not a guide or incentive to action. For action was no longer possible:

> I have not touched politics. Whether for the experienced or inexperienced, it is vain. The first can select what they will on their own accord, the second can not rightly use even what they have selected.[29]

Philology, not politics, was serious business. Even the writing of political handbooks was nothing but a cheap and vulgar contest for fame. Almost certainly referring to Paschalius' commentary or *Observations,* just published, Lipsius declared:

> And now I hear there are some who make this their particular concern. I did what I could,[30] and I do not seek to hinder anyone from running for the palm of victory in that same circus.[31]

The same admonitions were repeated in his later editions of Tacitus (1585, 1588, 1589, 1600, 1607). Lipsius, it is clear, was now interested only in correcting old manuscripts.

Indeed, philology provided a good way to escape from the world he lived in. But it was pathetically difficult to study in times so troubled. Observing the ruins of the burned library at the University of Louvain in 1593, he sadly exclaimed that "peace requires the arts of peace, but in vain if now we do not care for their high priests and worshipers."[32] Lipsius lived through the years of the Revolt of the Netherlands. To suffer as little as possible he locked himself away and turned out one brilliant work after another of philological acumen: the first book of Livy (1579), *Electorum liber primus* (1580), the second book in 1582, *Epistolica institutio* (1580), *De amphitheatro liber* (1584), notes on Valerius Maximus (1585), etc.—and these outside his more famous works: *De constantia* (1584) and the *Politicorum sive civilis doctrinae libri sex* (the *Politica*) (1589), which he believed would last as long as Latin literature. He studied as best he could within his own "beata tranquillitas," and he sought only to be untouched by "the conflicts of the world, news of the war, and the gossip and anger of the Dutch." What, after all, do such things matter?[33]

They mattered very little. Indeed, how else could Lipsius have been a Catholic at his birth in 1547, have become a Lutheran in 1572 at Jena, a Catholic again at Louvain from 1573 to 1578, a Calvinist at Leiden from 1578 to 1591, and finally, back at Louvain, a Catholic until his death in 1606? He cannot be said to have been a hypocrite. He was merely impartial: "for all religion and no religion are to me one and the same."[34] Such was his view in 1582; but seven years later, in the *Politica,* he stated that one basis for the best state was one religion, enforced by the king, "with fire and sword" if necessary.[35] Its validity was not a question here. When pressed by the ardent Calvinist Theodore Coornhert to define just what the "one religion" was, Lipsius hedged and never did answer. He refused even to answer the question implied in the title: What is the best form of government? Instead he simply brought together a huge pile of classical citations under chapter rubrics like "On Succession," "The End of the State," "On the Examples of Princes," "On Justice," "On Clemency," etc. Thus the value of an ancient author depended not upon the wisdom or the applicability of what he said but upon the number of citations he provided. Tacitus supplies more than any other "because he alone told us more than all the rest together." Moreover, "he is intimate with us, and he offers himself without being asked."[36] If Tacitus has anything to teach a modern reader, that's up to the reader, not the editor, to discover. Lipsius' work therefore, was a monument of scholarship. It was "learned and laborious," as Montaigne put it (*Essays* i. 26).[37] And it was nothing else.

Lipsius continued to write some of his best classical studies while professor of Latin at Louvain from 1591 until his death: *Fax historica* (1595), *Admiranda, sive de magnitudine Romana* (1597), *Manuductio ad Stoicam philosophiam* (1604), *Physiologia Stoicorum* (1604), and other works on various aspects of Roman life and thought.

Only once did he come close to touching upon practical problems; this was in his testimonials to orthodoxy: the *Diva Virgo Hallensis* (1604), and the *Diva Virgo Sichemiensis* (1605). But these works had no connection with scholarship. They were rather compendia of the most ridiculous miracle stories that Lipsius' contemporaries had heard in some time. Scaliger and Casaubon were shocked. Indeed, Lipsius himself realized that something was out of joint. In 1605 he wrote that "because of my continued ill health and the heavy burden of the times, I begin to mistrust my judgments, and I fear that my present writings are not up to my former reputation."[38] But he still was no hypocrite. He was faced with a spiritual problem. His idea of Christianity was on a much higher plane than that of contemporary polemicists. And these works were mere bones, which he could have thrown as well to one pack of dogs as to the other.

Lipsius' own religion was a form of Christian Stoicism—a synthesis of Seneca and Epictetus with early Christian theology similar to the one he had seen in the Latin Fathers, especially in Tertullian. The synthesis had defects, to be sure: when faced with the ticklish doctrine of suicide, Lipsius quickly ran from Seneca to Epictetus; and he thus found it easy to accommodate the Stoic *fatum* with Christian Providence. This tactic, however, was no longer acceptable in an age which demanded theological rigor. Lipsius himself may have realized the shortcomings of Christian Stoicism. On his deathbed, one of the attending Jesuits is reported to have asked him if his Stoic tenets gave him constancy in the face of death. "These things are vain," he supposedly replied; and pointing to the crucifix, he added, "there is the true patience."[39] But this deathbed scene may have been, as some of his friends said, a Jesuit lie. How far he himself thought he had succeeded in reconciling Christianity and Stoicism is still an open question.

It is a much less open question why he submitted to official orthodoxy in the end. Throughout his life he had resisted the influence of the Jesuits,[40] though frequently professing his love for them. He stoically withstood their annoying clamor for his conversion, just as he patiently bore the papal impositions of silence. In spite of his repeated emendations of his works, he was unable to have many of them taken off the Index; for the ecclesiastical authorities constantly complained of such indiscretions as "papal cruelty and the Spanish Inquisition." The *Politica* was placed on the Index in 1593, and his pleas to Francesco Benci, the philologian in Rome, to Cardinal Cesare Baronio, the famous historian of the popes, and to Cardinal Robert Bellarmine, the great Jesuit theologian, for suggestions on how to correct it produced such a welter of conflicting advice that he gave up. He turned his back on the recent, retired into *mores antiquos,* and threw his persecutors the *De cruce* (a study of crucifixion in Roman times), in 1593, as a sop.

On the plateau of classical studies he was "safe." One last attempt to descend from it—in the patriotic *Lovanium* of 1605—turned out to be badly written, lethargic, and devoid of color. His friends pitied him. His enemies nettled him. But he was too tired or too indifferent to fight back. He didn't really care. Years before, when the Dutch scholars were abusing him for his recently published *Politica,* he had answered: "It doesn't pay to respond; it's useless."[41] He did not bother now, either. Besides, he was too busy with his philological research. And his research included the preparation of a seventh edition of Tacitus (published one year after his death, in 1607). Here, at least, he was not apathetic. In 1602, when an anonymous enemy viciously attacked his sixth edition of Tacitus, he was on his own ground: his defense was forceful and brilliant; his counterattack was fast, poignant, and ingenious.[42] It is not for nothing that, even in his own lifetime, he had earned the title "Sospitator Taciti."

Lipsius' fame as a Tacitan philologist rested on his objectivity; and his objectivity, in turn, was the result of his isolation from the world he lived in. But the consequence was as harmful for the humanist tradition as it was beneficial to pure philology. The text became more perfect. But it was dead. When once or twice Lipsius forgot himself, he ended up in melodramatic moralizing. Apropos of Tacitus' remark (*Germania* xxiv) about the passion for gambling among the Germans, Lipsius quoted a long passage from Saint Ambrose on the vice of gambling among the Huns, and then concluded: "O how disgusting! O how barbarous! And I know that among certain Northern peoples today, this insanity is rampant."[43] Even this reference later appeared to him to be too immediate. The Germans might take offense. Lipsius accordingly removed all unflattering remarks about them from the personal correspondence he later published in the *Centuries*. Usually he fled from a possible contemporary reflection as rapidly as he could. Tacitus' observations on usury, for example, in *Germania* xxvi shows the rule. Tacitus wrote of the Germans: "To charge interest and to extend the same to usury is unknown, and the principle accordingly better observed than if there had been actual prohibition." It could not but have reminded him of a very current dispute, but he deliberately obfuscated the relevancy of it:

> "*Observed*"? What is observed? Indeed, "interest" is not observed, nor is "usury." There is a flaw in this sentence. Instead of "observed" [*servatur*], could it be "is scorned" [*spernitur*] or perhaps, in the subjunctive, "should be scorned" [*spernatur*]? The sentence requires this meaning. Or else it ought to be taken in the sense that it had first implied the interdict.[44]

A half-century earlier, Celtis had seen immense political implications in the same sentence. Lipsius saw nothing but a question of language.

Even his apologies for the utility of history in general are commonplace and hollow:

> There is great dignity in history, great fruit. To read the memorials of past ages, the wars among the highest kings, the misfortunes and downfall of peoples, affords dignity and enjoyment. Such readings not only feed the soul but invigorate it also. However, there is

> great utility in noting in history the varieties of examples, the causes of events, and from these fountains to derive precepts for private and public life.[45]

Hunting for what might be valuable turns into a game, as intricate as it is fruitless:

> Single pages—nay, why do I say pages? Single *lines* embody dogmas, counsels, admonitions. But they are often brief and hidden, and it is necessary to have a certain sagacious mind for smelling them out and pursuing them.[46]

Or else it becomes merely an excuse for trying out another metaphor, as in the *Monita et exempla politica libri duo, qui virtutes et vitia principum spectant* (written in 1605): ''the flower of the histories in the fields of antiquity, of the Middle Ages and of our own time—a Herculean work.''[47] Lipsius, obviously was never affected by the humanist tradition of politics and history. He helped, then, to remove the old Tacitus from any possible political application just when Botero was saying he should never have been used that way in the first place.

At the same time, two linguistic authorities—with the political use of Tacitus farthest from their minds—were turning Tacitus from merely one possible model into the sole authority for good writing, not only in Latin, but in the vernaculars as well. First of all, Henri Estienne, the great Hellenist, in publishing his *De la Préexcellence du langage françois* in 1579, was bent on demonstrating the superiority of French to all other languages. To back up his argument, he showed that the translation of two chapters of Tacitus on the Gauls (*Historiae* iv. 73–74) by his compatriot, Blaise de Vigenère (1576),[48] was shorter by nine words than the same chapters in the standard Italian translation by Giorgio Dati (1563). Estienne had long led a violent campaign to root out so-called unnatural and unnecessary Italianisms from the French language. He now made Tacitus the standard for this mission.

The second was Italy's defender against Estienne, Bernardo Davanzati,[49] already ''altered'' by his colleagues of the *Alterati* in Florence as ''Il Silente'' for his taciturnity and for his abbreviated style. He had recently begun his own translation of Tacitus' *Annales,* largely for the purpose of making the Italian more Tacitan. He said that Dati, with ''an ample and easy style,'' had been wrong ''to overflow and sweeten a text so stringent and tart.''[50] Then, to counter Estienne's boast, he set out to make the translation even more compact: ''to prove with fact the bad things said by Arrigo Stefani.''[51] By July 1583 he finished the first book of the *Annales* and finally published it in 1596. The Florentine language, he had demonstrated, could sharply express every idea in Tacitus with 37,000 letters fewer than French[52]—and with 5,000 fewer than Tacitus himself. His friends of the Academy were convinced by the undeniable ratio of Florentine: Latin: French:: 9:10:15. In 1600 Davanzati published the whole *Annales;* and before his death in 1606 he had completed his translation of Tacitus (eventually published in 1637). This translation became a minor classic of Italian literature and earned its maker the epithet "Tacito Fiorentino."

To be sure, Davanzati had other than purely linguistic reasons for doing his translation. It offered him a welcome relief from making money after his return from apprenticeship with the Capponi bank in Lyons in 1547. It was an intellectually respectable task, too, and one that permitted him to cut into the dominion of Lionardo Salviati, the "brilliant and unscrupulous dictator of linguistic propriety" (as Cochrane has called him).[53] Salviati was a master not only of proper Italian speech but also of copious bombast and Ciceronian style elaborated almost to the point of parody. At a certain point in his loquacious career he had picked up Tacitus, republished Dati's translation, and composed a little commentary on the opening words of the *Annales*.[54] Then, when he threatened to do another Tacitus of his own, Davanzati must have shuddered and hurried to parry the blow, as his friend, Francesco Bonciani, suggested. But Davanzati may have had a still more important reason for his work: that of using the enemy of tyrants as a silent weapon against the Medicean regime, which had, in Cochrane's words, "exiled his father, confiscated his patrimony, and barred his access to public office."[55] For example, on the first page of the *Agricola* (using a copy of Salviati's new edition of Dati) he wrote: "He [Tacitus] commemorates the evils of slavery; see and note."[56] And close to this note he added: "For us the bell calling us to counsel has been taken away, in order that we shall no longer be able to hear the sweet sound of liberty."[57] Indeed, the pages of his copy are loaded with comments of a similar nature—snaps at Duke Cosimo and Duke Ferdinando and reminiscences of Florence's last great *fuoruscito*, Filippo Strozzi. His hand is so cramped and tiny that one wonders whether he himself could have reread them. Certainly no one else did.[58]

"Self-censorship," Cochrane observes, in his article on the end of the Renaissance in Florence, "had apparently become second nature."[59] One is easily reminded of Tacitus in *Agricola* ii: "We should have lost memory as well as voice, had it been as easy to forget as to keep silence.'' But the attitude of the frustrated educated class under Domitian and the feeling of the contented intellectuals under Ferdinando de' Medici were extremely different. Aside from a few brooding malcontents like Davanzati, these Florentines were quickly losing their memory of former days, with pleasure. A coincidence of the stars, a crude and superficial historical parallelism, and a desire to believe their own eulogies of the prince and his family, all tended to convince them that the earlier time of republican disturbance and uncertainty had at last been superseded by the age of Augustus, Tiberius, and Trajan—i.e., of Cosimo, Francesco, and Ferdinando. Since Cosimo's ascension to the throne, they observed, the city had become firmly consolidated in its government, stronger in arms, more efficient in administration, more sure in the machinery of justice, more magnificent in architecture, musical composition, learned societies, and processions, and, most important of all, more ordered. In fact, Florence appeared to them as secure as it could possibly be. In this realization they were exceedingly comforted. With a shudder they remembered—every so often—the endless quarrels, the party conflicts, the street fights, and the mob violence of the past. But nowadays, they reflected with relief, such goings-on were absolutely impossible.

Still, politics, or rather political theory, fascinated them, and they debated endlessly on themes taken from their now unmentionable predecessor, Machiavelli: whether the Romans rose to greatness through virtue or fortune, whether courage or money is the sinews of war, whether a militia is more effective than a professional army, etc. But, unlike the discussions in the Oricellari Gardens long before, these debates in the Florentine academies were little more than games.[60] The solutions to the problems posed were not meant to have any connection with a political order they regarded as no longer subject to alteration. Only one of them suspected that Tacitus might be of use, not, certainly, to the subject, but at least to the prince. And he was a Florentine not by birth but by adoption. Scipione Ammirato,[61] the poet and genealogist from Lecce, who worked in Florence for thirty years until his death in 1601, probably became interested in Tacitus during the discussions in the Alterati of Davanzati's translation in 1583. In 1584 or 1585 he began to write his *Discorsi sopra Cornelio Tacito;* and he finally published them in 1594.

Ammirato was almost certainly influenced by Botero's *Della Ragion di Stato* (1589) while writing his *Discorsi*. Although he does not mention Botero by name, his frequent use of ''ragion di stato'' as a distinct concept and his attack on Machiavelli as an architect of it are both good reasons for this assertion. Moreover, Ammirato comes to conclusions similar to those of Botero on the relation between religion and politics and on the best form of government. Still, there are notable differences in their uses of Tacitus. First of all, although Ammirato and Botero agree that real political self-interest must further the interest of religion and the Church, Ammirato saves Tacitus from Botero's implicating him with the evil Machiavelli. He does this first by accepting *reason of state* (which Botero had branded as absolutely bad), next by associating it with Tacitus, then by subjecting it to the dictates of religion, and finally by using it against Machiavelli, who had shown the Christian religion to be incompatible with politics. Ammirato therefore avoids the confusion and inconsistency of Botero (who had quoted Tacitus, fosterer of corruption, many times to condemn the equally evil teachings of Machiavelli) by seeing Tacitus as Machiavelli's good alter ego, not as his accomplice. Botero had condemned Tacitus along with Machiavelli; Ammirato condemns—or, more exactly, contradicts—Machiavelli through Tacitus.

Second, concerning the best form of government, the very title of Ammirato's *Discorsi* on Tacitus shows that the work is directed against Machiavelli's *Discorsi* on Livy: the greatest Roman historian of the Principate posed against the greatest Roman historian of the Republic. If Livy was Machiavelli's number-one authority for the superiority of republican government, then Tacitus, for Ammirato, was the perfect counterauthority: "If thus this work [says Ammirato of the *Annales*] seems to be much in the hands of everyone these days, it is because, treating of the principate, it is more suitable to our times."[62] Besides the necessity to overlook Tacitus' frequent nostalgia for the Republic in the *Annales* and the *Historiae*, Ammirato was not unaware of other difficulties in using Tacitus as a counterbalance to Livy. For one, the portraits of the early Roman emperors were really not the most edifying models for imitation. For another, Tacitus is lacking in those examples of the transcendent moral principles according to which, Ammirato believed, a contemporary prince should be judged—if indeed, he could be judged at all. Finally, none of the rulers Tacitus wrote about was a Christian. In spite of such difficulties, however, Ammirato was sure he could convince his readers that Tacitus could be used as a source of political maxims as safely as the Bible.

For example, one of Tacitus' absolutely valid axioms was even more important to Ammirato than it had earlier been to Bodin. He calls it that "memorabilissima sentenza": "Every great example contains some injustice which is imposed upon individuals for public utility" (*Annales* xiv. 44).[63] Using it as a kind of "elastic clause," Ammirato deduces much throughout the *Discorsi* to sanction the status quo: acceptance of Spanish rule in Italy, maintenance of large armies, payment of heavy taxes to support them, obedience to the dictates of the Church, etc. The security and good order of the whole, in other words, demands some sacrifice and discomfiture of the parts. Della Casa had once denounced such deductions from *reason of state;* to him the freezing of things as they existed was unjust. But Ammirato now saw it as the most beneficial way of running a modern state. He felt that the basic structure of society could not be altered and that the present arrangement was preferable to any known alternative. Besides, any minor adjustments of it were no business of the subjects. Princes, who moved on a plane infinitely removed from ordinary human ways, were best left to their own inscrutable devices. At the most, one could hope to appeal to their conscience or to their vanity. A study of Tacitus, or any other classical author, may be interesting or intriguing, but actual policy, the reality of politics, was in the hands of the prince alone; and no one could have the moral prerogative to advise or even inform him. Thus, aside from the prince, political philosophy had become something to contemplate and not something to act upon. Even the basis of it, the study of history, had become (as Ammirato later admitted in his great *History of Florence*—the first part published in 1600, the second in 1641) merely an "incomprehensible delight" from which he acquired "fascinating bits of knowledge."[64]

Ammirato's method for acquiring such bits for contemplation and pleasure remained, however, Machiavellian: the formulation of general laws from an analysis of specific data of history, ancient and modern. An example of Ammirato's use of Machiavelli's method to contradict Machiavelli is shown in *Discorsi* xviii. 159. Machiavelli's thesis in his own *Discorsi* (ii. 10) was countered by Tacitus' offhand comment on money being the nerves of war. Ammirato shows his friends at the Academy that Tacitus was borne out not only by the theoretical statements of Pericles and Cicero but by the practical experience of Alexander, Hannibal, and the Venetians. He points out too that "the abovementioned author" had misread Herodotus iii and Justin xxv. 201 and had completely overlooked Thucydides, book i, on the strength of the Athenians. Moreover, "the author" had deliberately left out the sequel to the Battle of Agnadello in 1509, when the Venetians had bought back all they had lost to the pope, the emperor, and the king of France.[65] Thus, Ammirato concluded, the thesis of Tacitus was "as firm a proposition in the government of states as is [the axiom] among the mathematicians about the whole being greater than any of the parts."[66] And only the prince was expected to make any use of it at all.

The main result of the *Discorsi*, apparently, was to abolish the whole subject of politics once and for all; and Florentines, at least, followed Ammirato's advice and locked up Machiavelli in the cabinets of forbidden books for the next 150 years. Ammirato gave Italians (in the six further editions published over the next twenty years), Frenchmen (in the translations of 1618, 1628, 1633, and 1644), Germans (in the translations of 1609 and 1618), and any one else who could read the Latin (1609), a satisfying excuse to forget about politics. Those who did bother to refer to Ammirato's manual of easy solutions learned that the good in their political order was actually the better and that the defects of that order were really blessings. Readers could not easily notice Ammirato's inconsistencies and contradictions. The *Discorsi* were not planned to be read straight through but rather a chapter at a time, with the index rather than the table of contents serving as a guide. Besides, Ammirato's interesting style, full of witty anecdotes, cute asides, and fast-moving periods, influenced by Sallust, Guicciardini, and Tacitus, provided good entertainment. At the least, readers tasted the *Discorsi* for pleasure; at the most they read them for philosophy. But they never looked into them for practical guidelines, with political activity in mind. The effect of the *Discorsi* on Tacitan studies was thus similar to that of Lipsius' great editions: there was no point in looking further in Tacitus for lessons in politics, because politics was either outside the realm of human control or was the business of princes alone. The humanistic tradition of the use of Tacitus which had grown since Bruni was now dead. In its place stepped the followers of Botero; and they were now busily proving to princes that Tacitus was, despite Ammirato's view, just as evil as Machiavelli.

If Plato's dictum of no man knowingly doing evil may be extended to the humanists and their recommendations of classical authors as guides to political activity, it can certainly apply to all users of Tacitus before Botero's condemnation of him took hold. There is but one exception; and he was the great Italian patriot and propagandist, Traiano Boccalini.[67] In his famous *Ragguagli di Parnaso* (Venice, 1612–13) he gave "the great Tacitus," "the true master of prudence," "the prince of political writers," his due.[68] Boccalini saw Tacitus as the greatest

Machiavellian who ever lived; he saw him as "the discoverer of modern heresy," "the architect of fallacy," and "the impious Tacitus"; but for precisely these reasons he praised him rather than buried him beneath opprobrium. Botero was right: Tacitus and Machiavelli were both counselors of evil. But Botero was wrong in thinking that evil was wrong. In the *Ragguagli* he cites and quotes Tacitus hundreds of times and usually puts his own arguments in Tacitus' mouth. His intention is to transform his readers into Machiavellis, to give the sharp teeth of dogs to Italian sheep.[69] He obliges his readers to wear the "political spectacles" (*occhiali politici*) which Tacitus provides: through them (and along with his own training in their use) the reader can look into the secrets of princes, the art of politics. Before Tacitus revealed his findings, men were at least blessedly ignorant of how evil politics really were; but now, having put on Tacitus' glasses of political wisdom, men could not avoid looking at an ugly reality. "Happy the world," he sighs, "if Tacitus had remained taciturn."[70] Like Machiavelli, he was pained by his discovery. Also like Machiavelli, he knew that looking at political reality was not enough: it had to be dealt with. The Spanish dominators of Italy did not hesitate to dirty their hands in what politics necessitated; and Boccalini hoped, through Tacitus, to teach Italians the same art in order to resist them. Politics, then, may be evil. But this evil can be used to serve a just cause—namely, patriotism, which was Boccalini's driving passion.

Boccalini was not talking in a vacuum. As long as he was employed by princes, to be sure—and especially by the Hispanophile Pope Paul V—he had to remain silent, and the pamphlets he had been working on since 1607 were kept safely guarded. Then, in 1611, he moved to Venice, the capital of anticurial and anti-Spanish sentiment in Italy. Suddenly politics once again became possible; and what Machiavelli and Tacitus had discovered became susceptible to application in practice. True, Venice was not entirely safe. Paolo Sarpi, the great historian and the state theologian of Venice since the outbreak of the Interdict Controversy, had just escaped assassination, and Boccalini knew that his and his country's enemies would stop at nothing to get him. They did so in fact in September 1613; at least all the evidence supports the contemporary rumor that he was poisoned by assassins sent from Rome. Venice, however, was aided by allies more powerful than herself; and it was to one of them, James I of England, that Boccalini had poured out his miseries and his hopes. He considered James a wise and moderate king, one who was willing to work with, or at least listen to, his subjects. Moreover, Boccalini had probably learned that James was himself a student of Tacitus; and he may have heard that Francis Bacon, the renowned philosopher and public official, could appeal to James's wisdom with lessons from Tacitus.[71] So Boccalini wrote to James from Venice, on 27 August 1612, for the purpose of presenting to him as a gift the first half of the *Ragguagli*, published in that year.[72]

The first sentence of the letter is a quotation from Tacitus (*Annales* iv. 35): "And so one is all the more incited to laugh at the stupidity of men who suppose that the despotism of the present can actually efface the remembrances of the next generation." He then half translates and half quotes the famous line from *Agricola* ii about its not being as easy to lose memory as to lose speech. The nauseating historical writing of the present suffers from "the most cruel triumvirate" of ambition, hypocrisy, and avarice, which has proscribed the better writers of history. He ends by calling James "a secure asylum for all things virtuous," whose subjects, like those of Trajan (quoting *Historiae* i. 1), enjoy "the rare happiness of times, when we may think what we please, and express what we think."

Luckily, before his assassination, he managed to publish the second half of the *Ragguagli* and to complete most of another book, the *Osservazioni sopra Cornelio Tacito*, which was to come to light, and then clandestinely, only in 1677.[73] Boccalini thought of his *Osservazioni* as a more serious endeavor and as more explicit instruction to his fellow Italians than his famous *Ragguagli*.[74] They did not need the disguise of the dialogue form and of metaphor, as in the *Ragguagli:*

> My *Ragguagli di Parnaso* are passing through the hands of so many wise men that it is superfluous for me to reflect on what benefit they have caused while wearing a mask: without eyes, they have opened the eyes of men who, blindly sleeping, let authority guide them by the nose, not knowing or not observing the artifices of princes. But how much benefit ought this, my present work, produce if it is put before the view of everyone not wearing a mask. Of what force?[75]

Force enough to throw out the Spanish and the many Italian princes who supported them, he ardently hoped. For this job, he intended to help readers of the *Osservazioni* by removing at least some of the difficulty of deciphering Tacitus. Of course, this service was possible only because he himself had gained mature insight through his political experience. Without it, it is impossible to discourse, in however mediocre a way, on any writer at all. Great and new secrets, many of them, can be discovered in Tacitus every day. Tacitus is now the order of the day (not Livy, who, writing on republics, is fitting for those who live in them): "I speak in some appropriate places in Tacitus of the princes of our time also—to the operations and interest of whom I see fitting the teachings of our author."[76] And he feels that he himself is the best man to decipher Tacitus for use in his own time:

> I believe myself to have so much understanding of the humors of this age that I shall not easily be mistaken if it be declared (so I go on imagining) that when these commentaries—worked out on my own, out of the spirit of Tacitus—come to light, they shall be judged, not as a whole but in part, of comparable quality [to Tacitus].[77]

But then, a few lines later, he modestly admits to having a talent which cannot work miracles but which must follow the dry road of a secure method.

One example of Boccalini's method (which he learned from Machiavelli) is shown by his comments on Tacitus' first sentence in the *Annales,* that "Rome at the beginning was ruled by kings." He elaborates on it with about 400 words of observation.[78] The main points are these: first, Romulus suppressed the Roman people and thereby enabled subsequent kings to become tyrants; second, ancient kings were modest in authority—being little more than "magistrates"—and were not absolute, as today; third, monarchy was unusual in ancient days and it was limited, but now republics are rare and kings can do what they please.

Another example, hundreds of pages later, in his observations on the *Agricola,* may be seen in his comments on that sentence of Tacitus which had served as the keynote of his letter to James I: "We should have lost memory as well as voice, had it been as easy to forget as to keep silence." "Without any doubt," he begins,

> the prince is not the lord of the soul of men, that is to say, of those powers which they are not able to repress, being, as they are, invisible to him . . . but the prince is lord only of the mouth and the other externals of a man.[79]

Thus, he continues—drawing on the recent examples of the Turks and King Sigismund of Poland—realistic rulers demand only obedience and tribute from their subjects, not caring a jot for what they believe in their hearts. But Queen Elizabeth of England, who prohibited by an edict ("which I have seen") internal or spiritual diversity of belief, was silly.

Her successor does not think this way, Boccalini declares—mindful of his friend; he could not even imagine doing such a thing. Thus, he concludes, ''our Tacitus'' would like to imply that the Romans had accommodated themselves so much to the cruel servitude of their tyrants that, ''as far as they could, they would have learned forgetfulness of their evils, and also not to speak of them.''[80] In other words, Boccalini means that they chose to remember, or could not help remembering, the cruelty—just as Boccalini could not help remembering the cruelty of the Spanish.

Boccalini, it is clear, was trying his best not to let Italians forget that there were alternatives to living under Spanish tyranny and that Tacitus could teach them how to change for something better—even if it had to come about by fighting evil with evil. When he said that it were better if Tacitus had kept his mouth shut, he meant that the world was far happier before ruler and subjects knew the art of successful politics which Tacitus (and then Machiavelli) had revealed. Tacitus' teaching and a realistic approach to politics were, in short, the same thing. However, aside from some Venetians, most people educated about Tacitus by Botero believed that Tacitus should in fact be silenced so that everything might go on just as it was. It was Botero, then, not Montaigne, Ammirato, or Boccalini, who set the tone (aside from England) for the seventeenth-century attitude toward the use of Tacitus in politics. Those who thought about politics at all condemned him; the others, scholars like Lipsius, didn't care anyway. Tacitus in Renaissance political thought had come to an end.

7 The Legacy of the Renaissance Political Use of Tacitus

The tradition of the application of Tacitus to political reality, which had begun with Bruni in 1403, did not survive the death of Boccalini in 1613. Thereafter, anti-Tacitists needed only to show that Tacitus had never, in fact, been really practical to begin with. Besides continuing their attacks on Tacitus' morality—as had Botero and his disciple, the Jesuit theologian Pedro Ribadeneyra[1]—they now began to undermine the very historical validity of Tacitus' writings. They showed that Tacitus was not only a bad man but a bad historian as well. And now that Boccalini was known as Tacitus' arch-defender, it followed that a certain Girolamo Briani[2] would begin the attack on his historiography with an *Aggiunta* (''addition to'') *ai Ragguagli di Parnaso* in 1614. In Briani's opinion, neither the one nor the other had been a good historian. For a good historian describes only pleasant events: he avoids inconvenient questions, and, most of all, he does not trouble himself with the unrealistic search for *arcana imperii*—which is just what Boccalini and Tacitus had seen as the chief fruit of historical investigation.

Briani, however, was merely preliminary to the man who really initiated, in 1617, a full-blown crusade against everything Tacitus stood for as a historian. This crusader was Famiano Strada, a Jesuit and professor of rhetoric at the Collegio Romano.[3] In the *Prolusiones academicae*, a massive hodgepodge of bits on stylistics, politics, morals, etc., he devoted some space to showing that Tacitus and the Tacitan historians who imitated him were bad historians. They ignored Lucian's directive that history ought to be both pleasurable and truthful. They broke the first imperative by their dreary accounts of tyrants, dwelling on their crimes and their cruelty. They broke the second by their exaggerated suppositions and wild investigations into *arcana imperii*.

> Therefore, watch out for whoever reveals I-know-not-what hidden arts and secrets of ruling while putting together a history: if he is pernicious to religion (which ought to be the first concern in each and every thing), and is pernicious to the state and to the ways of

> men, he will hardly, I think, be judged by you to be a good citizen. And the very one from whom seems to flow this kind of writing is, in a word, Cornelius Tacitus.[4]

Tacitus created egotists prone to disloyalty, breeders of contumacy, and wreckers of confidence in rulers. As an antidote to the poisoning of the body politic, Strada prescribed Livy—Livy and the whole catechism of Ciceronian orthodoxy which had been thrown over by Patrizi.

So popular and so influential became Strada's work that even the University of Padua reverted to the old dogmatism, which Patrizi had once destroyed there.[5] Indeed, so sweeping were the effects of Strada's work that his single critic, Gasparo Scioppio,[6] a German Italianate philologian and a vitriolic hater of Strada and all Jesuits, was, in his *Infamia Famiani* (about 1618), reduced to absolute confusion. He never did actually answer Strada, and he ended up in a long disquisition about style and grammar. He was certain about one thing only: Tacitus' history taught the evil Jesuits all they knew; and Tacitus, not Livy, was their real master. Scioppio is an example of ineffectual resistance in the face of Strada's campaign to put Livy back on the throne of historiographical tyranny. "Thus," concludes Spini, "the anti-Tacitan campaign rode to victory all over Italy."[7] Its triumph was celebrated by Agostino Mascardi,[8] Strada's successor to the chair of rhetoric in Rome, in his *Arte istorica* of 1636, a book which was accepted as the last word on the subject by an entire generation. And the captive enemy was publicly humiliated by one of Mascardi's best friends and admirers, Cardinal Guido Bentivoglio.[9] He showed what became typical of Tacitus' reputation as both man and historian when he wrote his *Memorie* (between 1640 and 1644). Tacitus, according to Bentivoglio, was the evil demon dwelling within Giovan Battista Deti, the worst cardinal of the whole college:

> He showed himself too much devoted to the senses, and therefore he was given to a sort of life which touched much more of the profane than of the ecclesiastical. He was a chief of that way of life, stored up with a thousand tumults within himself, completely full of Tacitus, a worshiper of his *sententiae,* with Tiberius always in his mouth and always in his example; at court it is usually said that he would have been much more well adapted to the Rome of Tiberius than to the Rome of the present.[10]

The line from Botero to Strada to Bentivoglio is a clear one: by the middle of the seventeenth century many people, Italians especially, generally saw Tacitus as both evil and useless.

Among other groups—the Spanish, the Germans, and the French—Tacitus was somewhat less demeaned and just a bit more useful in certain areas. But in these lands too, by the mid-1600s, Tacitus came to have little in common with the humanistic, practical political use of him in the Renaissance. In Spain,[11] first of all, the change began in 1595, when Pedro Ribadeneyra, the Jesuit follower of Botero and an apologist for Philip II, first introduced Tacitus to his countrymen. They had scarcely heard of Tacitus before, and now, with Ribadeneyra, they were told that they had not been missing very much. Ribadeneyra, in defending his king's governance by God's laws against those princes who used Satan's rules of *ragion di stato*, attacked the archadvocates of this noxious creed: Machiavelli, Bodin, and Tacitus. All were atheists. Tacitus, in particular, "the pagan historian and enemy of Christianity," was also a "debauched man" and generally "impious."[12] None of Ribadeneyra's compatriots, for almost twenty years, argued against him; yet none of them hurried to agree with him, either.

The Spaniards' neglect of Tacitus in this period was the result of their basic ignorance of his writings. No one had ever published them in Spain; no one had ever used them in a commentary or in a history there; and no one had yet translated them into Spanish. Indeed, in this period they learned of Tacitus rather indirectly: to some extent from Bodin, Ammirato, Botero, and Ribadeneyra, but especially from Lipsius. Still, they ignored Lipsius' many fine editions of Tacitus. Instead, they became acquainted with Tacitus merely at second hand, and in fragments, via Lipsius' *Politica* (1581), his laborious potpourri of maxims, and his *De constantia* (1585), his exposition of Stoicism. It is a wonder that even these works became available to them, considering the effects of the censorship law of 1558 and the revised Index of 1559,[13] which together made it quite difficult to obtain foreign books, Lipsius' included. He himself frequently had difficulties with the Roman Inquisition, and his *Politica* was placed on the Index in 1593. However, with sporadic relaxations of the censorship restrictions, at least a few copies of some of Lipsius' works filtered into the hands of Spaniards. Even then they might not have begun to develop much of an interest in Tacitus from these books had it not been for Manuel Sueyro, a captain with the Spanish armies in Lipsius' war-ravaged homeland. Sueyro was the first to translate Tacitus into Spanish, at Antwerp in 1613. Only then did Tacitus become generally available to his countrymen.

Still, Sueyro's translation did not, by itself, stimulate Spaniards to think about Tacitus in political terms. No, they arrived at that line of thought one year later, through the example set by Balthasar Alamos de Barrientos, adviser to Philip III. Inspired by Sueyro, he published his *Tácito Español* along with some *aforismos*, or medicinal prescriptions for the body politic, based on the text of Tacitus.[14] He had been working on the translation itself for some years. He had begun it in 1579–98 when he was in prison, from which he was freed only upon the death of Philip II, who had punished him for supporting his patron, Antonio Perez, the famous rebel. However, although he had been back in circulation for fifteen years and had been reinstated by his incarcerator's son, he had done nothing with his translation until encouraged by Sueyro. Moreover, somewhere along the line he must have read Lipsius, because his aphorisms are almost entirely derived from the pages of the *Politica*. Like Lipsius, Alamos attempted to demonstrate that politics, like medicine, is a science; but, unlike Machiavelli, he left the reader to discover the remedies for himself. For Alamos the truths contained in the maxims were *encerrados*, or "locked up"; and their existence lay in these maxims intrinsically, apart from their particular historical and political context. Then, through a study of human psychology, which these maxims revealed, an understanding of these truths via a "similitudo temporum" was supposed to emerge. In all, Alamos' intention to make Tacitus useful for anything actual and relevant was as tacit as with Lipsius; and his method was just as vague and unmanageable.

Nevertheless, Alamos' work appeared as something of a threat to at least one contemporary. Alvia de Castro, a Portuguese scholar armed with Ammirato's *Discorsi* on Tacitus, hastened to attack Alamos only two years later. Alvia argued in his *Verdadera razón de Estado* that politics is not really a science, such as medicine; instead, it is a batch of isolated items of experience. Thus, he asserted, the proper approach to Tacitus' maxims is to debate on their content and not on their context. Alvia, it seems, was inspired by Alamos' own handling of Tacitus rather than Alamos' statements about how he was intending to handle Tacitus. In general, Alvia's criticism of Alamos must have been effective, because, aside from a half-dozen mimics of Alamos over the next seventy-five years, his aphorisms aroused little interest. Even his translation (and Sueyro's, too) was commonly replaced, after 1629, by one done by Carlos Coloma, a historian and military commander in the Milanese territory; and, after Coloma, there were only two or three other translators of Tacitus all the way down to the end of the eighteenth century. Alamos then, was superseded linguistically by Coloma and politically by Alvia; and the latter's really useless method set the tone for years to come.

Even about twenty-five years later, other students of Tacitus still walked in Alvia's footsteps. One of them was Diego Saavedra Fajardo, royal emissary to Italy and Germany, who wrote his *Idea de un Principe cristiano representada en cien Empresas* in 1640. Agreeing with Alvia, he thought that a science of politics was impossible, and he used Tacitus, along with Aristotle and the Bible, to prove that Machiavelli's approach was erroneous. However, he went one step beyond Alvia in removing Tacitus still further from any real political usefulness: to Fajardo the important thing was to discover how princes *ought* to act.

Finally, removing even princes from Fajardo's formulation of Tacitus' ideal relevancy, there came Baltasar Gracián, a Jesuit moralist and author of the *Oráculo Manual* (1647). With Gracián's book Tacitus lost even that last vestige of political significance that he had retained in Fajardo's book. With Gracián's handbook Tacitus was reduced to being a mere moral guide. The text is a collection of about three hundred aphorisms, around eighty of them derived from Tacitus. In compiling them, Gracián emphasized his predecessors' regard for Tacitus' keen insight into human psychology. Like Alamos, Alvia, and Fajardo, he saw great value in Tacitus' treatment of simulation, dissimulation, feigning, disguise, etc. Unlike them, however, he recommended the practice of these abilities, not particularly for success in dealing with princes, but for private ethics, for personal life. Thus, although Spaniards, despite Ribadeneyra, eventually came to appreciate Tacitus more highly than did Italians by the mid-seventeenth century, they too saw him as useless for political action.

In Germany,[15] meanwhile, the decline in the Renaissance political use of Tacitus since the days of Rhenanus was somewhat reversed, though briefly, at the beginning of the seventeenth century. The spark for this momentary vivification came from Arnold Clapmarius, professor of law at the University of Altdorf, who was the first to import *reason of state* into Germany. He performed this service in his book *De arcanis rerum publicarum,* which he published in 1605. It was heavily influenced by Ammirato, with whom Clapmarius corresponded. Like his Italian predecessor, he masked the evil Machiavelli with the neutral or, at best, acceptable Tacitus. However, unlike the Spaniards of his generation, he had ready access to Tacitus' works, and he had no scruples in not following the "hard line" of Botero and his disciples on

Tacitus' impiety and immorality. On the contrary, he was, like Ammirato, able to deal with Tacitus as a substitute for Machiavelli while still applying Machiavelli's method. Therefore, like Ammirato, he could derive political and legal principles from his historical understanding of the text. In short, he did not feel compelled to shroud Tacitus' value within veiled maxims. Instead, his open analysis of Tacitus led him to something which, in the judgment of Friedrich Meinecke, the famous modern historian, was "very vital" in his theory about the *simulacra imperii seu libertatis* ("semblances of imperium or of liberty"): in return for real rights and freedoms, rulers give their subjects useful illusions of justice and freedom.[16] For the validity of this Tacitan principle Clapmarius could point to many examples among contemporary German princes, who were becoming absolute rulers while gradually undermining the real constitutional rights of the three estates. And, although Clapmarius' book was widely read, republished, and imitated, the absolutism which it sanctioned became, by mid-century, a stultifying ideology which helped to smother any further vital uses of Tacitus.

Already by 1617, Matthias Bernegger, professor of history at Strassburg, began to remove Tacitus from even the limited usefulness which Clapmarius had understood. In that year he published his *J. Lipsii Politicorum libri ad disputandum propositi.* Its method, inspired by Lipsius and applied by Bernegger in his lectures on Tacitus since 1614, was to take striking words and phrases from Tacitus, use them as *loci communes,* and from them elaborate themes for philosophical and moral reflection. Its message was, in a word, Prudence: just as Lipsius had understood it. This book was later used by Johannes Freinsheim, professor, librarian, and Bernegger's son-in-law, in his *Specimen paraphraseos Cornelianae* (1641). It was the result of his many years' work of compiling, collating, and annotating foreign translations of Tacitus' *Annales* (including those of Micyllus, de la Planche, Grenewey, Dati, and Sueyro). And that's all it was. Although Freinsheim had lived and suffered through the Thirty Years' War, contemporaries could never detect his experiences in war and exile from studying his work. As with his father-in-law, Lipsius was probably at the core of his prudence and taciturnity. The same was true for Freinsheim's friend, Johann Heinrich Boecler, a professor of history, who wrote his *Bibliographia historico-politico-philologica* about 1652 (published only in 1677). Boecler's work expresses his belief that politics is not a science but a philosophic area of logical analysis, a part of Aristotelian ethics. At most, he felt that Tacitus was of some use as a weapon against tyrants. But, according to Else-Lilly Etter, in her study of Tacitus in this period, Boecler's insight here is "dry school wisdom" and "lacking in experience and contemporaneousness."[17] Her judgment can apply, as well, to all other German students of Tacitus for the rest of the century.

In France the story is similar.[18] The legacy of Tacitus from the Renaissance survived mainly in a debased inheritance of Montaigne's use of him for Stoicism. The first heir was Pierre Charron, Montaigne's friend and visitor to his tower. His handling of the theme shows how the younger Montaigne's original and subtle Stoical understanding of Tacitus had lost its verve less than ten years after Montaigne's death. Charron merely rummaged through Tacitus to extract choice words and phrases on the theme of Stoical prudence. His *Thresor de la Sagesse* of 1601 shows, in its very title, this devolution. The work is nothing but a collection of "virtues"; marginal rubrics tag paragraphs of hoarded snippets from ancient authors, mainly Plutarch and Seneca. Charron uses Tacitus almost exclusively under the heading "Prudence," and the chief value in learning it is to enable one to live with princes in this world. Charron's chief foundation appears to be Lipsius rather than Montaigne. Another basis was Ammirato, diluted by Charron's comprehension of *reason of state*, according to which individuals are forced to bear with particular injustices, which, in the larger context (determined by the prince), really add up to justice.

This aspect of *reason of state* was stressed also in the notes of Jean Baudouin, who in 1610 translated Tacitus and joined to it his translation—the first in French—of Ammirato's *Discorsi* on Tacitus. Gabriel Naudé, librarian for Cardinal Richelieu, was another who saw this connection between *reason of state* and Stoical forbearance as the chief reason for studying Tacitus. In his *Bibliographia politica* of 1633, he, like Charron, arranged his classical citations under various ideal themes, with Tacitus again providing lessons in political prudence: caution in dealing with princes, who, compelled by larger exigencies of *reason of state*, may choose to destroy with a nod. And what Naudé lacked in practical political application he made up for with bombast. In one place, for example, he speaks of Tacitus as a *deus ex machina*, occupying a seat above the theatrical stage of history, "from which, amid stupor and amazement, he resolves political difficulties"; for this, "he is venerated silently, as befits a deity."[19] Whatever Naudé was saying, one thing is clear: he has nothing in common with the tradition of Tacitus which flourished with Bodin and Montaigne.

Other Frenchmen throughout the century sang similar paeans to

Tacitus and, like Naudé, filled their flower baskets with his maxims. Only one of them, by mid-century, tired of this habit. Nicholas Perrot d'Ablancourt, in the dedication to his translation of Tacitus (1650), remarked that "people have made maxims out of every line of him" and that "if one were to have collected all the books which have been written to praise him or to clarify him, one would have a large library."[20] He himself did not waste the effort. Most people disapproved of this neglect. Many years later, for instance, another translator, Nicholas Amelot de la Houssaie, still could not forgive d'Ablancourt, and he berated him because "his version is almost entirely devoid of those sentences, and of those maxims of state, which collide at every period of the original."[21] Amelot voiced his complaint in his essay "De la Flaterie" (1686),[22] a collection of Tacitus' remarks on the subject. In it he frankly admitted that a subject cannot avoid flattering princes. Moreover, Peter Burke, in his essay on Tacitism, in commenting on Amelot's dedication to Louis XIV in another work—his translation of Gracián's *Oráculo Manual*—says that "his own ethic was one of 'accommodation.' "[23] In all, by 1650 and after, Frenchmen had certain uses for Tacitus, but these uses were not "political"—at least not in the sense that the Renaissance gave to this word.

Only for Englishmen had political uses for Tacitus, by 1650, become drastically different from what had developed elsewhere in Europe. For them it all began just a few years before Boccalini wrote to King James (in 1612) about the freedom of speech his subjects enjoyed. In fact, James himself, his family, and his courtiers had prepared the way for dynamic political uses of Tacitus in England. Indirectly, they had only recently laid this foundation through their acceptance of Tacitus as a guide to good morals, a teacher of political philosophy, and, to some extent, as a historical text worth studying.

Prior to 1603 and James's ascent to the English throne, almost no one in England believed Tacitus worthwhile for these purposes—let alone for actual political application. James's predecessor, Queen Elizabeth, for one, remained ignorant of Tacitus until late in her reign, and through the entire sixteenth century only a few historians, etiquette writers, and grammarians were much better informed. In fact, neither Elizabeth nor her people as a whole were much excited by Tacitus even after the first English translations appeared in the 1590s. Their lack of enthusiasm is clear from the statements of Henry Savile, Tacitus' first English translator and a tutor to Elizabeth.[24] In presenting his versions of the *Historiae* and *Agricola* to her in 1591, he made excuses for Tacitus' difficulty: "for Tacitus I may say without partialitie, that he hath written the most matter with the best conceite in the fewest words of any Historiographer ancient or modern. But he is harde."[25] Tacitus provided a lot of interesting information, but the style was difficult. In fact, Savile simply didn't like it. Expressing his own sentiments or allowing his friend Robert Devereux, the famous earl of Essex, to say them for him under "A. B. to the Reader,"[26] he tells Elizabeth that "if thy stomach be so tender as thou canst not digest Tacitus in his own style, thou art beholding to Savile, who gives thee the same food, but with a pleasant and easie taste."[27] Later, in a critical footnote, Savile was even more specific when he identified "that bastard Rhetoricke" of those writers of old, "infected with that heresie of style begun by Seneca, Quintilian, the Plinies, and Tacitus."[28] Yet, despite Tacitus' distasteful style, Savile had two reasons for translating as much of Tacitus as he did: first, as princes make history, so history "magnifies" princes; second, as readers learn of Rome, full of tumult and anarchy under tyrants, they will more appreciate England, rich with peace and security under Elizabeth.[29]

Though Elizabeth herself may have been "magnified" in the process, her stomach remained just as tender as Savile thought it was. Some seven years later it is clear that she still believed Tacitus wrote in an unseemly style. In a letter of 22 June 1597 by Robert Cecil, the queen's intimate councillor, to Thomas Burgh, lord deputy of Ireland, her attitude is indirectly revealed. Cecil writes apropos of Burgh's negotiations with Hugh O'Neill, earl of Tyrone, the famous rebel:

> Her majesty is exceedingly well satisfied with your purposes, your endeavors in particular, and with your answers to the rebel. Yet I must add this, that your style to the rebel is held too curious, and that you do in all your writings a little too much imitate the succinctness of Tacitus, which for a man to write to a council is not held so proper.[30]

A few years later, in 1599, Elizabeth probably acquired another reason for not encouraging Tacitus' popularity: she may have learned that Tacitus incited treason. Francis Bacon, her philosophical adviser, many years later (in 1625) recalled an incident from this year which supports this connection. Drawing heavily on Tacitus, John Hayward, a member, with Bacon, of the circle around Essex, had just published a history of Henry IV. When the book came to Elizabeth's notice, she asked Bacon "whether there was no treason contained in it?" And Bacon responded,

"No, Madam, for treason I cannot deliver opinion that there is any, but very much felony . . . because he has stolen many of his conceits out of Tacitus."[31] Apparently Elizabeth had read neither Savile's translation nor Richard Grenewey's supplement to it (the *Annales* and the *Germania,* 1598)[32] too carefully. Otherwise she might have detected Hayward's source. And even if she had read them well, she somehow got the idea on her own, or certainly from Bacon, that Tacitus could at least provide information, if not inspiration, for treason. In any case, there is no cause to regard Bacon's anecdote as apocryphal—if we keep in mind the belated development in England of political applications of Tacitus.

All of that began to change in 1603, when James became king of England. In that year James himself republished his *Basilikon Doron* or *Precepts on the Art of Governing*—this time with references to Tacitus and other classical authors, which he had not included in the first edition of 1599. But these references, and those to Tacitus in particular, are vague, being little more than textual parallels which came to mind when James, or perhaps a learned friend, reread the text before its second publication.[33] Still, whatever James's method, he apparently wanted readers to recognize his knowledge of Tacitus. And Ben Jonson, the famous playwright, may have been encouraged by this to publish his *Sejanus* in 1603. The play is deeply permeated with Tacitus' account of that insidious councillor and traitor to Tiberius. Jonson annotated the edition with marginal references to Tacitus—fifty-nine in Act I alone. Now, with Elizabeth dead, Jonson may have had Essex in mind as a parallel to Sejanus; at least this is what some contemporaries suspected.[34] Finally, in the same year also, Bacon dedicated to James his *Briefe Discourse Touching the Happie Union of the Kingdoms of England and Scotland;* in it he used Tacitus politically for the first time.[35] He included Tacitus' account (in *Annales* xi. 23–24) of the Emperor Claudius' admission of Gauls into the senate over strong senatorial objections. Bacon, who needed a job, was at the least greeting James with this historical allusion to Claudius' political synthesis of two cultures; at most, he may have been hinting that Scotsmen might someday be represented in Parliament. At any rate, Bacon, whose career had long been stunted while serving Elizabeth, felt no hesitation in citing an author whom his potential new employer also used.

Perhaps Bacon had learned that James's elder son, Henry, might already have developed an interest in Tacitus. It is certain that, a few years later, Henry was a hard-working young student of Tacitus' language; and John Harrington, his tutor, frequently helped the lad over the more difficult passages.[36] Moreover, Henry had his own father's example, in the *Basilikon Doron*, to show him that moralisms gleaned from Tacitus were worth a ruler's time and interest. Henry's younger brother, Charles, was not forgotten here, either. His tutor was John Cleland,[37] a friend of both Prince Henry and Harrington, who in 1607 wrote for him the *Propaedeia, or the Institution of a Young Noble Man*. In it he too, like the king, gleaned moral advice from Tacitus for the boy's instruction. Thus, with such backing in the royal household, it is no wonder that Tacitus became more widely accepted and understood in England.

Among those at court Bacon was probably most responsible for showing other Englishmen some ways in which Tacitus could be interesting.[38] His uses of Tacitus in the *Advancement of Learning* (1605), *De sapientia vetorum* (1609), the *Essays* (1597, 1612, and 1625—though exclusively in the latter two, expanded, editions), and the *De augmentis scientiarum* (1623) certainly popularized this ancient author, hitherto so largely neglected.[39] Bacon's method of using Tacitus in these works is confined to rounding out and completing his own ideas with Tacitus' pointed phrases and acute sentences. Whether for political maxims or for historical information, and whether for moralisms or for stylistic examples, Bacon seems to have used Tacitus as a kind of commonplace book of neat lines. One example, from "Of Seditions and Troubles" (written between 1607 and 1612 but not published until 1625), not only shows his typical method but ironically cautions others, rulers at least, not to follow it: there is harm, Bacon says in this essay, if princes deliver witty and sharp speeches—witness Galba, the Roman emperor, who ruined himself by causing his troops to lose hope for a donative when he couldn't resist saying that he "levied his soldiers, he did not buy them" ("legi a se militem, non emi"—*Historiae* i. 5).[40] In fact, there seem to be only two places, in his literary publications, where Bacon expresses direct praise of Tacitus as opposed to simply taking information and sentences from him. In one of these he prefers Tacitus, "who utters the very morals of life itself," over Aristotle and Plato and their doctrines; in the other he compares Tacitus to Suetonius, who is not as credible.[41] Thus, although Bacon said almost nothing about Tacitus himself, Englishmen read Bacon's vast literary output and at least became more accustomed to Tacitus' name, his clever style, his historical information, and his moralistic value.

What Bacon did not do, in all his published works, was to make Tacitus better understood for political application to immediate political circumstances. His early *Discourse* on the union of England and Scotland (1603) may be an exception; nevertheless, his purpose for using Tacitus in it is quite indirect and can only be surmised. Even less directly related to political actuality, aside from Bacon, was Jonson's *Sejanus:* it was only possibly written with relevance to Essex and Elizabeth; moreover, it was hardly political, in any immediate sense, after their deaths. Likewise, little argument for political immediacy could be derived from the interests of King James, Harrington, Prince Henry, and Cleland.

No, it seems that no one in England really applied Tacitus to politics until Bacon himself did, in a way completely detached from his literary production, in 1610. In that year, serving James as solicitor general (an office he had occupied since 1607, four years after being knighted by James), he made two speeches in which he used Tacitus for particular political effect. The first was to the king on behalf of the Commons. Bacon compared James to the emperors Nerva and Trajan, who united *imperium* and *libertatem* (*Agricola* iii), a compliment, he added, "by one of the wisest writers to two of the best emperors."[42] In the second speech, to the Commons on behalf of the king, he used the same example to praise James in order to urge the members to desist from further question of receiving the king's messages.[43] In both cases Bacon tried to reconcile the two parties with respect to the difficult problems of James's royal prerogative (the core of his sovereignty or "imperium") and Parliament's rights and liberties. More specifically,[44] the Parliament of 1610 was strongly opposed to James's uninhibited use of proclamations (which, it said, created new offenses unknown to the law) and impositions (which, it said, James was now using to tax trade beyond what commerical protection required). In still a third area, writs of prohibition (restricting the limits of ecclesiastical jurisdiction), James opposed Parliament in his belief that the king possessed all spiritual and temporal jurisdiction, while Parliament, on the other hand, asserted the rights of the courts of common law to issue such writs when necessary. In all, problems of *imperium* and *libertas* were clearly the immediate political questions of the day in Bacon's two speeches. Bacon was trying to convince both sides that Tacitus' Nerva and Trajan pointed to a solution through compromise. Indeed, some resolution of the dispute over impositions, at least, was under way when, with fresh conflicts developing, James dissolved Parliament in February 1611.

In the interval between it and the next Parliament, of 1614, James fell upon bad days. Not only did Henry, his son, die, but so did Cecil, his wise secretary of state. Bacon, still full of ambition, and with memories of his frustration under Elizabeth, applied for the vacant position. In a letter of 31 May 1612, he wrote to James, saying

> I will be ready as a chessman to be wherever your Majesty's royal hand shall set me. Your Majesty will bear me witness, I have not suddenly opened myself thus far. . . . I see the distractions and I fear Tacitus will be a prophet. "magis alii homines quam alii mores" ["other men, not other manners"—*Historiae* ii. 95].[45]

Still, Bacon knew he would really serve James better than had the freedmen and informers of the emperors Otho and Vitellius—apropos of the context from which he quoted. Nevertheless, James passed over him and chose, instead, Robert Carr, "a Scottish upstart . . . a man without experience and without ideas," as J. R. Tanner, the renowned constitutional historian, identifies him.[46] To mollify Bacon, James raised him from solicitor general to attorney general in 1613.

If Bacon had been more highly regarded by Elizabeth, he could have enjoyed this position long before, in 1593. Instead, she had chosen Edward Coke, the present chief justice and Bacon's lifelong rival (he had even stolen Bacon's lady friend and had married her).[47] But now, in 1616, James dismissed Coke from his position for his failure to comply with the king's policy on *Commendams,* or ecclesiastical benefices presented as the king willed, according to his prerogative. So now, Bacon was only too ready to apply for his enemy's vacant post. To get the job, Bacon wrote to James (on 21 November 1616) promising, once again, to be his pliant tool:

> But while your Majesty peruseth the accounts of Judges in circuits your Majesty will give me leave to think of the Judges here in his upper region. And because Tacitus saith well "opportuni magnis conatibus transitus rerum" ["periods of transition suit great attempts"—*Historiae* i. 21]. Now upon this change . . . I shall endeavor, to the best of my power and skill, that there may be a consent and united mind in your Judges, to serve you and strengthen your business.[48]

Bacon never did get the job, but he was honored the following year with the office of lord keeper of the great seal and, in 1618, with that of lord chancellor. Bacon continued to serve James as best he could amid the ever-increasing conflict between king and Parliament. Tacitus, as is clear from the examples given, was readily at Bacon's fingertips to provide guidelines for political action in the various political situations with which he had to deal. But Bacon never attained the power he had always yearned for, with which he could give Tacitus full rein in the political world; and James, not so wise as he usually thought he was, could perhaps have profited from Bacon's applications of Tacitus' lessons. Tanner sums up both men pretty well:

> Bacon was not a king, and James was not really a philosopher. The philosopher had fallen on evil days, for the kings were Stuarts; and what was really needed was the conservation of existing liberties against encroachment, and not the efficient paternal government which Bacon and Strafford [Charles I's conservative and very loyal supporter] dreamed of but which James and Charles could never hope to attain.[49]

Tanner is basically correct here, despite the vague causation implied in "evil days" and the inevitability implied in the wider context. He could have added that Bacon was not really a philosopher either—at least not when he took bribes and was impeached in 1621. And then too his use of Tacitus for political activity was over also.

Other politicians, no doubt inspired by Bacon's own example and educated in Tacitus through Bacon's wide uses of him in his literary work, now quite frequently began using Tacitus to affect immediate political circumstances. There are many instances. Coke, for one—active once again—spoke to the Commons in 1625 on the need to stop the publication of certain "popish" writings; in arguing for unity in the observance of correct religion, he cited Tacitus' remark, in *Agricola* xii, that British tribal disunity had allowed them all to be conquered.[50] Archbishop William Laud, Charles I's stout defender of the religious establishment, provides another instance; in the same Parliament he used the same source, but to argue for religious unity within the Church of England.[51] Moreover, in the following year, Laud was instrumental in silencing Isaac Dorislaus, a Dutch professor of history at Cambridge, for his lectures on Tacitus. In them, Dorislaus had applied Tacitus' statements to events in the Revolt of the Netherlands: by using Tacitus to denounce monarchic Spain, Dorislaus appeared to Laud to be denigrating monarchy in general.[52] Also in 1626 is another instance. John Eliot, the famous Puritan politician, gave a speech to the Commons in which he argued at some length that no one so resembled Sejanus, evil Tiberius' evil councillor, as did George Villiers, the ill-starred duke of Buckingham. King Charles, immediately learning of the speech, exclaimed, "Implicitly, he must intend me for Tiberius!" and ran to the House of Lords.[53] Eliot was arrested but soon released. Buckingham was stabbed to death in 1628. Charles dissolved Parliament, which was as angry as the king, in 1629. He did not call it again until 1640.

In the "Eleven Years' Tyranny," and on into the '40s, Tacitus continued to be used, mostly by Puritans, during the worsening relations between the Crown and the disbanded Commons. For example, William Prynne, the rabid Puritan, was tried for treason in the Star Chamber for his use of *Annales* xv. 65, 67. In these passages Tacitus recounts how Subrius Flavus, a soldier, plotted Nero's assassination. Flavus' hatred of the emperor was in part inspired by Nero's having been an actor. Prynne accordingly said that Flavus was justified in his plot, for Prynne was convinced that England, like Nero's Rome, was being corrupted by plays. Prynne also referred to the disgrace of Roman ladies forced onto the stage by Nero. Since the ladies of Charles's court had recently acted in a masque, Prynne was brought to trial, sentenced, and imprisoned.[54] Only at the beginning of the revolutionary Long Parliament, in 1640, was Prynne released and compensated by his colleagues. He then contributed his share toward bringing the Commons into open revolt against the king in 1642. But the Commons itself was by then split between the advocates of "limited episcopacy" and the "root and branch" men, who wanted no episcopacy at all. The former position had been put forward the year before by James Ussher, archbishop of Armagh. Sometime earlier, Ussher had written *The Power communicated by God to the Prince, and the Obedience required of the Subject;* in it he used Tacitus to back up many of his arguments. Charles had specially commanded the work and was pleased with the result.[55] It shows that Tacitus was by no means the monopoly of Puritan antimonarchists. Contemporaries were not much influenced by it, however, because it got "lost" on the way to the printer. In 1649 Charles himself lost his head.

In the '50s the use of Tacitus in the debate between antimonarchists, of the various kinds, and monarchists, hoping for the "restoration" with Charles II, nevertheless continued. At the beginning of the decade a certain "Salmasius" became widely known for his *Defense of the King*. It stirred enough interest to induce John Milton to write a counterattack in his *Defense of the People of England* (1651).[56] In it he took Salmasius to task for his abuse of the context in the way he used one particular quotation from Tacitus. In his detailed argument Milton declared that Tacitus "is an approved Writer, and of all others the greatest Enemy to Tyrants. . . ."[57] Six years later, the same opinion, minus Milton's astute exegesis, led an obscure fanatic, Captain Titus, author of *Killing No Murder,* to use several lines in Tacitus to show that Oliver

Cromwell, the Protector, had to be assassinated.[58] Luckily, Cromwell died on his own before Titus could inflict Tacitus' judgment upon him! But then, in 1659, Jeremy Taylor, author of *A Rule of Conscience,* dedicated to Charles II, showed even greater skill in ransacking Tacitus to support the rightful rule of the king. Thus, through four decades, Englishmen used Tacitus as an important source in their political struggles.

With Charles's restoration to the monarchy in May 1660, the polemics over the evil and good of monarchy ceased. Tacitus' political application in England ceased with them. Thereafter he was used by historians, like Edward Hyde, the earl of Clarendon, in his great *History of the Rebellion and Civil Wars in England;* he was used by political philosophers like Thomas Hobbes, the famous author of the *Leviathan;* and, in general, he was read more often, in some thirty-five Latin and English editions issued down to the year 1800. But the intense tradition of his political use, in the years 1610 to 1660, did not survive the Restoration. He then became as useless for politics in England as he had become on the Continent after 1613; even the Glorious Revolution of 1688–89 encouraged no revival. Still, the dynamic political uses of Tacitus in England in the first half of the seventeenth century stand in very sharp contrast to his fate at that time in France, Germany, Spain, and Italy; and in England, unlike elsewhere, Tacitus received no abuse for immorality either before or after the Restoration. These are some obvious differences. But there are still two very important questions which remain unanswered. First, the influences, if any, of Tacitus upon Englishmen from Boccalini, Lipsius, Muret, Montaigne, Ammirato, Bodin, Machiavelli, and others has not yet been analyzed. Second, possible influences of English uses of Tacitus upon other Europeans have not been traced at all. Toffanin, von Stackelberg, and Etter—scholars who have attempted a wide synthesis of "Tacitism" in the seventeenth century—have simply ignored England. Tenney and Benjamin, on the other hand, are scholars who have investigated particular aspects of Tacitus in England but have avoided the Continental context, although the latter asserts them without evidence. And it is beyond the scope of this book—on Tacitus in the age of Renaissance humanism—to provide more than the sketch already given in this chapter. Any deeper study will probably have to begin, as here, with Bacon.

It was Bacon, too, who indirectly inspired the renewed signs of a more practical context for Tacitus back on the Continent. His contribution is clear even from a brief survey of his effect on the use of Tacitus by Giambattista Vico, the great Italian philosopher.[59] Vico found

Tacitus' information and insights of much worth for his thinking about the classics, philology, literature, education, myth, history, and—most valuably—law and political theory; in his most famous work, the *Scienza Nuova* (published in three editions, from 1725 to 1744, in which his thought was constantly developing), he used Tacitus specifically over sixty times—and Bacon may have inspired many of them. For Bacon, along with Tacitus and Plato, was one of Vico's three favorite authors. To Vico—as he reveals in his *Autobiography* (1725)—Bacon was the greatest synthesis of statesman and philospher: a union of Tacitus, the unexcelled statesman, and Plato, the unexcelled philosopher:

> With an incomparable metaphysical mind, Tacitus contemplates man as he is, Plato as he should be. And as Plato with his universal knowledge explores the parts of nobility which constitute the man of intellectual wisdom, so Tacitus descends into all the counsels of utility whereby, among the infinite chances of malice and fortune, the man of practical wisdom brings things to good issue.[60]

And Bacon, correcting and expanding on these two men, transformed them into reality by way of his method, which pointed the way to a true science of civilization.[61] Vico's study of all three authors led him to vast and profound ramifications of thought in all areas of human mentality and activity.[62] Tacitus, in particular, remained of consistent value for him throughout it all.

Essentially, Vico saw Tacitus as providing statesmen "with a body of facts objectively appraised," as Santino Caramella, one of Vico's best modern students, has it.[63] Moreover, Santino accurately observes that the way Tacitus " 'descends into all counsels of utility' was not interpreted by Vico in the tendentiously Stoic or theological manner that had prevailed among the Tacitists."[64] Their ideal, reflected in Tacitus' maxims, was the incorruptible prince. Indeed, it is here, in Vico's break with the tradition of the Tacitists, in the context of their reason-of-state commentaries, that Tacitus again becomes really useful after his neglect since the early 1600s.

Vico accomplished this revitalization of Tacitus by using him to support a good or just *ragion di stato,* which is the old *ragion di stato* (known only to the ruler) but placed midway between divine reason (known only to God) and natural reason (known to all men). This third kind, natural reason, embodying full justice, was the "true" *ragion di stato;* and Vico sees it fitting in his time for both popular states and popular monarchies. In the latter government the authority of the prince should therefore have the morality of the democratic conscience as its condition. Thus, Vico saw Tacitus as a source for political science within the context of the subjugation of political reality to natural reason. Vico's own political reality, in Naples, was the establishment by Philip V, in 1702, and Charles III, 1734, of their new Bourbon dynasties. For Vico, Tacitus had most immediate practical value as a stabilizer and corrective of these new monarchies under which he lived. In this framework, then, Vico helped Tacitus to become both politically useful and politically beneficial once again.

Another important founder of Enlightenment thought, Charles Montesquieu,[65] was also helping Tacitus in this direction. But Montesquieu's practical goal was different. In his most important work, *De l'Esprit des Lois* (1748), his purpose for using Tacitus was the discovery of natural law. His example later inspired such propagandists as Denis Diderot, Honoré Mirabeau, Camille Desmoulins, and André Chenier.[66] Chenier, a poet of the Revolution, frequently used Tacitus, "whose name pronounced makes tyrants pale";[67] and he, like the others, commonly identified with Tacitus and praised him as a tyrant-hater and, more generally, as a detester of monarchs, whose very existence represented an abuse of natural law.

Other revolutionaries, in America, generally began from arguments of natural law and natural reason and, like their French counterparts, used Tacitus to support their antimonarchical polemics.[68] Benjamin Franklin, for instance, as early as 1722, at the age of sixteen, used Tacitus for his work on free speech, the *Dogwood Papers*. For it he used a translation of the *Annales* and the *Historiae* for historical material. In fact, one line from the latter work struck him so much that he took the trouble to dig out the original Latin from somewhere.[69] This line was Tacitus' statement (in i. 1) about the "rara temporum felicitate . . ."—"the rare happiness of times, when we may think what we please, and express what we think." Moreover, throughout Franklin's long life Tacitus remained one of his favorite authors. Other patriots, like John Adams and Thomas Jefferson, valued Tacitus greatly.[70] Despite the differences between them over the degree of direct democracy desired in the new constitution, both men saw the fundamental problem of *Annales* iv. 33, in which the mixed form of government is seen as something "easy to commend but not to produce." They knew the difficulty of getting divergent groups of people to work in concerted action. And no one knew this better than another American, Jonathan Boucher, a rigid Tory and a fiery preacher.

Before he left for England in August 1775, he had preached for over twelve years against toleration, republicanism, and the will of the people. In these sermons he said that the colonies would never manage to function together, and he backed this up with Tacitus' remark on the ancient Britons (*Agricola* xii): "Our greatest advantage in coping with tribes so powerful is that they do not act in concert."[71] Boucher shows that Tacitus in eighteenth-century America was not necessarily viewed as a supporter of revolution. Ever since Bruni and Decembrio, after all, there had been two sides to every political issue—a fact which most modern practitioners of *Ideengeschichte* somehow ignore. But in Bruni's time as in Boucher's, both sides at least agreed that Tacitus was both beneficial and useful for political reality.

However, there is another side, even to this more positive aspect of the political use of Tacitus in the Enlightenment: it shows a generally negative regard for him. Gains in Tacitus' reputation were largely annulled by the great Voltaire, who suspected Tacitus of being a liar in almost every sentence of the *Germania* and who, after several readings of Tacitus' account of Nero in the *Annales,* "was tempted to believe nothing."[72] Another great Enlightenment author felt the same way. He was Simon Linguet, the great writer of the nineteen-volume *Annales politiques civiles et littéraires*. In another work, his important *Histoire des révolutions de l'Empire romain* (2 vols., 1766) he made this remark about the historical authority of Tacitus: "It is with trembling that I dare to contradict Tacitus . . . but, in the end, I ask that one forget, if one can, the Authorities, and that one weigh reasons only."[73] Finally, with regard to Tacitus' description of the revolt of the Pannonian Legions (*Annales* i. 16, etc.), he said, "I don't believe a word of it."[74] Moreover, in England, at about the same time, at least one man had the same opinion: Thomas Hunter, author of some *Observations on Tacitus* (London, 1752), said that Tacitus "is void of Candor, wants Judgment, exceeds Nature, and violates Truth."[75]

From Italy, and also right in the middle of the halcyon days of the Enlightenment, comes still another example of a continuing negative regard for Tacitus. It is provided by Giovan Francesco Pagnini del Ventura, an economic theorist and historian. In his *Della Decima, e di varie altre gravezze imposte dal cumune di Firenze* (Florence, 1765), he tried to demonstrate that the great days of commercial prosperity of the fifteenth century could be brought back by simply changing the current system of legislation. With this purpose in mind, he then tried to show that the causes of the commercial decadence of Italy were all moral, not physical. He backed up his argument by citations from all recent economic writers in France, England, and Spain. He then added:

> However, these just hopes remain not the least embittered by the wicked [trista] reflection suggested by Tacitus, by which you are reminded that "cure operates more slowly than disease, and as the body itself is slow to grow and quick to decay, so also it is easier to damp men's spirits and their enthusiasm than to revive them: nay, listlessness itself has a certain subtle charm, and the languor we hate at first we learn to love." [From *Agricola* iii.][76]

In short, it is clear that in Italy, England, and France, Tacitus was a thorn in the side of many Enlightenment optimists.

With the passing of the Enlightenment and its revolutions, the general feeling toward Tacitus was set forth by Napoleon I himself:

> I know of no other historian who has so calumniated and belittled mankind as he. In the simplest transactions he seeks for criminal motives: out of every emperor he fashions a complete villain, and so depicts him that we admire the spirit of evil permeating him, and nothing more. It has been said with justice that his *Annals* are a history, not of the Empire, but of the Roman criminal tribunals—nothing save the accusations and men accused, persecutions and the persecuted, and people opening veins in baths. He speaks continually of denunciations, and the greatest denouncer is himself.[77]

His nephew, Napoleon III, felt the same way.[78] But Victor Hugo, the great novelist, in his hatred for this dictator, dropped Virgil, courtier of a tyrant, and began to admire Tacitus.[79]

In the early nineteenth century, however, even such statements as these were mere expressions of personal feeling and opinion rather than carefully thought-out arguments based on the classics. Besides, people no longer knew how to apply the classics to political reality; and now, with the Romantic reaction against them in favor of medieval life and thought, people forgot about the classics entirely—except for the scholars, that is. And they, the scholars, were quickly developing into the superoffspring of that lineage which had continued without interruption since Lipsius: scholarship for scholarship alone. One branch of it, flourishing between 1870 and 1900, produced the 369 philological dissertations on Tacitus (mostly German) listed in the *Catalogus Dissertationum Philologicarum Classicarum* (2d ed., Leipzig, 1910). Another branch finally produced the first study of the history of Tacitus in European intellectual development in Felice Ramorino's *Cornelio Tacito nella storia della cultura* (Milan: Hoepli, 1897), and still another produced scores of ever finer critical editions of Tacitus' works. All in all, nineteenth-century students of Tacitus were unconcerned one way or another about Tacitus' morality and never conceived of him as providing useful tools for dealing with their own political reality.

In the twentieth century, when students of Tacitus (and, for that matter, of all classical authors) are so very few, it is difficult to tell what the trend is with regard to Tacitus as a useful political guide. For example, the use made of the *Germania* by the Nazis is an open question. There is at least one indication, though, in Hans Drexler, author of *Tacitus: Grundzüge einer politischen Pathologie* (Frankfurt a.m.: Verlag Moritz Diesterweg, 1939), who declares that since 1933, thanks to National Socialism, the "problem of the races" has guided historical investigation of the ancient Greeks and Romans.[80] Great historians, Tacitus in particular, are studied, he says, because in them "the image" (*Bild*) and "the artist" (*Bildner*) are united; thus, Tacitus' ideas and judgments were coordinated with his world,[81] which was sick and dying from many causes, though, at bottom, from the deeper cause of race.[82] Each race, indeed, has value depending on the degree to which it concentrates on eternity and is fulfilled by "the necessity of destiny" ("die Notwendigkeit des Schicksals").[83]

Not so indiscernible is the common opinion *about* the Nazis' use of Tacitus. Meinecke, for example, in a historical article appearing in 1948, on an entirely different subject, muses that the German "habit of obedience" may have been "an original or native trait." He asks, "[was it] perhaps the spirit of fealty described by Tacitus?"[84] More explicit is Lionel Trilling, the American literary critic, writing in 1950:

> The German racists overlooked all the disagreeable things which Tacitus observed of their ancestors, took note only of his praise of the ancient chastity and independence, and thus made of the *Germania* their anthropological primer.[85]

Finally, Momigliano, in a lecture given in Copenhagen in 1954 on "Some Observations on Causes of War in Ancient Historiography," tells us that no international enterprise has yet compiled a list of "the hundred most dangerous books ever written":

> When it is done, I suggest that Homer's *Iliad* and Tacitus' *Germania* should be given high priority among these hundred dangerous books. This is no reflection on Homer and Tacitus. Tacitus was a gentleman and, for all that I know, Homer was a gentleman too.

> But who will deny that the *Iliad* and the *Germania* raise most unholy passions in the human mind? It is fortunately not my task to speak here about the influence of Tacitus' *Germania*. One horror is enough for one day.[86]

To say the least, Tacitus' image, to the small extent it is cared about it in the twentieth century, has not thrived well since the Nazis.

However, there are four or five recent signs that Tacitus has not been wholly forgotten in the context of other recent political events—although they, too, are gloomy. The first, in 1950, comes from the same Trilling who commented on the uses the Nazis made of the *Germania:* "But these are the aberrations," he qualifies, and "the influence of Tacitus in Europe has been mainly in the service of liberty, as he intended it to be."[87] And, although Tacitus has never meant much in America, a

> reason for our coolness to Tacitus is that, until recently, our political experience gave us no ground to understand what he is talking about. Dictatorship and repression, spies and political informers, blood purges and treacherous dissension, have not been part of our political tradition as they have been of Europe's. But Europe has now come very close to us, and our political education of the last decades fits us to understand the historian of imperial Rome.[88]

Later Trilling speaks of Tacitus as endowed with poise, intellect, love of virtue, and energy but also as a man "utterly without hope" and full of despair.[89] Indeed, Tacitus' subject was not Rome at all "but rather the grotesque career of the human spirit" in a society enduring for no other reason than the maintenance of anarchy—and here lies "his relevance to us now."[90] A second sign, just as dour, was written in 1953 by Francesco Saverio Nitti (1868–1953), a disillusioned old man who had been prime minister of Italy in 1920–21. "Tacitus," he says in his *Memorie e ricordi* (Bari, 1958), "rightly notes that the people are always very inconstant and at the same time fear and desire revolutions."[91] Thus, like Trilling, he too sees Tacitus of value in a time of anarchy and revolution. A third sign, coming in 1968 from Donald R. Dudley, a historian and author of *The World of Tacitus,* offers, like Nitti, a political lesson based on Tacitus which is not very cheerful. He implies a decline of our political vigor and astuteness. He quotes Thomas Jefferson, who in his old age declared that he had "given up newspapers for Tacitus and Thucydides, Newton and Euclid." He then is quick to add that "in our times, the march of progress has established newspapers rather than Tacitus as the required reading for Presidents of the United States.''[92] Of course, Dudley did not then know of Watergate and the resignation of President Nixon; but his comment is all the more poignant from our perspective in 1975. Finally, in July–August 1968, a poem by a certain Christopher Pollock appeared in the *Catholic Worker*, a Chicago newspaper. Its title is ''Pax Americana'':

Dragged backward from sleep
By an embryonic fear
Into the smothered
Darkness of the room
I hear the chronic
Muttering of drains
And dimly hear
The tolling bells
In all the scattered
Valleys of the world
Mourning the young war dead

A volume of Tacitus
Haunts my mind,
Parched blood on the earth
The stones with sticky lips
Crying out,
Prodigies creeping from wombs
And the Roman people
Hiding their eyes
With their hands.

Perhaps the second half of the twentieth century may return to the tradition of the Renaissance. And Tacitus, long buried in classics libraries, may come to life once again.

Notes

Introduction

1. Though Cicero's *De oratore* (discovered in 1422) and others of his principal works rest on very weak manuscript traditions, he has enjoyed one of the most successful survivals of all classical authors. Virgil was also preserved very well, in dozens of manuscripts, at least eight of them being of the fourth and fifth centuries. Caesar is extant in thirty-five complementary manuscripts, Livy in forty-one (though the fifth Decade appears in one only). In general, see the standard references: John Edwin Sandys, *A History of Classical Scholarship*, 3 vols. (New York: Hafner, 1958); Hilda Buttenwieser, "Distribution of the Manuscripts of the Latin Classical Authors in the Middle Ages" (unpublished Ph.D. diss., University of Chicago, 1930), and her article "Popular Authors in the Middle Ages," *Speculum*, vol. 17 (1942); and R. R. Bolgar, *The Classical Heritage and Its Beneficiaries* (New York: Harper & Row, 1964). See also the introductions in the Loeb Classical Library editions.

2. Montaigne, *The Complete Essays of Montaigne*, ed. Donald M. Frame, 3 vols. (New York: Doubleday-Anchor, 1960), 2:376–77. The story about the Emperor Tacitus (A.D. 275–76) comes from Flavius Vopiscus or another author of the unreliable *Historia Augusta* x. 3.

3. Krantz: *Saxonia* (Cologne, 1520), fol. 2, a, verso; cited in Gerald Strauss, *Sixteenth-Century Germany: Its Topography and Topographers* (Madison: University of Wisconsin Press, 1959), pp. 8–9.

4. Tertullian: "ille mendaciorum loquacissimus" (*Apologia* xvi. 3). He devoted a whole page to a brief summary of Tacitus' account of how the Jews, and, from them, the Christians, came to worship the ass (*Historiae* v. 3–4); he then goes on to claim that even Tacitus' account of Pompey in the temple is a fake. Orosius: *Historiae adversum Paganos* i. 5; i. 10; iv. 20; v. 3; vii. 10, 27. There are a few passages, however, where Orosius refrained from criticism and insult: vii. 3 and 9. In one place, vii. 10, he seems to credit Tacitus with being a careful historian, for he says that he "composed this story with the greatest care"—though perhaps he implies "with lying subtlety." Nonetheless, he goes on to argue that Tacitus, like other Roman historians, willfully suppressed the truth on Roman military losses.

5. Saint Jerome: *Commentarii in Zachariam*, iii. 4 (referring to both the *Annales* and the *Historiae* together): "Cornelius Tacitus, qui post Augustum usque ad mortem Domitiani vitas Caesarum triginta voluminibus exaravit." Jerome speaks of "thirty books" because the *Historiae* originally had twelve and the *Annales* eighteen. See Ronald Syme, *Tacitus*, 2 vols. (Oxford: Clarendon Press, 1958), 1:211; 2:686–87; note also John Jackson's introduction to the *Annales* in the Loeb Classical Library, pp. 234–35, n. 2.

6. Severus: *Historiae sacrae* ii. 28. 2 and 29. 1–3.

7. Sidonius: "Carmen ad Consentium" in *Carmina* xxiii. 152–53: "et qui pro ingenio fluente nulli, / Corneli Tacite, es tacendus ori." The pun was translated by W. B. Anderson in the Loeb edition. Sidonius brought in Tacitus here only in a list of Roman authors whom he praises—to show that his friend Consentius is part of a long tradition of genius.

8. Sidonius: *Epistolae* iv. 14 (c. 471–72) to Polemius. See also letter iv. 22 (date uncertain), to Leo, minister of King Euric of the Visigoths and a learned jurist. Leo had advised Sidonius to drop his epistolary art and take up history instead. Sidonius answers that the writing of history is a task better suited to Leo and recalls that Pliny the Younger had turned down a similar request from Tacitus. Sidonius is confused about the letter of Pliny (v. 8), which was not to Tacitus but to Titinius Capito.

9. Cassiodorus: *Variae* v. 2 (edition of Venice, 1533, p. 110): "Haec quodam Cornelio scribente, legitur in interioribus insulis oceani ex arboris succo defluens, unde et succinum dicitur, paulatim solis ardore coalescere." Based on *Germania* xiv.

10. Jordanes: *De origine actibusque Getarum* ii. 13: "Cornelius etiam, annalium scriptor, enarrat metallis plurimis copiosam, herbis frequentem et his feraciorem omnibus, quae pecora magis, quam homines alant: labi vero per eam multa quam maxima relabique flumina gemmas margaritasque voluentia." This passage is the only one in the work in which Jordanes makes a direct reference to Tacitus. In other places (ii. 10–13 and iii. 21) he simply paraphrased him on various details, all from the *Agricola* x–xiii.

11. A good summary, with full references for the many conflicting views by the chief scholars on the question, is provided by Mary Frances Tenney, "Tacitus through the Centuries to the Age of Printing," *University of Colorado Studies* 22, no. 4 (1935): 347–52. And, in particular, see Felice Ramorino, *Cornelio Tacito nella storia della cultura* (Milan: Hoepli, 1898), and F. Haverfield, "Tacitus during the Late Roman Period and the Middle Ages," *Journal of Roman Studies* 6 (1916): 196–220. On Peter of Blois and his assertion that he read Tacitus in his adolescence, see a recent criticism by R. W. Southern, *Medieval Humanism* (New York: Harper & Row, 1970), pp. 117–18: Peter merely copied a statement from John of Salisbury (*Policraticus* viii. 18); and John himself never even read Tacitus. On Otto see the resemblances and parallels hinted at by Charles Christopher Mierow, trans., *The Deeds of Frederick Barbarossa by Otto of Freising and His Continuator, Rahewin* (New York: Norton, 1966), pp. 24, n. 2; 25, n. 3.

12. On the fact of Tacitus' not being in any medieval library catalogues, see Buttenwieser, "Distribution of Manuscripts," p. 160. On the few mentions in the glossaries, see ibid., p. 158, about a negligible thirteenth-century manuscript (Med. Gad. Plut. LXXXIX, Inf. 41) containing a group of historical texts, among them a single passage from the *Annales*. In any case, Tenney, in "Tacitus through the Centuries," p. 347, emphatically states that medieval glossaries "contain not a single comment" on Tacitus; but she could easily have missed Buttenwieser's notice. Also, Remigio Sabbadini, *Le scoperte dei codici latini e greci ne' secoli XIV e XV*, 2 vols. (Florence: Sansoni, 1905–14), 2:8, quotes from the *Flores moralium autoritatum* (Capitolare di Verona, CLXVIII—155), circa 1329: "Cornelius Tacitus, quem Titus imperator suae praefecit biliothecae, Augusti gesta descripsit atque Domitiani." Sabbadini comments that "ciò mostra che non la conosceva" and questions whence "gli deriverà la notizia che sia stato bibliotecario di Tito?" See also below, note 18.

13. Only a rough summary of the salient points of each discovery will follow. The problems are absolutely immense. Indeed, Jürgen von Stackelberg, the recent investigator of the intricacies involved (in *Tacitus in der Romania: Studien zur literarischen Rezeption des Tacitus in Italien und Frankreich* [Tübingen: Max Niemeyer, 1960]), has almost thrown up his hands in despair: "neuere Forschungen [than Sabbadini's] haben, zum Teil

durch kritische Untersuchungen des Bekannten, zum Teil durch neue Funde zu einer Veränderung der Situation, zu Komplikationen geführt, Ungewissheiten und Schwierigkeiten zutage gefördert, die eine entgültige Darstellung nicht mehr oder noch nicht zulassen'' (p. 44). But things are not so complicated as to provide Donald R. Dudley, *The World of Tacitus* (London: Secker & Warburg, 1968), p. 234, any grounds for asserting that these texts were ''discovered about 1430''!

14. E. A. Lowe, ''The Unique Manuscript of Tacitus' *Histories,* Montecassino,'' *Cassinensia* (1929), pp. 264–70, argues a German origin of the manuscript in a very detailed argument resting mainly on the name ''abbas raynaldus'' written on the eleventh-century manuscript in a twelfth-century hand and on the fact that two pages of the Mediceus II were retraced in the thirteenth century. See also Tenney, ''Tacitus through the Centuries,'' pp. 351–52.

15. Boccaccio's friend and student, Benvenuto Rambaldi da Imola, describes (in his commentary on canto xxii of Dante's *Paradiso*) his master's visit to Monte Cassino. Though he mentions no Tacitus manuscript, it is likely that it was there, along with so many others later mined from the library, ''while the grass was growing on the window-sills and the dust reposing on the books and bookshelves. Turning over the manuscripts, he found many rare and ancient works, with whole sheets torn out, or with margins ruthlessly clipped [the former to make psalters; the latter, amulets, to sell to local people]. As he left the room, he burst into tears.'' Cited in Sandys, *History of Classical Scholarship,* 2:13.

16. For example, K. J. Heiling, ''Ein Beitrag zur Geschichte des Mediceus II des Tacitus,'' *Wiener Studien* 53 (1935): 109. See von Stackelberg, *Tacitus in der Romania,* p. 46, who caught the error.

17. According to Heiling, ''Ein Beitrag,'' p. 109.

18. Boccaccio finished *De claris mulieribus* in 1362. The chief support for the assumption that the sections assimilated from Tacitus were added only later, after 1371, is based on Petrarch's ignorance of the discovery. To support the date 1362, it must be assumed that Petrarch did hear of his friend's find but that the evidence for this has been lost; but this would be a rash assertion, built on silence. It is certain that Petrarch was ignorant of Tacitus' writings—though he may have read his name somewhere, perhaps in Saint Jerome or in Severus, or perhaps from his friend Guglielmo da Pastrengo, who heard of Tacitus. Pastrengo, in *De orig. rerum,* fol. 18, quotes the exact strange statement as in note 12 above, about Tacitus' having been Titus' librarian. On Pastrengo, see Georg Voigt, *Die Wiederbelebung des classischen Altertums: Oder, das erste Jahrhundert des Humanismus,* 3d ed., 2 vols. (Berlin: Georg Reiner, 1893), 1:249. But even if Petrarch had read the *De claris mulieribus,* he would not have learned of Tacitus, because Boccaccio used Tacitus without acknowledgment in this work.

19. All citations which I draw directly from Tacitus come from the Loeb Classical Library editions (Cambridge: Harvard University Press): the *Annales,* edited by John Jackson (1962–63); the *Historiae,* by Clifford H. Moore (1962); the *Dialogus,* by Sir William Peterson (1963); the *Agricola* and the *Germania,* by Maurice Hutton (1963). All translations, unless otherwise specified, come from Alfred John Church and William Jackson Brodribb, trans. and ed., *The Complete Works of Tacitus* (New York: Modern Library, 1942).

20. Tacitus *Annales* xiv. 3: ''Anicetus the freedman, placed in charge of the fleet at Misenum and the tutor of the young years of Nero, came upon the idea . . . that it was possible [to construct] a ship'' (my translation).

Boccaccio: ''Agrippina,'' 90: ''by Anicetus, prefect of the fleet before Misenum and his guardian from youth, it was disclosed that a fragile ship could be [built]. . . .'' Cited, along with proof of the parallel, in Pierre de Nolhac, ''Boccaccio et Tacite,'' *Mélanges d'archéologie et d'histoire* 12 (1892): 132.

The passages relate to Nero's consideration of various methods for doing away with his mother.

21. Boccaccio: ''Quaternum quem asportasti Cornelio Tacito quaeso saltem mittas, ne laborem meum frustraveris et libro deformitatem ampliorem addideris.'' Cited in de Nolhac, ''Boccaccio et Tacite,'' pp. 129–30.

22. For example, Roberto Weiss, *The Renaissance Discovery of Classical Antiquity* (Oxford: Basil Blackwell, 1969), p. 43. For another example, see Hans Baron, *The Crisis of the Early Italian Renaissance,* 2d rev. ed. (Princeton: Princeton University Press, 1966), p. 475, n. 21. Weiss and Baron follow Giuseppe Billanovich in his review of von Stackelberg's *Tacitus in der Romania* in *Romance Philology* 17, no. 3 (February 1964): 696. Billanovich earlier expressed this view in *I primi umanisti e le tradizioni dei classici latini* (Fribourg, Switz.: Edizioni universitarie, 1953).

23. Such noncommittal citations no doubt can support Hans Nachod (in his introduction to the Petrarch section of Ernst Cassirer et al., *The Renaissance Philosophy of Man* [Chicago: University of Chicago Press, 1963], p. 26), who contends that Boccaccio may have known some authors who had escaped the attention of Petrarch, ''but lacking Petrarch's imagination he remained satisfied with the factual knowledge to be derived from classical literature by dry though devoted application.''

24. Sicco Polentone: ''Librorum eius [Taciti] numerum affirmare satis certe non audeo: fragmenta equidem libri undecimi et reliquos deinceps ad vigesimum primum vidi, in quis vitam Claudii et qui fuerunt postea Caesares ad Vespasianum usque ornate ac copiose enarravit'' (Cod. Riccardiano 121, fol. 65). Cited in Remigio Sabbadini, *Storia e critica di testi latini,* 2d ed. (Padua: Editrice Antenore, 1971), p. 186. This edition, the first since 1914, contains an important bibliography (pp. xi–xli) of Sabbadini's widely scattered writings. See also Tenney, ''Tacitus through the Centuries,'' p. 355, n. 114.

25. Poggio to Niccoli: ''Cornelium Tacitum, cum venerit, observabo penes me occulte. Scio enim omnem illam cantilenam, et unde exierit, et per quem, et quis eum sibi vendicet, sed nil dubites, non exibit a me ne verbo quidem.'' From *Poggii Epistolae . . . ordine chronologico disposuit notisque illustravit,* ed. Thomas de Tonnelis, 3 vols. (Florence: Typis L. Marchini & typis delle Murate, 1832–61), vol. 3, letter no. 14, of 27 September 1427. Other letters concerning the Mediceus II are nos. 5 (23 October 1426), 15 (21 October 1427), and 17 (5 June 1428). The letters are now translated into English by Phyllis Walter Goodhart Gordon, *Two Renaissance Book Hunters: The Letters of Poggius Bracciolini to Nicolaus de Niccolis,* Records of Civilization: Sources and Studies, vol. 91 (New York: Columbia University Press, 1974). For the letter at hand, Gordon dates it *25* September 1427—her no. LI. For the other Mediceus II letters listed, see her nos. XLVIII (which she dates *21* October 1426), LII, and LVII.

26. Poggio to Niccoli, *Poggii Epistolae,* vol. 3, no. 15 (21 October 1427): ''Misisti mihi librum Senecae et Cornelium Tacitum, quod est mihi gratum; at is est litteris longobardis, et maiori ex parte caducis, quod si scissem liberassem te eo labore. Legi olim quemdam apud vos manens litteris antiquis, nescio Colucii ne esset an alterius. Illum cupio habere vel alium, qui legi possit. Nam difficile erit reperire scriptorem, qui hanc codicem recte legat; ideo cura ut alium habeam si fieri potest, potueris autem si volueris nervos intendere.'' Cf. Gordon, *Two Renaissance Book Hunters,* letter no. LII.

27. Poggio to Niccoli, *Poggii Epistolae,* vol. 3, no. 17 (5 June 1428): ''Dedi Bar-

tholomaeo de Bardis Decadem Livii, et Cornelium Tacitum, ut illos ad te mittat: in tuo Cornelio deficiunt plures chartae variis in locis." Cf. Gordon, no. LVII.

28. See M. Lehnherdt, "Enoche von Ascoli und die *Germania* des Tacitus," *Hermes* 33 (1898): 499–505. For the views of Clarence W. Mendell and Remigio Sabbadini, see below in the text.

29. Poggio to Niccoli, *Poggii Epistolae,* vol. 3, no. 14 (27 September 1427): "De Cornelio Tacito, qui est in Germania, nil sentio; expecto responsum ab illo monacho. Nicolaus Treverensis nondum recessit. De libris nil postea audivi. Heri, cum ipsum hac de re interrogassem, dixit se nil certa habere. Omisi hanc curam librorum absentium, et ad eos, qui adsunt nobis animum converti: nam nil audio praeter fabulas." Cf. Gordon, no. LI. Other letters concerning the "minor works" are vol. 2, no. 34 (3 November 1425—the first hint of their existence; cf. Gordon, no. XLII) and vol. 3, nos. 12 (17 May 1427; cf. Gordon, no. XLIX—which she dates *15* May 1427) and 29 (26 February 1428; cf. Gordon, no. LXVI—which she dates 26 February *1429*).

30. Vol. 2, no. 34 (3 November 1425): "aliqua opera Cornelii Taciti nobis ignota."

31. See the large extracts from their letters in Sabbadini, *Storia e critica,* pp. 195–200, and the excellent analysis following.

32. The list is published by Rodney P. Robinson, "The Inventory of Niccolò Niccoli," *Classical Philology* 16 (1921): 251–55.

33. Note especially *Tacitus: The Man and His Work* (New Haven: Yale University Press, 1957); "Tacitus: Literature: 1948–1953," *Classical Weekly,* vol. 48/49 (1955); and, particularly for the context at hand, "The Discovery of the Minor Works of Tacitus," *American Journal of Philology* 56 (1935): 113–30, and "Manuscripts of Tacitus' Minor Works," *Memoirs of the American Academy in Rome* 19 (Yale University Press, 1949): 135–45.

34. "Manuscripts of Tacitus' Minor Works," p. 136. Mendell says it was Herbert Bloch who discovered this quotation from the *Agricola* by Peter in 1941; see Bloch's "A Manuscript of Tacitus' *Agricola* in Monte Cassino about A.D. 1135," *Classical Philology,* vol. 36, no. 2 (1941).

35. Mendell, "Manuscripts of Tacitus' Minor Works," p. 142.

36. Remigio Sabbadini (1850–1934) is still a standard authority in many works on the revival of classical antiquity during the Renaissance, most notably in *Storia e critica di testi latini* and *Le scoperte,* both cited above.

37. Sabbadini, *Le scoperte,* p. 166, provided Decembrio's whole lengthy account.

38. Ibid., pp. 141–42: "che otto fogli del codice hersfeldese, contenenti il nucleo di nezzo dell' *Agricola,* sono state recentissimamente ritrovati a Iesi, . . . e descritto dal Decembrio . . .; [and] donde conchiudiamo che Enoch portò seco l'archetipo hersfeldese."

39. It was not until Justus Lipsius' great Tacitus edition of 1574 that six and not five books were differentiated.

40. Letter of Soderini, cited in von Stackelberg, *Tacitus in der Romania,* p. 52; "Videbis enim nostros homines supra millesimum et quingentesimum annum Florentinos appellatos apud Populum Romanum in honore fuisse: si quidem ex Germania nobis allatus fuit proxime pervetustus in membrana codex, descriptus litteris non multum distantibus a longobardis cuius auctor inscribitur P. Cornelius in quinque libros digestus, ab excessu divi Augusti usque ad interitum Tiberii acta populi Romani domestica externaque complectens. Et nomen auctoris, et stili gravitas, et ordo narrationis faciunt, ut iudicemus id opus esse Cornelii Taciti; sed quicumque sit auctor, liber est antiquus et pene venerandus. In eo narrantur Florentini auditi fuisse, cum nollent Clanim in Arnum derivari, et eorum

postulatis ex S. C. [senatu consulto] fuisse satisfactum. Verba auctoris hac epistola inclusimus, ut tu, et vetustate patriae nobiscum gaudeas. . . .'' The praenomen initial ''P'' for Publius, appearing in Mediceus I at the subscriptions to books i and iii of the *Annales* is the first instance of this name. Sidonius Apollinaris twice uses ''Gaius.'' See Syme, *Tacitus,* 1:59 (cited in n. 5, above).

41. See Giovio, quoted in von Stackelberg, *Tacitus in der Romania,* p. 67.

42. Tacitus is itemized as the seventh book in the fifth bank. The inventory (October 1451) is published by M. Goldmann, ''Drei italienische Handschriftenkataloge, s. XIII–XV,'' *Centralblat für Bibliothekswesen* 4 (1887): 137–55. But there are more problems over the early manuscript tradition of Mediceus II just because of this inventory item (p. 151). For, although the scribe correctly gave the beginning words of *Historiae* i. 1, he ended the entry with ''finis vero in penultima carta *machina acessura erat,*'' words which do not occur in any known portion of Tacitus, nor does anyone seem to know whether any other extant ancient used them—especially since it is known that Tacitus was bound with some Apuleius in this library.

43. See the quotations from this letter of Sarzana in Sabbadini, *Storia e critica,* pp. 251–52.

44. Ibid., p. 252. Bessarion, cardinal of Tusculum and legate to Bologna, had it copied in Bologna in October 1453. The copyist received fourteen ducats for his work. I refer to the *Cento codici bessarionei: Catalogo di mostra,* of the Marciana Library in Venice (Venice: Liberia Vecchia del Sansovino, 31 May–30 September 1968), exhibit no. 97, pp. 93–94. An appendix contains the Latin text of Bessarion's own inventory of his 482 Greek and 264 Latin volumes, which he bequeathed to Venice.

45. Sabbadini, *Storia e critica,* p. 252.

46. Ibid.

47. Though there are tantalizing ''leads'' here and there. For example, Hutton, in his introduction to the *Agricola* in the Loeb Classical Library edition, refers to an *Agricola* MS recently found in Toledo, copied between 1471 and 1474. Note also those in Paul Oskar Kristeller, *Iter Italicum: A Finding List of Uncatalogued or Incompletely Catalogued Humanistic Manuscripts of the Renaissance in Italian and Other Libraries,* 2 vols. (London: Warburg Institute, 1967): vol. 1, p. 60 (*Germania*—Ferrara); p. 189 (*Germania*—Florence); p. 241 (*Agricola*—Genoa); vol. 2, p. 319 (*Agricola*—Rome); p. 440 (*Dialogus*—Rome).

48. As listed by Maria Valenti, *Saggio di una bibliografia delle edizioni di Tacito nei secolo XV–XVII* (Rome: Edizini de ''L'Italia che scrive,'' 1951). Valenti gives 113 items in all, dating from 1470 to 1687, including reprints of different versions. See also the introductions to the Loeb Classical Library editions.

49. Puteolanus or his publisher may have heard that Pomponeo Laeto, the famous Roman antiquarian and troublemaker for Pope Paul II, had to go through the trouble of making his own copy of the *Agricola* for insertion into the leaves of his Vindelinus edition. On Laeto's manuscript see Hutton, introduction to Loeb ed., p. 149. It is listed in Kristeller, *Iter Italicum,* 2:319.

50. This probability is only my conjecture concerning Puteolanus' connection with the Hersfeld MS and Decembrio—and it is likely to remain so. Puteolanus' MS of the *Agricola* (probably used in preparation of his edition), along with the MS of the dedicatory epistle, was almost certainly lost in Genoa in World War II; see Kristeller, *Iter Italicum,* 1:241. I bring up my conjecture again in chapter 1.

51. For information on translations I rely mainly on four lists: (1) Else-Lilly Etter's, in

her *Tacitus in der Geistesgeschichte des 16. und 17. Jahrhunderts* (Basel: Helbing & Lichtenhahn, 1966), pp. 214–15; (2) von Stackelberg's tables in his *Tacitus in der Romania*, pp. 275–76; (3) Bolgar's, in his *The Classical Heritage* (see n. 1 above), appendix II, pp. 536–37; and (4) the various introductions to Tacitus' works in the Loeb editions.

52. See M. Radlkofer, "Die älteste Verdeutschung der *Germania* des Tacitus durch Johann Eberlin," *Blätter für das Bayerische Gymnasialschulwesen* 23 (1887): 1–16.

Chapter 1

1. Of much importance to this chapter is Hans Baron's *Crisis of the Early Italian Renaissance*. There are two editions, published by Princeton University Press in 1955 and 1966. The first, in two volumes with continuous pagination, contains more complete documentation. In these notes the editions will be referred to as "Baron, *Crisis*, 1955" and "Baron, *Crisis*, 1966." The former is cited only when necessary.

2. " . . . che è giunto il Messia," as Francesco di Vannozzo of Padua put it. See Baron, *Crisis*, 1966, pp. 37, 471.

3. Tacitus *Historiae* i. 1. And compare the first sentence of the *Dialogus*, where Tacitus decries the blight of ignorant orators. Of course, Bruni could not have known of this work.

4. Bruni: *Laudatio florentinae urbis*, L, fol. 144v: "Nam posteaquam res publica in unius potestatem deducta est, preclara illa ingenia (ut inquit Cornelius) abiere." Translated by Baron and cited in *Crisis*, 1966, pp. 58 and 475, n. 20. Baron notes that Bruni must have been quoting Tacitus from memory, for, where Bruni has "preclara illa ingenia," Tacitus said "magna illa ingenia." The change from "great" to "brilliant" betrays an unconscious exaggeration on Bruni's part. Poggio too, arguing against Guarino da Verona (see later in the chapter), uses the words "illa praeclara ingenia"; but see Baron, *Crisis*, 1966, pp. 478–79, n. 41. The first printed edition of the *Laudatio* is in Baron's *From Petrarch to Leonardo Bruni: Studies in Humanistic and Political Literature* (Chicago: University of Chicago Press for the Newberry Library, 1968), pp. 232–63. On Tacitus, see ibid., p. 247.

5. Baron, *Crisis*, 1966, p. 58.

6. "Cornerstone" is not too much of an exaggeration for Baron's reference to the Bruni quotation from Tacitus as "the pivot" (*Crisis*, 1966, p. 66), upon which turned the further development of civic humanism in the debate between Poggio and Guarino. See also Baron, *From Petrarch to Leonardo Bruni*, p. 154, where a similar point is made.

7. Baron, *Crisis*, 1966, pp. 59, 60. Baron's emphasis on Bruni's exaggeration of Tacitus' statement in *Historiae* i. 1, cannot be questioned. As to the larger context, however, note that Michael Grant (*Roman Literature*, rev. ed. [Baltimore: Penguin, 1964], p. 108) stresses the fact that the evil of rule by one man is perhaps the "central point" of Tacitus' philosophy. Baron, differing somewhat, admits Tacitus' "acceptance of the imperial monarchy as an historical necessity" (*Crisis*, 1966, p. 59). Of related interest is Donald J. Wilcox' criticism of Baron in *The Development of Florentine Humanist Historiography in the Fifteenth Century* (Cambridge, Mass.: Harvard University Press, 1969), p. 73, where he says that Baron missed an element of Tacitus used by Bruni—the idea that the republic died from internal causes and that the empire was a necessary evil. Still, he cautions, Bruni was not *thoroughly* receptive to this Tacitan element. Finally, note my text, pp. 22–23.

8. See Baron, *Crisis*, 1966, p. 62, and his bibliography on p. 477, nn. 30, 31.

9. Frances Tenney, "Tacitus through the Centuries to the Age of Printing," *University of Colorado Studies* 22 (1935): 354 and n. 105, suggests (basing herself on opinions of Felice Ramorino and Gerhard Voigt) that Rambaldi may have cited from memory or may have taken his material from Boccaccio's works.

10. On *Inferno* v. 63, on Cleopatra: "Cleopatra adulterata est cum omnibus regibus orientalibus, ut dicit Cornelius Tacitus" ("Cleopatra committed adultery with all the kings of the Orient, as Cornelius Tacitus says"); cited by Tenney, ibid., p. 354, n. 105.

On the death of Seneca: "ille intravit balneum cum flebotomia, prout haec patent apud Cornelium Tacitum" ("he entered the bath and opened up his veins, according as these things are revealed by Cornelius Tacitus"), on *Inferno* iv. 141, cited by Tenney, ibid., n. 106.

11. Bandino (c. 1335–c. 1418) spent half his life compiling his *Fons*. He probably began it around 1370. Jürgen von Stackelberg says that it was 1370 or later (*Tacitus in der Romania: Studien zur literarischen Rezeption des Tacitus in Italien und Frankreich* [Tübingen: Max Niemeyer, 1960], p. 270); Tenney implies that it was after 1373 ("Tacitus through the Centuries," p. 354); Pierre de Nolhac simply says that it was toward the end of the fourteenth century ("Boccaccio et Tacite," *Mélanges d'archéologie et d'histoire* 12 [1892]: 297).

12. The *Fons* manuscript: Cod. Laur. Aedil., fols. 170, 171, 172. The Tacitus citations on the women, influenced by Boccaccio's uses, are in fol. 172, except for Venus (fol. 171). It has never been published. See Tenney, "Tacitus through the Centuries," p. 354, nn. 108, 109, where most of the Tacitus citations are collected.

13. "Cornelius Tacitus, orator et hystoricus eloquentissimus, prout eius probant hystorie quas cum multo lepore legimus." From "De viris claris" in the *Fons*, Cod. Laur. Aedil., fol. 172c. 120A, cited in Tenney, p. 354, n. 109. It is also cited in Francesco Novati, ed., *Epistolario di Coluccio Salutati*, 4 vols. (Fonti per la storia d'Italia, vols. 15–18) (Rome: Forzani e C. Tipografi del Senato, 1891–1911), 2:297.

14. "sed singulariter perierunt hystorie; de quo quidem mecum nequeo consolari. ubinam sunt annales Ennii, Quadrigarii, Gnei Gellii, Q. Claudii, L. Pisonis aut Fabii? . . . ubi Cornelius Nepos, ubi Tacitus, ubi Tranquillus? . . . ubi sunt et alii infiniti?" In a letter of Salutati to Juan Fernandez di Heredia of 1 February 1392(?) from Florence; published in Novati, ed. *Epistolario di Coluccio Salutati*, 2:297. This letter used to be dated 1 February 1377, but Novati, in a long and very detailed argument, proposes 1 February 1392. The later date is not questioned by B. L. Ullman in his "Observations on Novati's Edition of Salutati's Letters," *Studies in the Renaissance* (Rome: Edizioni di Storia e Letteratura, 1955), chap. 9, pp. 201–40, esp. p. 222. By early 1392, then, Salutati still had not read Tacitus.

Of course, one could assert that Salutati, having read what was available, complained only of those *parts* of Tacitus still lost, but there is no evidence to support this view. If Bandino had read Tacitus (about whom he was so enthusiastic) before 1392, would he not have mentioned this to his dear friend, Salutati? From reading the dozen letters of Salutati to Bandino (none of Bandino's replies is extant) and from the affectionate and ecstatic biography of Salutati by Bandino (see Novati, 4:501–8), it is impossible to deny the depth of their friendship. The letters reveal a constant exchange of information and of books between them. Noteworthy here is the *elenchus* of all his books which Bandino sent to Salutati in 1377 (Novati, 1:276), which, apparently did not contain a Tacitus—for the latter was still ignorant of him in 1392. Considering the Tacitus problem in the light of this *elenchus* of 1377, Novati was probably right, in one of his suggestions (note in 2:297) that "il Bandini venisse più tardi in possesso di un codice Tacitiano." Thus, if Salutati had no knowledge of Tacitus before 1392, it is probable that Bandino also had none. But by 1 August 1395 (see the following note) Salutati had read Tacitus. So Bandino could have read Tacitus for the first time, and passed him on to Salutati, any time between 1 February 1392 and 1 August 1395.

15. "Nam quid de Cornelio Tacito referam, qui, licet eruditissimus foret, nedum proximos illos equare non potuit, sed a Livio, quem non sequendum solum hystorie serie, sed imitandum eloquentia sibi proposuit, longe discessit?" Salutati, *Epistolario*, Novati ed., 3:76–91, 81–82. Dated 1 August 1395, Florence, to Cardinal Bishop Bartolommeo Oliari.

16. Rambaldi, translated by Baron, *Crisis*, 1966, p. 51; and the Latin on p. 478, n. 36: ". . . sed quando, quomodo, vel per quem fateor me nescire" (from the *Commentum* on *Inferno* xv); see also Baron, *Crisis*, 1955, pp. 463–64 for much longer quotations from the same passage.

17. Ronald Witt, in "Coluccio Salutati and the Origins of Florence," *Il Pensiero Politico* 2, no. 2 (August 1969): 161–72, provides a good analysis of the literary and political interconnections behind Salutati's conclusion.

18. Baron, *Crisis*, 1955, p. 61, says that Salutati's argument was "a critical performance which has no parallel in Bruni's *Laudatio*."

19. Rambaldi: "Sic adeo mors illa indignissima visa est displicuisse Deo et hominibus." Cited in Baron, *Crisis*, 1966, p. 498, n. 19, and translated on p. 154. Petrarch (*De gestis Caesaris*) concluded: "ut evidenter ostenderetur caedem illam nec Deo nec hominibus placuisse." Cited in Baron, *Crisis*, 1966, p. 499, n. 19.

20. Rambaldi: "sed uterque petebat regnum, uterque ingratus patriae, . . ." Again, close to Petrarch: "ut utriusque partis merita non usque adeo, ut putantur, imparia et utrumque . . . regnare voluisse . . . constaret." Both passages are cited in Baron, *Crisis*, 1966, p. 499, n. 22.

21. Salutati: *De tyranno*, iv. 19–20: "Quare concludamus illos Cesaris occisores non tyrannum occidisse, sed patrem patrie et clementissimum ac legitimum principem orbis terre. . . ." Cited in Baron, *Crisis*, 1955, p. 503, n. 36, but not translated by Baron in his discussion of the passage on pp. 135–36. See also the 1966 edition, esp. pp. 146–51.

22. It is almost unnecessary to say that Salutati considered Giangaleazzo a true tyrant; the *Invectiva* (written in 1397–98) is only the strongest proof of this fact. And even though Salutati defended Caesar in the *De tyranno*, the contrast is only apparent and not real. Hence the surprise of some scholars is unwarranted. Baron (*Crisis*, 1966, p. 100) exclaims that "the composition of a book so monarchical in tenor as the *De tyranno*, by the chancellor of Florence, in the midst of the Florentine-Milanese struggle, is an astounding phenomenon." Berthold L. Ullman, in *The Humanism of Coluccio Salutati* (Padua: Editrice Antenore, 1963), p. 33, is equally disturbed at this ostensible contradiction: "It is surprising that Coluccio, brilliant defender of free Florence, should defend Caesarism and monarchy." Still, Baron attempts to resolve his problem by distinguishing between Salutati the chancellor (author of the *Invectiva*) and Salutati the humanist (author of the *De tyranno*). Ullman, trying to resolve the difficulty, states that perhaps the *De tyranno* was merely an *opus ad hoc*, i.e., to answer a few questions put by a young Paduan student.

However, there is no need for such bifurcation of either the man or his works. Salutati, as both chancellor and humanist, was not contradictory in his views because he sanctioned Caesar, a legitimate ruler (hence, not a tyrant) but denounced Giangaleazzo, an illegitimate ruler (a tyrant). Salutati was not Bruni the revolutionary, who objected to any one-man rule. To Salutati, one-man rule by Caesar was all right because Caesar was accepted by the Roman people (hence he was not a ruler *defectu tituli* and therefore not a tyrant) and because his rule was most clement (hence he was not a ruler with *superbia* and therefore not a tyrant). Besides, in Salutati's time a republic and a monarchy were often held by one man but with different ends in view.

23. Baron, *Crisis*, 1966, pp. 147 and 242.

24. *De laudibus Mediolanensium urbis panegyricus*. The version of 1436 has not been preserved. The work is published today, after an edition from Decembrio's last years (around 1473) in *Archivio Storico Lombardo*, 4th ser. 8 (1907): 27–45. See also Baron, *Crisis*, 1966, pp. 69–70, and the appropriate notes there.

25. Decembrio, *Panegyricus:* "Pene oblitus es: Ciceronem, Livium et in primis Maronem, divina ingenia, Cesaris et Augusti temporibus . . . floruisse. Quo igitur illa preclara ingenia, ut Cornelius inquit, abiere?" Cited in Baron, *Crisis*, 1966, p. 481, n. 44, and paraphrased by Baron on p. 70.

26. See Baron, *Crisis*, 1966, pp. 66–69 and 478–80, nn. 41–43b.

27. Poggio: *Defensiuncula contra Guarinum Veronensem*. In the passage cited in the next note, Poggio used the words "praeclara ingenia." Baron (*Crisis*, 1966, pp. 478–79, n. 41) calls attention to these words from the *Laudatio* to prove that Poggio had it in mind when he wrote.

28. Translated by Baron, *Crisis*, 1966, pp. 66–67, and cited on pp. 478–79, n. 41: Poggio, having just made a full quotation from *Historiae* i. 1, continues: "Cum ergo et Senecae verbis, quibus illa praeclara ingenia Ciceronis aetate nata esse, deinde in deterius decrevisse affirmat, et Taciti testimonio asserentis [edition of 1538: asserentes] magna illa ingenia post imperium ad unum delatum defecisse apertissime constet quanta iactura sit secuta in literis latinis libertate amissa, rectissime scripsisse me dico . . . latinam eloquentiam corruisse."

29. Translated by Baron, *Crisis*, 1966, p. 67.

30. For these ideas, both in Bruni's works and in works by later authors, on Rome's fate under the empire, see Baron, *Crisis*, 1966, p. 66, and esp. *Crisis*, 1955, p. 465. Baron refers to the "rich collection of the material" of authors later than Bruni in E. Santini, "La fortuna della Storia Fiorentina di L. Bruni nel Rinascimento," *Studi Storici* 20 (1911): 177–95. For the influence of Florentine writers on non-Florentines, Baron refers to the first chapter of W. K. Ferguson's *The Renaissance in Historical Thought* (Boston, 1948).

31. B. L. Ullman, *The Humanism of Coluccio Salutati*, p. 14, mentions Salutati's own account of the incident in 1391 (cf. Novati, 4:251).

32. See the Introduction. Poggio complained of the barely legible manuscript Niccoli had sent him. Despite Poggio's promises to keep secret what must have been the archetype, Niccoli probably never complied. So Salutati now asked Niccoli for the good manuscript that he remembers Niccoli once allowed him to read. It is hard to say whether Poggio ever got it. However, the point here is that not many good copies were available.

33. See Nicolai Rubinstein, *The Government of Florence under the Medici* (Oxford: Oxford University Press, 1966).

34. Bruni wrote the pamphlet in Greek: Περὶ τῆς πολιτείας τῶν Φλωρεντίνων. See Baron, *Crisis*, 1966, pp. 427–28 and 559–60, nn. 37–39, where Baron cites large passages from a Latin translation.

35. From a letter of a certain Nicodemo, an intimate of Cosimo and servant of Francesco Sforza, of 8 August 1458. Cited in Ferdinand Schevill, *Medieval and Renaissance*

Florence, 2 vols. (New York: Harper & Row, 1963), 2:366. See also Rubinstein, *The Government of Florence under the Medici*, chap. 5, "The Parlamento of 1458 and the Consolidation of the Régime," pp. 88–135, esp. 105–6. Note also Paul O. Kristeller, *Renaissance Thought II: Papers on Humanism and the Arts* (New York: Harper & Row, 1965), esp. pp. 46–47. Finally, see Eugenio Garin, "The Humanist Chancellors of the Florentine Republic from Coluccio Salutati to Bartolomeo Scala," in *Portraits from the Quattrocento*, translated by Victor A. Velen and Elizabeth Velen (New York: Harper & Row, 1972), pp. 1–29, esp. 18–19.

36. Alberti's five uses of Tacitus were based, respectively, on *Historiae* ii. 49 (where Alberti missed the correct meaning of "modicum et mansurum"; what Tacitus meant was "would endure if modest because it would not be despoiled"); *Annales*, xv. 43 (referring to volcanic stone); *Historiae* v. 11; and *Annales* xv. 43. I have not been able to place the last reference (having to do with the space next to city walls). Tenney, "Tacitus through the Centuries," p. 357, n. 129, was of help for two of the references.

37. For biographical information on Biondo and information on his works, consult three fine studies: Denys Hay, "Flavio Biondo and the Middle Ages," *Proceedings of the British Academy* 45 (1959): 97–128; Bartolomeo Nogara's 183-page introduction to his edition of the *Scritti inediti e rari di Biondo Flavio* (Rome: Tipografia Poliglotta Vaticana, 1927); and Alfred Masius, *Flavio Biondo: Sein Leben und seine Werke* (Lepizig: B. G. Teubner, 1879), a work still very useful even after Nogara.

38. Flavio Biondo, *Roma instaurata; De origine et gestis Venetorum;* and *Italia illustrata* (n.p., 1481–82); the same works, together with the *Decades* (Basel: Froben, 1531). Using the latter edition, Tenney, "Tacitus through the Centuries," p. 357, n. 128, points out eleven references to Tacitus in the *Roma instaurata:* i. 43, 45, 64, 72, 99; ii. 55, 89, 108, 114; iii. 42, 77. These, and one that she missed—the reference to the Lacus Curtius (*Roma instaurata* ii. 45)—are all in the incunabulum I used.

39. Hay, "Flavio Biondi and the Middle Ages," p. 121.

40. Hanna H. Gray, "History and Rhetoric in Quattrocento Humanism" (Ph.D. diss., Radcliffe College, 1957), p. 264. Gray illustrates her argument by a thorough examination of Giovanni Pontano's *Actius*. (On Pontano, see below in the text.) Also, see Gray's "Renaissance Humanism: The Pursuit of Eloquence," in *Renaissance Essays*, ed. Paul O. Kristeller and Philip P. Wiener (New York: Harper & Row, 1968), pp. 199–216; this essay originally appeared in the *Journal of the History of Ideas* 24, no. 4 (1963): 497–514. Note too that Charles Trinkaus comes to similar conclusions on the close association between rhetoric and history. See his analysis of Bartolomeo della Fonte's *Oratio in historiae laudatione* (1482) in "A Humanist's Image of Humanism: The Inaugural Orations of Bartolomeo della Fonte," *Studies in the Renaissance* 7 (1960): 90–147.

41. Moreover, after Poggio's discovery of Cicero's *De oratore* in 1422, humanists had Cicero's authority with which to buttress their condemnation of "the advocate's stinging epigram" (*De oratore* ii. 15) as unsuitable to good historiographical style. More than a century later this trait became one of Tacitus' best stylistic distinctions.

42. *Laurentii Vallae in Barptolemaeum* [sic] *Facium Ligurem invectivarum seu recriminationum libri iv*, in *Opera Omnia*, edited by Eugenio Garin, 2 vols. Monumenta politica et philosophica rariora, nos. 5 and 6 (Torino: Bottega d'Erasmo, 1962), 1:460–632. The *Recriminations* is an offprint of the 1540 Basel edition. Both Sabbadini, *Le scoperte*, p. 253, n. 3, and Tenney, "Tacitus through the Centuries," p. 357, n. 129 (following Sabbadini), note six references, though without context. In the Garin edition: p. 475 (*Annales* xi. 29); p. 516 (*Annales* xv. 67); p. 518 (*Annales* xiii. 48—incorrectly

given as xiii. 47 by Sabbadini); p. 529 (*Annales* xii. 5); p. 531 (*Annales* xiv. 47, xv. 6 and *Historiae* iii. 73); and p. 595 (*Annales* xiv. 49). The reference on p. 518 is to the legation from Puteoli (modern Pozzuoli), near Naples. In the other references—e.g., the one on page 516, where Tacitus is shown to have used the words "sesquipes" and "sesquiplaga"—Valla quotes from Tacitus. For details on the conflict with Fazio, see Roberto Valentini, "Le invettive di Bartolomeo Facio contro Lorenzo Valla," *Atti della R. Accedemia dei Lincei,* Classe di Scienze morali, storiche, e filologiche ser. 5, 15 (1906): 493–550. I follow Felix Gilbert, *Machiavelli and Guicciardini: Politics and History in Sixteenth Century Florence* (Princeton: Princeton University Press, 1965), p. 217, on Valla's historical realism.

A hitherto unnoticed reference of Valla to Tacitus occurs in the *Opera Omnia* (Garin ed., 2:125). It is contained in the *Epistolae familiares* (2:115–30), which is an offprint of the Venice edition of 1503. The letter—number six of the collection—is to Ioannes Aretino; it is important because in it Valla says he has just read Tacitus. Unfortunately, unlike some of the others, it is undated, though the whole collection dates from 1435–38, when Valla was with King Alfonso.

43. In Valla's *Disputatio ad Alphonsum,* cited in H. J. Erasmus, *The Origins of Rome in Historiography from Petrarch to Perizonius,* Bibliotheca classica vangorcumiana, no. 11 (New York: Van Gorcum, 1962), p. 29.

44. For instance, by Federigo da Montefeltro, duke of Urbino and enthusiastic bibliophile—but along with almost any ancient author he could get his hands on. In Tacitus he was not especially involved. Instead, it was Caesar whom (according to Vespasiano) "he praised beyond measure" and Livy whom he had read to him at meals. See *Vespasiano: Renaissance Princes, Popes and Prelates. The Vespasiano Memoirs: Lives of Illustrious Men of the XVth. Century,* translated by William George and Emily Waters (New York: Harper & Row, 1963), pp. 99–105, esp. p. 100. This being the case, there is no basis for Denis Mark Smith's statement that Federigo "was especially fond of Tacitus and the *Commentaries* of Caesar" in "Federigo da Montefeltro," *Renaissance Profiles,* ed. J. H. Plumb (New York: Harper & Row, 1965), p. 134.

45. Puteolanus: "quae me ita afficit, delectat, tenet, ut nihil unquam pari voluptate legerim." From Puteolanus' prefatory epistle to Jacobus Antiquarius, secretary to the duke of Milan, in his edition of the *Agricola,* published together with works of Pliny the Younger and Petronius (Milan, 1476; an edition not listed by Valenti, *Saggio*). The preface is published in B. Botfield, ed., *Praefationes et epistolae editionibus principibus auctorum veterum* (Cambridge, Eng.: At the University Press, 1861), pp. 158–60.

46. Puteolanus, in a preface to the same Antiquarius, but in his edition of all Tacitus' works then known (Milan, c. 1475–80); published in Botfield, ed., *Praefationes,* pp. 160–63; see esp. p. 162: "multis vigiliis intentissimoque studio."

47. Ibid., p. 162: "Veneti enim impressores adeo inculcaverant ac foedaverant hoc divinum opus ut non modo Cornelianae facundiae majestas inquinaretur, sed vix sensus ullus conjectari posset. Quid ego effecerim judicent docti, sed collatis exemplaribus."

48. See above, Introduction, page 14, and n. 50.

49. In Botfield, ed., *Praefationes,* pp. 162–63: "Quo artificio omnes mea sententia facile vicit, ita creber rerum frequentia, ut verborum prope numerum sententiarum numero sequatur. Ita dein verbis aptus et pressus, ut nescias utrum res oratione, an verba sententiis illustrentur. In contionibus (audeo enim promere quod sentio) Livio quoque anteferendus, magis tamen Salustii argutam densitatem quam hujus amplitudinem imitatus, . . . semper artificiosa docebit varietate, immensaque jucunditate delectabit."

50. Published in *Giovanni Pontano: I Dialoghi*, edited, with an introduction, by Carmelo Previtera (Florence: Sansoni, 1943), pp. 123–239. On the *Actius* see the following: Myron P. Gilmore, *Humanists and Jurists* (Cambridge, Mass.: Harvard University Press, 1963), pp. 44–49; Gilbert, *Machiavelli and Guicciardini*, pp. 203–5; and Gray, "History and Rhetoric," esp. the appendix, pp. 265–326, which contains a translation from the Previtera edition, pp. 192–203, 208–31—the main sections of Altilius on history.

51. Translated by Gray, "History and Rhetoric," pp. 325–26, from the Previtera edition, p. 231: "Quid, obsecro, tam est adversum quam vanitas historiae, quae vitae magistra esse dicitur? Elegantiam iccirco dicendi maximam hac praesertim in parte exigimus, quod haec ipsa scribendi pars permultis sit aliis laudibus ac virtutibus caritura. Itaque compensetur utique elegantia quod deerit de cultu coeteroque splendore, . . . nam quanquam et Tacitus et Curtius abunde sunt laudibus ac virtutibus ornati suis, laus tamen omnis Latinae historiae penes duos putatur existere diversoque in dicendi genere, Livium ac Sallustium. Ad haec iniquitas temporum Trogum nobis omnino abstulit, et Curtium ac Tacitum quasi mutilatas videmus statuas, licetque suspicari potius ac coniicere quam omnino de iis iudicium aliquod absolutum ac certum tradere."

52. All three references are in the *Actius* (in the Previtera edition): on page 137, two examples from Tacitus on the use of "plenus" (*Dialogus* xxxiii. 23 and *Historiae* i. 2) and, on page 220, that Sallust wrote about the origin of the Mauri (Moors) and Tacitus on the Jews. Pontano adds that these things are pleasant to read but that they should be related with great care and discretion, "since matters of this kind are either doubtful or mythical" (Gray translation, in "History and Rhetoric," p. 306).

53. " . . . longe abest a pristina dignitate et gratia." Rucellai, in a letter to Roberto Acciaiuoli, published in *Sylloges Epistolarum a viris illustribus scriptarum*, edited by Petrus Burmannus, 2 vols. (Leiden, 1727), 2:202, and cited in Gilbert, *Machiavelli and Guicciardini*, p. 205.

Chapter 2

1. Anthony Bosman, *Hieronymus Bosch* (New York: Barnes & Noble, 1963), pp. 27, 29, 76. See also Gilbert Highet, "The Mad World of Hieronymus Bosch," *Horizon* 12, no. 2 (Spring 1970): 66–80, esp. on "The Hay Wagon," pp. 78–80.

2. Tacitus *Agricola* iii: "nunc demum redit animus."

3. Johannes Trithemius, cited in Lewis W. Spitz, *Conrad Celtis: The German Arch-Humanist* (Cambridge, Mass.: Harvard University Press, 1957), p. 64.

4. It followed the example of Enea Silvio's *Europa* (part of his unfinished *Historia rerum ubique gestarum locorumque descriptio*) and *Commentaries* and Biondo's four works, described in chapter 1.

5. *Aeneas Silvius: Germania und Jakob Wimpfeling "Responsa et Replicae ad Eneam Silvium,"* edited by Adolf Schmidt (Cologne: Böhlau, 1962), pp. 9–10. Wimpfeling's "Response" was written later, in 1515. Abridged translations of both texts can be found in Gerald Strauss, trans. and ed., *Manifestations of Discontent in Germany on the Eve of the Reformation* (Bloomington: Indiana University Press, 1971), pp. 35–48.

6. *Aeneas Silvius: Germania*, p. 9: "Excogitantur mille modi, quibus Romana sedes aurum ex nobis tanquam ex barbaris subtili extrahat ingenio."

7. Ibid., p. 10.

8. Ibid., pp. 47–48: "His ferociora de Germania scribit Cornelius Tacitus, quem in Adriani tempora incurrisse perhibent. Parum quidem ea tempestate a feritate brutorum

maiorum tuorum vita distabat. Erant enim plerumque pastores, silvarum incole ac nemorum, cuiusmodi vitam inertem ac pigerrimam esse Aristoteles auctor est. Nec munite his urbes erant neque oppida muro cincta, non arces altis innixe montibus, non templa sectis structa lapidibus visebantur. Aberant ortorum ac villarum delicie, nulla viridaria, nulle consitiones, nulla tempe, nulla vineta colebantur. Prebebant largos flumina potus, lacus et stagna inserviebant lavacris, et siquas natura calentes produxerat aque. Rarum apud eos argentum, rarius aurum; margaritarum incognitus usus, nulla gemmarum pompa, nulla ex ostro vel serico vestimenta. Nondum metallorum investigate minere, nondum miseros in viscera terre mortales truserat auri sitis. Laudanda hec et nostris anteferenda moribus. At in hoc vivendi ritu nulla fuit litterarum cognitio, nulla legum disciplina, nulla bonarum artium studia. Ipsa quoque religio barbara, inepta, idolorum cultrix etque adeo demoniorum illusionibus labefacta, ut humanis sepe hostiis litatum esse apud illos non sit ambiguum. Latrocinia laudi fuerunt, omnia feda, omnia tetra, aspera, barbara et, ut propriis utamur vocabulis, ferina ac brutalia.''

9. Tiedemann: ''Hier fiel ihnen ganz unerwartet ein strahlendes Licht auf die germanische Vorzeit.'' Hans Heinrich Louis Max Tiedemann, *Tacitus und das Nationalbewusstsein der deutschen Humanisten: Ende des 15. und Anfang des 16. Jahrhunderts* (Berlin: Ebering, 1913), p. 7.

10. Campano's speech is more fully described by Gerald Strauss, *Sixteenth-Century Germany: Its Topography and Topographers* (Madison: University of Wisconsin Press, 1963), pp. 9–10.

11. Campano wrote to a friend: ''Compono me in adventum Caesaris habiturus orationem, qualem Italia legat, Germania non capiat'' (cited in Paul Joachimsen, ''Tacitus im deutschen Humanismus,'' *Neue Jahrbücher für das klassische Altertum* 27 [1911]: 705).

12. Campano: ''non ad mores modo; sed ad nomen quoque Germaniae subnaseo,'' cited in Tiedemann, *Tacitus und das Nationalbewusstsein,* p. 2.

13. According to Spitz, *Conrad Celtis: The German Arch-Humanist,* p. 94.

14. For general background, see Rudolf Hirsch, ''Printing and the Spread of Humanism in Germany: The Example of Albrecht von Eyb,'' in *Renaissance Men and Ideas,* ed. Robert Schwoebel (New York: St. Martin's Press, 1971), pp. 23–37.

15. The publisher of the Bologna edition, Baldassare Azzoguidi, gave it the appellation ''libellus aureus.'' He appended it to Poggio's translation of Diodorus Siculus' *Bibliotheca historiarum.*

16. A text ''marred by numerous stupid blunders,'' according to Rodney Potter Robinson in *The Germania of Tacitus: A Critical Edition* (Middletown, Conn.: American Philological Association, 1935), p. 329.

17. Celtis' role is especially clear here, considering that Enea Silvio himself, as pope, was almost directly responsible for the actual spread of printing and printers in Germany. His support of Adolf of Nassau against Archbishop Diether of Isenberg (Mayer's superior) and their enlisting the printers of Mainz—Gutenberg included—for their vigorous polemics are behind the extension of the role of printing. For the printers, too, Adolf's conquest of Mainz, in late October 1462, forced some of them to move to Cologne, Strassburg, and other cities—carrying the new invention with them. This knowledge comes to me from Florence A. Gragg, trans., and Leona S. Gabel, ed., *Memoirs of a Renaissance Pope: The Commentaries of Pius II: An Abridgment* (New York: Putnam, 1959), p. 300, n. 3. Thus I make the point of Celtis' *Oratio* being of some influence in awakening interest in Enea Silvio's and Campano's letters—despite the German printers'

earlier interest in Enea Silvio. Enea Silvio's tractate-letter to Mayer had missed their attention until after Celtis' oration.

18. According to Spitz, *Conrad Celtis: The German Arch-Humanist*, p. 12.

19. For the wider context of the beginnings of humanistic instruction at German universities, and at Ingolstadt in particular, see Terrence Heath, "Logical Grammar, Grammatical Logic, and Humanism in Three German Universities," *Studies in the Renaissance* 18 (1971): 9–64; note esp. p. 37, where Heath designates Celtis as the first "poeta" to hold his position at Ingolstadt in his own sphere, i.e., not in another faculty. For earlier background, see Frank Baron, ed., *Stephen Hoest: Reden und Briefe: Quellen zur Geschichte der Scholastik und des Humanismus im 15. Jahrhundert* (Munich: Wilhelm Fink, 1971).

20. Celtis: *Oratio in gymnasio in Ingelstadio publice recitata,* sentences 43–44: "O liberum et robustum populum, o nobilem et fortem gentem et plane dignam Romano imperio, cuius inclitum maris portum et claustra Oceani nostri Sarmata et Dacus possident! Ab oriente autem valentissimae gentes serviunt, Marcomanni, Quadi, Bastarnae et Peucini et quasi a corpore Germaniae nostrae separatae vivunt." The text, with English translation, is in Leonard Forster, ed., *Selections from Conrad Celtis: 1459–1508* (Cambridge, Eng.: At the University Press, 1948). For reasons that are clear from the organization of my argument, I have taken the liberty of transposing Celtis' Latin names for tribes back into the translation and removing Forster's translated tribal names into my own text.

21. Letter of 1505 from Vienna, in Hans Rupprich, ed., *Der Briefwechsel des Konrad Celtis* (Munich: C. H. Beck, 1934), no. 328.

22. Translated by Forster. The same is true for all quotations from the *Oratio*.

23. For this metaphor of rampart mountains separating irreconcilable enemies, Tacitus' imagery could have been the source of Celtis' inspiration—at least in part. A much more direct source, specifying the Alps in particular (although in this case they are dividing Italians from Gauls, not Germans), is Cicero *De provinciis consularibus* xiv. And still more direct is Petrarch, in his famous "Italia Mia": "Nature provided well for us when she placed the shield of the Alps between us and the German frenzy" (David Thompson, ed. and trans., *Petrarch, A Humanist among Princes: An Anthology of Petrarch's Letters and Selections from His Other Works* [New York: Harper & Row, 1971], pp. 55–56).

24. Similar in sentiment is Tacitus on the Britons in *Agricola* xxi: "Step by step they were led to things which dispose to vice, the lounge, the bath, the elegant banquet. All this, in their ignorance, they called civilization, when it was but a part of their servitude."

25. Celtis met Hasilina, of noble family, in Cracow in 1490. After a year, he rejected her and later caused her much embarrassment by his poems, for example, "De nocte et oscula Hasilinae, Erotice." This poem, along with others by Celtis, can be found in Harry C. Schnur, trans. and ed., *Lateinische Gedichte deutscher Humanisten* (Stuttgart: Reclam, 1967), pp. 40–41; the Latin text faces the translations. For English, see the translation of Forster, *Selections from Conrad Celtis,* pp. 26–27. Note that after a most detailed examination of the "four corners of Germany," Celtis was made ill from "the Italian disease" (also known as "the French disease" and "the Spanish disease") in 1496; a second bout with it, in 1498, left him an aged-looking man; he died of syphilis in 1508.

26. Rudolf Buchner, *Maximilian I: Kaiser an der Zeitenwende* (Göttingen: Musterschmidt, 1959), p. 66: "Der Bilanz der Jahre seit 1496 war erschreckend: eine lange Kette schwerer äusserer Misserfolge, die teilweise ganz persönlich dem König und seiner unbedachten Politik zur Last fielen." Cf. R. W. Seton-Watson, *Maximilian I: Holy Roman Emperor* (Westminster: Archibald Constable, 1902), p. 47: "the House of

Hapsburg was finally excluded from the cradle of its greatness'' by these events. See also the astute analyses of Maximilian's problems with the estates by Fritz Hartung and Karl Siegfried Bader in Gerald Strauss, ed., *Pre-Reformation Germany* (New York: Harper & Row, 1972), pp. 73–135, 136–61. For wider general background see Gerhard Ritter, *Die Neugestaltung Deutschlands und Europas im 16. Jahrhundert* (Frankfurt a.M.: Ullstein, 1967).

27. After several attempts at imitating Celtis' somewhat cramped hexameters, I have resorted to prose translations. Celtis' poetic style and imagery are very complex in places:

> Pectoribus similes ingentes corporis artus,
> Prodiga cui natura dedit per lactea colla
> Candida proceris tollentes corpora membris.
> Flava come est, flavent oculi flavoque colore
> Temperie iustam retinent sua membra staturam.

(from the *Germania generalis* ii. 11–15, in *Conradus Celtis Protucius, Quattuor Libri Amorum secundum quattuor latera Germaniae. Germania generalis,* edited by Felicitas Pindter, Bibliotheka Scriptorum Medii Recentisque Aevorum, Saecula XV–XVI, edited by Ladislaus Juhasz [Leipzig: B. G. Teubner, 1934]). Celtis' source was *Germania* iv; but his extreme amplification of the imagery, as well as his avoidance of negative points, is obvious.

28. Celtis: *Germania generalis* ii. 1. 5–7:

> Gens invicta manet toto notissima mundo
> . . . .
> Indigena, haud alia ducens primordia gente,
> Sed caelo producta sua, Demogorgonis alvus
> Protulerat patualas ubi cuncta creata sub auras.

Celtis' source was *Germania* iv: ''For my own part, I agree with those who think that the tribes of Germany are free from all taint of intermarriages with foreign nations, and they appear as a distinct, unmixed race like none but themselves.''

With ''Demogorgon'' Celtis expanded Boccaccio's adaptation of this medieval mythical founder of the whole race of gods to be the generator of the German people also. See Frank L. Borchardt, *German Antiquity in Renaissance Myth* (Baltimore: Johns Hopkins University Press, 1971), p. 108.

29. See the word ''taint'' in the preceding note. In Latin, Tacitus says, ''nullis aliarum nationum conubiis *infectos*'' (italics mine). Cf. *Germania* xlvi: ''conubiis mixtis nonnihil in Sarmatarum habitum *foedantur*'' (italics mine).

30. Celtis: *Liber amorum* ii. 9. 113–14: ''Fenus et usuram nemo illo in tempore norat / Dum patrio tantum caespite victus erat.'' His source is Tacitus *Germania* xxvi: ''Faenus agitare et in usuras extendere ignotum. . . .'' The close similarity between the passages was pointed out by Ludwig Sponagel, *Konrad Celtis und das deutsche Nationalbewusstsein* (Bühl-Baden: Konkordia, 1939).

31. Celtis: *Norimberga* iii: ''Armenta etiam equorum multa, quae publice / Aluntur, nullo mortali opere contacti.'' His source is Tacitus *Germania* x: ''Publice aluntur [equi] isdem nemoribus ac lucis, candidi et nullo mortali opere contacti.'' This parallel has also been pointed out by Sponagel.

32. If Bosch had any particular emperor in mind, it was probably Frederick III.

33. *Ulrichi Hutteni Equitis Germani Opera quae reperiri potuerunt Omnia,* edited by

Eduard Böcking, 7 vols. (Leipzig: B. G. Teubner, 1859–62), 3:124–58. Hereafter cited as *Opera omnia*.

34. Ibid., pp. 331–40. In Hutten's revised text of 1518 (ibid.—above the 1511 version), any ambiguity between modern and ancient "primores" was avoided by the poem's new title: "Quod ab illa antiquitus Germanorum claritudine nondum degeneraverint nostrates."

35. However, Borchardt (*German Antiquity in Renaissance Myth*, p. 25) sees Hutten's reliance on Tacitus in a peculiar context: "A certain school of patriotic humanists, including Ulrich von Hutten, recognized the value of Tacitus for historical and propagandistic purposes, and used him to those ends. But far more influential than the works of Tacitus themselves was their appearance in the forgery published under the name of Berosus. It tied the classical option to the biblical, placing the Germanic antiquity of Tacitus in the context of the children of Noah. This was perhaps not as 'modern' as the services rendered by Hutten, but it was far more typical of the Renaissance." Borchardt here refers to the Pseudo-Berosus, Annius of Viterbo, librarian of Alexander VI, who published his forgeries, *Auctores vetustissimi nuper in lucem editi* in Venice in 1498 and his *Commentaria* about them in Rome in the same year. Among many classical and medieval authors, some real and some contrived, Annius worked Tacitus' *Germania* into his fictitious texts and observations. An especially persistent Annian influence on the German humanists was the connection of Tacitus' Tuisco and Mannus (*Germania* ii) as descendants of Noah. Heinrich Bebel (c. 1505) and Conrad Peutinger (c. 1510) gave full credence to this point. Gerald Strauss, in his biography of Aventinus, the important German humanist discussed in the next chapter, shows his subject to have borrowed heavily from the Annian material. Even Beatus Rhenanus, a cautious philologian, was—at first—fooled by this and other elements of the forgery. But Rhenanus' growing skepticism causes Borchardt (p. 156) to label his progress and critical sense as "unimportant" in his context, just as he considers Hutten to be too "modern." Although such categories become difficult for him to handle, and although he is too narrow in his awareness of Tacitus' direct influence, Borchardt is valuable for his main purpose: to show the survival and revival of medieval myth in Renaissance literature.

36. Though, of course, Hutten does not mention the details about the livestock of the ancient Germans (*Germania* v): "[they are] rich in flocks and herds, but these are for the most part undersized, and even the cattle have not their usual beauty or noble head. It is number that is chiefly valued. . . ."

37. *Opera omnia*, 3:338–39, ll. 116–20:

> Nos etiam argentum, nos nobile mittimus aurum,
> Nos legimus gemmas; et qua non aspera quondam
> Dicta magis tellus alia est, nunc omnia gignit
> Vina etiam pulchrumque crocum vestesque superbas
> Velleraque et pecudes; nos quasdam invenimus artes,
> Quarum nulla satis laudem celebraverit aetas.

Hutten's inclusion of clothing [*vestes*], into a list of nature's gifts to the Germans, is, at first sight curious—until one realizes that *Germania* xvii was his source: there the emphasis lies on the fact of the Germans' apparel consisting of things of nature and the earth. There are frequent echoes of other passages of the *Germania* throughout the poem.

38. Tacitus *Germania* v: "Silver and gold the gods have refused to them, whether in kindness or in anger I cannot say. I would not, however, affirm that no vein of German

soil produces gold or silver, for who has ever made a search? You may see among them vessels of silver, which have been presented to their envoys and chieftains, held as cheap as those of clay."

39. Tacitus referred to the horses and cattle ("indeed the only riches of the people," *Germania* v); wealth of cereals, "wild fruit, fresh venison, curdled milk" (*Germania* xxiii); barley, wheat, beer ("in quandam similitudinem vini corruptus," *Germania* xxiii); and the many thick forests. In the last quotation from Hutten, he referred to "crocum"; this was a dye produced from certain plants in Thuringia. Perhaps Tacitus was referring to this dye when he described the German women's garments as "striped with purple" (*Germania* xviii).

40. *Opera omnia,* 3:208, no. 4, "De Caesare": "Christus habet coelos, infra regit omnia Caesar; / Nec nisi coelestum respicit hic dominum."

41. Ibid., pp. 207–68.

42. Ibid., p. 210, no. 10, "De magnitudine Maximiliani ad Germaniam," ll. 1–10:

> Quid veteres mirare tuos, Germania, reges?
>   Quid repetis priscos in tua secla duces?
> Ne pete Gambrivios natosque Tuisconis omneis
>   Visaque sub Manno fortia corda deo,
> Hermionasve alacreis natosque Ingaevones armis,
>   Cymbrorum proceres Teutonicumque genus,
> Quique domi tibi quique foris peperere decorem,
>   Neve Ariovistos Arminiumque ferum.
> Crede mihi, temere praesens revocatur ad aevum
>   Corolus, ut fortis, magnus ut ille fuit.

43. Ibid., 3:353–400.

44. Ibid., p. 279, in "Omnia Romae pecunia redimi."

45. As is evident from the poem quoted on p. 41. Aside from Tacitus' *Annales* xi. 16–18 and xi. 55, his sources were probably Velleius Paterculus, Florus, and, to a lesser extent, Suetonius.

46. Hajo Holborn, *Ulrich von Hutten and the German Reformation,* trans. Roland H. Bainton (New York: Harper & Row, 1966), p. 77.

47. All in *Opera omnia,* the first two in 3:389–400, the third in 1:106–13.

48. Duke Ulrich had murdered Hutten's cousin, Hans von Hutten, in 1515. Duke Ulrich lusted after Hans's wife and, his advances rejected, he found a simple if stupid solution—he killed Hans. The duke's wife, Sabine, sister of Duke Wilhelm of Bavaria, fled her monstrous husband, and all southern Germany was aflame with the issue. Hutten wrote many orations against the duke.

49. In *Opera omnia,* vol. 5.

50. Ibid., 3:107–14. See further discussion below.

51. Ibid. David F. Strauss provided a German translation of this dialogue, *Febris I,* along with nine others, in his *Ulrich von Hutten,* 3 vols. (Leipzig: F. A. Brockhaus, 1860), vol. 3: *Gespräche von Ulrich von Hutten. Febris II* appeared in 1520.

52. *Opera omnia,* 4:269–308.

53. See Thomas W. Best, *The Humanist Ulrich von Hutten: A Reappraisal of His Humor* (Chapel Hill: University of North Carolina Press, 1969). For a lighthearted view, in pictures, of the *Germania* itself, enjoy H. E. Köhler, *Tacitus: Germania: Mit 45*

Zeichnungen von H. E. Köhler (Munich: Friedr. Bassermann'sche Verlagsbuchhandlung, 1968).

54. *Opera omnia*, 4:285–86: "Hoc non dico quidem, illud vero ipsa ostendit res, multa melius facere eos quam ullos alios sobrios, multa prudentius disponere. Sequuntur autem proverbium quoddam apud se divulgatum, 'de mane concilium, de vespere convivium' nam a cibo in multam usque noctem perbibunt, mane de republica et gravibus negotiis ieiuni consultant." See *Germania* xxii; and note how Hutten avoids *Germania* xxiii.

Martin Luther, however, could not pass the vice off as "imbibing nourishment." In *Against Hanswurst* (1541) he condemns "all of Germany, which is plagued with excessive drinking. We preachers speak and preach against it; unfortunately that does not help much. It is an old and evil custom in Germany, as the Roman Cornelius wrote" (*Luther's Works*, ed. Helmut T. Lehmann and Jaroslav Pelikan, 55 vols. [Philadelphia: Fortress Press (Concordia), 1955–66], 41:239; trans. Eric W. Gritsch).

55. *Opera omnia*, 4:286–87: "At non habeant communes, sed fidem ostentant hac in re suam: neque fere custodita alibi pudicitia mulierum illibatior est quam hic neglecta et in periculum missa; adulteria vero nusquam rariora sunt, nusquam religiosius colitur matrimonium et sanctis habetur." The bases here are *Germania* xix ("nemo enim illic vitia ridet . . .") and xx ("Sera iuvenum venus . . ."). See also *Germania* xviii.

56. *Opera omnia*, 4:292–93: "Audies. A principio nullae fuerunt in Germania urbes neque contigua fuerunt aedificia, verum sua cuique et secreta domus." Cf. *Germania* xvi.

57. *Opera omnia*, 4:292–93: "PHAETHON: Scio. SOL: Nec tum mercatores accedebant qui peregre aliquid importarent, utebantur apud se natis omnes, hisque solis, ferarum vestientes pellibus; in cibo autem utentes quae produxisset patrium solum, externa ignorabantur passim. Quo tempore fraudabant nulli quempiam institores; quaedam rigida fuit passim probitas, hanc sequebantur omnes; pecuniam nondum viderat quisquam, nec argentum habebant vel aurum. PHAETHON: Hoc fuit optimum Germaniae tempus." All of this is based on various sections of the *Germania*. In connection with the merchants in particular, and the Germans' small contact with them, Hutten was thinking of the sparseness of notices of them: *Germania* v ("Quamquam proximi ob usum . . ."); xv ("Iam et pecuniam accipere docuimus"); and xxiii ("Proximi ripae et vinum mercantur").

58. *Opera omnia*, 4:294: "bellicae imprimis gloriae studiosus, pecuniae contemptor, exercebatque se venando, et tranquilli impatiens odio habebat quietam, . . ." See *Germania* xiv ("Si civitas, in qua orti sunt, longe pace et otio torpeat . . .") and xv ("Quotiens bella . . .").

59. Here, on the dating, I follow Holborn, *Ulrich von Hutten*, p. 77, n. 8. For an examination of the sources, detailed content, and development of the Arminius legend, see Richard Kuehnemund, *Arminius, or the Rise of a National Symbol in Literature from Hutten to Grabbe*, University of North Carolina Studies in Germanic Languages and Literature, no. 8 (Chapel Hill: University of North Carolina Press, 1953). Note also Dieter Timpe, *Arminius-Studien* (Heidelberg: Carl Winter, 1970), and the translated selections in Gerald Strauss, trans. and ed., *Manifestations of Discontent*, pp. 75–82 (see n. 5, above).

60. Machiavelli, in the *Discorsi*, was the very first to make political application of the new texts. See chapter 4.

61. Della Gandy, "A Comparison of the Treatment of the Germans in the *Germania* and the *Annales* of Tacitus" (Master's thesis, University of Chicago, 1903), pp. 12–13, says that Arminius, in the *Annales*, is shown as "treacherous and craven." This generalization is too extreme. *Annales* ii. 88 by itself proves that Gandy is mistaken. But see, in addition, *Annales* ii. 9 and 17. Kuehnemund, *Arminius*, p. 3, is more balanced in arguing

that Tacitus' genuinely tragic perspective, though marred by some malicious joy in an enemy's weaknesses, was "filled equally with fear and admiration."

62. The following comparison agrees with most of the points in Gandy's study.

63. Cited in Paul Joachimsen, "Tacitus im deutschen Humanismus," p. 716: "Nam candidus imprimis fuit et quo nemo sincerius scripserit historiam minusque affectibus tribuerit. Etiam autem Germaniam viderat et gentis eius mores descripsit ac rerum ibi gestarum fuit perquam studiosus."

64. With some caution, based on Peter Burke's statistics in "A Survey of the Popularity of Ancient Historians: 1450–1700," *History and Theory* 5, no. 2 (1966): 135–52, esp. p. 141.

65. I refer to Aventinus' translation of his *Annales ducum Boioriae* into the *Bayerische Chronik*. Joachimsen ("Tacitus im deutschen Humanismus," p. 717) believes that the name change occurred in 1529, since Aventinus was then working on the second book of the translation, where the name first was translated.

66. *Luther's Works,* 13:59: It is brought up in the commentary on verse 4: "Rescue the small and the poor, deliver them out of the hand of the godless." Translated by C. M. Jacobs.

67. *Andreae Althameri Brenzii scholia in Cornelium Tacitum Rom. historicum, de situ, moribus populisque Germaniae* (Nuremberg, 1529).

68. Melanchthon: *Ausgabe der "Germania," mit Vorwort und Beilage: Vocabula regionum enarrata et ad recentes appellationes accommodata* (Wittenberg, 1538); republished in 1557. Melanchthon had published an earlier version of the work at Wittenberg in 1517: *Vocabula regionum et gentium quae recensentur in hoc libello Tacito.* It probably stems from his classroom instruction needs.

69. According to David F. Strauss, *Ulrich von Hutten: His Life and Times,* trans. G. Sturge (London: Daldy, Isbister, & Co., 1874), p. 216. The same work, unabridged, was cited in the original three-volume edition in note 51, above.

70. Cited ibid., p. 337.

71. Luther: *An Appeal to the Ruling Class of the German Nationality as to the Amelioration of the State of Christendom,* in John Dillenberger, trans. and ed., *Martin Luther: Selections from His Writings* (New York: Doubleday, 1961), p. 421. See also pp. 419–20 for two passages in which Luther tells what popish cardinals think about the drunken and silly Germans.

72. In a commentary on Psalm 101 (written in 1534), in *Luther's Works,* 13:218.

Chapter 3

1. Aventinus: "Ioannis Aventini sum. Chunradus Celtis praeceptor meus." From the *Haus-Kalendar,* in *Johannes Turmairs genannt Aventinus Sämmtliche Werke,* edited by Georg Leidinger, 6 vols. (Munich: C. Kaiser, 1880–1908), 6:5.

2. In his *Ritratto delle cose della Magna.* See the next chapter, where this work and two others of Machiavelli's on Germany are analyzed for Tacitan influence.

3. Aventinus: *Haus-Kalendar,* in *Sämmtliche Werke,* 6:12: "Plinius: Multum refert, in quae tempora cuiusque virtus inciderit. Ita de Valentino imperatore optimo, si licuisset ei uti melioribus consultoribus. Ita virtus Maximiliani in iniqua inciderit."

4. Aventinus: from the first verse of the poem in *Sämmtliche Werke,* 1:626:

Teutonum custos pater atque princeps
Caesar invictis metuendus armis,

Faustus advenit: lyrico saluto
Carmine divum.

5. Cited in Gerald Strauss, *Historian in an Age of Crisis: The Life and Work of Johannes Aventinus: 1477–1534* (Cambridge, Mass.: Harvard University Press, 1963), p. 80.

6. Ibid., p. 116.

7. Aventinus: from the "Einleitung" to the *Bayerische Chronik* in *Sämmtliche Werke,* 4:4: "Cornelius Tacitus hat geschriben von den breuchen, sitten, gelegenhait, altem herkommen der Teutschen bei kaiser Traiani zeiten. Sein nachkommen sein römisch kaiser gewesen. Niemant hat mêr bei den alten Römern, des püecher wir noch hieten, von uns geschriben." He refers, of course, to the Emperor Tacitus, A.D. 275–76.

8. Ibid., p. 843: "Aber (als Tacitus und Plinius der jung . . . selber schreiben) so haben die Teutschen vil anzal volks, ganze her, all guet krieger haufenweis erlegt, erschlagen, aussgetilgt, gefangen dermassen, das die Römer nit allain besorgten, si müesten die alten grenitz des römischen reichs . . . verlieren."

9. "Vom gotsdienst, wie in künig Tuitscho gesetzt hat" is based on *Germania* ix–xi, xxxix, xl, and xliii.

10. "Von der ê [Ehe] und kinderzucht" is based on *Germania* vii, viii, xvii, xix, xx, xxv, and xl.

11. "Von den landschaften, irrung und rechtsprechen." There is much on landscape and climate throughout the *Germania.* On justice, see *Germania* xii, xix, and xxi.

12. "Von erbschaft" is based mainly on *Germania* xx.

13. *Bayerische Chronik* (1:12), in *Sämmtliche Werke,* 4:82: "Wie man das übel strafen, das guet belonen sol: Macht er und schuef, das gegen den übertrettern die priester und pfaffen solten handeln, nach denselbigen greifen, si fâhen, pinden und mit rueten ausstreichen, als ob solchs nit zue einer straf oder durch gewalt des Fürsten, sunder geschähe auss besonderm pefelch und willen des almechtigen gots, welches die geistlichen, 'schergen' und 'herolden' haben genent."

14. Ibid., 2:53: "In fact, he permitted only the priests to give capital punishment, to imprison, and to flog, and not as though penalties, or by order of the leader, but as if by the inspiration of God."

15. Gerald Strauss, *Historian in an Age of Crisis,* p. 110.

16. *Bayerische Chronik* (1:12), in *Sämmtliche Werke,* 4:77: "Vom gotsdienst, wie in künig Tuitscho gesetzt hat: Am ersten ordnet er den gotsdienst also: pauet gar kein kirchen noch altar nit, etlich paum, hölzer und wäld weihet er und verpants, das sie niemants abe dorft hauen, in und zue denselbigen liefen die leut, so si peten wolten, geistliche werk üeben, ir andacht und gotsdienst under den wolken und offnem himel verbringen solten. Er hielt's dafür und gab's also aus under die leut, das got, so im himel wont, waer untödlich und grösser, dan das man in in stain und wänd in gepeu und stainhaufen, von tödlicher hand zam gesetzt, einschliessen solt."

17. Ibid., 2:53: "Besides, he had groves and coppices consecrated in which sacred things were duly performed. He thought that the heavenly Being, by reason of his majesty, should not be confined within walls or be made into any likeness of the human face and the appearance of a transient thing."

18. In *Sämmtliche Werke,* 1:171–242.

19. In general see Robert Schwoebel, *The Shadow of the Crescent: The Renaissance Image of the Turk, 1453–1517* (New York: St. Martins Press, 1968); and, more particularly here, see John W. Bohnstedt, *The Infidel Scourge of God: The Turkish Menace as*

Seen by German Pamphleteers of the Reformation Era, Transactions of the American Philosophical Society, n.s. 58, pt. 9 (Philadelphia: American Philosophical Society, 1968). Wholly out of spirit with these studies, however, are the sentiments of Myron P. Gilmore in *The World of Humanism: 1453–1517* (New York: Harper & Row, 1962), pp. 19–21, where the Turkish threat is minimized and the humanists and other writers are seen as exaggerators.

20. *Ursachen,* in *Sämmtliche Werke,* 1:175; cited and translated by Strauss, *Historian in an Age of Crisis,* p. 159.

21. Ibid., pp. 227–28; cited and translated by Strauss, p. 197.

22. Ibid., pp. 228–29; cited and translated by Strauss, p. 198.

23. Ibid., p. 240; cited and translated by Strauss, pp. 222–23.

24. From the "Preface" to book 3 of the *Bayerische Chronik* in *Sämmtliche Werke,* 5:2; cited and translated by Strauss, p. 145.

25. Gerald Strauss, *Sixteenth-Century Germany: Its Topography and Topographers* (Madison: University of Wisconsin Press, 1959), p. 70. See also his "Topographical-Historical Method in Sixteenth-Century German Scholarship," *Studies in the Renaissance* 5 (1958): 87–101, and his more recent essay "The Course of German History: The Lutheran Interpretation," in *Renaissance Studies in Honor of Hans Baron,* edited by Anthony Molho and John H. Tedeschi (Florence: Sansoni, 1971), pp. 663–86. In the same volume, note Lewis W. Spitz, "Humanism in the Reformation," pp. 643–62, and, on historiography in particular, pp. 654–55.

26. Remember that Wimpfeling was also the author, ten years later (1515), of the work cited in chap. 2, n. 5. Its full title is *Responsa et replice ad Eneam Silvium ad salutem et decorem sacrosancti imperii Romani amore patriae Germanicaeque nacionis.* This work is the most direct example of the effect Enea Silvio's letter had, even some fifty years later.

27. Strauss, *Sixteenth-Century Germany,* p. 34.

28. Cited by Strauss, ibid., p. 114.

29. G. R. Elton, *Reformation Europe: 1517–1559* (Cleveland: World Publishing Co., 1962), p. 153.

30. According to Strauss, *Sixteenth-Century Germany,* p. 114.

31. Cited by Strauss, ibid., p. 27. The statement does not come from the *Cosmographia* but from a plea in an earlier work which the *Cosmographia* satisfied. The earlier work was a thirty-page study on sundials, *Erklerung des newen Instruments der Sunnen . . .* (Oppenheim, 1528). The statement occurs in its second part, titled "Exhortation and Plea of Sebastian Münster to All Practitioners of the Gentle Art of Geography, to Aid Him in the Truthful and Rightful Description of the German Nation." Strauss (pp. 26–27) provides a long quotation from this section.

32. Strauss, *Sixteenth-Century Germany,* p. 66.

33. In the words of Münster, *Cosmographia* (Basel, 1544), p. 93; cited and translated by Strauss, *Sixteenth-Century Germany,* p. 147. See also pp. 147–49 of his book for a general discussion and further examples of the "Golden Age" theme in these historians.

34. Strauss, *Sixteenth-Century Germany,* p. 145.

35. Aventinus to Rhenanus: *Sämmtliche Werke,* 1:643–46; also in *Briefwechsel des Beatus Rhenanus,* edited by Adalbert Horawitz and Karl Hartfelder (Leipzig: B. G. Teubner, 1886), pp. 345–46. On Rhenanus being impressed: Rhenanus to Michael Hummelberg, December 1525, *Sämmtliche Werke,* 6:88, n. 1. I owe the notice of both these references to Strauss, *Sixteenth-Century Germany,* p. 25.

36. The details on Rhenanus' life and works may be found in two articles by Adalbert

Horawitz: "Beatus Rhenanus: Ein biographischer Versuch," and "Des Beatus Rhenanus literarische Thätigkeit in den Jahren 1508–1531," *Sitzungsberichte der kaiserlichen Akademie der Wissenschaften* 70 (1872): 189–244; and 72 (1874): 323–76.

37. *Beati Rhenani vita per Ioannem Sturmium* in Horawitz and Hartfelder, eds., *Briefwechsel,* p. 10: "Post lectionem aut scriptionem domesticam in hortos suos suburbanos exire deambulatum solebat. Prandio horam decimam, coenae sextam dederat, . . . domum quoniam libidinibus et impudicitiae clausam tenuit, comessationes admittebat nullas: convivia rara eaque optimis parabat."

38. Ibid., p. 9: "Magna fuit illius domus solitudo."

39. These three editions are each of the complete works of Tacitus. In 1539 Rhenanus published a separate edition of the *Dialogus* with notes; he had some doubts of its authenticity because of its "un-Tacitan" style.

40. That is, in his *castigationes* and *scholiae*. They first appear in the edition of 1533 (Basel: Froben). In 1534 (Venice) they were printed with those of Andrea Alciato (on Alciato, see the next chapter). In 1542 (Lyons: Gryphius) Rhenanus' notes appear with those of Aemilio Ferretti, Alciato, and Beroaldus.

41. *P. Cornelii Taciti equitus romani annalium . . . sive Historiae Augustae . . . per Beatum Rhenanum . . . Libellus de Germanorum populis . . . Dialogus de oratoribus . . . Vita Julii Agricolae . . .* (Basel: Froben, 1533) p. 425: "Quoties autem hodieque contingere videmus ut in contrariis aciebus ab utraque parte Germanica auxilia conspiciantur."

42. Ibid., p. 429: "Hactenus esse nobis exemplo Turce, quorum item initio neque obscurius quicquam, neque incertius: si modo licet citra piaculum, nostratem optimeque meritam de Christiana pietate gentem, cum truclentissimis hostibus nostris conferre: cum quibus nuper, quod bene ac feliciter vertat, iustum piumque bellum suscepimus, auspiciis & ductu Caroli Augusti atque Ferdinandi Caesaris."

43. Tacitus: "Nemo enim illic vitia ridet, nec corrumpere et corrumpi saeculum vocatur." Similarly, the chapter ends: "plusque ibi boni mores valent quam alibi bonae leges." On Heinrich Bebel's ingenious use of this statement to account for the absence of philosophers and lawgivers among the ancient Germans, note Paul Joachimsen's comments in "Humanism and the Development of the German Mind," pp. 162–224 in Gerald Strauss, ed., *Pre-Reformation Germany* (New York: Harper & Row, 1972), p. 185.

44. Rhenanus: *P. Cornelii Taciti* . . . , p. 426: "Quanto sanctiores fuere nobis ethnici. Nam quotusquisque hodie vel vitia non ridet, vel quantumvis enormibus flagitiis non praetexit illud. Sic seculum est. Si quis aliena matrimonia contaminantem aut puellis illudentem damnet, statim audit, Sic seculum est. Si bonus vir pessimam istam potandi consuetudinem reprehendat, mox adest qui excuset quod sic hodie seculum sit. Si quis improbet morem quo iuvenes in militiam temere proficiscuntur ad nullum non scelus patrandum erudiendi, huic mox dicetur, Sic seculum est. Si quis miretur sacerdotum in parandis praebendis insatiabilitatem, audit, Sic seculum est. Si quis immodicum mortalium studium in parandis divitiis, questum illicitum, atque contractuum iniquitatem detestetur, huic tanquam nesciente allegabitur, Sic nunc seculum est. In summa, nullis non erratis, nequitiis, criminibus, obtendimus, Sic seculum est. Dissimiles igitur maioribus nostris vitia ridemus nobisque blandimur, & corrumpentes ac corrupti, decipientes alios ac circumscribentes culpam in seculum reiicimus."

45. Bebel: *De laudibus atque philosophia Germanorum* (1508). And note H. Hermelink, "Die Anfänge des Humanismus in Tübingen," *Württembergische Vierteljahrshefte für Landesgeschichte* 15 (1906): 39–41.

46. *Beati Rhenani Selestadiensis rerum Germanicarum libri tres* (Strassburg: Lazarus

Zetzner, 1610), p. 5: "Populi Germaniae veteris in summa libertate vixerunt. Ne tamen putes libertatem in anarchiam exisse, Reges ex nobilitate quaeque; natio [*non licuit*], duces ex virtute sumebant, ut scribit Tacitus."

47. Rhenanus: *P. Cornelii Taciti . . .*, unpaginated preface: " . . .quemadmodum hic non meritam mortem fortiter subierit, quid alius in ius calumniose vocatus dixerit aut fecerit, quam agendum caute cum his qui solo nutu perdere possunt, quam parce fidendum, et his similia exempla multum conferant ad legentis pectus prudentiae monumentis instruendum." I was led to this important reference by Jürgen von Stackelberg, *Tacitus in der Romania*, p. 7 (see chap. 1, n. 11).

48. Friedrich Meinecke, *Machiavellism: The Doctrine of Raison d'Etat and Its Place in Modern History*, trans. Douglas Starck (New Haven: Yale Univeristy Press, 1957), p. 132.

49. See page 87, below.

Chapter 4

1. For background on Machiavelli I rely on the best authorities. Among biographies: Roberto Ridolfi, *The Life of Niccolò Machiavelli*, trans. Cecil Grayson (Chicago: University of Chicago Press, 1963), and J. R. Hale, *Machiavelli and Renaissance Italy* (New York: Crowell-Collier, 1963). Among general interpretations of his thought: Rudolf von Albertini, *Das florentinische Staatsbewusstsein im Übergang von der Republik zum Prinzipat* (Bern: Francke, 1955); Felix Gilbert, *Machiavelli and Guicciardini: Politics and History in Sixteenth Century Florence* (Princeton: Princeton University Press, 1965); Federico Chabod, *Machiavelli and the Renaissance*, trans. David Moore (New York: Harper & Row, 1965). For the genesis and chronology of his thought: Hans Baron, "The *Principe* and the Puzzle of the Date of the *Discorsi*," *Bibliothèque d'Humanisme et Renaissance* 18 (1956): 405–28; Gennaro Sasso, *Niccolò Machiavelli: Storia del suo pensiero politico* (Naples: Nella sede dell'istituto, 1958). (This is not the place to enter into the problems which lie between the approaches and conclusions of Baron and Sasso. They are not so great as to create an obstacle to a unified interpretation of Machiavelli's thought. This has been shown by Eric Cochrane in the conclusion to his "Machiavelli: 1940–1960," *Journal of Modern History* 33 [1961]: 113–36.) For critical editions of Machiavelli's works: Sergio Bertelli, ed., *Opere*, 8 vols., Biblioteca de classici italiani (Milan: Feltrinelli, 1960–64)—particularly vol. 1, *Il Principe e Discorsi* (1960) and vol. 2, *Arte della guerra e scritti politici minori* (1961) (Bertelli's edition is excellent for its very thorough indexes and helpful introductions. It is regrettable, however, that Bertelli, in his critical introduction to volume 1, does not take account of the thesis of Hans Baron and overlooks fhe considerable evidence for the separate compositions of the *Prince* and the *Discorsi*); Mario Bonfantini, ed., *Opere* (in the series La Letteratura Italiana: Storia e Testi, vol. 29) (Milan: Ricciardi, 1954). The translations used here are *The Discourses on the First Ten Books of Titus Livius*, by Christian E. Detmold, and *The Prince*, by Luigi Ricci, both in the Modern Library edition (New York: Random House, 1950), and *The History of Florence*, by Allan Gilbert, in *Machiavelli: The Chief Works and Others*, 3 vols. (Durham, N.C.: Duke University Press, 1965).

2. Pasquale Villari, *Niccolò Machiavelli e i suoi tempi*, 3 vols. (Florence: Le Monnier, 1877–82). The basis for this information on Villari comes from the excellent criticism of Sergio Bertelli (in his introduction to his edition of the *Arte della guerra e scritti politici minori*, pp. 186–87), with whom I concur.

3. Daniel Waley, "The Primitivist Element in Machiavelli's Thought," *Journal of the History of Ideas* 31 (1970): 91–98, esp. pp. 96–97.

4. Bertelli, in his introduction to the *Arte della guerra* . . . , pp. 186–87, admittedly follows Sasso, *Niccolò Machiavelli*, pp. 161–63.

5. Bertelli, in his introduction to the *Arte della guerra* . . . , p. 187, refers to Villari as their "paragone" for the error. But without specifying any of "gli altri," it is difficult to determine whom he has in mind among those listed in his bibliographical note on p. 192. One, for sure, is A. Renaudet (*Machiavelli*, 1942) whom even Waley (p. 96) considers oversimplified and exaggerated.

6. Bertelli ed., p. 202 (but my translation): "e godono in questa lor vita rozza e libera, e non vogliono ire alla guerra se tu non gli soprappaghi; e questo anco non li basterebbe, se le comunità non li comandassero." Bertelli, in his introduction, p. 187, pointed out the passage; but, in citing it, he seems to use a text quite variant from his own: "cosí godono quella lor rozza vita e libertà e per questa causa non vogliono ire alla guerra se non soprappagati; né ciò anche basterebbe, se non fossero comandati dalle loro comunità."

7. Pointed out by Bertelli, ibid., p. 210, n. 5

8. My article, "Tacitus in the Political Thought of Machiavelli," *Il Pensiero Politico* 4, no. 3 (1971): 381–91, is a summary of my arguments on Machiavelli in this chapter. In both, the chronology is Baron's.

9. All translations from the *Prince* and the *Discourses* are from the Modern Library edition.

10. But Jürgen von Stackelberg, *Tacitus in der Romania*, pp. 69–70 (see chap. 1, n. 11) while pointing out the verbal parallels, abandons the problem of any connection almost immediately by considering it "ein Gemeinplatz humanistischer Denkweise" and by referring to a sentence of a similar sense in Cicero's *De amicitia* ix. 31. Besides, he says that the thought is "weder spezifisch taciteisch noch etwa besonders typisch für Machiavelli"!

11. The definition is Hans Baron's, "The *Principe* and the Puzzle of the Date of the *Discorsi*," p. 406. The *Discourses* are not a prorepublican work only. Many students of Machiavelli err on this point.

12. The chronology here is that determined by Baron, ibid. The question has become extremely complex ever since Felix Gilbert aroused great interest in it with his famous article "The Structure and Composition of Machiavelli's *Discorsi*," *Journal of the History of Ideas* 14 (1953): 136–56. The particular point I am making is that the references to Tacitus in the *Discourses*, specifically those within bk. i, chaps. 1 through 18, were included when these chapters were first written, i.e., after 1515, and not before the Tacitus references in the *Prince*.

Bertelli pointed out the dependence of *Discourses* i. 10 on Tacitus in a speech in Perugia in autumn 1969 during the Machiavelli Conferences (and see also *Il Pensiero Politico* 2, no. 3 [1969]: 507). Moreover, Bertelli has shown me that Machiavelli's extensive use of Tacitus here gives proof to Gilbert's argument on the structure of the *Discourses:* the structure of the first eighteen chapters does not adhere to the progression of a step-by-step commentary on Livy manifest in the rest of the work; thus, *Discourses* i. 10, being based entirely on Tacitus, adds proof to the argument concerning the looser structure of the first eighteen chapters. However, this conclusion does not support Gilbert's thesis of a pre-*Prince* origin of these chapters. Baron also accepts the fact of their deep difference from the rest of the *Discourses* but sees them, and rightly so, as conceived and written after the *Prince* and after the commentary-on-Livy sections.

13. The parallel to Tacitus' statement was pointed out by von Stackelberg, *Tacitus in der Romania*, p. 70.

14. The Emperor Galba's speech to Piso on the advantages of adoption in *Historiae* i. 16 may have helped Machiavelli find the answer.

15. This parallel was pointed out by von Stackelberg (p. 70).

16. Detmold translation, p. 410. For the textual criticism which follows, the original Italian must be given for the final lines: "E veramente quella sentenzia di Cornelio Tacito è aurea, che dice: che gli uomini hanno ad onorare le cose passate e ad ubbidire alla presenti, e debbono desiderare i buoni principi, e comunque ei si sieno fatti, tollerargli. E veramente chi fa altrimenti, il piú delle volte rovina sé e la sua patria.

"Dobbiamo adunque, entrando nella materia, considerare prima contro a chi si fanno le congiure; e troverreno farsi o contro alla patria o contro ad uno principe." (Bertelli ed., pp 390–91.)

17. Tacitus: "Ulteriora mirari, praesentia sequi; bonos imperatores voto expetere, qualiscumque tolerare."

On account of the length of this *discorso*, references to the page numbers of both the translation and the Bertelli text will be provided in these notes.

18. Von Stackelberg, *Tacitus in der Romania*, pp. 71–72: "Ob man jedoch Herrscher jeglicher Art hinnimmt, *wie sie sind*, oder ob man die Herrscher duldet, wie auch immer *sie zu solchen geworden sind* (si sieno fatti) ist freilich nicht dasselbe. Das eine kurze Wörtchen 'si' in Machiavellis Wiedergabe der Tacitusstelle biegt den Sinn des Satzes in folgenschwerer Weise um: Tacitus' 'goldene Sentenz' wird so zu einem machiavellistischen Grundsatz. Wen einer wie Cesare Borgia nur energisch und geschickt genug ist, sich zur Herrschaft emporzuschwingen, gleich mit welchen Mitteln, so wäre er—gemäss Tacitus—nach Machiavelli als Herrscher zu dulden. Machiavellis Sehnsucht nach einem Ende der politischen Unordnung in Italien spricht hieraus—nicht etwa ein grundsätzlicher Konservatismus."

19. Thus, von Stackelberg (ibid., p. 72), adds that the later Tacitists corrupted Machiavelli's meaning into a support not of illegitimate rulers but of evil rulers.

20. For example (page references are first to the Detmold translation, then to the Bertelli edition): p. 411 (p. 391): "A prince should not threaten or menace his subjects"; p. 411 (p. 391): "A man's property and honor are the points upon which he will be most keenly sensitive. A prince, then, should be most careful to avoid touching these"; p. 423 (p. 401): "As is always the case with bad rulers, they are in constant fear lest others are conspiring to inflict upon them the punishment which they are conscious of deserving"; p. 423 (p. 401): "Therefore princes should guard against indulging in menaces." But these are only a few examples. There are many others, and here Machiavelli refers the reader to them (p. 411 [p. 391]): "A prince, then, should avoid incurring such universal hatred; and, as I have spoken elsewhere of the way to do this, I will say no more about it here." The reference is to chapter 19 of the *Prince*, for which this chapter in the *Discourses* provides the fuller, more republican context. *Prince* 19 also deals with conspiracies and is entitled: "That We Must Avoid Being Despised and Hated." The following advice is given: avoid being rapacious and usurping the property and women of the subjects; avoid becoming despicable through being thought changeable, frivolous, effeminate, timid, irresolute; keep the people satisfied and contented; have a parliament like the king of France; keep the great people in check and favor the lesser people; do not live licentiously; do not be considered effeminate, and do not be ruled by your mother; avoid committing a grave injury against anyone near you; do not have a cruel

and bestial disposition; avoid contemptible actions; if you are of base blood, you may be hated; do not be ferocious; keep down the avarice and cruelty of the army so as not to hurt the people.

21. One is reminded here of the tracts *De tyrannide* of John of Salisbury and *De tyranno* of Coluccio Salutati because both argued that not everyone had the right to assassinate a tyrant. Instead, it is implied, a group of the big men in the state should decide and act on it. But Machiavelli is more "liberal" on this point than the other two. Immediately following the given quotation, he says: "Still, if one of this class of [low] persons should be daring enough to attempt such an undertaking, he would merit praise rather for his intention than for his prudence."

22. Detmold trans., pp. 428–29; Bertelli ed., p. 406.

23. Bonfantini, in his edition of Machiavelli's *Opere* (in the series La Letteratura Italiana: Storia e Testi, vol. 29, p. 320) says: "Dobbiamo perciò pensare che questa generica protesta fosse da lui collacata sul principio della sua trattazione per motivi prudenziali, onde non inimicarsi i principi del tempo suo, e soprattutto i Medici."

24. Detmold trans., pp. 417, 420, 421; Bertelli ed., pp. 396–97, 400. See Tacitus *Annales* xv. 49–50; xv. 54–56; xv. 51–53.

25. Detmold trans., end of p. 430 to the middle of p. 433; Bertelli ed., middle of p. 408 to middle of p. 410. Aside from this section, there are only two or three short scattered comments pertaining to republics, i.e., on conspiring against them.

26. Detmold trans., p. 431; Bertelli ed., p. 408: "Questo s'intende in una republica dove è qualche parte di corrozione; perché in una non corrotta, non vi avendo luogo nessuno principio cattivo, non possono cadere in uno suo cittadino questi persieri."

27. And here it is hard not to remember *Discourses* i. 10 about Julius Caesar, who sent his country to hell in a basket, so to speak. And here, in *Discourses* iii. 6 (Detmold trans., p. 432; Bertelli ed., p. 409): "And it is not everyone that controls an army, like Caesar, or Agathocles, or Cleomenes, and the like, who by a single blow made themselves masters of their country."

28. The Latin of Machiavelli's quotation from Tacitus (Bertelli ed., p. 198): "'Proclivius est iniuriae, quam beneficio vicem exsolvere, quia gratia oneri, ultio in quaestu habetur.'" The line is taken from Tacitus *Historiae* iv. 3 with only slight variation: "Tanto proclivius est iniuriae quam beneficio vicem exsolvere, quia gratia oneri, ultio in quaestu habetur." The new emperor, Vespasian, allowed the rebellious town of Capua to be punished, although he sent no assistance to Tarracina. The contexts are parallel in that both are concerned with an ungrateful prince; but in Machiavelli the object of the ingratitude is generals, while in Tacitus it is a town.

29. Von Stackelberg, *Tacitus in der Romania*, pp. 72–73; see also pp. 50–55 and 66–68 for the basis of this denial, i.e., that Machiavelli did not know of the first part of the *Annales*. See also below, n. 31.

30. The Latin is from the Bertelli edition, p. 443.

31. Because of the contradiction, Bertelli (ibid., n. 2) has qualified his cross-reference to Tacitus with a "però." Leo Strauss, however, in his *Thoughts on Machiavelli* (Seattle: University of Washington Press, 1969; first published in 1958), pp. 160–65, is not so excessively scrupulous and rightly sees Machiavelli mindful of, though misquoting, Tacitus' statement. Von Stackelberg, however, remains unconvinced of the connection. He objects to L. J. Walker, *The Discourses of Niccolò Machiavelli*, 2 vols. (New Haven, Conn., 1950), 2:183, who pointed out Machiavelli's use of *Annales* iii. 55 here. Von Stackelberg, on the contrary, argues that there is little similarity in the wording—

mentioning that it is identical in *obsequium* and *poena* only; moreover, an analysis of the context in Machiavelli "schliesst eine Erinnerung an den Passus aus Tacitus geradezu aus." His argument here is that Machiavelli spoke of the masses, the *multitudo*, while Tacitus mentions no such thing. However, von Stackelberg then rightly sees a problem in the fact that Tacitus in this sentence—which Machiavelli quoted wrongly—speaks of just the opposite.

But, more generally, von Stackelberg's argument here is only a particular deduction from his larger thesis (pp. 50–55 and 66–68), that Machiavelli had absolutely no knowledge of the first part of the *Annales*. But here von Stackelberg has a problem over the reference to *Annales* i. 79 in bk. ii, chap. 2 of Machiavelli's *History of Florence*. But on this problem and all its ramifications, see note 37, below.

32. Strauss, *Thoughts on Machiavelli*, pp. 160–65, clearly demonstrates these chapters (i. 19–23) to be a "Tacitean subsection."

33. Perhaps it was of some influence on Carlo Pasquali (Paschalius), who published the first political commentary *specifically dedicated to Tacitus* (in 1581). See chapter 5, below.

34. *Annales* iii. 52: "stringent legislation was apprehended against the luxury which had reached boundless excess"; "fear that a prince who clung to old-fashioned frugality would be too stern in his reforms"; "moderate measures could not stop the evil." *Annales* iii. 53: "the corruptions withwhich we cannot cope"; "restraining and cutting down to the old standard." *Annales* iii. 54: "demand some restriction"; "can be checked only by sharp and painful treatment"; "quenched only by remedies as strong"; "if any of our officials give promise of such energy and strictness as can stem the corruption."

35. As in the quotation on p. 79, above. The italics are mine.

36. This whole section of my analysis of the *Discourses* demonstrates the truth of Baron's allusions and hints concerning specific Tacitan elements in this republican tradition which influenced Machiavelli in particular (Hans Baron, *Crisis of the Early Italian Renaissance: Civic Humanism and Republican Liberty in an Age of Classicism and Tyranny*, rev. ed. [Princeton: Princeton University Press, 1966], esp. p. 70).

37. Von Stackelberg, *Tacitus in der Romania*, pp. 50–55, 66–68 (and see nn. 29 and 31, above, on the author's denial that Machiavelli used *Annales* iii. 55 in *Discourses* iii. 19). On the *History of Florence* reference, von Stackelberg asserts that Machiavelli got his knowledge of the passage only indirectly: his source is supposed to have been the quotation from *Annales* i. 79 attached to the letter of Cardinal Francesco Soderini to Marcello Virgilio, Machiavelli's colleague in the Soderini government, in 1509 (see pp. 16–17 of my Introduction). Cardinal Soderini informed Virgilio of the newly discovered manuscripts and the comments in them about the Florentines. Machiavelli, so the argument runs, got the letter from Virgilio because Paolo Giovio, the famous historian, later remarked that Virgilio was accustomed to loaning texts to Machiavelli. This argument is more ingenious than realistic. Indeed, if Machiavelli could have read the *same* words in an edition of Tacitus or the words of Tacitus quoted by Soderini, it really says nothing about his necessarily getting them from the latter. And the point about Virgilio loaning texts to Machiavelli is not significant at all: one may as well assume that Machiavelli got his Livy, his Seneca, his Caesar, and every other text from Virgilio as well. And even if Machiavelli did get the letter from his friend, it is realistic to expect that he would have excitedly awaited the day when the new texts would be published—especially after 1513, having liked Tacitus enough to quote him once or twice in the *Prince*. And, after using Tacitus with such high regard in the *Discourses* (including the passage from *An-*

nales iii. 55, which was among the newly discovered sections), it is clear that he had read Tacitus directly: almost certainly in the new Beroaldus edition of 1515.

But aside from the reference in the *History of Florence*, von Stackelberg tries to show that Machiavelli never knew the first section of the *Annales*, on the grounds that he passed up "chances" to use it. Von Stackelberg asserts that in this or that place in Machiavelli's writing he could have used this or that passage of Tacitus. This approach is worthless. There are plenty of "chances" Machiavelli passed up even in Livy, to say nothing of the "chances" he passed up in those parts of Tacitus which von Stackelberg admits he knew.

38. Translated by Allan Gilbert in his edition of the *History of Florence*, 3:1082. The passage is based on *Annales* i. 79: "A question was then raised in the Senate by Arruntius and Ateius whether, in order to restrain the inundations of the Tiber, the rivers and lakes which swell its waters should be diverted from their courses. A hearing was given to embassies from the municipal towns and colonies, and the people of Florentia begged that the Clanis might not be turned out of its channel and made to flow into the Arnus, as that would bring ruin on themselves."

39. Allan Gilbert's edition of the *History of Florence*, 3:1028. Giannotti, in Machiavelli's last years (1525–27) was very likely involved in an anti-Medici plot and in the '30s was an exile and a determined Medici opponent. He explicitly admitted his indebtedness to Machiavelli's writings about conspiracies. See Randolph Starn, ed., *Donato Giannotti and His "Epistolae"* (Geneva: Librairie Droz, 1968), pp. 20–22, 39.

40. See my Preface also.

41. Giuseppe Toffanin, *Machiavelli e il "Tacitismo": La "politica storica" al tempo della Controriforma* (Padua: A. Draghi, 1921), p. 43: "influenza dell'uno sull'altro ben più dinamica, ma più inconscia nel mistero delle assimilazioni spirituali." See von Stackelberg, *Tacitus in der Romania*, pp. 64–66, where this quotation and other examples from Toffanin serve as a basis for his acute and witty criticism of the author.

42. Giuseppe Prezzolini, *Machiavelli Anticristo* (Rome: Gherardo Casini, 1954). The author has also written the historical romance, *Vita di Niccolò Machiavelli*, which Theodor Lücke for some reason or other thought merited a German translation (Dresden: Widerstandsverlag, 1929). For Prezzolini's warm acknowledgment of Toffanin (aside from the great implicit influence) see *Machiavelli Anticristo*, p. 300, among other places. The text is also available in English translation, *Machiavelli*, by Giocanda Savine (New York: Farrar, Straus & Giroux, 1967).

43. Prezzolini, *Machiavelli Anticristo*, p. 109: "Una volta Machiavelli cita Tacito (D. III. XIX, 228b) e invece di scrivere 'quando dice,' scrive 'quando *ait*.' Vorrei saper che cose direbbe un critico delle paroline. Vedrebbe probabilmente Machiavelli compresso d'ammirazione davanti a Tacito (che è citato col nome due volte sole da lui), che, non potendo altrimenti manifestare la sua ammirazione, avrebbe usato la parola latina, quasi che Tacito non potesse *dire* semplicamente come ogni mortale (come Dante, per es. *Lett.* 10 dicembre 1513), e l'operazione del pronunziare una sentenza fosse da significarsi soltanto con un *ait* più maestoso, più solenne, e magari più breve (d'una sillaba) dell' italiano." Of similar interest is Leo Strauss, *Thoughts on Machiavelli*, p. 325, n. 171: "Machiavelli introduces the citation [in *Discourses* iii. 19] with the Latin *ait:* he draws our attention to the fact that he can write Latin; he thus prepares us for his writing some Tacitean Latin."

44. All cited in Sasso, *Niccolò Machiavelli*, pp. 268–69, n. 66: Walker, *Discourses of Machiavelli*, 2:285; C. Marchesi, *Tacito* (Milan, 1944), pp. 171–73; P. Beguin, "Le 'Fatum' dans l'oeuvre de Tacite," *L'Antiquité Classique* 20 (1951): 315–34.

45. Sasso, *Niccolò Machiavelli*, pp. 268–69, n. 66.

46. Ibid., p. 192: "che la fortuna non è una trascendente divinità ma la conseguenza di un limite della natura umana, e può perciò esser sempre riportata a quella radice umana che è la sua stessa condizione. Il Machiavelli si era proposto di comprendere i termini reali di una situazione storica, di chiarire al suo pensiero una realtà angosciosa e tragica." This pertains specifically to the conception of Fortuna which Machiavelli revealed in a letter to Piero Soderini (late December 1512–January 1513). However, though the conception was greatly elaborated by Machiavelli as time went on, it remained basically founded in the concept explained by Sasso.

47. On Alciato, the following material is essential: Paul Émile Viard, *André Alciat: 1492–1550* (Paris: Société Anonyme du Recueil Sirey, 1926); the long introduction by Gian Luigi Barni, ed., *Le Lettere di Andrea Alciato Giuresconsulto* (Florence: Le Monnier, 1953); Roberto Abbondanza, "Premières considérations sur la méthodologie d'Alciat," *Pédagogues et juristes*, Congrès du Centre d'Etudes Supérieures de la Renaissance de Tours, 1960 (Paris: Vrin, 1963), pp. 107–18—abridged and translated by Eric Cochrane, ed., *The Late Italian Renaissance: 1525–1630* (New York: Harper & Row, 1970), pp. 77–90; and Abbondanza's "Tentativi medicei di chiamare l'Alciato a Pisa (1542–1547)," *Annali di storia del diritto* 2 (1958): 361–403. For Alciato's works (aside from the letters) there are many old and good editions but no modern critical ones.

48. It is a question how much Alciato was influenced by Budé's work. The two did not meet personally until about 1520, when Alciato was teaching in Avignon. There was increasingly bitter rivalry between them. Along with Ulrich Zazius, their German counterpart, they were considered a "triumvirate" in advancing the new legal scholarship, the *mos Gallicus* as opposed to the old *mos Italicus* of the Bartolus tradition.

49. Viard, *André Alciat*, p. 43.

50. On Ferretti's life and his painstaking examination of many Tacitus manuscripts—including the Mediceus codices—in the years 1531–42 see Else-Lilly Etter, *Tacitus in der Geistesgeschichte des 16. und 17. Jahrhunderts* (Basel: Helbing & Lichtenhahn, 1966), pp. 31–32.

51. Baudouin, *De institutione historiae universae* . . . , in Johan Wolfius, ed., *Artis historicae penus*, 2 vols. (Basel: Petrus Perna, 1579), 1:677: "et superstites reliquias iuris studiosis ludenter commendo: neque temere factum esse profiteor, quod duo aetatis nostrae nobilissimi interpretes iuris, And. Alciatus et Aemilius Ferrettus, in emendandis atque explicandis Taciti annalibus multum operae posuerint." Baudouin's work is printed here among many Renaissance *artes historicae*.

52. Ibid. As if aware of Alciato's slighting of Livy for Tacitus, Baudouin does his ultimate to demonstrate that Tacitus really lived about the same time as Livy anyway! He also wants to show that Tacitus praised Livy. For the first point, he says that the adolescent Tacitus could actually have heard the old Livy. Perhaps Baudouin didn't know that Livy died in 17 A.D., and that Tacitus was born around 55 A.D. The only possible grounds I can imagine (aside from the difficulty of determining, from internal evidence, Tacitus' probable age from his writings) for Baudouin's assertions is in the *Dialogus* xvii, where Aper, the speaker for modern eloquence, tries to show that the notion that Cicero and others are "the ancients" is false: "only a hundred and twenty years from the death of Cicero to the present day. No more than the life of an individual." Aper then goes on to mention the man in Britain he spoke to who said he had fought against Caesar when the latter tried to invade the island. In support of his second point, that Tacitus praised Livy, Baudouin is probably thinking of *Annales* iv. 34 (the only line in which Tacitus explicitly

names Livy), which, however, occurs in a speech and so does not necessarily express Tacitus' own sentiment: "Livy, with a fame for eloquence and candor second to none, . . . " But Baudouin may somehow have forgotten that the line ends in a way that is not at all in support of Livy's candid eloquence: ". . . lavished such eulogies on Pompey that Augustus styled him 'the Pompeian'; yet it was without prejudice to their friendship." Baudouin makes one other comment on the proximity in time of the two historians. Both should be read, he says, because the law student will find in them everything he needs to learn about Rome: not too many years lie between the end of Livy's *History* and the beginning of Tacitus' *Annales* (Wolfius, ed., *Penus,* 1:676).

53. The preface, of course, was published in the three editions of the *Annotationes* following the first, but it was also published separately in 1530 (Hagenau) under the title *Historiae encomium* (and this, aside from its specific attention to Tacitus, is exactly what it is) in a volume along with J. Bracellus' *De bello Hispano* and G. Pontano's *De bello Neapolitano.* The preface is a dedicatory epistle to Alciato's friend, Galeazzo Visconti. The source for my description and quotations is the text edited by Barni, pp. 221–24. See also chapter 5, below, for the important discussion over Alciato's remark (in a letter to Paolo Giovio) that Tacitus' style was "full of thorns." The letter is probably spurious.

54. Baudouin (in Wolfius, ed., *Penus,* 1:676) similarly makes a point about the Romans being more valuable than the Greeks for the study of law. Unlike Alciato, however, he does not call them dishonest; he only says that not much on law is to be found in the Greek historians. For which reason he would rather read Livy, Sallust, Caesar, and Tacitus than Polybius, Dionysius, Diodorus, Plutarch, Appian, and Dio.

55. Alciato (Barni ed., p. 223): "at senatorum varias sententias, ingentes quorundam etiam instante fato spiritus, rerum gestarum consilia, principum varios motus et pacis tempore necessarias artes apud alios non aeque offendas. Sed et nobis prae Tacito sordescet Livius, cum ille clarorum virorum [the opening two words of the *Agricola*—and, perfectly relevant also, in the *Historiae* i. 3] exemplo plurimis nos praeceptis instructos dimittit, quemadmodum in caput autorum scelera, vertantur, quantum nominis ex constantia animique fortitudine nobis quaeramus, quam caute cum malis principibus agendum, quam modestos cum omnibus esse conveniat." For the whole passage Alciato may have Tacitus' own account of his own type of history in mind (*Annales* iv. 32–33). Note, too, that there are many passages in classical writings where statements of Stoic "withdrawal" are voiced in similar tone. Seneca, for example, in *Epistle* 105. 1–6: with influential persons "it will profit you to engage but not entangle yourself, lest the cure may cost you more than the risk. Nothing, however, will help you so much as keeping still—talking very little with others and as much as may be with yourself." Cited by Thomas W. Africa, *Rome of the Caesars* (New York: Wiley, 1965), pp. 95–96.

56. See pages 64–65, above.

57. The composition dates of Tacitus' works: for the *Dialogus* (scholars vary widely), A.D. 75, 78–81, 84–85, 95, 97, 97–98, or even, according to Syme, the best authority, c. 102–106/7; the *Agricola,* between October 97 and January 98; the *Germania,* 98; the *Historiae,* 98–109; and the *Annales,* again according to Syme (*Tacitus,* 465–80), completed as late as 117–18 or even 120–23, with Tacitus beginning them about 109.

58. Puteolanus, in Botfield, ed., *Praefationes,* p. 162 (see chap. 1, n. 45): "Absolvisse omnem historiae legem; nam cum suorum temporum majore ex parte memoriae consuluerit, id pari eloquentia ac libertate praestitit; debebat tribus deinceps gentis Flaviae imperatoribus ab iis ad maximos honores evectus, quos incorruptam rerum fidem professus ut nullo odio sic nullo amore rettulit, nihil falsi dicere, nihil veri omittere ausus."

Puteolanus is thinking primarily of *Historiae* i. 2—i.e., on Tacitus' honors under the Flavians.

59. Beroaldus, in Botfield, ed., *Praefationes*, p. 307: "Ac mihi quidem videtur per tot secula Cornelius non tam caput [*sic*] suum perdidisse, quam ultro ipse occultasse. Audiebat enim eam esse ignaviam temporum, eum bonarum litterarum contemptum ut non modo non quemquam videre, sed ne a quoquam videri quidem dignum esse existimaret." The basis for Beroaldus' last clause is *Agricola* xlv: "With Domitian it was the chief part of our miseries to see and to be seen."

60. Domitian, whom Tacitus feared and hated, had been dead for over a year when Tacitus began to write the *Agricola* and, thereafter, all his other works. But the nightmare of his life under this ruler may have poisoned his views of earlier emperors. For example, check Naphtali Lewis and Meyer Reinhold, skilled editors of the valuable *Roman Civilization: Sourcebook II: The Empire* (New York: Harper & Row, 1966), p. 93, who state that recent scholarship shows Tiberius to have been correct and moderate in his application of the treason law and that "it seems clear that Tacitus retrojected to the time of Tiberius the reign of terror through which he lived under Domitian." Still, despite Tacitus' possibly warped impressions, he wrote in admittedly happy times.

61. According to Viard, *André Alciat*, pp. 91–111, esp. 91–93.

62. *Oratio habita Ferrariae MDXLIII cum primum professurus illuc venit*. See Viard, *André Alciat*, pp. 103–4.

63. On Sadoleto and the Avignon incident see Viard, *André Alciat*, pp. 79–80, and, on Alciato's shifting tactics to get hired at Bourges, see Peter G. Bietenholz, *Basle and France in the Sixteenth Century: The Basle Humanists and Printers in Their Contacts with Francophone Culture* (Toronto: University of Toronto Press, 1971), p. 227. In March 1529 Alciato (in the same letter that contained the Avignon incident) asked Sadoleto to help get him a job at the University of Bologna. Sadoleto was equivocal in his answer: If you *really* want me to, I will write for you. But why do you want to return to a land so ruined by war anyway? (See Viard, pp. 79–80). See Viard also on the items immediately following: on the king of France, pp. 82–83; on Ludovico II, p. 86, n. 3; on the *Contra vitam monasticam*, p. 171 and esp. the long note on pp. 135–36.

64. This description, more clear than most attempted, is by Henry Green, *Andrea Alciati and His Book of Emblems: A Biographical and Bibliographical Study* (New York: Burt Franklin, n.d.; reprint of 1872 edition, London: Trübner), p. 10; see also p. 1. However, the word's definition still escapes an answer: see the review of Arthur Henkel and Albrecht Schöne, eds., *Emblemata: Handbuch zur Sinnbildkunst des XVI. und XVII. Jahrhunderts* (Stuttgart: J. B. Metzlersche Verlagsbuchhandlung and C. E. Poeschel Verlag, 1967), by William S. Heckscher and Cameron F. Bunker in *Renaissance Quarterly* 23, no. 1 (Spring 1970): 65: "I suspect that diligent search might help in uncovering the reason for Alciati's choice of the word *emblema* which started the ball rolling." The reviewers then offer a few suggestions.

65. Green, *Andrea Alciati and His Book of Emblems*, p. 9 and passim, says that Alciato most probably printed a book of emblems, of 100 items, in 1522 but that because it was so badly executed he withdrew it in disgust and destroyed whatever copies he could lay his hands on. Green tries to reconstruct which of the eventual 212 items were in this 1522 edition, assuming there was one.

66. Described ibid., pp. 41, 43. The first, "Firmissima Conveli non posse," with an oak tree in a storm and an ode to Charles V on raising the siege by Suleiman the Magnificent on 16 October 1529, first appeared in the 1531 edition. The second, "Laurus," with a laurel tree, celebrates Charles's defeat of Barbarossa.

67. Described ibid., pp. 43–44.

68. Alciato's *emblema* "Respublica liberata" in *Andr. Alciati iuriscons. mediolanensis in Decretalium titulos aliquot . . . Commentaria . . . Tractatus, Orationes, Adnotationes in C. Tacitum, & Emblemata* (Lyons, 1560), p. 348v:

> Caesaris exitio, ceu libertate recepta,
> Haec ducibus Brutis c[a]usa moneta fuit.
> Ensiculi in primis, queis [quibus] pileus in super adstat,
> Qualem missa manu servitia accipiunt.

The *emblema* first appeared in the collection, with eighty-six new items, of 1546 (Venice, the Aldine Press). It appears on leaf twenty-six. It is enumerated as item 150 and item 151, respectively, in the more standardized editions of 1574 and 1621.

The verse is elegiac. The sentiment of utmost contempt is most skillfully packed into the most subtle language. The English translation cannot convey Alciato's sneers. I thank my friend, Dieter Hoffmann, with whom, as a fellow student at the University of Tübingen, I debated and analyzed the innuendoes in these lines.

Later I was much helped by learning that Alciato had an actual Roman coin in mind. It is itemized and pictured in David R. Sear, *Roman Coins and Their Values,* The Seaby Catalogue, rev. ed. (London: Stockwell, 1970), p. 76, as item no. 320, valued at 500 pounds. There is a photograph of it also in Fred Reinfeld, *New Treasury of the World's Coins* (New York: Bantam, 1967), p. 45; and, on page 31 there, it is stated that the liberty cap of Roman freedmen appeared on many early American coins.

69. Sometimes directly, sometimes indirectly; see the following chapters, esp. chap. 5.

70. Which is not to imply that everyone liked what he did or, for that matter, even liked him. Luigi Firpo, at the Machiavelli Conferences (September and October 1969) demonstrated, with many contemporary references, Machiavelli's disagreeable personality; see his article, "Le origini dell'anti-Machiavellismo," *Il Pensiero Politico* 2, no. 3 (1969): 337–67.

71. From Viard's study it seems that Alciato married when young but that his wife died within a year or two, before he took up his first position at Avignon. But, according to Quirinus Breen, *John Calvin: A Study in French Humanism,* 2d ed. (n.p.: Archon Books, 1968), p. 51, he left his wife in Milan during his four years in Avignon. Breen, by the way, tries too hard to give Calvin some backing for his view that Alciato was a frivolous Italian. Breen implies that Alciato was some kind of dirty old man: for portraying many nudes in his *emblemata,* for showing the Cupid figure frequently in them, and for his liking to deal with the theme of student love. Breen gives no specific evidence for these points. At any rate, Alciato had a son, but there is only one small reference to him in all of Alciato's letters (see the Barni edition).

72. According to Nicolai Rubinstein, however, Machiavelli's role in the government was limited to making suggestions on policy; he had no part in adopting it or carrying it out. See Cochrane's note on the Conferences in *Renaissance Quarterly* 22, no. 4 (Winter 1969): 424–29, esp. p. 427.

73. My authorities for Guicciardini are von Albertini, *Das florentinische Staatsbewusstsein;* Gilbert, *Machiavelli and Guicciardini;* Roberto Ridolfi, *Vita di Francesco Guicciardini* (Rome: Angelo Belardetti, 1960) (translated since by Cecil Grayson, *The Life of Francesco Guicciardini* [London: Routledge & Kegan Paul, 1967]); Vittorio de Caprariis, *Francesco Guicciardini: Dalla politica alla storia* (Bari: Laterza, 1950). For Guicciardini's works I used the nine-volume *Opere* edited by Roberto Palmarocchi for the Scrittori d'Italia series (Bari: Laterza, 1936); the *Carteggi di Francesco*

Guicciardini, edited by Roberto Palmarocchi (vols. 1–4) and Pier Giorgio Ricci (vols. 5–17) in the series Fonti per la Storia d'Italia (Rome: Istituto Storico Italiano per l'Età Moderna e Contemporanea, 1938–70); *Le cose fiorentine*, edited by Roberto Ridolfi (Florence: Olschki, 1945); and the *Ricordi*, in the critical edition by Raffaelo Spongano (Florence: Sansoni, 1951). For standard translations I used the *Maxims and Reflections of a Renaissance Statesman* (*Ricordi*), translated by Mario Domandi (New York: Harper & Row, 1965); and the *History of Florence* with the *History of Italy*, translated by Cecil Grayson and edited and abridged by John R. Hale (New York: Washington Square, 1964). These editions of Guicciardini's works have useful introductions also.

74. The dating of the individual *ricordi* is of great importance for my analysis of Guicciardini. My study of the Tacitus *ricordi* helps, in fact, to give some grounds for dating a few of them. Regardless of which other *ricordi* in the "B" series were or were not composed in April 1528, my analysis shows that the three on Tacitus were likely written in 1528 (or even 1526–28, without my thesis being seriously affected): in the context of that period they take on a significance which would be lacking otherwise. On the other hand, there is no argument on the two Tacitus *ricordi* of collection "C" (1530–32); everyone agrees on those dates of composition for the whole collection. Other problems and some possible solutions will become clear. See Spongano on the enormous problems involved in dating the *Ricordi*.

75. All translations of the *Ricordi* are from the Domandi edition.

76. Guicciardini may be confused here. Tacitus mentions no certain conversations at Augustus' death. He says only that it has not been ascertained whether Tiberius "found Augustus still breathing or quite lifeless" (*Annales* i. 5). But then, Tacitus (*Annales* i. 13) mentions some "last conversations" of Augustus, at which Tiberius does not seem to be present but which he heard of. Also, Guicciardini's allusion to the thoughts of tyrants is too vague to apply here with confidence. Perhaps, too, he was thinking of Suetonius' report, in his life of Augustus, chap. 91.

77. In this case, Guicciardini is definitely mindful of *Annales* iii. 65.

78. However, aside from the few comments following below in the text, this statement is made on loose grounds. There is nothing in the words of either B-78 or B-79 or in the related *ricordi* on tyranny—B-81, B-82, B-83—to suggest that Guicciardini is thinking specifically of a princely as opposed to a demogogic tyranny. Similarly with B-101: the words do not strongly suggest either one meaning or the other; and, in this case, there are no corollary *ricordi* either preceding or following to help explain its object more definitely. Thus, the basis for my statement is supposition alone. But then there are the questions of exactly when in 1530 Guicciardini could have added the final comment to B-79 (see a few sentences below in the text) and of exactly when he decided to drop B-101 in this year (if not, indeed in 1531 or 1532). And, along this line, it is noteworthy that Tacitus was moved up almost to the beginning of the "C" collection, while in the "B" collection he was sandwiched in the middle. But these are all the vaguest speculations. Regardless of the particular target of the individual *ricordi* (princely or demagogic tyranny), my thesis remains basically unaffected. Besides, if neither way can be proved, it should be assumed that Guicciardini referred to both forms of tyranny in each *ricordo*. And this was probably his reason for keeping the idea so general.

79. I owe the finding of this reference to Ridolfi, *Vita*, p. 217 (in the Grayson translation, p. 138): Guicciardini writes: "Altrimenti solo prevalerà a tutti, non per maggiori forze ma, come Cornelio Tacito, *fatali omnium ignavia*." In his notes, on p. 471 (Grayson trans., p. 302), Ridolfi cites this letter as being to Guicciardini's friend, Cesare

Colombo, and the advice to be shown to the pope—including the Tacitus reference—contained therein. Ridolfi was unable to supply the source of the Tacitus phrase. It comes from *Annales* xv. 61, pertaining to the death of Seneca.

I have found no use of Tacitus by Guicciardini earlier than this letter of 1526. For most of his works the search has not been difficult. For the *Carteggi* however, still without an index, my quest was made tedious by having to scan through each volume, page by page, looking for "Tacitus" and Latin quotations and words, which are italicized. But even if I missed any references before 1526 (or even after 1526, up to the *Ricordi* of 1530–32) my argument would not be seriously affected unless Guicciardini expressed the sentiments of *ricordo* C-18 in one of them.

In fact, I have discovered no evidence that Guicciardini had ever even read Tacitus before 1526. Ridolfi, on the contrary (*Vita,* p. 10; Grayson trans., p. 5), states that he read Tacitus before he was sixteen years old, i.e., before 1499. His statement, supported with a reference to the *Cose fiorentine*, is strongly suspect. But first, a little background on the context of the problem: Guicciardini's unfinished *Cose fiorentine* was begun by him around 1526 or 1527. In it he used Tacitus, along with Frontinus, for information on the origin and name of Florence (*Le cose fiorentine,* Ridolfi ed., p. 5; cf. *Opere,* de Caprariis ed., p. 347): "Et Cornelio Tacito conferma el nome medesimo di Florentia; el quale fu sì pocho distante dalla età da Plinio, che la cità in si breve tempo non potecte havere tale augumento che facessi convertire el nome suo in Florentia, che è la causa della mutatione assegnata da coloro che hanno havuto opinione che da principio la si chiamassi Fluentia. Credo adunche che el nome suo proprio et primo fussi Florentia, et me persuado che el medesimo harebbono creduto Lionardo, el Poggio et gl'altri, se havessino havuto facultà di leggere questi scriptori, l'uno de' quali venne in luce non molti anni sono, *dell'altro e' primi tre libri, che parlano di Florentia colonia, furono ritovati nella adolescentia mia.*" (Italics mine.) Although confusing the number of the books, a question easily open to debate (until Lipsius straightened everyone out), he bases his description on the reference in *Annales* i. 79, as had Machiavelli. On Frontinus, thinking of the *De aquaeductibus,* Guicciardini confuses the text's discovery (by Poggio at Monte Cassino in 1429) with its first publication by the printer Eucharius Silber, about 1486. Poggio apparently did not use it for his *History*.

Now, Ridolfi (*Vita,* p. 10) is suspect on three points for quoting this *Cose fiorentine* reference to support his argument that Tacitus was among the authors Guicciardini studied in his boyhood: "I suoi primi studi di umanità saranno stati conformi alle consuetudini e alle regole pedagogiche del tempo; nè i suoi scritti dell'età matura ci mostrano in modo particolare un lungo studio e un grande amore per gli antichi scrittori, fatta eccezione per gli storici: principalmente, dopo Livio, Senofante, Tucidide e il suo Tacito." He then quotes from the *Cose fiorentine* on Tacitus and Frontinus. First of all, then, Ridolfi has weak grounds for providing proof, twenty-seven years after the context of the statement. Second, and more serious, the reference Guicciardini points to is from the first part of the *Annales,* which he could not have read before he was twenty-six (1509, when the texts were first discovered) or thirty-two (when the texts were first published by Beroaldus in 1515): both ages rather late for "adolescentia mia." But here, Guicciardini may have used the term in the classical Latin sense, which was very broad: ranging anywhere from the early teens to forty-five years of age (watch for a forthcoming article by George Javor, a philologist at Northern Michigan University). Considering then, the wide span Guicciardini may have had in mind, Ridolfi's position could be extremely shaky. Third, Guicciardini nowhere says he *read* Tacitus in his adolescence; he only says they were *discovered* then. In all, if Ridolfi has proof for his assertion, he chose a very problematic reference for support. Moreover, even if he has better evidence (which he for some reason fails to cite) for Guicciardini's boyhood knowledge of other works of Tacitus, my own analysis shows why Guicciardini waited so long to use his Tacitus: it was that he was not prompted to do so prior to his own political crises in the years 1526–32.

80. According to the nonliteral but more effective translation of the line from *Annales* xv. 61 by John Jackson in the Loeb series.

81. *Opere,* edited by Palmarocchi, 9:219, ''Leggete in Cornelio Tacito, scrittore gravissimo, che Augusto insino al dí che morei, insino al punto che spirava l'anima, ancora che per la vecchiaia ed infirmità avessi gia consumato el corpo e lo spirito, lasciò per ricordo a Tiberio, successore suo, che erano quegli di chi non doveva fidarsi.'' I have not been able to place Guicciardini's reference. And neither *Annales* i. 5 nor i. 13 (noted already, n. 76, above) seems to apply.

82. See n. 79, above.

83. Thomas W. Africa, in his very enjoyable *Rome of the Caesars* (New York: John Wiley, 1965), p. 170, hints at a deeply psychological cause for Guicciardini's fascination with Tacitus: ''Though they lived centuries apart, both Guicciardini and Tacitus had bloodied their hands in political purges, groveled before princes at Rome, and later relieved their guilt by libeling rulers who were safely dead. Assessing a kindred spirit, Guicciardini remarked that . . .''; he then quotes *ricordo* C-18. Africa also draws a parallel between Montaigne's criticism of Guicciardini (in *Essays* ii. 10) as applicable to Tacitus as well.

84. Classical authors in the *Ricordi:* Livy (B-149), who mentions the decree of the Syracusans on the killing of the daughters of tyrants; Aristotle (?), ''the philosopher'' quoted (C-58) on there being no truth about future contingencies; and Seneca (*Epistolae ad Lucilium* cvii), quoted (B-80): ''Ducunt volentes fata, nolentes trahunt.'' Saint Augustine, though not strictly a classic, is cited twice (C-33 and B-65).

85. Alessandro, cited in Cochrane, *Florence in the Forgotten Centuries: 1527–1800: A History of Florence and the Florentines in the Age of the Grand Dukes* (Chicago: University of Chicago Press, 1973), p. 26.

86. Ibid.

87. Guicciardini, *History of Italy* i. i; translated by Grayson in the Hale edition, p. 85.

88. See Abbondanza, ''Tentativi medicei di chiamere l'Alciato a Pisa (1542–1547)'' (cited in n. 47, above).

Chapter 5

1. See the Introduction for other translators relative to this period. Another is an anonymous translation of the *Historiae* (Venice, 1544) listed by von Stackelberg, *Tacitus in der Romania: Studien zur literarischen Rezeption des Tacitus in Italien und Frankreich* (Tübingen: Max Niemeyer, 1960), pp. 247, 275. In general, translations of Tacitus were not too frequent until after the 1570s and 1580s. Before then, Tacitus was almost always read in Latin. For an analysis of French translations for the whole sixteenth century, see von Stackelberg, ibid., pp. 251–52, and a notice on p. 161. For the Italian, see ibid., pp. 245–49. And note carefully that any political sentiment or motivations in these translations mentioned in von Stackelberg are all well outside my thirty-three year period after 1533.

2. For Erasmus, I have referred to Tenney, ''Tacitus in the Middle Ages and the Early

Renaissance and in England to about the Year 1650'' (Ph.D. diss., Cornell University, 1931), pp. 289–98. On Erasmus' recommendation of Tacitus for schoolchildren, see his letter to Petrus Episcopus of Cracow (entitled *In Senecam*) of 1529 (in *Opus epistolarum Des. Erasmi Roterdami,* 12 vols., ed. P. S. Allen [Oxford: Clarendon Press, 1906–58], 8:33); and note also a letter of 1527 (ibid., 6:482). But Tenney correctly notes that Tacitus is absent in Erasmus' tracts on education (*De ratione studii, De pueris instituendis . . . , De scribendis epistolis*) or in works on the training of a prince, such as the *Institutio principis Christiani*. This absence may be surprising, considering that Erasmus (in his famous letter to Martin Dorp of 1515 [see *Opus Epis.* 2:90–114]) recognized an undesirable point in Tacitus—his anti-Christian sentiments—but recommended that despite this he ought to be read for his erudition.

For Vives, see the *Libri de disciplinis,* part 2: *De tradendis disciplinis seu de institutione Christiana libri vi* (here in the German translation by Friedrich Kayser, *Johannes Ludovicus Vives: Pädagogische Schriften,* Bibliothek der katholischen Pädagogik, vol. 8 [Freiburg i.B.: Herder, 1896]). There are four references, as follows. Bk. 3, chap. 6, p. 263: there is much cruelty described in Tacitus, which is certainly dangerous to imitate, but, still, Tacitus is noble, splendid, sharp, etc. Bk. 4, chap. 4, p. 293: for the broad historical style, read Livy; for the presentation of ideas read Tacitus. Bk. 5, chap. 2, p. 322: Tacitus is very valuable for his emphasis on guiding principles, especially in regard to war and peace. Bk. 5, chap. 2, p. 324: among historians who have written of single men there is Tacitus on his father-in-law, Agricola.

In the same volume there is one other reference to Tacitus which ought to be singled out. It is in the *De institutione feminae Christianae ad Sereniss. D. Catharinam Hispanam Anglicae Reginam,* of April 1523, ed. Kayser, p. 366: Vives speaks of the delicacy of the impressionable age of children, of their first years, when morals should be inculcated in them. ''For an explanation of what I mean, I submit the words of Cornelius Tacitus about the spiritual dispositions of the ancient Romans.'' He then quotes a long passage from the *Dialogus* (xxviii): ''In the good old days'' to ''virtuous accomplishments'' in the Loeb edition. Vives then adds: ''So Tacitus. One sees thereby in what manner and with what means these ancient Romans had climbed to the apex of virtue.''

3. Tenney, ''Tacitus in the Middle Ages,'' pp. 278–80 (see also page 5 of an abstract of the same, published under the same title [Ithaca, N.Y.: Cornell University Press, 1932]).

4. Ibid., pp. 299–301, with quotations. Tenney refers to the *De emendata structura latini sermonis libri sex,* 1st ed. (London, 1524). Others followed in 1527, 1529, 1530, 1533, 1540, etc.

5. Ibid., pp. 292–93, with a list of Erasmus' sentences.

6. Baldessare Castiglione, *The Book of the Courtier,* translated by Charles S. Singleton (New York: Doubleday, 1959), pp. 62–65. True, the interlocutors leave the debate hanging, but the argument favoring Tacitus and Italicus (i.e., that they are equal to Cicero and Virgil) is implicitly Castiglione's own. Remember that Castiglione, in the dedicatory epistle to the work, says, ''Neither do I understand why so much more authority should be granted to one manner of speech than to another'' (p. 5).

7. Tenney, ''Tacitus in the Middle Ages,'' pp. 312–14.

8. See chapter 7.

9. Arnaldo Momigliano, ''The First Political Commentary on Tacitus,'' *Contributo alla storia degli studi classici* (Rome: Edizioni di Storia e Letteratura, 1955), pp. 38–59, esp. p. 47. The article first appeared in the *Journal of Roman Studies* 37 (1947): 91–101.

10. Tenney (''Tacitus in the Middle Ages'') provided the facts. Polydore Vergil,

Edward Hall, John Leslie, et al., are all duly listed, and perhaps every single Tacitus citation is quoted or at least mentioned. Tenney sometimes devotes pages to English historians to show that Tacitus was *not* used by them—for example, John Leland (pp. 115–19). Still, even this information (or lack of it) is of significance, as will be clear later in this paragraph.

11. There are numerous sixteenth-century editions of the *Anglica historia*. On Polydore Vergil and his work see Denys Hay, *Polydore Vergil: Renaissance Historian and Man of Letters* (Oxford: Oxford University Press, 1952); Hay's thirty-four-page introduction to his translation (with Latin text) of bks. xxvi and xxvii (printed version) in *The Anglica Historia of Polydore Vergil: A.D. 1485–1537,* Camden Series, vol. 74 (London: Royal Historical Society, 1950); Sir Henry Ellis' edition of bks. i through viii, from an early English translation, in the Camden Series (London, 1848); and Tenney, "Tacitus in the Middle Ages," pp. 88–99, who quotes and briefly analyzes scores of Vergil's borrowings from Tacitus. Vergil had already used Tacitus in his *De inventoribus rerum* (Venice, 1499), a brilliant work of antiquarian research. Finally, note the introduction to the Ellis volume for the letter of Vergil to James IV of Scotland, written in 1509, complaining that Tacitus was unknown and unused in England. Vergil, unable to obtain a commission to do the work from King Henry VII (whom he goes out of his way to call a stingy old man, time and time again in the history), finally convinced Henry VIII to patronize him.

12. On Cheke, see Tenney, "Tacitus in the Middle Ages," p. 303; on Haddon, see ibid., p. 304.

13. Ibid., p. 302.

14. Ibid., pp. 312–16. Only in 1607 with John Cleland, tutor to Charles I, and his *The Institution of a Young Nobleman,* was Elyot's appreciation of Tacitus revived for this genre. On Cleland, see Tenney, pp. 315–19.

15. For the broader historical context, see Arthur B. Ferguson, " 'By Little and Little': The Early Tudor Humanists on the Development of Man," in *Florilegium Historiale: Essays Presented to Wallace K. Ferguson,* ed. J. G. Rowe and W. H. Stockdale (Toronto: University of Toronto Press, 1971).

16. For Tacitus in Boece and the other British historians in this paragraph, I rely, though always with caution, on Tenney's dissertation, "Tacitus in the Middle Ages."

17. But Tenney (ibid., p. 148) qualifies that this first English translation of the *Agricola* may have been inserted into the *Chronicles* by their immediate continuators, John Hooker and others.

18. See ibid., p. 168. Note also H. R. Trevor-Roper, *Queen Elizabeth's First Historian: William Camden and the Beginnings of English Civil History,* Neale Lectures in English History, 1971 (London: Cape, 1971), and F. Smith Fussner, *Tudor History and the Historians* (New York: Basic Books, 1970).

19. As paraphrased by Paul F. Grendler, *Critics of the Italian World, 1530–1650: Anton Francesco Doni, Nicolò Franco, and Ortensio Lando* (Madison: University of Wisconsin Press, 1969), pp. 149–50. Lando's *La Sferza de' Scrittori* (Venice: Arrivabene, 1550) is, according to Grendler, "a mockery on ancient and modern authorities." Lando has nothing especially against Tacitus; indeed, all the ancients have imperfections. Among historians: Diodorus told fables, Thucydides exaggerated, Xenophon wrote fictions and was prolix, etc.

20. For the origins of the Ciceronian dogmatism in historiography I refer to Hanna H. Gray, "History and Rhetoric in Quattrocento Humanism" (Ph.D. diss., Radcliffe, 1957) and her article, "Renaissance Humanism: The Pursuit of Eloquence," *Journal of the*

History of Ideas 24 (1963): 497–514. For the period at hand, see Beatrice Reynolds, "Shifting Currents in Historical Criticism," *Journal of the History of Ideas* 14, no. 4 (1953): 471–92 (also in Paul O. Kristeller and Philip P. Wiener, eds., *Renaissance Essays* [New York: Harper & Row, 1968], pp. 115–36), where she analyzes the *artes historiae* of Francesco Robortello, Giovanni Pontano (though Gray, in her dissertation and article, is the chief authority on Pontano), Francesco Patrizi, François Baudouin, and others. Reynolds' source for these is the convenient anthology produced by Wolfius, already referred to (chap. 4, n. 51). Note also the important article by William J. Bouwsma, "Three Types of Historiography in Post-Renaissance Italy," *History and Theory* 4, no. 3 (1965): 303–14. Check, too, the good survey by Paul F. Grendler, written with a more specific genre in mind, "Francesco Sansovino and Italian Popular History: 1560–1600," *Studies in the Renaissance* 16 (1969): 139–80. But for what follows I found one study especially valuable for its fine synthesis of many problems handled less comprehensively in the other studies. I refer to Giorgio Spini, "The Art of History in the Italian Counter Reformation," in the translation by Cochrane of "I trattatisti dell'arte storica nella Controriforma italiana" (in *Contributi alla storia del Concilio di Trento e della Controriforma* [Florence: Vallecchi, 1948]) in *The Late Italian Renaissance: 1525–1630* (New York: Harper & Row, 1970), pp. 91–133.

21. Curione, cited and translated into German by Markus Kutter, *Celio Secondo Curione: Sein Leben und sein Werk, 1503–1569* (Basel: Helbing & Lichtenhahn, 1955), p. 275. It is from a letter to Boniface Amerbach written in February 1548.

22. For the description which follows, see ibid., pp. 242–43. On Curione the historian and *ars*-historiographer, see pp. 234–45.

23. Curione, from the *De historia legenda sententia,* translated by Burke, "A Survey of the Popularity of the Ancient Historians, 1450–1700," *History and Theory* 5, no. 2 (1966): 150. Burke himself cites it from Wolfius, *Penus,* 2:600.

24. Description from Kutter, *Celio Secondo Curione,* pp. 242–43.

25. Spini, in the Cochrane translation, *Late Italian Renaissance,* p. 107.

26. According to Kutter's description, pp. 237–38.

27. I have used the Latin translation in Wolfius, ed., *Penus,* 1:397–543: *De historia dialogi X*. Reynolds, "Shifting Currents" (see n. 20, above), has a three-page summary of it; but the best analysis is in Spini. On Patrizi the philosopher, see Paul Oskar Kristeller, *Eight Philosophers of the Italian Renaissance* (Stanford, Cal.: Stanford University Press, 1964), pp. 110–26.

28. The phrase, in summary, occurs in Wolfius, ed., *Penus,* 1:537, and in other places also: "autor, occasio, tempus, locus, modus agendi, et instrumenta." These elements are handled throughout in the context of such subjects as history's definition, diversity, universality, etc.

29. Patrizi, ibid., 1:529: "ex aequali aequale . . . ut verum profiteatur, et tantum verbis exprimat, quantum res ipsa continent."

30. Ibid., pp. 531–35. Cicero is brought up on p. 531.

31. Ibid., pp. 535–36.

32. Ibid., p. 515: "ut multifariam ex iis [ancient and recent histories] utilitatem, ad gubernandam hanc Remp. & pacem illius conservandam, consequerentur: intentique esse in earum rerumpub. imitatione, quae longo tempore floruerunt." And the three particular categories for this political utility are war, peace, and sedition.

33. Ibid., p. 532: on Livy, Thucydides, and Sallust (on Polybius see n. 35, below): "Livius, Thucydides, Sallustius & alii plures" are mentioned as "the most excellent

historians,'' who, nevertheless, have used many speeches in their writings. There follows a discussion about the type of oratory (if any) fit for inclusion in histories. Though there is debate on this matter, there is none over the epithet given the three examples. Besides, these three historians and Polybius are the subjects of 90 percent of Patrizi's analyses.

34. Burke, ''A Survey of the Popularity of Ancient Historians, 1450–1700,'' p. 145.

35. Patrizi, in Wolfius, ed., *Penus,* 1:536: ''Secunda ergo, quae historico praescribitur lex, non Polybium modo, verum etiam alios, qui tale aliquid faciant, coarguit. Dum enim res gestas enarrant, manent intra limites historici: sed ubi rerum causas & rationem scrutantur, philosophi munus obeunt.'' Probably the source of Burke's error is in the lines which follow immediately: ''[CAMILLUS:] 'In truth, I should have desired, that all historians possessed something philosophical, as Polybius' [Ego vero cuperem, inquit, omnes historicos, quiddam philosophicum, uti Polybius, obtinere]. [PATRIZI:] 'I think little of that' [Id, inquam, ego parvi facio].'' In these lines ''id'' pertains to ''quiddam philosophicum'' and not to Polybius, of course. Or perhaps Burke was confused, if he used the popular *Penus* edition by Wolfius, by the use of ''inquit'' and ''inquam'' in the Tenth Dialogue. In the other dialogues each speaker is introduced by the abbreviation of his name; but in the Tenth Dialogue, strangely enough, readers of the *Penus* edition must pay close attention to, for example, ''Camillus inquit,'' ''Et Cataneus . . .'' etc., which are the only guidelines among dozens of *inquit*s and *inquam*s per page. With three, four, or five speakers, it is no fun. Unfortunately, I was unable to refer to another edition.

36. Ibid., p. 535: Camillus, one of the speakers, questions: ''Sed quo pacto damnare potes hasce *tanti viri tam egregias, & ad civilem vivendi rationem tam utiles disputationes?*'' And Patrizi answers: ''*Ita est Camille, ut dicis, & merito mihi id obijicis:* sed erravi ego prius, quod alteram historiae legem non adiecerem'' (italics mine); he then goes on to quote the second law, as in my text. Thus, even Polybius' philosophical disputations within his history are useful to civic life (to the civic life of Venice). Reynolds (''Shifting Currents,'' p. 491) is correct, therefore, when she says that Polybius is the crux of the whole change in historiography which began with Patrizi.

37. Patrizi, in Wolfius, ed., *Penus,* 1:510.

38. Ibid., p. 422.

39. Ibid., p. 447: ''Nullus est enim historicus, qui non in eum finem scribat, ut in publicum edatur.'' Good advice!

40. Possibly the only hint (and that the slightest) that Patrizi, in this work, was even aware of Tacitus' existence is the phrase ''ac aliusquidam Germaniam'' brought up concerning ''mixed history''—i.e., including those who write ''praeter locorum descriptionem, etiam gentium mores, animantium & plantarum quarundam formas explicent.'' Leander (?), who described Italy, is in this category ''ac aliusquidam Germaniam,'' and he must be thinking of Tacitus, or Pliny, or Mela, or Strabo? (Patrizi, ibid., p. 415.)

41. The two others are a certain Robert Breton, who wrote *De optimo statu reipublicae liber* (Paris, 1543), and Jerome Garimberto, bishop of Gallese, who wrote *De' regimenti publici de la città* (Venice, 1544) and *Fatti memorabili d'alcuni Papi* (Venice, 1567).

42. Jean Bodin, *Methodus ad facilem historiarum cognitionem,* in Pierre Mesnard, ed., *Oeuvres Philosophiques de Jean Bodin,* Corpus Général des Philosophes Français, Auteurs Modernes, vol. 5, no. 3 (Paris: Presses Universitaires de France, 1951), p. 167, col. B, ll. 1–7. Only Mesnard's Latin text (Paris: Marinus Juvenus, 1572) of Bodin is used here and not Mesnard's translation, which follows in the same edition. The translations from Bodin's book are mostly my own, although for a few of them and for swifter general reading I have used the English translation by Beatrice Reynolds, ''*Method for the Easy Comprehension of History*'' *by John Bodin* (New York: Columbia University Press,

1945). Her edition is very valuable for identifications of the more obscure personages in the work.

For the place of my quotation, see Reynolds, ed., *Method* . . . , p. 154. But note that her text does not include Thomas More among the names Bodin lists there. This discrepancy and others are probably due to the fact that she used the 1583 edition and not the 1572 edition, as here. And, because this book stresses the genetic development of ideas, I have used the 1566 edition (at the University of Tübingen) to check very crucial passages—for example, the one just quoted. It would be of no little significance for my thesis if Patrizi had not been named in the 1566 edition. See page 178 of the same.

43. Mesnard, ed., *Oeuvres . . . de Jean Bodin,* p. 109, col. B, ll. 15–28; Reynolds, ed., *Method* . . . , p. 8—whom I follow here.

44. Patrizi, in Wolfius, ed., *Penus,* 1:409: "Ad primam quid dicam sane nescio, nisi quod historiae qualitates prius sciri nequeant, quam quid ea ipsa sit." (Ad secundam): "Docere quidem Pontanum, ex quibus historia constet, & quis sit illius finis, sed non monstrare quid illa sit, cum tamen is primus noster scopus fuerit."

45. Mesnard, p. 167, B.18–29; Reynolds, p. 154—whom I follow here.

46. All these points are contained within a few pages: Mesnard, p. 134, A.37–p.135, A.43; Reynolds, pp. 68–71. All, that is, except for Tacitus and his use of documents, for which see Mesnard, p. 126, A.40; Reynolds, p. 46.

47. Mesnard, p. 135, A.43; Reynolds, p. 71.

48. Mesnard, p. 135, B.19–20; Reynolds, p. 72.

49. Mesnard, p. 134, B.30–33; Reynolds, p. 69.

50. Mesnard, p. 134, A.51–53; Reynolds, p. 69.

51. Mesnard, p. 134, B.40–41; Reynolds, p. 70—whom I follow here.

52. Mesnard, p. 134, B.41–55; Reynolds, p. 70—with some crucial differences, of interpretation, from my translation. Note the Latin: "Sed me lacerat & conficit quorundam reprehensio, quae refutatione minus egeret, nisi auctoritate plurimum valerent. nam ausus est Alciatus historiam illam plane divinam senticeta vocare, in ea epistola quam ad Jovium scripsit. & quidem propter asperum dicendi genus ab iis repudiari solet, qui leviores Grammaticorum nugas malunt, quam gravissimas eorum narrationes qui totum vitae suae tempus in Repub. gerenda consumpserunt. quanquam non video cur Alciatus tantum virum contemnere; ipse de eloquentia triumphare debeat: nisi quod Decius illum ex albo Jurisconsultorum eximens Ciceronianum vocavit: non aliter ac Hieronymus qui se ante Christi tribunal verberibus caesum scripsit, quod Ciceronianus esset non Christianus. sed hic verberibus; ille contumelia nullo suo merito affectus est extra jocum."

53. I have not been able to discover Bodin's basis for saying that Decius called Alciato a Ciceronian and that he removed him from the list [?] of jurisconsults.

54. Giovio published a letter, which he said he had received from Alciato, in the first pages of his *Historiarum sui temporis tomus primus (secundus),* . . . (Florence, 1550). Giovio claimed it was an accident—that Alciato's letter just happened to be grabbed up with the manuscript of the book when he sent it to the publisher and that the publisher, by mistake, printed it. The letter, besides describing Tacitus' style as like "thorn patches," was damaging to Alciato in other ways, too—for example, in its explicit dislike of Pope Paul III. Contemporaries of Giovio believed the letter spurious and believed Giovio was vicious. The letter is dated from Ticino, 7 October 1548. My source is the edition of Giovio's *Historiae sui temporis,* edited by Visconti Ferraro and Giuseppe Guido Ferraro, 4 vols. (Rome: Istituto Poligrafico della Stato, 1956–57), 2:1–3. Giovio's excuses over the accident are in a letter to a friend (dated 19 September 1550), ibid., 2:173–76.

55. Mesnard, p. 130, B.52—p. 131, B.6; Reynolds, pp. 60–61.

56. Mesnard, p. 176, A.50–51, and p. 162, B.7–8; Reynolds, pp. 173 and 141.

57. On Bodin's life and thought I used Roger Chauviré, *Jean Bodin: Auteur de la "République"* (Paris: Champion, 1914); the biographical sketch in Mesnard, pp. vii–xxi, as well as his introductions to the works he presents; J. W. Allen, *A History of Political Thought in the Sixteenth Century* (New York: Barnes & Noble, 1960), pp. 394–444; and Julian H. Franklin, *Jean Bodin and the Sixteenth Century Revolution in the Methodology of Law and History* (New York: Columbia University Press, 1963). The last must be used with some caution.

58. "... ipso historiae parente": Mesnard, p. 131, A.37; Reynolds, p. 61.

59. Mesnard, p. 136, A.18–19; Reynolds, p. 73.

60. Mesnard, p. 136, B.16–18; Reynolds, p. 74.

61. Mesnard, p. 136, B.45–46; Reynolds, p. 75.

62. Mesnard, p. 129, B.42–45; Reynolds, p. 57.

63. According to Spini, "I trattatisti . . . ," in the Cochrane translation, p. 112. My own close reading of Patrizi definitely supports Spini here.

64. Mesnard, p. 128, B.59–p. 129, A. 6–8; Reynolds, p. 54—whom I follow here. Also mentioned for this talent in another passage, in the same breath with Machiavelli, are Guicciardini, Tacitus, and Plutarch: Mesnard, p. 129, B.42–45.

65. Mesnard, p. 167, A.50–55 (which also agrees with the 1566 edition, p. 178); Reynolds, p. 153—whom I follow here. The fact that everyone was speaking Machiavelli's views on government, according to Bodin in the 1566 edition—and that it was not a later inclusion—is obviously an important point for my approach. See at the end of this chapter, too, on Botero's similar report.

66. Mesnard, p. 149, B.41–50; Reynolds, p. 109.

67. On the chancellor: Mesnard, p. 190, B.28–31; Reynolds, p. 211. On the king: Mesnard, p. 209, B.10–11; Reynolds, p. 256.

68. Mesnard, p. 177, A.19–27; Reynolds, p. 178.

69. Mesnard, p. 205, A.3–p. 206, B. 20; Reynolds, pp. 245–49.

70. Mesnard, p. 206, A.25–28; Reynolds, p. 248.

71. Mesnard, p. 214, A.29–44; Reynolds, p. 267.

72. Mesnard, p. 215, A.52–56; Reynolds, p. 270.

73. Mesnard, p. 167, A.55–59; Reynolds, p. 153. The edition of 1566, p. 178, agrees also.

74. Mesnard, p. 129, A.2; Reynolds, p. 54.

75. Mesnard, pp. 177, B.15 and following; Reynolds, pp. 179–86.

76. All in Mesnard, p. 130, B.10–p. 131, A.33; Reynolds, pp. 59–60.

77. Mesnard, p. 177, A.19–27; Reynolds, p. 178.

78. Reynolds, p. 272. It is in the Mesnard edition too, but I have lost my exact reference to it.

79. For the *République* I used two editions: *Les Six Livres de la République de I. Bodin Angeuin: Ensemble une apologie de René Herpin* (Paris: Jacques de Puis, 1583), in the facsimile edition (n.p.: Scientia Aalen, 1961), and *The Six Bookes of a Commonwealth: A Facsimile Reprint of the English Translation of 1606 Corrected and Supplemented in the Light of a New Comparison with the French and Latin Texts*, edited by Kenneth Douglas McRae (Cambridge, Mass.: Harvard University Press, 1962). The index of the latter has been helpful.

80. Mesnard, p. 217, B.56–58; Reynolds, p. 276—whom I follow here. Bodin follows

with a severe criticism of Venice, with its multitude of magistrates, whom the Venetians spent most of the year choosing, etc.

81. For Lipsius see also the bibliography in the notes of chap. 6, below. But for what follows here on Lipsius' life I use Jason Lewis Saunders, *Justus Lipsius: The Philosophy of Renaissance Stoicism* (New York: Liberal Arts Press, 1955), a book which now must be read only in conjunction with the discoveries of Hendrik D. L. Vervliet, in *Lipsius' Jeugd 1547–1578: Analecta voor een kritische Biografie,* Mededelingen van de koninklijke Vlaamse Academie voor Wetenschappen, Letteren en schone Kunsten van België, Klasse der Letteren, vol. 31, no. 7 (Brussels: Palais der Academiën, 1969); see my review of this in *Renaissance Quarterly* 25, no. 1 (spring 1972): 86–87.

82. The *Variae lectiones* were finished in late 1567 or early 1568 but were not published until 1569 in Antwerp. They are a collection of conjectures and commentaries on ancient authors, and Lipsius already shows his perfect knowledge of Latin and his philological skill. Saunders, *Justus Lipsius,* p. 8, calls them one of the finest examples of sixteenth-century Ciceronian prose. Lipsius later called them a "folly of his youth." But here he was mindful of something more serious than its un-Tacitan prose and its youthful erudition. Indeed, as Vervliet, *Lipsius' Jeugd,* pp. 12–24, has shown, its politically embarrassing dedication to Granvella was predated by Lipsius to 1 June 1566. Lipsius' personal ambitions in praising his patron were thus, with a stroke of the pen, made patriotically more excusable after the outbreak of the revolt in 1568.

83. Vervliet, *Lipsius' Jeugd,* pp. 29–30.

84. The inauguration oration, Oratio II: *Iusti Lipsii Isacni, habita Jenae anno 1572 cum inciperet publice interpretari Cornelium Tacitum.* It is enumerated as "Oratio II," in *Iusti Lipsii orationes octo Jenae potissimum habitae e tenebris erutae et in gratiam studiosae iuventutis foras productae* (Darmstadt: Balthasar Hofmann, 1607), pp. 28–38. The authenticity of the "Oratio II" has been doubted by A. Roersch, *Juste Lipse* (1925) and, following him, by José Ruysschaert, *Juste Lipse et les Annales de Tacite* (Turnhout: Brepols Press, 1949), but Arnaldo Momigliano has successfully cleared up the difficulties in "The First Political Commentary on Tacitus," *Contributo,* pp. 57–58 (see n. 9, above).

85. "Oratio II," p. 31. And the line "O Deus immortalis, qua scelera & quod inaudita crudelitatis genus Hispani in miseros Belgos non ediderunt?" (ibid.) is typical. He then goes on to a detailed list of Spanish atrocities.

86. Ibid., p. 32: "& instituti inquisitores singulorum domus, colloquia, aditus, ut canes venatici, scrutarentur."

87. Ibid., p. 33: "& vestra expectationi satis facerem; nihil mihi aut vobis utilius, aut in his afflicta Reipub. ruinis accommodatius visum fuit, quam ut Cornelii Taciti, accuratissimi scriptoris, Annalium libros, publice vobis ex hos loco proponerem, & propositos interpretarer."

88. Ibid., p. 34: "sed tamen, quod ad Remp. & mores nostros attinet, quid afferre Livius potest, praeter bella, exercitus, & seditiones Tribunitias? jucundum auribus fateor; sed ego aurium voluptatem, cum animi utilitate coniunctam desidero."

89. Ibid., p. 35: "purus enim certe & latinus in dictione Tacitus est, etsi asper quibusdam videri possit, & difficulis: brevis tum in narrationibus, acutus in explicandis causas, & aequus iudex, de quo illud verissime possum dicere: Nemini placere Tacitum posse, nisi sapius lectum: Qui ut attentum lectorem mirifice delectat: sic supinum & aliud agentem praeterit, ac fallit."

90. Ibid.: ''Jam vero quam multa in eo, ad res civiles, ad motus communes, ad iurisprudentiam pertinentia, ut in similitudine similis Tyrannidis, quam multa exempla temporum nostrorum? Age vel Tyberius, fallax, continuis caedibus, & sanguine innocentium civium madens, nonne expressa imago sanguinolenti illius, & furiosi Tyranni, Ducis Albani?''

91. Ibid.: ''Quam prudenter de illa Tacitus, & quam apte ad tempora nostra de comburendis hareticorum libris! Scribit enim ille, cum quidam liberius quiddam de Cassio & Bruto scripsisset, damnatum a Tiberio, & scripta ejus per aediles conquisita, & exusta.'' Based on Tacitus *Annales* iv. 34–35.

92. See the quotation on page 118, above, and also the end of note 88.

93. *François Hotman: Francogallia,* the Latin text edited by Ralph E. Giesey and translated by J. H. M. Salmon (Cambridge, Eng.: At the University Press, 1972). Also, greatly abridged, in Julian H. Franklin, ed. and trans., *Constitutionalism and Resistance in the Sixteenth Century: Three Treatises by Hotman, Beza, and Mornay* (New York: Pegasus, 1969).

94. Fauchet, *Recueil des antiquitez gauloises et françoises* (Paris, 1579). The quotation is from von Stackelberg, *Tacitus in der Romania,* p. 161.

95. The quotation is from the same page of von Stackelburg. Fauchet merely reworked slightly the translation of Etienne de la Planche (c. 1548).

96. For the *Discours sur la servitude volontaire,* by Etienne de la Boétie (1530–63), I have used the most recent edition, that by Maurice Rat, published with an introduction and critical notes (Paris: Librairie Armand Colin, 1963). The only Tacitus reference is on p. 77: ''Et touteffois, de celui là, de ce boute-feu, de ce bourreau, de ceste beste sauvage [all pertaining to Nero] on peut bien dire qu'apres sa mort, aussi vilaine que sa vie, le noble peuple romain en receut tel desplaisir, se souvenant de ses jeus et desses festin, qu'il fut sur le point d'en porter le dueil; ainsi l'a escrit Corneille Tacite, auteur bon et grave, et des plus certeins [with a variant: ''et grave des plus, et certes croiable''].'' Boétie was thinking of the *Historiae* i. 4: ''Plebs sordida . . .'' (La Boétie's ''le noble peuple''!).

Von Stackelberg, *Tacitus in der Romania,* p. 163, has probably found an echo of Tacitus in another line. But that is all the Tacitus in the work. Suetonius and Plutarch are the predominating authorities and sources, along with Petrarch, Homer, Tacitus, etc. Von Stackelberg (p. 162) correctly points to a most significant fact about the *Discours:* ''die Erinnerung an Gelesenes dürfte dem Feuer von La Boéties Deklamation mehr Nahrung geboten haben als der Gedanke an politische Realitäten der Zeit.'' But von Stackelberg himself misses the importance of what he, at least generally, observes. First, I do not see anything *at all* pertaining to political reality in the *Discours.* Second, the work is a declamation which, unlike Valla's against the Donation of Constantine, *happens* to have been written with no connection with actual politics in mind. (Von Stackelberg erroneously seems to imply that a declamation is automatically devoid of actual political relevance.) According to Montaigne, whose friend he was, La Boétie wrote the *Discours* at the age of eighteen. The fact that he received his B.A. in law between 1548 and 1550 (closer determination is impossible; see Rat's edition, p. 12) then takes on some significance. Perhaps he wrote the declamation in some connection with his legal studies—as a kind of ''graduate paper'' or presentation piece. But this is only the vaguest speculation. At any rate, von Stackelberg, despite his minimal estimation of the political value of Tacitus in the work, states (pp. 163–64) that ''Tacitus als Tyrannenhasser wird uns in Frankreich erst *wieder* bei Autoren der Revolution begegnen'' (italics mine). But, in reality, La Boétie had no such conception of Tacitus. Von Stackelberg, very well versed in Enlightenment literature, reads too much into La Boétie. Besides, even if one were intent on finding a tyrant-hater in the *Discours,* one should point the finger at Suetonius and not at the one use (or possibly even two uses) of Tacitus. But, in all, it is very difficult to speak about La Boétie's views in the work. Declares Rat (pp. 34–35): "L'oeuvre d'ailleurs fut remaniée, retouchée par la suite. Et par qui? Par La Boétie? Par Montaigne? On ne sait."

97. *Più consigli et avertimenti di M. F. G. in materia di republica et di privata,* edited, with notes, by J. Corbinelli (Paris, 1576). Another edition appeared nine years later; its title, like the other, is interesting: *I precetti e sententie più notabili in materia di stato di M. F. G.,* edited by Luigi Guicciardini (Anversa, 1585).

98. *M. Antonii Mureti Opera Omnia ex MSS. aucta & emendata, cum brevi annotatione,* edited by David Ruhnken, 4 vols. (Leiden: Samuel & Johan Luchtmans, 1789), 1:299–300: "Paulus III. P. M. quo nullum sapientorem senem nostra vidit aetas, Tacitum saepe relegendo contriverat, neque ullum profanum scriptorem aeque libenter legebat." This quotation is from "Oratio XIII" (given 3 November 1580), an introduction to Muret's course on the first book of the *Annales;* it appears on pp. 294–301 of this volume. The next, "Oratio XIV," "sequitur in eodem argumento," is dated in November 1580 (specifically 4 November in some editions). One critic, the erudite Morris W. Croll (see below), believes instead that Muret delivered it in March 1581 as an opener for a second course on Tacitus—probably on book ii of the *Annales.* This oration is in pages 301–11. A third oration, "Oratio XV," is an introduction to Muret's course on book iii of the *Annales* and was given in November 1581 (see pages 311–18). A good summary and description of these orations is in von Stackelberg, *Tacitus in Romania,* pp. 106–15. But for understanding them within the context of Muret's career and the literary developments of the '60s and '70s in which they are a focal point, one must refer to the pioneering and unsurpassed work of Morris W. Croll, *Style, Rhetoric, and Rhythm,* edited by J. Max Patrick et al. (Princeton: Princeton University Press, 1966)—specifically, "Muret and the History of 'Attic Prose,'" pp. 107–62, and, on Tacitus in particular, pp. 150–54.

99. *Opera Omnia,* ed. Ruhnken, 1:300 ("Oratio XIII"): "Cosmus Medices, qui primus Magnus Etruriae Dux fuit, homo factus ad imperandum, qui eam, quae vulgo fortuna dicitur, in consilio & prudentia consistere docuit, Taciti libros in deliciis habebat: eorumque lectione avidissime fruebatur."

100. Ibid.: "Neque non hodie multi aut Principum, aut eorum, qui de summis rebus a Principibus in consilium adhibentur, eundem studiosissime legunt, & quasi pro magistro quodam prudentiae habent." Earlier students of Tacitus in the Renaissance have somehow missed this important reference, following, and of one piece with, those on Paul III and Cosimo I. It gives some basis to Botero's later report that Tacitus was on the lips of everyone. And see my note 65, above, on Machiavelli's popularity in this context.

101. Ibid., p. 299: "qui non inani verborum sono, sed bonitate & gravitate sententiarum ducerentur, praecipuo in honore Tacitum semper habuerint. . . ."

102. Ibid., p. 303 ("Oratio XIV"): "Quamquam autem Dei beneficio aetas nostra Tiberios, Caligulas, Nerones non habet: prodest tamen scire, quomodo etiam sub illis viri boni ac prudentes vixerint, quomodo et quatenus illorum vitia tulerint ac dissimulaverint, . . ."

103. Ibid., pp. 303–4: "Multa saepe sunt in Principibus, quae vir bonus laudare non potest, tegere et transmittere silentio potest. Ad ea connivere qui nesciunt, et sibi periculum creant et ipsos Principes plerumque deteriores faciunt. Multi enim, qui vitia

sua latere credunt, sponte eas paullatim exuunt, ne detegantur: et dum bonos haberi putant, boni fiunt.''

104. Etter, however, does try to argue that he was basically republican in his understanding of Tacitus. She attempts to show this as an essential element distinguishing him from later commentators of ''Tacitism.'' See Else-Lilly Etter, *Tacitus in der Geistesgeschichte des 16. und 17. Jahrhunderts* (Basel: Helbing & Lichtenhahn, 1966), pp. 57–58.

105. From ''Oratio XIV''; cited by Croll, *Style, Rhetoric, and Rhythm,* p. 153.

106. I follow Momigliano, ''The First Political Commentary on Tacitus,'' *Contributo.*

107. Cited in Momigliano, *Contributo,* p. 44: ''Magno principi cautio est adhibenda ne quicquid virium penes se est, id contractum unum in locum simul semperque habeat.''

108. Cited ibid.: ''Princeps et respublica eo vinculo sunt adstricti ut nihil alteri separatim accidere possit, quod idem ad alterum non pertineat. Hinc fit, ut nihil sibi princeps utile esse putet quod idem reip. non expediat.''

109. Ibid., p. 41.

110. Ibid., p. 52.

111. On Botero and his political thought I have used the following material. The best by far is Federico Chabod, *Giovanni Botero* (Rome: Anonima Romana, 1934); very valuable have been the short introductions to the bibliographical studies by Luigi Firpo, *Gli scritti giovanili di Giovanni Botero: Bibliografia ragionata,* Biblioteca degli Eruditi e dei Bibliofili, vol. 45 (Florence: Sansoni, 1960); Meinecke, *Machiavellism,* pp. 66–71, is standard (see next note); J. W. Allen, *A History of Political Thought* (see n. 57, above) is very good, especially on Botero's debt to Bodin.

112. Friedrich Meinecke, *Machiavellism: The Doctrine of Raison d'Etat and Its Place in Modern History,* trans. Douglas Starck (New Haven: Yale University Press, 1957), p. 46, n. 2.

113. Ibid., pp. 46–47, and n. 3—from a book of memoirs.

114. From a two-page excerpt in Massimo Petrocchi, *La Controriforma in Italia* (Rome: Anonima Veritas, 1947), pp. 188–89: ''Alcuni accecati nella avarizia, e nella cupidità loro, affermano, che Vostra Maestà non consentirà mai di lasciar Piacenza, che che disponga sopra ciò la ragion civile; con ciò sia che la ragion degli stati nól comporta; dico che questa voce è non solamente poco cristiana; ma ella è ancora poco umana. . . . [p. 189] Invano adunque si affaticano coloro, che fanno due ragioni, l'una torta, e falsa, e dissoluta, e disposta a rubare, et a mal fare; et a questa han posto nome ragion di stato.'' This oration is so essential for an understanding of the development of ''reason of state'' that it is a wonder that Meinecke did not mention it; perhaps he did not know of it. But maybe he did and for some reason chose not to deal with it. See Meinecke, *Machiavellism,* pp. 46–47, n. 3, where, after mentioning the phrase from the book of memoirs of 1525, he adds that ''more than twenty years intervened before the next mention of ragione di stato''; he then states that further decades were to elapse before Botero initiated the theoretical discussion of it. Yet, about the mention of ''more than twenty years'' later, he says nothing. It would correspond to the date of the Della Casa oration. Petrocchi himself quoted it from M. Fancelli, ed., *Orazioni politiche del Cinquecento* (Bologna: Zanichelli, 1941).

115. Luigi Firpo, *Gli scritti giovanili di Giovanni Botero* (Florence: Sansoni, 1960), p. 20: ''È questo il primo trattato politico del Botero, inspirato dal rigorismo e dal fervore di restaurazione cattolica suscitati dall'esempio di San Carlo Borromeo.''

116. There are many editions of Botero to which one may refer. Probably the most authoritative is the one edited by Luigi Firpo (Turin: UTET, 1948). Here I have used the

translation by P. J. Waley and D. P. Waley, *Giovanni Botero: The Reason of State. The Greatness of Cities* (London: Routledge & Kegan Paul, 1956). I have also referred to the edition translated and edited by George Albert Moore, *Practical Politics (Ragion di Stato) by Giovanni Botero: Religion and the Virtues of the Christian Prince against Machiavelli (abridged) by Pedro Ribadeneyra* (Washington, D.C.: Country Dollar Press, 1949).

117. Botero, in the dedication, Waley edition, p. xiii.

118. Ibid., p. xiv.

119. Ibid.

120. According to Momigliano, *Contributo*, p. 53.

121. For Meinecke, author of the classic work on "reason of state," it is merely that "Tacitus *became* the great teacher of raison d'état" (p. 25; italics mine); and, with as little explanation, Meinecke said that this happened after Lipsius' edition of 1574 (p. 26). Spini, though dealing essentially with late sixteenth-century historiography, has failed to explain that basic political connection so essential to his thesis. He says (in the Cochrane translation, p. 114), that the stylistic-political struggle between the Tacitists and the anti-Tacitists began when discussions about history "*became* associated with the contemporary discussions about the merits and demerits of the Roman historian Tacitus..." (italics mine).

122. Toffanin (*Machiavelli e il "Tacitismo"*) and von Stackelberg see "reason of state" and the "roots" of *Tacitismo* or "Tacitism," and Machiavellian-Tacitism, Tacitistic-Machiavellianism, etc. all over the place. Moreover, there are, everywhere, spoors, hints, and approaches to these things. All very confusing! And Etter, despite her precise analysis of cause and effect in some sections (most notably those on Muret and Lipsius), also, throughout her study, allows similar vague and general terms and processes (Ansätze, Übereinstimmungen, Zeitströmungen, etc.) to obscure and confuse her theses.

123. Momigliano, *Contributo*, p. 54.

124. See Gentillet's *Anti-Machiavel,* the original edition of 1576, edited with commentary by Edward C. Rathé (Geneva: Librairie Droz, 1968). Note, too, Donald R. Kelly, "Murd'rous Machiavel in France: A Post Mortem," *Political Science Quarterly* 85 (December 1970): 545–59. See also Salvo Mastellone, "Aspetti dell'antimachiavellismo in Francia: Gentillet e Languet," *Il Pensiero Politico* 2, no. 3 (1969): 376–415.

125. Botero's dedicatory statements are sufficient to demonstrate this opprobrious conjunction. But Burke, in his essay on "Tacitism" in T. A. Dorey, ed., *Tacitus* (London: Routledge & Kegan Paul, 1969), p. 165, implies that Botero didn't carry out his condemnation of Tacitus in the body of his work: "he is attacking Tiberius, not Tacitus, whom he quotes about seventy times in his book (compared to twenty-nine quotations from the Bible and twenty-one from Aristotle)." Burke however, has neither checked these quotations too carefully nor understood Botero's general orientation for making quotations at all. First of all, Botero does not attack Tiberius with any consistency: of seventeen mentions (usually with quotations from this emperor, with Tacitus as the source), eight are with praise of his words or deeds, six are with condemnation, and three are neutral; moreover, of the approximately seventy quotations from Tacitus, all except one are totally neutral: "Tacitus says....," "Tacitus reports....," etc. The exception is positive in tone because Botero says that Tacitus "nobly said of it..." (Waley translation, p. 159). Second, it is clear that Botero quoted his sources and authorities for information and for *sententiae,* regardless of the context or his general opinion of the author he uses. In short, Botero is showing how Tacitus' facts must be interpreted for a good political science—unlike the pernicious "ragion di stato" interpretation (by Machiavelli and Tacitus) of the

same factual and objective material. This was the way Botero was able to use an author he condemned. True, there is a certain inconsistency in this method; but Botero wasn't disturbed by it. A little later, Scipione Ammirato, the famous Florentine political thinker, cleared up this inconsistency (see pp. 142–43, above).

Chapter 6

1. On Tertullian and Orosius, see my Introduction. On Budé, see Else-Lilly Etter, *Tacitus in der Geistegeschichte des 16. und 17. Jahrhunderts* (Basel: Helbing & Lichtenhahn, 1966), pp. 61–62, and Jürgen von Stackelberg, *Tacitus in der Romania: Studien zur literarischen Rezeption des Tacitus in Italien und Frankreich* (Tübingen: Max Niemeyer, 1960), p. 160. The passages cited in the latter come from Budé's *De asse et partibus eius* (chap. 4): first, along with Suetonius and Pliny, he says that Tacitus has "invidia vaecors adversus Christianum nomen"; then, on Tacitus' statement that Nero persecuted Christians for their hatred of humanity, he lashes out at that "hominem nefarium Tacitum [qui] prodere hoc exemplum nefariae mentis non veritus sit"; and finally, he sends forth this barrage: "id iste scleratorie historiae stylo, toxico mendacii oblito, repetere instit, vaecordium omnium scriptorum perditissimus, si recte verba eius aestimentur."

2. In his letter to Dorp, cited in chap. 5, n. 2

3. Bodin, *Methodus* (following immediately upon the section about Alciato and Tacitus, quoted and analyzed above, pp. 111–12), in the Reynolds translation, pp. 70–71: "Budé sharply called Tacitus the most wicked of all writers, because he wrote something against the Christians. I think this was the reason why Tertullian called him most deceitful and why Orosius called him a flatterer. But just as the jurisconsult Marcellus answered that a prostitute did evil in being a prostitute, yet, granted that she was such, her acts were not base, so Tacitus acted impiously in that he was not a Christian, but he did not write impiously against us, since he was tied to pagan superstition. On the other hand, I would judge him lacking in scruple if he did not try to maintain whatever religion he considered to be the true one and to overthrow the contrary. Since the Christians and the Hebrews were daily dragged to punishment like poisoners and were associated with all crimes and lusts, what historian would refrain from contemptuous words? If ignorance deserves an excuse, then I suppose that Tacitus ought to be excused. . . . If this, then, is a crime, Ulpian is guilty of a much greater crime, since he wrote the seven books about torturing Christians, not for historical research, but for the rigor of the punishments."

4. In 1550, Ortensio Lando's assertion (see above, p. 105), that Tacitus told too many lies, does break the silence here; but considering the whimsical nature of the *Sferza,* its collecting of imperfections in all ancient writers, and its emphasis on some kind of "credibility gap" for all the historians, I find a very slim connection, if any, with my Budé context here.

5. See above, pp. 3–4 and esp., in this chapter, pp. 131–32.

6. On Muret, see above, p. 122. Note also Etter, *Tacitus in der Geistesgeschichte,* pp. 52–55.

7. For Montaigne I use the French text edited by Robert Barral and Pierre Michel, *Montaigne: Oeuvres complètes* (Paris: Editions du Seuil, 1967). I use the best translation available anywhere in English, that of Donald M. Frame, *The Complete Essays of Montaigne,* 3 vols. (New York: Doubleday, 1960). This edition was indispensable for me because it clearly shows Montaigne's later additions to earlier essays, even when these

consist of only a word or two. For Montaigne's life and thought I rely on Frame's *Montaigne's Discovery of Man: The Humanization of a Humanist* (New York: Columbia University Press, 1955).

8. That is, in his *Montaigne's Discovery of Man*. Etter and von Stackelberg completely ignore it. But this fact is no surprise, considering their particular approach to intellectual history.

9. In *Essays* iii. 8, where Montaigne discusses the closeness of style between Seneca and Tacitus. For its context, see below, this chapter.

10. Montaigne, thinking of *Dialogus* xxxix, errs in attributing the statement to Messalla, the speaker in defense of ancient rhetoric in the *Dialogus*. In fact it is Maternus, Messalla's supporter and the one who effects a kind of compromise in the end. However, Montaigne's error is easily forgiven in view of the fact that the "Great Lacuna" ends three chapters before his citation and that, within it, Messalla finished speaking and Maternus began. Of course, Montaigne could not be expected to know the results of the sophisticated criticism of Sir William Peterson in the Loeb Classical Library edition.

11. My knowledge concerning Seneca's style, and Silver Age Latinity in general, owes much to the 114-page introduction by Walter C. Summers (writing in 1910) in the *Select Letters of Seneca* (London: Macmillan, 1962). On Seneca I wish to note the excellent little chapter in Thomas W. Africa's *Rome of the Caesars*. Africa writes very enjoyably.

12. Here, my "very probably" is just about a "certainly," considering Montaigne's very thorough reading of the *Methodus* at this time, as is shown by his assiduous critique of Bodin's judgments on Plutarch in *Essays* ii. 32.

13. Close in name is Gra*n*ius Silvanus (Marcianus), who "laid hands on himself" (*Annales* vi. 38).

14. Seneca, *Thebais* 1. 1. Translated in the Frame edition, 2:19.

15. See Keith Cameron, "Montaigne and 'De la Liberté de Conscience,'" *Renaissance Quarterly* 26, no. 3 (Autumn, 1973): 285–94. At the very end of this acute analysis of the essay, Cameron declares: "No doubt more opinions about Montaigne's techniques and procedures would be revised after a careful reinstatement of his work in the political context of his age." No one should object to that.

16. Frame, *Montaigne's Discovery of Man,* p. 59.

17. In the Frame edition, 2:183. However, in aiming at the same point in another essay, Montaigne is willing to quote Tacitus in order to argue with him: in "On the Lame" (iii. 11) Montaigne says that he himself is dull-witted, thick, and given to what appears real. Then he says that he shuns the reproaches of the ancients, and he quotes Tacitus (*Historiae* i. 22), though without mentioning his name: "Cupidine humani ingenii libentius obscura creduntur" ("By a twist of the human mind, obscure things are more readily believed").

18. Frame, *Montaigne's Discovery of Man,* p. 72.

19. Ibid., p. 134.

20. The whole passage: "Quand je lus Philippe de Commines, il y a plusieurs années, très bon auteur certes, j'y remarquai ce mot pour non vulgaire: qu'il se faut bien garder de faire tant de service à son maître, qu'on l'empêche d'en trouver la juste récompense. Je devais louer l'invention, non pas lui, je la rencontrai en Tacite, il n'y a pas longtemps: 'Beneficia eo usque laeta sunt dum videntur exolvi posse; ubi multum antevenere, pro gratia odium redditur.'" Montaigne then quotes lines of similar meaning from Seneca and Cicero.

21. It is clear that Montaigne's interest in Tacitus here is not limited to the *Historiae*. A

few other elements of this passage makes it even clearer: Montaigne is uneven; he begins speaking of the *Historiae* but, after a few sentences, bases his comments on the *Annales* as well. For example: "belles morts comme s'il craignait nous fâcher de leur multitude et longeur," which is patterned on Tacitus' own words in *Annales* iv. 33. Another example: Montaigne's comments on Tiberius' letter to the senate are based on *Annales* vi. 6, and he quotes from it. Also, Montaigne himself speaks mostly of Tacitus personally and in general (though referring to him throughout merely as "il"). Finally, at the very end of his criticism, Montaigne specifically refers to the *Annales*.

22. This essay ("De L'Art de Conférer"), as well as the fuller context of judgment in Montaigne's thought, must be studied in Raymond C. La Charité, *The Concept of Judgment in Montaigne* (The Hague: Martinus Nijhoff, 1968). Note, in particular, p. 143: "Because the development of judgment and the study of human nature are inseparable, judgment and self-study become interdependent. Because judgment's principal function evolves from inspection and introspection, self-study constitutes a major expansion of the role of judgment." Also, ibid.: "The notion of 'essai,' 'essayer,' that is to experience, depicts the role and primary activity of judgment, for the whole of life is the proper test of judgment."

23. Montaigne devotes some space to these traits of Tacitus; he shows, for example, that Tacitus' discussion of Tiberius' letter to the senate (*Annales* vi. 6) goes very far beyond the actual evidence.

24. Besides the *Iusti Lipsii orationes octo Jenae . . . habitae* used in the preceding chapter, I here used the following editions of Lipsius' works: *Justi Lipsii Opera Omnia*, 4 vols. (Versaliae: Andreae ab Hoogenhuysen, 1675); *Opera Omnia*, 4 vols. (Antwerp: Plantin, 1603–17); Immanuel Bekker, ed., *Cornelius Tacitus ab I. Lipsio, I. F. Gronovio, N. Heinsio, I. A. Ernestio, F. A. Wolfio*, 2 vols. (Leipzig: Weidmann, 1831) (the first volume contains prefaces [pp. i–xi] from some of Lipsius' seven editions of Tacitus); *De constantia*, translated as *Two Bookes of Constancie* from an old English translation by Sir John Stradling (New Brunswick, N.J.: Rutgers University Press, 1939); *De bibliothecis syntagma*, translated by J. Dana as *A Brief Outline of the History of Libraries* (Chicago: A. C. McClurg, 1907) (translation of the second edition, Antwerp: Plantin, 1607). For secondary material the most useful, by far, has been Jason Lewis Saunders' *Justus Lipsius: The Philosophy of Renaissance Stoicism*, used in the preceding chapter (see chap 5, n. 81). I have also referred to José Ruysschaert, *Juste Lipse et les Annales de Tacite: Une méthode de critique textuelle au XVI*[e] *siècle* (Turnhout: Brepols Press, 1949); Charles Nisard, *Le Triumvirat littéraire au XVI*[e]*siècle: Juste Lipse, Joseph Scaliger, et Isaac Casaubon* (Paris: Amyot, 1852); J. E. Sandys, *A History of Classical Scholarship*, 3 vols. (New York: Hafner, 1958), vol. 2; Arnaldo Momigliano, "The First Political Commentary on Tacitus," *Contributo* (see chap. 5, n. 9, above); and Hendrik D. L. Vervliet, *Lipsius' Jeugd 1547–1578: Analecta voor een kritische Biografie* (see chap. 5, n. 81).

25. Saunders is the only one who approaches a comprehensive study, but it too is mainly on the philosophical side and is brief on the biographical and historical side. Saunders rightly says that there is almost nothing on Lipsius the Christian Stoic before his own book. Before Saunders, the latest biographical sketch was that of A. Roersch, *Juste Lipse* (Brussels, 1925). Other studies, on philological or other very particular questions, can all provide good material for someone ready to rescue Lipsius from the fragmentary and lifeless images appearing in the mostly old-fashioned glimpses that have so far been

given of him as a man. And, with Vervliet's "analecta," there are now signs of a flesh-and-blood Lipsius—but still not enough to begin a synthesis of his life.

26. Vervliet, *Lipsius' Jeugd,* pp. 33–37, argues, however, that Lipsius was much more convincing.

27. On Lipsius' wife, Vervliet (ibid., pp. 37–42) demonstrates that Lipsius was moved to marriage by passion and love and that Anna was neither a bossy wife nor the ultra-Catholic manipulator behind his political-religious metamorphoses.

28. "Iustus Lipsius ad Lectorem," in Lipsius' second edition of Tacitus: "Correctiones aliquot veteres firmavi, novas addidi. Neutrum ambitiose, quia certe peccamus iam nos critici in hanc partem, et ut olim vitiis, sic nunc remediis laboratur. Quaedam etiam in aliis scriptoribus passim animadversa, non quia adfectarim, sed quia dabant se sub manum. Ut in segete flores quidam internascuntur sua sponte, sic in his scriptis alieni generis notae. Historiae et moribus, cum opus fuit, praetuli facem, sed nonnisi cum opus" (in Bekker, ed., 1:i [see n. 24, above]).

29. Ibid., p. ii: "Politica non attigi. Sive enim peritis sive imperitis, frustra. Illi sponte eligere possunt, hi nec electis recte uti."

30. Momigliano, "The First Political Commentary on Tacitus," *Contributo,* p. 40, in quoting the same passage, makes no comment on this phrase. I think it very important because it supports his argument (ibid., pp. 57–58) against Roersch (1925) and Ruysschaert (1949), both of whom say that the Jena Oration is not by Lipsius.

31. Immediately following the quotation cited in note 29, above: "Et audio iam esse quibus proprie ea cura. Ego quod potui, id feci, nec impedio, si quis in eodem circu curret ad palmam." Lipsius was writing these words in August 1580, and Paschalius did not publish his *Observations* until 1581. Perhaps Lipsius added this comment to the preface in 1581 before his work went to press. Momigliano ("The First Political Commentary on Tacitus," p. 40) has a better solution, however. According to him, Lipsius could easily have heard what Paschalius, then with his learned circle of friends in France, was doing. Besides, in 1581 at least, Paschalius was corresponding with Lipsius' publisher, Christopher Plantin. I may add, moreover, that the next political commentary, that of Lionardo Salviati, Italy's mentor of proper literary style (a commentary on the first sentence of the *Annales;* see above, p. 141), didn't appear until 1582—too late to have been in Lipsius' mind here. And the next commentary, a much more ample one, that of Annibale Scoto, an intimate of Sixtus V, who borrowed heavily from Paschalius, was not published until 1589. So, Lipsius could have had only Paschalius' *Observations* in mind.

32. Cited in Saunders, *Justus Lipsius,* p. 42: "Pax artes pacis requiret, frustra, si nunc earum antisthites negligimus et cultores."

33. Cited ibid., p. 38 (Saunders' translation).

34. Cited ibid., p. 19: "Nam omnis religio et nulla religio sunt mihi unum et idem."

35. Cited ibid., p. 30: "Clementiae non hic locus. Ure, seca, ut membrorum potius aliquid quam totum corpus intereat."

36. From the preface to the *Politica,* in the Antwerp 1603–17 edition of the *Opera Omnia* (cited in n. 24, above), 3:19 (pagination separate for each title): "Auctores uno aspectu, si lubet, vide, è quorum scriptis hoc Opus. Inter eos eminet Corn. Tacitus extra ordinem dicendus: quia Causa in prudentia viri est, et quia creberrimus sententiis: atque etiam, quia familiaris nobis, et offerebat se non vocatus."

37. Montaigne, of course, recognized it for a-thing-put-together, a *potpourri* or "*centon.*" After damning such works not openly planned that way, he excepts those that are:

"Ceci ne touche pas des centons qui se publient pour centons; et j'en ai vu de très ingénieux en mon temps, entre autres un, sous le nom de Capilupus, outre les anciens. Ce sont des esprits qui se font voir, et par ailleurs et par là, comme Lipse en ce docte et laborieux tissu de ses *Politiques*" (*Essays* i. 26). This essay, "On the Education of Children," was written about 1574; the comment on Lipsius' *Politica* is therefore a later insertion. Montaigne liked Lipsius, however. In *Essays* ii. 12, "The Apology," he refers to him as "le plus savant homme qui nous reste, d'un esprit très poli et judicieux" and a close relative of his friend Adrien Turnèbe, the Hellenist and director of the royal press, who died in 1565.

38. Cited in Saunders, *Justus Lipsius,* p. 55.

39. Cited ibid., p. 56.

40. See Vervliet, *Lipsius Jeugd,* pp. 9–12, on Lipsius' schooldays, from the age of twelve, at the Jesuit school at Keulen in the years 1559–64. But he left abruptly in mid-year—probably because of the plague or because, when his parents heard that he had been induced to become a Jesuit (on 29 September 1562, according to the school's archives), they objected and removed him. Lipsius himself remained absolutely quiet about these early experiences with the Society of Jesus. They still remain a mystery.

41. Cited in Saunders, *Justus Lipsius,* p. 42: "Nec lubet respondere, nec ratio est."

42. Lipsius' attacker, obviously under a pseudonym, wrote *J. Lipsi in C. Corn. Tacitum notae cum manuscriptio cod. Mirandulano collatae a Pompeio Lampugnano* (n.p.: C. R. Borgami, 1602). Lipsius, proving the supposed manuscript to be a forgery, answered in *Dispunctio notarum Mirandulani codicis ad Corn. Tacitum* (Antwerp: Plantin, 1602). The text, of vii plus 40 pages, is at the end of vol. 4 of the 1603–17 *Opera omnia* edition. See also Saunders, *Justus Lipsius,* p. 53.

43. Bekker edition, 2:409, n. 8: "O foeda, O barbara! Et scio apud quosdam Septentrionalium hodie hanc insaniam pro parte vigere" (for Bekker, see n. 24, above).

44. Ibid., p. 410, n. 10: "*'Servatur'?* Quid servatur? Immo non servatur fenus, nec est eius usus. Aliquid in hac scriptura vitii: an *spernitur,* vel *spernatur?* Ac tale sententia petit. Aut pro sensu capiendum, quasi de interdicto praeivisset." And note that the translation of the Tacitus passage (in the text), better suiting my context here, comes from Hutton, of the Loeb edition. The Church and Brodribb translation, used throughout, does not "ring" as well here. Anyway, to understand Lipsius' philological problem, note Tacitus' Latin: "Faenus agitare et in usuras extendere ignotum; ideoque magis servatur quam si vetitum esset."

45. Ibid., 1:iv: from the preface edition to the fifth (?) edition of Tacitus, 1589: "Historiae . . . magna dignitas est, magnus fructus. Memorias legere prisci aevi, bella inter summos reges, populorum casus et occasus, dignitatem cum voluptate habet; nec pascitur solum ea lectione animus, sed adsurgit. Notare autem in historia varietatem exemplorum, causas eventorum, et ex iis fontibus praecepta derivare ad vitam privatam communemque, utilitas est, . . ."

46. Ibid., p. ix: from the preface to the 1607 edition of Tacitus (written in August 1605): "Singulae paginae—quid paginae? Singulae lineae dogmata, consilia, monita sunt: sed brevia saepe aut occulta, et opus sagace, quadam mente ad odorandum et assequendum."

47. Cited and translated in Saunders, *Justus Lipsius,* p. 50.

48. On Vigenère's translation, see above, p. 120.

49. For Davanzati, I use Enrico Bindi, ed., *Le Opere di Bernardo Davanzati,* 2 vols. (Florence: Le Monnier, 1852–53). Bindi has an excellent introduction (l:v–lx), "Della

Vita e delle opere di Bernardo Davanzati." Of much help here was Cochrane's *Florence in the Forgotten Centuries* (Chicago: University of Chicago Press, 1973), pp. 119–21.

50. Bindi edition of Davanzati, 1:lxxi: In the "Dedication to Baccio Valori" of 15 September 1595: "Volgarizare tutto Tacito non pare che occorra, avendol fatto Giorgio Dati con ampio stile e facile, credo per allargare e addolcire il testo sì stringato e brusco; . . ."

51. Cited by Bindi, ibid., p. xxxviii: "per riprovare col fatto il mal detto d'Arrigo Stefani."

52. This statistic and the following are cited in Cochrane, *Florence in the Forgotten Centuries,* p. 121. Davanzati's comparison to the French must have been based on the translation of *Annales* i–vi by Etienne de la Planche, published about 1548 and republished in 1555 and 1581; or on the de la Planche translation as reworked by Claude Fauchet, along with Fauchet's own translation of the rest of Tacitus, published in 1582 and republished in 1584, etc. De Vigenère, aside from the two chapters (in his edition of Caesar, as mentioned here and in the preceding chapter, p. 120) did only the *Germania* in 1575.

53. Cochrane, *Florence in the Forgotten Centuries,* p. 119.

54. Salviati, *Discorso sopra le prime parole di Cornelio Tacito Urbem Romam a principio reges habuere* in his edition of Dati's translation (Venice, 1582). Etter, *Tacitus in der Geistesgeschichte,* pp. 86–87, has a summary of it.

55. Cochrane, *Florence in the Forgotten Centuries,* p. 119.

56. Cited in the Bindi edition, 1:xix: "Servitutis mala commemorat; vide et nota." Bindi is quoting from the *zibaldone,* then in the possession of a certain Bigazzi but now in the Biblioteca Nazionale in Florence.

57. Cited in the Bindi edition, 1:xix: "A noi la campana del consiglio fu levata, acciò che non potessimo sentir più il dolce suono della libertà."

58. These comments on Davanzati's notes and his handwriting come from my scrutiny of the same *zibaldone* that Bindi used.

59. Cochrane, "The End of the Renaissance in Florence," *Bibliothèque d'Humanisme et Renaissance* 27 (1965): 7–29; see also *The Late Italian Renaissance,* ed. Cochrane, pp. 43–73.

60. Cochrane is the best source on the Florentine and Tuscan academies in this period and for the whole of the seventeenth and eighteenth centuries also. See especially his *Tradition and Enlightenment in the Tuscan Academies* (Chicago: University of Chicago Press, 1961). Specifically here, however, I rely mainly on his *Florence in the Forgotten Centuries.*

61. For Ammirato I rely very heavily on Cochrane's *Florence in the Forgotten Centuries,* esp. pp. 93–161, and, on Ammirato and Tacitus in particular, pp. 121–26. This chapter on Ammirato is one of the highlights of Cochrane's beautiful book. J. H. Whitfield, of the University of Birmingham, England, has reviewed it in the *Renaissance Quarterly* 27 no. 2 (Summer 1974): 215–18. Although Whitfield offers a few valid points of criticism on particular items, he has, on the whole, totally misunderstood the grace, charm, and refined spirit of this book. Von Stackelberg, *Tacitus in der Romania,* pp. 120–28, also provides some useful material on Ammirato and Tacitus. Moreover, I have used the best biography for the context of his political thought, that by Rodolfo di Mattei, *Il pensiero politico di Scipione Ammirato* (Lecce: Centro di Studi Salentini, 1959). For the text of Ammirato's *Discorsi* I have referred to the Latin translation, *Dissertationes politicae; sive Discursus in C. Tacitum . . .* (Helenopoli: I. T. Schönwetter, 1609).

62. Ammirato, in the preface to the *Discorsi*, cited in von Stackelberg, *Tacitus in der Romania*, p. 121: "si perchè questa opera si vede andar molto hoggi per le mani di ciascuno: e si perchè trattando di principato, più a tempi nostri si confà."

63. Ammirato, *Discorsi* xiv. 7.

64. Cited in Cochrane, *Florence in the Forgotten Centuries*, p. 148.

65. All according to Cochrane, ibid., p. 123.

66. Cited ibid., from Ammirato's *Discorsi*, xviii. 9.

67. For Boccalini, I use the *Ragguagli di Parnaso* edited by Luigi Firpo, Scrittori d'Italia, 3 vols. (Bari: Laterza, 1910–48). Volumes 1 and 2 were originally edited by Giuseppe Rua. Volume 3 has an excellent index and copious annotations by Firpo. He also supplies a section of *scritti minori*, including thirty-four letters by Boccalini. For the *Osservazioni sopra Cornelio Tacito*, I use *La Bilancia Politica del Boccalini di tutte le opere di Traiano Boccalini*, 3 vols. (Castellana: Giovanni Hermano Widerhold, 1678). This edition is edited by Ludovico Dumay (vols. 1 and 2) and Gregorio Leti (vol. 3). Volume 1 contains Boccalini's *osservazioni* on the first six books of the *Annales;* volume 2, those on the first book of the *Historiae* and on the *Agricola;* volume 3 contains forty letters. The *Osservazioni* have never been published in full. I have referred to Meinecke, *Machiavellism*, pp. 70–89; von Stackelberg, *Tacitus in der Romania*, pp. 131–46; Etter, *Tacitus in der Geistesgeschichte*, pp. 92–100; Robert H. Williams, *Boccalini in Spain: A Study of His Influence on Prose Fiction of the Seventeenth Century* (Menasha, Wis.: Banta, 1946); Claudio Varese, *Traiano Boccalini* (Padua: Livania Editrice, 1958); and Giorgio Spini, "I trattatisti . . ." in the Cochrane translation, pp. 121–23 (see chap. 5, n. 20, above). Finally, though offering nothing on Boccalini (because he lies outside its methodological framework), the best thing for general background on Venice is William J. Bouwsma's *Venice and the Defense of Republican Liberty: Renaissance Values in the Age of the Counter Reformation* (Berkeley: University of California Press, 1968).

68. These epithets are collected from the *Ragguagli* by von Stackelberg, *Tacitus in der Romania*, pp. 133–35. The same for those in the next sentence.

69. *Bilancia Politica*, 1:313.

70. Ibid., p. 305: "felice il mondo, se Tacito avesse taciuto."

71. For James I, Bacon, and others in England, see chapter 7.

72. I refer to the letter in the "Scrittori d'Italia" edition of the *Ragguagli*, edited by Rua and Firpo, 3:361–63.

73. Clandestinely, because the place, "Cosmopoli," and the publisher, "G. B. Dalle Piazze," are fictitious. But von Stackelberg (*Tacitus in der Romania*, p. 141), following Firpo, determines the place as Genf and the publisher as De Tournes. Williams (*Boccalini in Spain*, p. 7) points out that two of Boccalini's sons, Aurelio and Rodolfo, applied to the authorities of Venice to print the work but were denied permission because of the political allusions it contained. The brothers then ceded the manuscript to the government in return for a pension. Somehow, however, Dumay and Leti managed to get hold of a copy and publish it the next year, and this is the edition I use.

74. As Boccalini himself states in the opening words of his preface to the *Ragguagli* (Rua and Firpo ed., 1:3): "Quel tempo che avanza alle fatiche dé miei Commentari, che ogni giorno fabbrico sopra gli *Annali* e le *Istorie* del prencipe degli scrittori politici Cornelio Tacito, volontieri per mia ricreazione spendo nella piacevole composizione de *Ragguagli di Parnaso*. . . ."

75. Boccalini in the Introduction to his *Osservazzioni* [*sic*] *sopra gli Annali di Cornelio Tacito*, in the *Bilancia Politica*, unpaginated introduction, fourth page: "I Ragguagli del

mio Parnasso, passano per le mani di tani huomini di senno, che non m'è che superfluo il ricordare qual frutto habbino cagionato con la Maschera sul volto, mentre anche senz' occhi hanno fatto aprire gli occhi à gli huomini, che ciecamente dormendo, lasciavano guidarsi per il naso dall' auttorità, e dagli artifizii non conosciuti, ò non osservati de' Prencipi; Ma qual frutto doverebbero produrre queste mie presenti fatiche, che si metteranno alla vista di tutti, e senza maschera d'alcuna forte?''

76. Ibid.: ''Parlo in alcuni luoghi proprii di Tacito, anche de' Principi de nostri tempi, all' operazioni, & interessi de quali vedo adattarsi gli ammaestramenti del nostro Auttore.''

77. Ibid.: ''Mi credo haver tanta cognizione dell'humore di questo secolo, che facilmente non sole sarò per ingannarmi, se protesto, come vado imaginandomi, che quando saranno comparse alla luce queste Comentature, quali si siano, cavate da me solo, fuori dell' anima di Cornelio Tacito, non in tutto, ma in parte verranno guidicati per paradoni [*sic;* = paragoni].''

78. Ibid., p. 1. (With the beginning of the actual work, the pages are numbered.)

79. Ibid., 2:18: ''Senza dubbio alcuno, il Prencipe non è Padrone dell'Anima de gli huomini, cioè di quelle potenze, ch'egli non può frenare, come invisibili à lui, . . . mà solamente il Prencipe è Padrone della bocca, e de gli alti esterni dell'huomo.''

80. Ibid., p. 19: ''Vorrà dunque inferire Tacito nostro, che i Romani s'accommodarono tanta alla crudel servitù de' loro Tiranni, che sino sarebbonsi indotti all'oblivione de' loro mali, se havessero potuto, come potevano non parlarne.''

Chapter 7

1. On Ribadeneyra, see p. 152 and note 12, below.

2. For Briani I rely entirely on Giorgio Spini's article on historiography in the Counter-Reformation, ''I trattatisti . . . ,'' as translated by Cochrane (see chap. 5, n. 20, above). For other aspects of this section on Italy, I have referred also to Rodolfo de Mattei, *Dal Premachiavellismo all'antimachiavellismo* (Florence: Sansoni, 1969); André Stegmann, ''Le Tacitisme: Programme pour un nouvel essai de définition,'' *Il Pensiero Politico* 2, no. 3 (1969): 445–58; and to many of the authorities, cited in chaps. 5 and 6, on Botero, Ammirato, and Boccalini.

3. For Strada I used the selections from his *Prolusiones academicae* in Benedetto Croce and Santino Caramella, eds., *Politici e moralisti del Seicento* (Bari: Laterza, 1930); and the Spini article, ''I trattatisti . . . ,'' in the Cochrane translation.

4. *Politici e moralisti del Seicento,* p. 5: ''Age igitur, quicumque historiam contexendo latentes nescio quas artes et dominationis arcana interim aperit, si religioni, cuius prima esse debet in unaquaque re cura, si civitati hominumque consuetudini perniciosus erit, haud erit, opinior, vobis iudicibus civis bonus . . . ; ipsumque a quo defluxisse videtur haec scribendi ratio, uno verbo Cornelium Tacitum.'' And note pp. 8–9: ''Accede ad horum annales aut historias, . . . quid usquam apud illos sincere honesteque factum leges? quid non potius subdole? quid non veteratorie? quid non fraudulenter?'' etc.

5. Thus, according to Spini (Cochrane translation, p. 127), Strada jumps ''back all the way to Speroni and Robortello and to the *leges* of history, the *magistra vitae*.'' On Padua, see ibid., p. 128.

6. For Scioppio, I rely on the information ibid., pp. 127–28.

7. Ibid., p. 128.

8. For Mascardi I rely on the material ibid., pp. 129–31.

9. For Bentivoglio see ibid.; and, for Bentivoglio's praises of Mascardi, see p. 130 in particular.

10. Bentivoglio, *Memorie del Cardinal Bentivoglio* (Venice: G. E. Schultzio, 1752), p. 111 (a propos of Cardinal Deti): "Mostravasi troppo dedito al senso, e perciò s'era dato ad una sorte di vivere, che sentiva molto più del profano, che dell'Ecclesiastico. Era capo sopra modo, riservato con mille rivolte in se stesso, tutto pieno di Tacito, adoratore delle sue sentenze; con Tiberio sempre in bocca, e sempre in essempio; tal che dalla Corte si giudicava, ch'egli sarebbe stato molto più a proposito per la Roma d'all'hora che per la Roma presente."

11. For Spain I rely mainly on the studies, already cited, by Etter, Sanmarti-Boncompte, Tierno-Galván, Stegmann, Momigliano ("Il 'Tacito Español,' di B. Alamos de Barrientos e gli 'Aphorismos' di B. Arias Montano," in *Contributo alla storia degli studi classici,* pp. 61–66), and von Stackelberg; on Peter Burke, "Tacitism," in *Tacitus,* ed. T. A. Dorey (London: Routledge & Kegan Paul, 1969), and his "A Survey of the Popularity of Ancient Historians, 1450–1700," in *History and Theory,* vol. 5 (1966); and, finally, on the excellent article by Michael D. Gordon, "The Science of Politics in Seventeenth-Century Spanish Thought," *Il Pensiero Politico* 7, no. 3 (1974): 379–94.

12. Ribadeneyra, in his *Religion and the Virtues of the Christian Prince against Machiavelli* (Madrid, 1595), as translated by George Albert Moore in *Practical Politics (Ragion di Stato) by Giovanni Botero: Religion and the Virtues of the Christian Prince against Machiavelli (abridged) by Pedro Ribadeneyra* (Washington, D.C.: Country Dollar Press, 1949), p. 252: "These are the fountains from which the politicians of our times drink: . . . Tacitus, the pagan historian and enemy of Christians. . . ." And (ibid.), "it is enough to say that Cornelius Tacitus was a pagan, idolator, and enemy of Christ Our Redeemer and of the Christians (of whom as an impious and debauched man he speaks meanly and scornfully), . . . a man so against Religion, and likewise our enemy. . . ."

13. See J. H. Elliott, *Imperial Spain 1469–1716* (New York: New American Library, 1966), pp. 222–24.

14. *Tácito español ilustrado con aforismos* (Madrid). The aphorisms were translated into Italian by Girolamo Canini d'Anghiari with his edition of Tacitus (Venice, 1628), through which they were read more widely, especially in Italy, than in the original.

15. For Germany at this time I rely mainly on Etter, *Tacitus in der Geistesgeschichte* (see chap. 6, n. 1 above), and Meinecke, *Machiavellism* (see chap. 3, n. 48).

16. Meinecke, *Machiavellism,* pp. 132–33.

17. Etter, *Tacitus in der Geistesgeschichte,* p. 161: "Äusserungen, die sich als Waffen gegen einen Tyrannen gebrauchen liessen, finden sich auch in Boeclers Schriften, aber es sind Empfehlungen, die sich wie trockene Schulweisheit anhören. Es fehlt ihnen die eigene Erfahrung und die Gegenwartsnähe. . . ."

18. For France at this time, I use chiefly von Stackelberg (*Tacitus in der Romania;* see chap. 6, n. 1, above) and Etter.

19. Cited in Etter, *Tacitus in der Geistesgeschichte,* p. 41: "Quod idem de Cornelio Tacito dicerem, si cum reliquis promiscue in historiae theatri scaena conspiceretur; at vero quoniam sedet ipse velut omnium princeps ac imperator in orchestra, aut potius sedem sibi fecit in machina, ex qua cum stupore et admiratione politicas difficultates componit, virtutum suarum maiestate omne fastigium humanum excedens, certe consultius esse mihi persuadeo non hunc tenui sermone velut hominem, sed eloquenti silentio deitatis venerari."

20. Cited in Peter Burke, "A Survey of the Popularity of Ancient Historians, 1450–1700," *History and Theory* 5, no. 2 (1966): 149.

21. Cited in von Stackelberg, *Tacitus in der Romania,* p. 192: "sa version est presque toute dénuée de ces sentences et de ces maximes d'état, qui se rencontrent à chaque période de l'Original."

22. *La Morale de Tacite. Premier Essai: de la Flaterie* (Paris, 1686). Amelot never proceeded, beyond this first installment, with the larger plan he had for *La Morale.*

23. Peter Burke, "Tacitism," in *Tacitus,* ed. T. A. Dorey (see n. 11).

24. For Savile (1549–1622), I primarily use Mary Frances Tenney, "Tacitus in the Middle Ages," pp. 306–10 (see chap. 5, n. 2, above); I also checked the brief but usually valuable remarks and citations in Burke, "Tacitism," pp. 153–54; Etter, *Tacitus in der Geistesgeschichte,* p. 133; Donald R. Dudley, *The World of Tacitus* (London: Secker & Warburg, 1968), pp. 35, 38, 243, note 3; and Edwin B. Benjamin, "Bacon and Tacitus," *Classical Philology* 60, no. 2 (1965): 102–10, in particular on Savile: pp. 105, 110, n. 32.

Savile titled his translation *The Ende of Nero and the Beginning of Galba: Fower Bookes of the Histories of Cornelius Tacitus.* In reality, he attached his own invented "restoration" of the lost ending of the *Annales* to the beginning of his translation. Burke ("Tacitism," p. 153) provides an example of its embellished and somewhat pedestrian style: "Thus Nero, a prince in life contemptible, and hateful in government, having thereby disarmed himself both of the love and fear of his subjects," etc. Later, in 1672, someone published a Latin translation of Savile's "restoration" (see Burke, p. 154).

Note also that Savile failed to translate all but a small portion of the already fragmentary book v of the *Historiae.* His reason—if Ben Jonson, the famous playwright, can be assuming correctly—was "for the evill it contains of the Jews" (see Tenney, "Tacitus in the Middle Ages," p. 306, n. 2).

25. Cited in Dudley, *The World of Tacitus,* p. 35.

26. According to Tenney, "Tacitus in the Middle Ages," p. 307.

27. Cited ibid., p. 308.

28. Cited in Benjamin, "Bacon and Tacitus," p. 110, n. 32; the quotation is much longer there, and I extract the kernel of Savile's gripe.

29. The first reason is stated explicitly by Savile in his preface; the second is in "A. B. to the Reader," written either by Savile himself or by Essex, his friend and patron.

30. Cited in Tenney, "Tacitus in the Middle Ages," p. 325. Cf. *Calendar of State Papers Relating to Ireland, 1596–1597,* p. 320. Note Cecil's tone of indirect discourse and the words "is held"; both clearly show that he is reporting Elizabeth's sentiments and not his own.

31. Bacon relates this incident in his *Apophthegms New and Old* (1625). I use Burke's quotation from his "Tacitism" essay, p. 155.

32. Savile's translation appeared again with Grenewey's in 1598. Neither translator did the *Dialogus* because Lipsius, from a hint by Rhenanus, doubted its authenticity from an argument of style: it appeared too Ciceronian. Grenewey, moreover, like Savile, was far from any awareness of a possible political applicability for Tacitus. Instead he saw Tacitus of philosophic value, offering "instruction of life, for all times . . . nothing yielding to the best philosophers" (cited in Burke, "A Survey," p. 149 (see n. 20, above). Besides, Grenewey must have had greater difficulties than Savile with Tacitus' Latin: or Grenewey didn't take liberties with the text, as Savile often did, to make it smoother. Ben Jonson called Grenewey's translation a wretched work (according to Tenney, "Tacitus in

the Middle Ages,'' p. 308, n. 1). However, Jonson liked Savile's translation and his invention of ''the end of Nero'' section (see Burke, ''Tacitism,'' p. 154); and Lipsius, too, so far as he could read English, was pleased with Savile's work (see Etter, *Tacitus,* p. 133).

33. Tenney, ''Tacitus in the Middle Ages,'' p. 319; see also her ''Tacitus in the Politics of Early Stuart England,'' *Classical Journal* 37 (1941): 151–63, esp. p. 156.

34. According to Burke, ''Tacitism,'' p. 160.

35. In fact, with but one exception, it is Bacon's first use of Tacitus absolutely. Of his earlier writings, from 1585, only the first of them, *The Masculine Birth of Time,* contains a mention of Tacitus (see the text below and note 41). *The Misfortunes of Arthur* (1588), etc., including Bacon's early commonplace book, *Of Colors of Good and Evil* (1597), reveals no use of Tacitus. His first edition of the *Essays* (1597), only ten pieces, is equally void of Tacitus. To be sure, proving the rule with the isolated exception, Bacon may have remembered his conversation with Queen Elizabeth about Hayward's book because he himself may only recently have come really to know Tacitus, or at least to appreciate him more deeply.

36. Tenney, ''Tacitus in the Middle Ages,'' pp. 320–22. Henry died in 1612, leaving Charles (I) next in line for the throne.

37. On Cleland see ibid., pp. 315–19.

38. On Bacon and Tacitus see the three authorities who have said almost everything so far about the relationship: Tenney, ''Tacitus in the Middle Ages,'' pp. 356–69, and her article in the *Classical Journal,* vol. 37, esp. pp. 154–56; Benjamin's short ''Bacon and Tacitus,'' entirely on the subject; and Morris W. Croll, ''Attic Prose: Lipsius, Montaigne, Bacon,'' in *Style, Rhetoric, and Rhythm: Essays by Morris W. Croll,* ed. J. Max Patrick et al. (Princeton: Princeton University Press, 1966), pp. 167–202, esp. pp. 188–95. For other comment, see the few items scattered about in the bibliography listed in note 24, above, on Savile. Add to them the few comments by Norma P. Miller, ''Style and Content in Tacitus,'' in *Tacitus,* ed. Dorey, pp. 99–116, esp. pp. 114–15 (for Dorey, see n. 11, above).

For Bacon's massive corpus of writings, I used the edition by James Spedding, Robert Leslie Ellis, and Douglas Denon Heath, *The Works of Francis Bacon,* 15 vols. (New York: Hurd & Houghton; Boston: Taggard & Thompson, 1861–64). For biographies with general surveys of Bacon's thought: Benjamin Farrington, *Francis Bacon: Philosopher of Industrial Science* (New York: Collier, 1961); A. Wigfall Green, *Sir Francis Bacon* (New York: Twayne, 1966); J. Max Patrick, *Francis Bacon,* Writers and Their Work, no. 131 (London: Longmans, Green & Co. for the British Council of the National Book League, 1961). For some studies of specific aspects of his work: F. H. Anderson, *The Philosophy of Francis Bacon* (New York: Octagon, 1971), esp. chap. 1, pp. 1–12, ''Politics and Learning''; Enrico de Mas, ''La Politica di Bacone,'' *Il Pensiero Politico* 3, no. 2 (1970): 267–71; and Brian Vickers, *Francis Bacon and Renaissance Prose* (New York: Cambridge University Press, 1968).

39. Tenney, ''Tacitus in the Middle Ages,'' pp. 356–69, in this section on Bacon, surveys some of the citations of Tacitus in these works of Bacon—including an analysis of similarities and differences, and omissions and additions, of Tacitus references between the *Advancement* and its later expansion as *De augmentis scientiarum* (1623). Note too her list, on p. 362, of some Tacitus citations in Bacon in other places in his vast literary output.

40. Spedding, Ellis, Heath, eds., *The Works of Francis Bacon,* 12:130. See also Tenney, ''Tacitus in the Middle Ages,'' p. 359. For the dating of this essay, see Green, *Sir Francis Bacon,* pp. 76–87, esp. p. 78.

41. The first, in *The Masculine Birth of Time,* cited in Croll, "Attic Prose," p. 192. The second, in *The Advancement of Learning,* in Spedding, Ellis, Heath, eds., *The Works of Francis Bacon,* 6:235.

42. Cited in Tenney, "Tacitus in the Politics of Early Stuart England," p. 156; cf., Henry G. Bohn, ed., *The Works of Lord Bacon* 2 vols. (London: Reeves & Turner, 1854; reprint of 1879, ed.) 1:483.

43. Bacon, *Works,* Bohn ed., 1:488; cited in Tenney, "Tacitus in the Politics of Early Stuart England," p. 156.

44. My sources for the following political context were J. R. Tanner, *Constitutional Documents of the Reign of James I: A.D. 1603–1625, with an Historical Commentary* (Cambridge: At the University Press, 1961), and his *English Constitutional Conflicts of the Seventeenth Century: 1603–1689* (Cambridge: At the University Press, 1962).

45. Cited in Tenney, "Tacitus in the Politics of Early Stuart England," p. 155; also in her "Tacitus in the Middle Ages," p. 368. Cf. Edwin A. Abbott, *Francis Bacon: An Account of His Life and Works* (London: Macmillan, 1885), p. 180.

46. Tanner, *English Constitutional Conflicts,* p. 46.

47. On the long rivalry between Bacon and Coke and for a comparison of the two men, see ibid., pp. 40–42. As for the broad context of their ideological differences (pp. 41–42): "Thus Coke represented a rigid conservatism—the conservatism of contitutional liberties as they were; Bacon represented reform—but reform carried out by a philosopher-king wielding a sovereignty unlimited and half-divine." See also, Tanner, *Constitutional Documents,* pp. 176–77.

48. Cited in Tenney, "Tacitus in the Politics of Early Stuart England," p. 156; also in her "Tacitus in the Middle Ages," p. 368. Cf. Abbot, *Francis Bacon,* p. 254.

49. Tanner, *Constitutional Documents,* p. 177. Strafford, in the quotation, is Sir Thomas Wentworth, earl of Strafford, Charles I's loyal servant and an ally of Archbishop Laud in the "Eleven Years' Tyranny" of 1629–40.

50. For fuller descriptions, with quotations, see Tenney, "Tacitus in the Politics of Early Stuart England," p. 159.

51. Ibid., p. 158.

52. Ibid., pp. 157–58. See also Burke, "Tacitism," p. 164; Mark H. Curtis, "The Alienated Intellectuals of Early Stuart History," in *Crisis in Europe: 1560–1660,* ed. Trevor Aston (New York: Doubleday, 1967), pp. 309–31, esp. pp. 311–12; and Christopher Hill, *Puritanism and Revolution: The English Revolution of the 17th Century* (New York: Schocken, 1964), p. 64.

53. Tenney, "Tacitus in the Politics of Early Stuart England," p. 160; and the quotation.

54. Ibid., p. 161.

55. Ibid., p. 158.

56. Ibid., pp. 161–62.

57. Cited, in a fuller version, ibid., p. 162. Note that in another place, at least according to Michael Grant, Milton attacks Tacitus "as one who had despaired of the Republic." Grant adds, again without a reference, that "a French royalist," in reaction to Milton, praised Tacitus as a supporter of autocratic law and order. See Grant's *Roman Literature* (Baltimore: Penguin, 1964). I have not been able to track down Grant's sources on these points.

58. Tenney, "Tacitus in the Politics of Early Stuart England," p. 161; and see the quotation from Captain Titus' work there.

59. For Vico, I rely mostly on the essays edited by Giorgio Taglicacozzo and Hayden

V. White, *Giambattista Vico: An International Symposium* (Baltimore: Johns Hopkins University Press, 1969)—particularly the ones by Enrico de Mas (translated by Elio Gianturco), "Vico's Four Authors," and Santino Caramella (translated by A. William Salomone), "Vico, Tacitus, and Reason of State." Also helpful was von Stackelberg, *Tacitus in der Romania,* pp. 149–58, and, more generally, Giuseppe Giarrizzo, "La politica di Vico," *Il Pensiero Politico* 1, no. 3 (1968): 321–85.

60. De Mas, "Vico's Four Authors," *Symposium,* p. 5, quoting from Max H. Fisch and Thomas G. Bergin, trans., *The Autobiography of Giambattista Vico* (Ithaca, N.Y.: Cornell University Press, 1963), p. 138.

61. De Mas argues plausibly, however, that, in addition to Bacon, Vico placed as great a value on a fourth author: Hugo Grotius, the great jurisprudent. Vico needed Grotius because "Bacon was unable to give us a valid example of how to put his method into effect, how to transfer it from the scientific domain to that of social phenomena" ("Vico's Four Authors," *Symposium,* p. 12).

62. The *Symposium* volume alone makes this point clear.

63. Santino Caramella, "Vico, Tacitus, and Reason of State," *Symposium,* p. 30.

64. Ibid., p. 29.

65. On Montesquieu see von Stackelberg, *Tacitus in der Romania,* pp. 222–24. In general see Peter Gay, *The Enlightenment: An Interpretation: The Rise of Modern Paganism* (New York: Vintage, 1968).

66. See Gay, *The Enlightenment,* and, more particularly, von Stackelberg, *Tacitus in der Romania,* pp. 234–38, 239–44; and see, still more specifically, von Stackelberg's article on the subject, "Rousseau, d'Alembert et Diderot, traducteurs de Tacite," *Studi Francesi* 6 (1958): 395–407, and Donald R. Dudley, *The World of Tacitus* (London: Secker & Warburg, 1968), pp. 235–36.

67. Cited in Dudley, *The World of Tacitus,* p. 235.

68. For Tacitus in eighteenth-century America I rely on Richard M. Gummere, *The American Colonial Mind and the Classical Tradition: Essays in Comparative Culture* (Cambridge, Mass.: Harvard University Press, 1963).

69. Ibid., p. 126.

70. Ibid., p. 192.

71. Ibid., p. 166. Boucher's book, his main work: *A View of the Causes and Consequences of the American Revolution in Thirteen Discourses Preached in North America between the Years 1763 and 1775.*

72. Voltaire, cited, in French, in von Stackelberg, *Tacitus in der Romania,* p. 225.

73. Linguet, cited ibid., p. 227: "C'est en tremblant que j'ose contredire Tacite . . . mais enfin je demande qu'on oublie, si l'on peut, les Auteurs, et que l'on pèse seulement les raisons" (from the 1766 edition, vol. 1, p. 54).

74. Linguet, cited ibid., p. 227: "j'avoue aussi qu'en copiant tout cet épisode dont Tacite a orné sa narration, je n'en crois pas un mot" (from the 1766 edition, vol. 1, p. 80).

75. Cited in Norma P. Miller, "Style and Content in Tacitus," in *Tacitus,* ed. Dorey, pp. 99–116 (see n. 11, above).

76. Pagnini, from *Della Decima . . . ,* 4 vols. (Lisbon and Lucca [but really Florence]: G. Bouchard, 1765–66), 3:174: "Restano però non poco amareggiate queste giuste speranze dalla trista reflessione che vien suggerita da Tacito, per la quale ci si rammenta che 'Tardiora sunt remedia, quam mala; & ut corpora lente augentur, cito extinguuntur, sic ingenia, studiaque oppresseris facilius, quam revocaveris. Subit quippe ipsius inertiae dulcedo, & invisa primo desidia postremo amatur.' " The text of Pagnini's quotation from

Tacitus differs in a few unimportant words from that of the Loeb Classical Library, from which edition I take my translation in the text. For Pagnini in his own historical context see the half-dozen places in Cochrane, *Florence in the Forgotten Centuries*.

77. Cited and translated by John Jackson in his introduction to the *Annales* in the Loeb edition, p. 236. For similar statements by Napoleon I on Tacitus, see von Stackelberg, *Tacitus in der Romania,* pp. 239–41.

78. According to Jackson, in his introduction to the *Annales,* Loeb ed., p. 236, n. 1.

79. According to Gilbert Highet, *The Classical Tradition: Greek and Roman Influences on Western Literature* (London: Oxford University Press, 1967), p. 406.

80. Drexler, p. 6: "Zum Glück ist es dem Nationalsozialismus mit der Geschichte in solchem Masse ernst, dass ein Wort der Rechtfertigung nach dieser Richtung völlig überflüssig ist. Es kommt hinzu, dass die beiden antiken Völker, in stärkerem Masse die Griechen, in geringerem die Römer, als rassen- und artverwandt besonders starkem Interesse begegnen."

81. Ibid., pp. 7–8: "Es wird sich zeigen, dass bei Tacitus wie bei jedem grossen Historiker die Welt, ihr Bild und sein Bildner eine unlösliche Einheit sind. Darum sind auch die Urteilskategorien und Ideen des Tacitus—der Versuch angesehener Forscher, ihr Vorhandensein in Abrede zu stellen, ist vergeblich gewesen—und die Sinnkoordinaten dieser Zeit identisch."

82. Ibid., p. 195: "Was aber den Rassengedanken betrifft, so liegt der Grund für das Aussterben des alten römischen Volkes—der Pöbel in Rom verdiente diesen Namen schon lange nicht mehr—in dem Nachlassen seiner sittlichen Kraft." And note page 196: "die Kernfrage der Wissenschaft von der Rasse ist das Leib-Seele-Problem." And, on the science of race itself (p. 197): "Es ist eine wahrhaft kopernikanische Wendung, . . ."

83. Ibid.: "Auf den Rassengedanken angewendet bedeutet das: alle Rassen sind naturgegebene Individualitäten; ihre Rang- und Wertverschiedenheit jedoch beruht darauf, das sie in verschiedenem Grade die Idee der Menschheit verkörpern. . . . [and the idea of races] wir ihn am tiefsten verwirklichen, wenn wir die historische und individuelle Notwendigkeit des Schicksals, das sich an einem Volke vollzieht, aufzuzeigen versuchen."

84. Meinecke, "The Year 1848 in German History," *Review of Politics* 10 (1948): 475–92. I used it in an anthology, edited by Herman Ausubel, *The Making of Modern Europe: Book II: Waterloo to the Atomic Age* (New York: Dryden Press, 1951), p. 675.

85. Lionel Trilling: "Tacitus Now," pp. 198–204 in his collection of essays, *The Liberal Imagination* (New York: Doubleday-Anchor Books, 1950), p. 198. Trilling, at Columbia University for forty-four years, passed away in 1975.

86. Momigliano, in this lecture (delivered in the Aula Magna of the University of Copenhagen, 1954) published now in *Studies in Historiography* (New York: Harper & Row, 1966), pp. 112–26; the quotation in the text is from pp. 112–13; originally it appeared in the *Acta Congressus Madvigiani, Proceedings of the Second International Congress of Classical Studies 1954* 1 (1958): 199–211.

87. Trilling, *The Liberal Imagination,* p. 198.

88. Ibid.

89. Ibid., p. 199.

90. Ibid., p. 204.

91. Nitti, *Opere,* 18 vols. (Bari: Laterza, 1958–63), 15:633: "Tacito nota giustamente che il popolo è sempre molto incostante e nello stesso tempo teme e disidera le rivoluzioni." Nitti has *Annales* xv. 46 in mind here. Another interesting reference occurs in vol.

10, p. 468 (in the "Avvertenza" to *La tragedia dell'Europa*): after speaking of the necessity of Italy's attachments to America, Britain, and Russia as a result of the consciousness of the new elements in post–World War I Europe, Nitti ends with "da parte mia, io posso dire agli'italiani le parole che Tacito mette sul labbro di uno dei personaggi della sua storia [iv. 58]: 'Numquam apud vos verba feci aut pro vobis sollicitior aut pro me securior' " (written in October 1923).

92. Dudley, *The World of Tacitus,* p. 237.

Selected Bibliography

Abbondanza, Roberto. ''Premières considérations sur la méthodologie d'Alciat.'' In *Pédagogues et juristes*, pp. 107–18. Congrès du Centre d'Etudes Supérieures de la Renaissance de Tours, 1960. Paris: Vrin, 1963. English translation by Eric Cochrane, ''Jurisprudence: The Methodology of Andrea Alciato.'' In *The Late Italian Renaissance: 1525–1630*, edited by Eric Cochrane, pp. 77–90. New York: Harper & Row, 1970.

———. ''Tentativi medicei di chiamare l'Alciato a Pisa (1542–1547).'' *Annali di storia del diritto* 2 (1958): 361–403.

Africa, Thomas W. *Rome of the Caesars*. New York: John Wiley, 1965.

Albertini, Rudolf von. *Das florentinische Staatsbewusstsein im Übergang von der Republik zum Prinzipat*. Bern: Francke, 1955.

Allen, J. W. *A History of Political Thought in the Sixteenth Century*. New York: Barnes & Noble, 1960.

Allen, Walter. ''Beatus Rhenanus: Editor of Tacitus and Livy.'' *Speculum* 12 (1937): 382–85.

———. ''The Yale Manuscript of Tacitus.'' *Yale University Library Gazette* 11 (1937): 81–86.

Amelung, Peter. *Das Bild des Deutschen in der Literatur der italienischen Renaissance*. Munich: Max Huebner, 1964.

Anderson, F. H. *The Philosophy of Francis Bacon*. New York: Octagon Books, 1971.

Anglo, Sydney. *Machiavelli: A Dissection*. New York: Harcourt, Brace & World, 1969.

For reasons of economy, this bibliography is limited to modern authorities used for this book—and, even then, not every single one cited in the notes is included here. The early sources that are analyzed and quoted, all fully cited in the notes, are easily accessible and are therefore not repeated here.

Assandria, Giuseppe. *Giovanni Botero: Note biografice e bibliografiche*. Bene Vagienna: Francesco Vissio, 1928.

Baron, Hans. *The Crisis of the Early Italian Renaissance: Civic Humanism and Republican Liberty in an Age of Classicism and Tyranny*. Rev. ed. Princeton: Princeton University Press, 1966.

———. *From Petrarch to Leonardo Bruni: Studies in Humanistic and Political Literature*. Chicago: University of Chicago Press for the Newberry Library, 1968.

———. "The *Principe* and the Puzzle of the Date of the *Discorsi*." *Bibliothèque d'Humanisme et Renaissance* 18 (1956): 405–28.

———. "Zur Frage des Ursprungs des deutschen Humanismus und seiner religiösen Reformbestrebungen." *Historische Zeitschrift* 132 (1925): 413–46.

Battaglia, Felice. *Enea Silvio Piccolomini e Francesco Patrizi: Due politici senesi del Quattrocento*. Florence: Leo S. Olschki, 1934–36.

Beare, W. "Tacitus on the Germans." *Greece and Rome* 11 (1964): 64–76.

Bec, Christian. "La Politique de Giovanni della Casa." *Il Pensiero Politico* 7 (1974): 362–78.

Becker, Marvin B. *Florence in Transition*. 2 vols. Baltimore: Johns Hopkins University Press, 1968.

Benjamin, Edwin B. "Bacon and Tacitus." *Classical Philology* 60, no. 2 (April, 1965): 102–10.

Berner, Samuel. "Florentine Political Thought in the Late Cinquecento." *Il Pensiero Politico* 3, no. 2 (1970): 177–99.

Bertelli, Sergio. "Machiavelli and Soderini." *Renaissance Quarterly* 28, no. 1 (Spring, 1975): 1–16.

Best, Thomas W. *The Humanist Ulrich von Hutten: A Reappraisal of His Humor*. Chapel Hill: University of North Carolina Press, 1969.

Bietenholz, Peter G. *Basle and France in the Sixteenth Century: The Basle Humanists and Printers in Their Contacts with Francophone Culture*. Toronto: University of Toronto Press, 1971.

Bindi, Enrico. "Della Vita e delle Opere di Bernardo Davanzati." In *Le Opere di Bernardo Davanzati*, edited by Enrico Bindi. 2 vols. Florence: Le Monnier, 1852–53.

Boase, Alan Martin. *The Fortunes of Montaigne: A History of the Essays in France: 1580–1969*. New York: Octagon Books, 1969.

Bohnstedt, John W. *The Infidel Scourge of God: The Turkish Menace as Seen by German Pamphleteers of the Reformation Era*. Transactions of the American Philosophical Society, n.s. 58, pt. 9. Philadelphia: The Society, 1968.

Bolgar, R. R. *The Classical Heritage and Its Beneficiaries: From the Carolingian Age to the End of the Renaissance*. New York: Harper & Row, 1964.

———. *Classical Influences on European Culture: A.D. 500–1500*. Cambridge: At the University Press, 1971.

Borchardt, Frank L. *German Antiquity in Renaissance Myth*. Baltimore: Johns Hopkins University Press, 1971.

Bouwsma, William J. "Lawyers and Modern Culture." *American Historical Review* 78, no. 2 (April, 1973): 303–27.

———. "Three Types of Historiography in Post-Renaissance Italy." *History and Theory* 4, no. 3 (1965): 303–14.

———. *Venice and the Defense of Republican Liberty: Renaissance Values in the Age of the Counter-Reformation*. Berkeley: University of California, 1969.

Breen, Quirinus. *John Calvin: A Study in French Humanism*. 2d ed. n.p.: Archon Books, 1968.

Buchner, Rudolf. *Maximilian I: Kaiser an der Zeitenwende*. Göttingen: Musterschmidt, 1959.

Büchner, Karl. *Tacitus: Die historischen Versuche*. Stuttgart: A. Kröner, 1955.

Burke, Peter. *The Renaissance Sense of the Past*. New York: St. Martin's Press, 1970.

———. "A Survey of the Popularity of Ancient Historians, 1450–1700." *History and Theory* 5, no. 2 (1966): 135–52.

———. "Tacitism." In *Tacitus*, edited by T. A. Dorey, pp. 149–71. London: Routledge & Kegan Paul, 1969.

Buttenwieser, Hilda. "Popular Authors of the Middle Ages." *Speculum* 17 (1942): 50–55.

Cameron, Keith. "Montaigne and 'De la Liberté de Conscience.'" *Renaissance Quarterly* 26, no. 3 (1973): 285–94.

Caprariis, Vittorio de. *Francesco Guicciardini: Dalla politica alla storia*. Bari: Laterza, 1950.

Carsten, F. L. *Princes and Parliaments in Germany from the Fifteenth to the Eighteenth Century*. Oxford: Clarendon Press, 1959.

Chabod, Federico. *Giovanni Botero*. Rome: Anonima Romana, 1934.

———. *Machiavelli and the Renaissance*. Translated by David Moore. New York: Harper & Row, 1965.

Chauviré, Roger. *Jean Bodin, Auteur de la "République."* Paris: Librairie Ancienne Honoré Champion, 1914.

Chudoba, Bohdan. *Spain and the Empire: 1519–1643*. Chicago: University of Chicago Press, 1952.

Clough, Cecil H. *Machiavelli Researches*. Naples: Pubblicazioni della Sezione Romanza dell' Istituto Universitario Orientali, 1967.

Cochrane, Eric. "The End of the Renaissance in Florence." In *The Late Italian Renaissance: 1525–1630,* edited by Eric Cochrane, pp. 41–73. New York: Harper & Row, 1970.

———. *Florence in the Forgotten Centuries, 1527–1800: A History of Florence and the Florentines in the Age of the Grand Dukes*. Chicago: University of Chicago Press, 1973.

———. "Machiavelli: 1940–1960." *Journal of Modern History* 33, no. 2 (1961): 113–36.

———. *Tradition and Enlightenment in the Tuscan Academies*. Chicago: University of Chicago Press, 1961.

Croce, Benedetto. "La Crisi italiana del Cinquecento e il legame del Rinascimento col Risorgimento." *La Critica: Rivista di letteratura, storia e filosofia* 37 (1939): 401–11.

Croll, Morris W. *Style, Rhetoric, and Rhythm: Essays by Morris W. Croll*. Edited by J. Max Patrick et al. Princeton: Princeton University Press, 1966.

Curtis, Mark H. "The Alienated Intellectuals of Early Stuart England." In *Crisis in Europe: 1560–1660,* edited by Trevor Aston, pp. 309–31. New York: Doubleday, 1967.

D'Addio, Mario. *Il pensiero politico di Gasparo Scioppio e il machiavellismo del Seicento*. Milan: A Giuffrè, 1962.

D'Andrea, Antonio. "The Political and Ideological Context of Innocent Gentillet's Anti-Machiavel." *Renaissance Quarterly* 23, no. 4 (1970): 397–411.

Dickens, A. G. *Reformation and Society in Sixteenth-Century Europe*. New York: Harcourt, Brace & World, 1968.

Dorey, T. A., ed. *Tacitus*. London: Routledge & Kegan Paul, 1969.

Dudley, Donald R. *The World of Tacitus*. London: Secker & Warburg, 1968.

Dunn, E. Catherine. "Lipsius and the Art of Letter-Writing." *Studies in the Renaissance* 3 (1956): 145–56.

Elliott, J. H. *Imperial Spain: 1469–1716*. New York: New American Library, 1966.

Emerton, Ephraim. *Humanism and Tyranny: Studies in the Italian Trecento*. Cambridge, Mass.: Harvard University Press, 1925.

Erasmus, H. J. *The Origins of Rome in Historiography from Petrarch to Perizonius*. New York: Van Gorcum, 1962.

Esler, Anthony. *The Aspiring Mind of the Elizabethan Younger Generation*. Durham, N.C.: Duke University Press, 1966.

Etter, Else-Lilly. *Tacitus in der Geistesgeschichte des 16. und 17. Jahrhunderts*. Basel: Helbing & Lichtenhahn, 1966.

Farrington, Benjamin. *Francis Bacon: Philosopher of Industrial Science*. New York: Collier, 1961.

Ferguson, Arthur B. "'By Little and Little': The Early Tudor Humanists on the Development of Man." In *Florilegium Historiale: Essays Presented to Wallace K. Ferguson,* edited by J. G. Rowe and W. H. Stockdale, pp. 125–50. Toronto: University of Toronto Press, 1971.

Fiorentino, Francesco. "Trajano Boccalini ed i suoi Commentari sopra Cornelio Tacito." In *Studi e ritratti della Rinascenza,* pp. 475–504. Bari: Laterza, 1911.

Firpo, Luigi. *I "Ragguagli di Parnaso" di Traiano Boccalini: Bibliografia delle edizione italiane*. Biblioteca degli Eruditi e dei Bibliofili, vol. 12. Florence: Sansoni, 1955.

———. *Gli scritti giovanili di Giovanni Botero: Bibliografia ragionata*. Biblioteca degli Eruditi e dei Bibliofili, vol. 45. Florence: Sansoni, 1960.

———. "L'Utopismo del Rinascimento e l'età nuova." In *Lo Stato ideale della Controriforma,* pp. 241–61. Bari: Laterza, 1957.

———. "Political Philosophy: Renaissance Utopianism." Translated by Eric Cochrane. In *The Late Italian Renaissance,* edited by Eric Cochrane, pp. 149–67. New York: Harper & Row, 1970.

Fleisher, Martin, ed. *Machiavelli and the Nature of Political Thought*. New York: Atheneum, 1972.

Frame, Donald M. *Montaigne's Discovery of Man: The Humanization of a Humanist*. New York: Columbia University Press, 1955.

Franklin, Julian H. *Jean Bodin and the Sixteenth Century Revolution in the Methodology of Law and History*. New York: Columbia University Press, 1963.

Friedrich, Hugo. *Montaigne*. Bern: Francke, 1949.

Fueter, Eduard. *Geschichte der neueren Historiographie*. Munich: R. Oldenbourg, 1911.

Fussner, F. Smith. *Tudor History and the Historians*. New York: Basic Books, 1970.

Gandy, Della. "A Comparison of the Treatment of the Germans in the *Germania* and the *Annales* of Tacitus." Master's thesis, University of Chicago, 1903.

Gay, Peter. *The Enlightenment: An Interpretation*. Vol. 1: *The Rise of Modern Paganism*. New York: Vintage, 1966.

Giarrizzo, Giuseppe. "La Politica di Vico." *Il Pensiero Politico* 1, no. 3 (1968): 321–85.

Gilbert, Felix. *Machiavelli and Guicciardini: Politics and History in Sixteenth Century Florence*. Princeton: Princeton University Press, 1965.

Gilmore, Myron P. "Freedom and Determinism in Renaissance Historians." *Studies in the Renaissance* 3 (1956): 47–60.

———. *Humanists and Jurists*. Cambridge, Mass.: Harvard University Press, 1963.

———, ed. *Studies on Machiavelli*. Biblioteca Storica Sansoni, n.s. 50. Florence: Sansoni, 1972.

———. *The World of Humanism: 1453–1517*. New York: Harper & Row, 1952.

Gordon, Mary L. "The Patria of Tacitus." *Journal of Roman Studies* 26 (1936): 145–51.

Gordon, Michael D. "The Science of Politics in Seventeenth-Century Spanish Thought." *Il Pensiero Politico* 7, no. 3 (1974): 379–94.

Grant, Michael. *Roman Literature*. Rev. ed. Baltimore: Penguin, 1964.

Gray, Hanna Holborn. "History and Rhetoric in Quattrocento Humanism." Ph.D. dissertation, Radcliffe, 1957.

———. "Renaissance Humanism: The Pursuit of Eloquence." *Journal of the History of Ideas* 24 (1963): 497–514. Reprinted in *Renaissance Essays*, edited by Paul O. Kristeller and Phillip P. Wiener, pp. 199–216. New York: Harper & Row, 1968.

Green, A. Wigfall. *Francis Bacon*. New York: Twayne, 1966.

Green, Henry. *Andrea Alciati and His Books of Emblems: A Biographical and Bibliographical Study*. New York: Burt Franklin, n.d. 1st ed., London: Trübner, 1872.

Grendler, Paul F. *Critics of the Italian World, 1530–1560: Anton Francesco Doni, Nicolò Franco, and Ortensio Lando*. Madison: University of Wisconsin Press, 1969.

———. "Francesco Sansovino and Italian Popular History 1560–1600." *Studies in the Renaissance* 16 (1969): 139–80.

Gummere, Richard M. *The American Colonial Mind and the Classical Tradition: Essays in Comparative Culture*. Cambridge, Mass.: Harvard University Press, 1963.

Gundersheimer, Werner L., ed. *French Humanism, 1470–1600*. New York: Harper & Row, 1969.

Häussler, Reinhard. *Tacitus und das historische Bewusstsein*. Heidelberg: Karl Winter, 1965.

Haggis, D. R., et al., eds. *The French Renaissance and Its Heritage: Essays Presented to Alan M. Boase*. London: Methuen, 1968.

Hale, David George. *The Body Politic: A Political Metaphor in Renaissance English Literature*. The Hague and Paris: Mouton, 1971.

Hay, Denys. *The Italian Renaissance in Its Historical Background*. Cambridge: At the University Press, 1961.

———. "Italy and Barbarian Europe." In *Italian Renaissance Studies*, edited by E. F. Jacob, pp. 48–68. London: Faber & Faber, 1960.

———. *Polydore Vergil: Renaissance Historian and Man of Letters*. Oxford: Clarendon Press, 1952.

Heath, Terrence. "Logical Grammar, Grammatical Logic, and Humanism in Three German Universities." *Studies in the Renaissance* 18 (1971): 9–64.

Highet, Gilbert. *The Classical Tradition: Greek and Roman Influences on Western Literature*. London: Oxford University Press, 1967.

Hirsch, Rudolf. "Printing and the Spread of Humanism in Germany: The Example of Albrecht von Eyb." In *Renaissance Men and Ideas*, edited by Robert Schwoebel, pp. 23–37. New York: St. Martin's Press, 1971.

Hogrefe, Pearl. *The Life and Times of Sir Thomas Elyot Englishman*. Ames: Iowa State University Press, 1967.

———. *The Sir Thomas More Circle: A Program of Ideas and Their Impact on Secular Drama*. Urbana: University of Illinois Press, 1959.

Horawitz, Adalbert. "Beatus Rhenanus: Ein biographischer Versuch." *Sitzungsberichte der kaiserlichen Akademie der Wissenschaften, Philosophisch-historische Classe* 70 (1872): 189–244.

———. "Des Beatus Rhenanus literarische Thätigkeit in den Jahren 1508–1531." *Sitzungsberichte der kaiserlichen Akademie der Wissenschaften, Philosophisch-historische Classe* 72 (1874): 323–76.

Huppert, George. *The Idea of Perfect History: Historical Erudition and Historical Philosophy in Renaissance France*. Urbana: University of Illinois Press, 1970.

Hurstfield, Joel, ed. *The Reformation Crisis*. New York: Harper & Row, 1966.

Joachimsen, Paul. *Geschichtsauffassung und Geschichtsschreibung in Deutschland unter dem Einfluss des Humanismus*. Beiträge zur Kulturgeschichte des Mittelalters und der Renaissance, vol. 6. Leipzig: Teubner, 1910.

———. "Tacitus im deutschen Humanismus." *Neue Jahrbücher für das klassische Altertum* 27 (1911): 696–717.

Kallen, Gerhard. *Aenea Silvio Piccolomini als Publizist in der Epistola de ortu et auctoritate imperii romani*. Stuttgart: Petrarca-Haus, 1939.

Kelly, Donald R. *Foundations of Modern Historical Scholarship: Language, Law, and History in the French Renaissance*. New York: Columbia University Press, 1970.

———. "François Baudoin's Conception of History." *Journal of the History of Ideas* 25 (1964): 35–57.

———. "Murd'rous Machiavel in France: A Post Mortem." *Political Science Quarterly* 85 (1970): 545–59.

Kisch, Guido. *Gestalten und Probleme aus Humanismus und Jurisprudenz*. Berlin: Walter de Gruyter, 1969.

Klaus, Arnold. *Johannes Trithemius (1462–1516)*. Würzburg: Kommisionsverlag Ferdinand Schöningh, 1971.

Knod, Gustav C. "Aus der Bibliothek des Beatus Rhenanus: Ein Beitrag zur Geschichte des Humanismus." *Die Stadtbibliothek zu Schletttstadt: Festschrift zur Einweihung des neuen Bibliotheksgebäudes am 6. Juni 1889*. Strassburg: M. Du Mont–Schauberg, 1889.

Kristeller, Paul Oskar. *Eight Philosophers of the Italian Renaissance*. Stanford: Stanford University Press, 1964.

———. *Iter Italicum: A Finding List of Uncatalogued or Incompletely Catalogued Humanistic Manuscripts of the Renaissance in Italian or Other Libraries*. 2 vols. London: Warburg Institute, 1965–67.

———. *Latin Books before 1600: A List of the Printed Catalogues and Unpublished Inventories of Extant Collections*. Rev. ed. New York: Fordham University Press, 1960.

———. *Renaissance Thought: The Classic, Scholastic, and Humanistic Strains*. New York: Harper & Row, 1961.

———. *Renaissance Thought II: Papers on Humanism and the Arts*. New York: Harper & Row, 1965.

Kuehnemund, Richard. *Arminius or the Rise of a National Symbol in Literature (from Hutten to Grabbe)*. University of North Carolina Studies in Germanic Languages and Literature, no. 8. Chapel Hill:

University of North Carolina Press, 1953.

La Charité, Raymond C. *The Concept of Judgment in Montaigne*. The Hague: Martinus Nijhoff, 1968.

Laistner, Max Ludwig Wolfram. *The Greater Roman Historians*. Berkeley: University of California Press, 1963.

———. *Thought and Letters in Western Europe: A.D. 500–900*. New York: Dial Press, 1931.

Langosch, Karl, et al., eds. *Geschichte der Textüberlieferung der antiken und Mittelalterlichen Literatur*. 2 vols. Vol. 2: *Überlieferungsgeschichte der mittelalterlichen Literatur*. Zurich: Atlantis Verlag, 1964.

Laugier, J. -L. *Tacite*. Paris: Editions du Seuil, 1969.

Leidinger, Georg. "Zur Geschichte der Entstehung von Aventins 'Germania illustrata' und dessen 'Zeitbuch über ganz Teutschland.' " *Sitzungsberichte der Bayerischen Akademie der Wissenschaft, Philosophisch-historische Abteilung*, vol. 3, pp. 3–33. Munich: C. H. Beck, 1935.

Mas, Enrico de. "La Politica di Bacone." *Il Pensiero Politico* 3, no. 2 (1970): 267–71.

Masius, Alfred. *Flavio Biondo: Sein Leben und Seine Werke*. Leipzig: Teubner, 1879.

Mattei, Rodolfo de. *Dal Premachiavellismo all'antimachiavellismo*. Florence: Sansoni, 1969.

———. *Il pensiero politico di Scipione Ammirato*. Lecce: Centro di Studi Salentini, 1959.

McKisack, May. *Medieval History in the Tudor Age*. New York: Oxford University Press, 1971.

Meinecke, Friedrich. *Machiavellism: The Doctrine of Raison d'Etat and Its Place in Modern History*. Translated by Douglas Starck. New Haven: Yale University Press, 1957.

Mendell, C. W. "The Discovery of the Minor Works of Tacitus." *American Journal of Philology* 56 (1935): 113–30.

———. "Manuscripts of Tacitus' Minor Works." *Memoirs of the American Academy in Rome* 19 (1949): 135–45.

———. "Tacitus: Literature 1948–1953." *Classical Weekly*, no. 48/49 (1955).

———. *Tacitus: The Man and His Work*. New Haven: Yale University Press, 1957.

Mestica, Giovanni. *Trajano Boccalini e la letteratura critica e politica del Seicento*. Florence: B. Barbèra, 1878.

Miller, Norma P. "Style and Content in Tacitus." In *Tacitus,* edited by

T. A. Dorey, p. 99–116. London: Routledge and Kegan Paul, 1969.

Momigliano, Arnaldo D. "The First Political Commentary on Tacitus." In *Contributo alla storia degli studi classici,* edited by Arnaldo D. Momigliano, pp. 38–59. Rome: Edizioni di Storia e Letteratura, 1955. Originally published in *Journal of Roman Studies* 37 (1947): 91–101.

———. "Il 'Tacito Español' di B. Alamos de Barrientos e gli 'Aphorismos' di B. Arias Montano." In *Contributo alla storia degli studi classici,* edited by Arnaldo D. Momigliano, pp. 61–66. Rome: Edizioni di Storia e Letteratura, 1955.

———. *Studies in Historiography*. New York: Harper & Row, 1966.

Nisard, C. *Le Triumvirat littéraire au XVIe siècle: Juste Lipse, Joseph Scaliger, et Isaac Casaubon*. Paris: Amyot, 1852.

Nolhac, Pierre de. "Boccaccio et Tacite." *Mélanges d'Archéologie et d'Histoire* (Ecole française de Rome) 12 (1892): 125–48.

Paratore, Ettore. *Pensiero politico e oratoria nell'Agricola di Tacito*. Rome: Edizioni dell'Ateneo, 1962.

Parel, Anthony, ed. *The Political Calculus: Essays on Machiavelli's Philosophy*. Toronto: University of Toronto Press, 1972.

Patrick, Max. *Francis Bacon*. London: Longmans, Green & Co. for the British Council of the National Book League, 1961.

Petrocchi, Massimo. *La Controriforma in Italia*. Rome: Anonima Veritas, 1947.

Prezzolini, Giuseppe. *Machiavelli Anticristo*. Rome: Gherardo Casini, 1954.

Raab, Felix. *The English Face of Machiavelli: A Changing Interpretation: 1500–1700*. London: Routledge & Kegan Paul, 1964.

Ramorino, Felice. *Cornelio Tacito nella storia della cultura*. Milan: Hoepli, 1898.

Renaudet, A. *Préréforme et humanisme à Paris pendant les premières guerres d'Italie., 1494–1517*. Paris: H. Champion, 1916.

Reynolds, Beatrice. "Latin Historiography: A Survey, 1400–1600." *Studies in the Renaissance* 2 (1955): 1–66.

———. "Shifting Currents in Historical Criticism." *Journal of the History of Ideas* 14 (1953): 471–92. Reprinted in *Renaissance Essays,* edited by Paul O. Kristeller and Philip P. Wiener, pp. 115–36. New York: Harper & Row, 1968.

Ridolfi, Roberto. *The Life of Francesco Guicciardini*. Translated by Cecil Grayson. London: Routledge & Kegan Paul, 1967.

———. *The Life of Niccolò Machiavelli*. Translated by Cecil Grayson. Chicago: University of Chicago Press, 1963.

———. *Vita di Francesco Guicciardini*. Rome: Angelo Belardetti, 1960.

Robathan, Dorothy M. "A Fifteenth-Century History of Latin Literature." *Speculum* 7 (1932): 239–51.

Roersch, Alphonse. "Juste Lipse." *Biographie nationale de Belgique* 12 (1892): 239–89.

———. *L'humanisme belge à l'époque de la Renaissance: Etudes et portraits*. Brussels: G. van Oest, 1910.

Rothenberg, Gunther E. "Aventinus and the Defense of the Empire against the Turks." *Studies in the Renaissance* 10 (1963): 60–67.

Rowse, A. L. *The Elizabethan Renaissance: The Cultural Achievement*. New York: Charles Scribner's Sons, 1972.

Rubinstein, Nicolai. *The Government of Florence under the Medici*. Oxford: Oxford University Press, 1966.

Ruysschaert, José. *Juste Lipse et les Annales de Tacite: Une méthode de critique textuelle au XVIe siècle*. Turnhout: Brepols Press, 1949.

Sabbadini, Remigio. *Le scoperte dei codici latini e greci ne'secoli XIV e XV*. 2 vols. Florence: Sansoni, 1905–14.

———. *Storia e critica di testi latini: Cicerone, Donato, Tacito, Celso, Plauto, Plinio, Quintilliano, Livio e Sallustio, Commedia ignota*. 2d ed. Padua: Editrice Antenore, 1971.

Sandys, John Edwin. *A History of Classical Scholarship*. 3 vols. New York: Hafner, 1958.

Sanmarti-Boncompte, Francisco. *Tacito en España*. Barcelona: Consejo superior de investigaciones cientificas instituto "Antonio Nebrija" (Delegacion de Barcelona), 1951.

Sasso, Gennaro. *Niccolò Machiavelli: Storia del suo pensiero politico*. Naples: Nella sede dell'istituto, 1958.

Saunders, Jason Lewis. *Justus Lipsius: The Philosophy of Renaissance Stoicism*. New York: Liberal Arts Press, 1955.

Seton-Watson, R. W. *Maximilian I: Holy Roman Emperor*. Westminster, Eng.: Archibald Constable, 1902.

Schellhase, Kenneth C. "Tacitus in the Political Thought of Machiavelli." *Il Pensiero Politico* 4, no. 3 (1971): 381–91.

———. Review of Hendrik D. L. Vervliet, *Lipsius' Jeugd 1547–1578: Analecta voor een kritische Biografie*. *Renaissance Quarterly* 25 (1972): 86–87.

Schwarzenfeld, Gertrude. *Karl V: Annherr Europas.* Hamburg: Schröder, 1954.

Schwoebel, Robert. *The Shadow of the Crescent: The Renaissance Image of the Turk: 1453–1517.* New York: St. Martins Press, 1968.

Shennan, Joseph Hugh. *Government and Society in France: 1461–1661.* London: Allen & Unwin, 1969.

Simone, Franco. *The French Renaissance: Medieval Tradition and Italian Influence in Shaping the Renaissance in France.* Translated by H. Gaston Hall. London: Macmillan, 1969.

Spini, Giorgio. "I trattatisti dell'arte storica nella Controriforma italiana." In *Contributi alla storia del Concilio di Trento e della Controriforma,* "Quaderni di Belfagor," pp. 109–36. Florence: Vallecchi, 1948. English translation, "The Art of History in the Italian Counter Reformation." Translated by Eric Cochrane. In *The Late Italian Renaissance: 1525–1630,* edited by Eric Cochrane, pp. 91–133. New York: Harper & Row, 1970.

Spitz, Lewis W. *Conrad Celtis: The German Arch-Humanist.* Harvard University Press, 1957.

———. "Humanism in the Reformation." In *Renaissance Studies in Honor of Hans Baron,* edited by Anthony Molho and John H. Tedeschi, pp. 643–62. Florence: Sansoni, 1971.

———. "The Philosophy of Conrad Celtis." *Studies in the Renaissance* 1 (1954): 22–37.

———. *The Religious Renaissance of the German Humanists.* Cambridge, Mass.: Harvard University Press, 1963.

Sponagel, Ludwig. *Konrad Celtis und das deutsche Nationalbewusstsein.* Bühl-Baden: Konkordia, 1939.

Stackelberg, Jürgen von. "Rousseau, d'Alembert et Diderot, traducteurs de Tacite." *Studi Francesi* 6 (1958): 395–407.

———. *Tacitus in der Romania: Studien zur literarischen Rezeption des Tacitus in Italien und Frankreich.* Tübingen: Max Niemeyer, 1960.

Stegmann, André. "Le Tacitisme: Programme pour un nouvel essai de définition." *Il Pensiero Politico* 2, no. 3 (1969): 445–58.

Strauss, David Friedrich. *Ulrich von Hutten.* 3 vols. Leipzig: F. A. Brockhaus, 1858–60. English translation by G. Sturge, *Ulrich von Hutten: His Life and Times.* London: Daldy, Isbister & Co., 1874.

Strauss, Gerald. "The Course of German History: The Lutheran Interpretation." In *Renaissance Studies in Honor of Hans Baron,* edited by Anthony Molho and John H. Tedeschi, pp. 663–86. Florence: Sansoni, 1971.

———. *Historian in an Age of Crisis: The Life and Work of Johannes Aventinus: 1477–1534*. Cambridge, Mass.: Harvard University Press, 1963.

———, ed. and trans. *Manifestations of Discontent in Germany on the Eve of the Reformation*. Bloomington: Indiana University Press, 1971.

———, ed. *Pre-Reformation Germany*. New York: Harper & Row, 1972.

———. *Sixteenth-Century Germany: Its Topography and Topographers*. Madison: University of Wisconsin Press, 1959.

———. "Topographical-Historical Method in Sixteenth Century German Scholarship." *Studies in the Renaissance* 5 (1958): 87–101.

Strauss, Leo. *Thoughts on Machiavelli*. Seattle: University of Washington Press, 1969.

Struever, Nancy S. *The Language of History in the Renaissance: Rhetoric and Historical Consciousness in Florentine Humanism*. Princeton: Princeton University Press, 1970.

Syme, Ronald. *Tacitus*. 2 vols. Oxford: Clarendon Press, 1958.

———. *Ten Studies in Tacitus*. Oxford: Clarendon Press, 1970.

Tagliacozzo, Giorgio, ed. *Giambattista Vico: An International Symposium*. Baltimore: Johns Hopkins University Press, 1969.

Tanner, J. R. *English Constitutional Conflicts of the Seventeenth Century: 1603–1689*. Cambridge: At the University Press, 1962.

Tenney, Mary Frances. "Tacitus in the Middle Ages and the Early Renaissance and in England to about the Year 1650." Ph.D. dissertation, Cornell University, 1931.

———. "Tacitus in the Politics of Early Stuart England," *Classical Journal* 37, no. 3 (1941): 151–63.

———. "Tacitus through the Centuries to the Age of Printing." *University of Colorado Studies* 22, no. 4 (1935): 341–63.

Tierno-Galván, E. *El Tacitismo en las doctrinas politicas del siglo de oro español*. In *Annales de la Universidad de Murcia,* Curso 1947/1948, pp. 895–975.

Timpe, Dieter. *Arminius-Studien*. Heidelberg: Carl Winter, 1970.

Toffanin, Giuseppe. *Machiavelli e il "Tacitismo," la "politica storica" al tempo della Controriforma*. Padua: A. Draghi, 1921.

Trevor-Roper, H. R. *Queen Elizabeth's First Historian: William Camden and the Beginnings of English Civil History*. London: Cape, 1971.

Ullman, Berthold L. *The Humanism of Coluccio Salutati*. Padua: Editrice Antenore, 1963.

———. "L. Bruni and Humanist Historiography." *Medievalia et Humanistica* 4 (1946): 44–65.

Valenti, Maria. *Saggio di una bibliografia delle edizioni di Tacito nel secolo XV–XVIII*. Rome: Edizioni de "L'Italia che scrive," 1951.

Valenti, Roberto. "Le invettive di Bartolomeo Facio contra Lorenzo Valla." *Atti della R. Accademia dei Lincei, Classe di scienze morali, storiche, e filologiche* 5th ser. 15 (1906): 493–550.

Varese, Claudio. *Traiano Boccalini*. Padua: Liviana Editrice, 1958.

Vervliet, Hendrik D. L. *Lipsius' Jeugd 1547–1578: Analecta voor een kritische Biografie. Mededelingen van de koninklijke Vlaamse Academie voor Wetenschappen, Letteren en Schone Kunsten van België, Klasse der Letteren,* 31, no. 7. Brussels: Palais der Academiën, 1969.

Viard, Paul Émile. *André Alciat: 1492–1550*. Paris: Société Anonyme du Recueil Sirey, 1926.

Vickers, Brian. *Francis Bacon and Renaissance Prose*. New York: Cambridge University Press, 1968.

Villari, Pasquale. *Niccolò Machiavelli e i suoi tempi*. Florence: Le Monnier, 1877–82.

Voigt, Georg. *Die Wiederbelebung des classischen Altertums: Oder, das erste Jahrhundert des Humanismus*. 2 vols. 3d ed. Berlin: Georg Reiner, 1893.

Waley, Daniel P. "The Primitivist Element in Machiavelli's Thought." *Journal of the History of Ideas* 31 (1970): 91–98.

Weiss, Roberto. *The Renaissance Discovery of Classical Antiquity*. Oxford: Basil Blackwell, 1969.

Welschinger, Henri. "Napoléon et Tacite." *Séances et travaux,* n.s. 81 (1914): 89–105.

Wilcox, Donald J. *The Development of Florentine Humanist Historiography in the Fifteenth Century*. Cambridge, Mass.: Harvard University Press, 1969.

Williams, Robert Haden, *Boccalini in Spain: A Study of His Influence on Prose Fiction of the Seventeenth Century*. Menasha, Wis.: George Banta, 1946.

Witt, Ronald. "Coluccio Salutati and the Origins of Florence." *Il Pensiero Politico* 2, no. 2 (1969): 161–72.

Zippel, G. *Giunte e correzioni al Giorgio Voigt's Il Risorgimento dell'antichità classica*. Florence: Sansoni, 1897.

Index of Names

Acciaiuoli, Angelo di Monte (bishop of Pozzuoli), 7
Acciaiuoli, Roberto, 185 n.53
Adam of Bremen, 5
Adams, John, 167
Adolf of Nassau, 186 n.17
Agathocles, 199 n.27
Agricola, 209 n.2
Agrippina the Elder, 122
Agrippina the Younger, 6, 19, 67, 176 n.20
Alamos de Barrientos, Baltasar, 16, 153–54
Alba, duke of (1507–82), 117–19, 135
Albert of Brandenburg, 41–43
Alberti, Leon Battista, 14, 25–26, 183 n.36
Albrecht the Wise (duke of Bavaria), 51
Albrecht V (duke of Bavaria), 55
Albucilla, 130
Alciato, Andrea, 15, 65, 84–94, 96–97, 99, 101–2, 106, 111–12, 119–20, 122, 129, 133, 195 n.40, 202 nn.48, 52, 203 nn.53, 54, 55, 204 nn.63, 64, 65, 205 nn.68, 71, 213 nn.53, 54, 220 n.3
Alciato, Francesco (cardinal), 128
Alexander VI (pope), 189 n.35
Alexander the Great, 46, 76, 144
Alfonso V (king of Aragon), 13, 27, 184 n.42
Althamer, Andreas, 47, 58, 101
Alvia de Castro, 153–54
Ambrose, Saint, 139
Amelot de la Houssaie, Nicolas, 157
Amerbach, Basil, 106
Amerbach, Boniface, 211 n.21
Ammanati, Giacomo Piccolomini (cardinal), 34
Ammirato, Scipione, 65, 142–45, 149, 152–53, 155–56, 165, 220 n.125
Anicetus, 6
Annius of Viterbo, 189 n.35
Antiquarius, Jacobus, 184 n.45
Aper, Marcus, 128, 202 n.52
Apollo, 44–45
Appian, 203 n.54
Appius Claudius the Decemvir, 78–80
Apuleius, 178 n.42
Aratus of Sicyon, 76
Arcimbaldo, Angelo, 12
Aretino, Ioannes, 184 n.42
Ariovistus, 41
Aristides, Aelius, 86
Aristotle, 16, 20, 25, 28, 33, 97–98, 105, 154–55, 160, 208 n.84, 219 n.125
Arminius, 12, 30, 41–42, 45–48, 191–92 n.61
Arruntius, Lucius, 130, 201 n.38
Ascham, Roger, 103
Atanagi da Cagli, Dionigi, 105
Atticus, 16
Augustine, Saint, 3, 16, 124, 132, 208 n.84
Augustus (emperor), 4, 12, 19, 22, 53, 95, 97, 142, 174 n.12, 203 n.52, 206 n.76
Aurelius. *See* Marcus Aurelius
Aventinus, Johannes, 32, 47–63, 119, 189 n.35, 192 n.65
Azzoguidi, Baldassare, 186 n.15

Bacon, Francis, 147, 158–63, 165–66, 230 nn.35, 39, 231 n.47, 232 n.61
Bandino d'Arezzo, Domenico, 7, 19–20, 180 n.11, 180–81 n.14
Barbaro, Francesco, 13

Barbarossa (pirate), 90, 204 n.66. *See also* Frederick I Barbarossa
Bardi, Bartolomeo d'Andrea de, 9
Baronio, Cesare (cardinal), 138
Bartolus of Sassoferreto, 202 n.48
Baudouin, François, 85–86, 104, 119, 202–3 nn.52, 54, 211 n.20
Baudouin, Jean, 156
Bautru des Matras, Jean, 116
Bebel, Heinrich, 63, 189 n.35, 195 n.43
Bellarmine, Robert (cardinal), 138
Bellenden, John, 104
Bembo, Pietro, 105, 107
Benci, Francesco, 101, 117, 138
Bentivoglio, Guido (cardinal), 151
Bernegger, Matthias, 155
Beroaldus, Philippus, 12–13, 15, 34, 42, 69, 78, 85, 87–88, 101, 195 n.40, 207 n.79
Berosus [Pseudo-Berosus]. *See* Annius of Viterbo
Bessarion, Johannes (cardinal), 13, 178 n.44
Bidernutio, Alphonso, 110
Biondo, Flavio, 14, 25, 103, 107, 185 n.4
Boccaccio, Giovanni, 5, 6, 7, 8, 19–20, 131, 175 n.18, 176 n.23, 180 n.9, 188 n.28
Boccalini, Aurelio, 226 n.73
Boccalini, Rodolfo, 226 n.73
Boccalini, Traiano, 145–49, 150, 157, 165, 226 n.74
Bodin, Jean, 109–16, 119–20, 122, 126–27, 129, 133, 143, 152, 156, 165, 213 n.42, 213 n.53, 214 n.65, 218 n.111, 220 n.3, 221 n.12
Boece, Hector, 103, 210 n.17
Boecler, Johann Heinrich, 155–56, 228 n.17
Boétie, Etienne de la, 120, 216–17 n.96
Bohemus, Johannes, 59
Bonciani, Francesco, 141
Boniface VIII, 19
Borgia, Cesare, 69, 73–74, 198 n.18
Borromeo, Charles, 124–25, 128
Borromeo, Federico (cardinal), 125
Bosch, Hieronymus, 31, 39, 188 n.32
Botero, Giovanni, 123–28, 134, 140, 142–43, 145–46, 149–52, 154, 214 n.65, 217 n.100, 218 nn.111, 114, 219–20 n.125
Boucher, Jonathan, 167–68
Bracellus, Jacobus, 203 n.53
Brant, Sebastian, 31, 59
Breton, Robert, 212 n.40
Briani, Girolamo, 150
Bruni, Leonardo, 7, 8, 13, 16–17, 19–22, 24–25, 38, 66, 68–70, 80–81, 101, 145, 150, 168, 179 nn.3, 4, 7, 181–82 n.22, 182 n.34, 207 n.79
Brutus, Marcus Junius, 19, 21–22, 91, 119
Buckingham, duke of. *See* Villiers, George
Budé, Guillaume, 85, 102, 112, 127–28, 202 n.48, 220 n.1, 220 n.3
Burgh, Thomas, 158

Caesar, Julius, 3, 19–23, 36–37, 41, 53, 67, 69–71, 87, 91, 106, 120, 173 n.1, 181–82 n.22, 184 n.44, 199 n.27, 200 n.37, 202 n.52, 203 n.54, 225 n.52
Cajetan, Cardinal (Tommes de Vio), 43–44
Caligula (emperor), 121–22
Calixtus III, 32
Calvin, John, 113, 131, 205 n.71
Camden, William, 104
Camerarius, Joachim, 117
Campano, Giovanni Antonio, 33–34
Canini d'Anghiari, Girolamo, 228 n.14
Capilupus (writer of compilations), 224 n.37
Cappel, Ange, 15
Capponi, Niccolò, 95–96
Carbo Papirius, 36
Carlo Emmanuele I (duke of Savoy), 123, 125
Carr, Robert, 162
Casaubon, Isaac, 135, 137
Cassiodorus, 4
Cassius, Gaius, 21–22, 119
Cassius Longinus, 36
Castiglione, Baldassare, 102, 209 n.6
Catherine of Aragon, 102
Catiline, 21
Cato the Elder, 53
Catullus, 112
Cecil, Robert, 158, 161, 229 n.30
Celtis, Conrad, 30–32, 34–39, 42, 46,

48–49, 50, 52, 57–60, 63–64, 101, 139, 186–87 n.17, 187 nn.19, 25, 188 nn.27, 28
Cerialis. *See* Petillius Cerialis
Cesarini, Giuliano (cardinal), 10
Charlemagne, 41, 53
Charles I (king of England), 160, 163–64, 210 n.14, 230 n.36
Charles II (king of England), 164–65
Charles III (king of Naples), 167
Charles V (emperor), 45, 48, 57, 61–62, 89–90, 96, 124, 204 n.66
Charles VIII (king of France), 29
Charron, Pierre, 131, 156
Cheke, John, 103
Chenier, André, 167
Cicero, 3, 16, 20–23, 86, 102, 105–7, 129, 144, 173 n.1, 183 n.41, 187 n.23, 197 n.10, 202 n.52, 209 n.6, 221 n.20
Clapmarius, Arnold, 65, 154–55
Claudius (emperor), 8, 119, 159
Claudius, Appius. *See* Appius Claudius
Claudius, Quintus. *See* Quadrigarius
Cleland, John, 160–61, 210 n.14
Clement VII (pope), 82, 96, 98, 207 n.79. *See also* Medici, Giulio de'
Cleomenes, 199 n.27
Cleopatra, 19
Cocceius Nerva (the jurist), 130
Coke, Edward, 162–63, 231 n.47
Coloma, Carlos, 153–54
Colombo, Cesare, 206–7 n.79
Colonna, Aegidius, 19
Commines, Philippe de, 221 n.20
Coornhert, Theodore, 137
Cortona, Cardinal of, 82
Corvini d'Arezzo, Giovanni, 13
Creussner, Frederick, 34
Cromwell, Oliver, 165
Cujas, Jacques, 103, 113
Cupid, 205 n.71
Curione, Caelio Secondo, 105–6, 114
Curtius, Quintus, 29, 87

Da Cagli, Dionigi Atanagi, 105
Dante Alighieri, 19–22, 83, 175 n.15
Dati, Giorgio, 15, 102, 140–55
d'Avalos, Alphonso, 89
Davanzati, Bernardo, 15, 140–42, 225 n.58
Decembrio, Angelo, 13–14
Decembrio, Pier Candido, 10–11, 13–14, 22–23, 25, 178 n.50, 182 n.24
Decius, Philipp, 111–12, 213 n.53
Della Casa, Giovanni, 124, 144, 218 n.114
Della Fonte, Bartolomeo, 183 n.40
Demogorgon, 39, 188 n.28
Desmoulins, Camille, 167
Deti, Giovan Battista (cardinal), 151
Devereux, Robert (earl of Essex), 158–59, 161, 229 n.29
Diderot, Denis, 167
Diether von Isenberg (archbishop), 186 n.17
Dietrich von Raitenau, Wolf, 125
Dio Cassius, 203 n.54
Diodorus Siculus, 86, 186 n.15, 203 n.54, 210 n.19
Dionysius of Halicarnassus, 203 n.54
Domitian (emperor), 4, 142, 174 n.12, 204 nn.59, 60
Dorislaus, Isaac, 163
Dorp, Martin, 209 n.2
Dürer, Albrecht, 37
Du Vair, Guillaume, 131

Eberbach, Peter, 40, 48
Eberlin von Günzburg, Johann, 15
Eck, Leonhard von (chancellor), 51
Edward VI (king of England), 103
Einhard, 5
Eliot, John, 163
Elizabeth I (queen of England), 103, 148–49, 157–59, 161–62, 229 n.30, 230 n.35
Elyot, Thomas, 102–3, 210 n.14
Ennius, 20
Enoch of Ascoli, 9–11, 14
Epicharis, 6–7, 130–31
Epictetus, 129, 138
Epicurus, 134
Eprius, Marcellus, 73
Erasmus, Desiderius, 31, 45, 48–49, 54, 63–64, 90, 102–3, 127, 131, 208–9 n.2
Ernst (son of Albrecht the Wise), 51
Essex, earl of. *See* Devereux, Robert

Estienne, Henri, 140
Euclid, 171
Eugenius IV (pope), 25

Fabius Pictor, Quintus, 20
Fauchet, Claude, 15, 119–20, 216 n.95, 225 n.52
Fazio, Bartolomeo, 27
Federigo da Montefeltro, 184 n.44
Ferdinand I (emperor), 62
Ferdinand of Aragon, 27
Fernandez de Heredia, Juan, 20
Ferretti, Aemilio, 15, 86, 101, 103, 195 n.40, 202 n.50
Flavius Vopiscus, 173 n.2
Florus, 190 n.45
Francis I (king of France), 62, 89–90, 96, 204 n.63
Franck, Sebastian, 58
Franklin, Benjamin, 167
Franz von Sickingen. *See* Sickingen, Franz von
Frederick I Barbarossa (emperor), 39
Frederick III (emperor), 10, 31–32, 188 n.32
Frederick the Wise (duke of Saxony), 47
Freinsheim, Johannes, 155
Froben, John, 45
Frontinus, Sextus Julius, 81, 207 n.79

Galba (emperor), 160, 198 n.14
Gambrivus, 41
Garimberto, Jerome (bishop of Gallese), 212 n.41
Gellius, Aulus, 20
Gentillet, Innocent, 126
Germanicus, Caesar, 122
Giannotti, Donato, 81, 201 n.39
Giles of Rome. *See* Colonna, Aegidius
Giovio, Paolo, 13, 105, 107, 111–12, 200 n.37, 203 n.53, 213 n.54
Gonzaga, Ferrante (governor of Milan), 89
Gracchus, Tiberius, 72
Gracián, Baltasar, 154, 157
Granvella, bishop of. *See* Perrenot, Antoine
Grebenstein, Heinrich von, 10, 11
Grenewey, Richard, 16, 155, 159, 229 n.32
Grotius, Hugo, 232 n.61
Gryphius, Sebastian, 15, 195 n.40
Guarino da Verona, 10, 14, 22–23, 179 n.4
Guibert of Nogent, 5
Guicciardini, Francesco, 29, 65, 94–99, 101, 106, 114, 116, 120–21, 124, 126, 127, 145, 206 nn.71, 74, 76, 78, 206–8 n.79, 208 n.83, 214 n.64, 217 n.97
Guicciardini, Luigi, 217 n.97
Guillomet (obscure translator of Tacitus), 15
Gutenberg, Johann, 186 n.17

Haddon, Walter, 103
Hadrian (emperor), 33
Hall, Edward, 210 n.10
Hannibal, 46, 144
Harrington, John, 159–61
Harrison, William, 104, 210 n.17
Hasilina of Cracow, 187 n.25
Hayward, John, 158–59, 230 n.35
Henry III (king of France), 123
Henry IV (king of England), 158
Henry VII (king of England), 210 n.11
Henry VIII (king of England), 210 n.11
Henry, duke of Guise, 132
Henry of Navarre, 132
Henry Stuart (son of James I), 159–61, 230 n.36
Herman the German. *See* Arminius
Hermiones, 41
Herodotus, 86, 144
Hessius, Eobanus, 40, 48
Hobbes, Thomas, 165
Hochstraten, Jakob von, 48
Holinshed, Raphael, 104, 210 n.17
Homer, 170, 216 n.96
Hooker, John, 210 n.17
Horace, 23
Hotman, François, 119–20
Hugo, Victor, 169
Hummelberg, Michael, 194 n.35
Hunter, Thomas, 168
Hutten, Hans von, 190 n.45
Hutten, Ulrich von, 12, 30, 32 39–49, 52, 57–58, 63–64, 101, 119, 189 nn.34, 36, 37, 190 nn.39, 45, 48, 191 n.54
Hyde, Edward (earl of Clarendon), 165

Ingevon, 41
Irenicus, Franciscus, 58–59
Italicus, Silicus, 209 n.6

James I (king of England), 146–49, 157, 159–63
James IV (king of Scotland), 210 n.11
Jefferson, Thomas, 167, 171
Jerome, Saint, 4, 105, 111–12, 175 n.18
Jesus Christ, 19, 41, 111–12
Johann Friedrich (duke of Saxony), 47
John of Salisbury, 5, 174, n.11, 199 n.21
Jonson, Ben, 159, 161, 229 n.24, 230 n.32
Jordanes, 5, 174 n.80
Josephus, 4
Judas Iscariot, 19
Julius II (pope), 41
Justin, 144

Krantz, Albert, 3

Laeto, Pomponeo, 85, 178 n.49
Lamola, Giovanni, 10
Lampugnanus, Pompeius (pseud.; attacker of J. Lipsius), 138, 224 n.42
Lando, Ortensio, 105, 210 n.19, 220 n.4
Latini, Latino, 101, 117
Laud, William (archbishop of Canterbury), 163, 231 n.49
Leander (describer of Italy mentioned by Patrizi), 212 n.40
Lefèvre d'Etaples, Jacques, 54
Leland, John, 210 n.10
Leo (jurist and minister of King Euric of the Visigoths), 174 n.8
Leo X (pope), 12, 14, 43, 68, 85
Leslie, John, 210 n.10
Linacre, Thomas, 102–3
Linguet, Simon, 168
Lipsius, Anna, 135, 223 n.27
Lipsius, Justus, 15, 61, 117–21, 126–27, 133–40, 145, 149, 152–53, 155–56, 165, 169, 177 n.39, 207 n.79, 215 nn.82, 85, 219 n.122, 222–23 n.25, 223 nn. 26, 27, 30, 31, 224 nn.37, 40, 42, 229–30 n.32
Livy, 3, 9, 20, 22–23, 27–29, 36, 69, 82–83, 86–87, 94, 97–98, 103, 105, 107, 115–17, 136, 148, 151, 173 n.1, 184 n.44, 197 n.12, 200–201 n.37, 202–3 n.52, 203 n.54, 207 n.79, 209 n.2, 211–12 n.33
Lottini, Gianfrancesco, 120
Louis XII (king of France), 38
Louis XIV (king of France), 157
Lucan, 20
Lucian, 7, 46, 105, 150
Ludwig of Bavaria (son of Albrecht the Wise), 51
Ludwig the Bavarian, 53
Luther, Martin, 43–45, 47, 49, 54, 56, 58, 64, 191 n.54,192 n.71
Lycurgus, 55

Machiavelli, Niccolò, 12–13, 25, 29, 51, 65–84, 91–95, 98, 100–101, 109, 114–16, 119–20, 122–26, 128, 142–46, 148–49, 152–55, 165, 191 n.60, 192 n.2, 196 n.1, 197 nn.6, 10, 11, 12, 198 nn.14, 18, 19, 198–99 n.20, 199 nn.21, 23, 25, 27, 28, 29, 199–200 n.31, 200 n.36, 200–201 n.37, 201 nn.39, 43, 202 n.46, 205 nn.70, 72, 214 n.65, 217 n.100, 219 n.125
Manelli, Giovanni Maria, 15
Mannus, 35, 41, 189 n.35
Manuzio, Aldo, 101
Manuzio, Paolo, 101, 117
Marcellus (jurisconsult), 220 n.3
Marcus Aurelius, 129
Margaret of Parma, 117
Marguerite de Valois, 123
Martin V (pope), 10
Mary of Burgundy, 51
Mascardi, Agostino, 151
Maternus, Curatius, 221 n.10
Maximilian I (emperor), 31–32, 35, 38–43, 45, 48, 51–52, 57, 66, 187–88 n.26
Maximilian II (emperor), 117
Maximinus (emperor), 71
Mayer, Martin (chancellor of Mainz), 11, 30, 32, 187 n.17
Medici family, 9, 66, 75, 92, 95–96, 98, 141, 199 n.23, 201 n.39
Medici, Alessandro de' (duke of Florence), 82, 98–99

Medici, Cosimo de' (the Elder), 13, 23–24, 82, 182 n.35
Medici, Cosimo I de' (duke of Florence; grand duke of Tuscany), 99, 105, 120–21, 141–42, 217 n.100
Medici, Ferdinando I de' (grand duke of Tuscany), 141–42
Medici, Francesco de' (grand duke of Tuscany), 142
Medici, Giovanni de', 12. *See also* Leo X (pope)
Medici, Giuliano de' (son of Lorenzo the Magnificent), 68, 69
Medici Giulio de', 82. *See also* Clement VII (pope)
Medici, Ippolito de' (cardinal), 82
Medici, Lorenzo de' (duke of Urbino), 68–70, 82
Medici, Lorenzo de' (the Magnificent), 68, 81–82, 92
Medici, Lorenzo di Pierfrancesco de' (Lorenzaccio), 99
Medici, Piero de', 68
Meginhard, 5
Mela, Pomponius, 20, 212 n.40
Melanchthon, Philip, 47, 58, 105, 117, 192 n.68
Mercury, 46
Messalina, 19
Messalla, Vipstanus, 221 n.10
Micyllus, Jacobus, 15, 102, 155
Milton, John, 164, 231 n.57
Minos (king of Crete), 46
Mirabeau, Honoré, 167
Montaigne, Michel de, 3, 120, 128–34, 137, 149, 156, 165, 208 n.83, 216–17 n.96, 221 nn.9, 10, 12, 15, 17, 20, 221–22 n.21, 222 nn.22, 23, 223–24 n.37
Montefalcone, Niccolò di, 6
Montesquieu, Charles, 167
Moravus, Augustinus, 35
More, Thomas, 93, 109, 213 n.42
Moses, 4
Münster, Sebastian, 59–60, 194 nn.31, 33
Muret, Marc-Antoine, 117, 121–22, 126, 128, 131, 133, 165, 217 n.98, 219 n.122

Napoleon I, 169
Napoleon III, 169
Naudé, Gabriel, 156–57, 228 n.19
Nepos, Cornelius, 20
Nero (emperor), 4, 20, 25, 26–27, 67, 72–73, 75, 121, 129, 164, 168, 176 n.20, 216 n.96, 220 n.1, 229 n.24
Nerva (emperor), 6, 88, 161
Newton, Isaac, 171
Niccoli, Niccolò, 8–11, 13, 23, 182 n.32
Nicholas V (pope), 9–10, 32
Nicholas of Cusa, 10
Nicodemo (intimate of Cosimo de' Medici the Elder), 182 n.35
Nitti, Francesco Saverio, 233–34 n.91
Nixon, Richard M., 172
Noah, 189 n.35

Oecolampadius, Johannes, 64
Oliari, Bartolommeo (cardinal), 181 n.15
O'Neill, Hugh (earl of Tyrone), 158
Origen, 61
Orosius, 3–4, 127, 173 n.4, 220 n.3
Ostorius Scapula the Younger, 130
Otho (emperor), 162
Otto of Freising, 5

Pagnini del Ventura, Giovan Francesco, 168
Panormita, Antonio, 10
Parrhasius, Aulo Giano, 85
Paschalius, Carlo, 122–23, 125–26, 136, 200 n.33, 223 n.31
Pasquali, Carlo. *See* Paschalius, Carlo
Pastrengo, Guglielmo da, 175 n.18
Paterculus. *See* Velleius Paterculus
Patrizi, Francesco, 107–10, 114, 151, 211 n.20, 213 n.42
Paul II (pope), 178 n.49
Paul III (pope), 120–21, 127, 213 n.54, 217 n.100
Paul V (pope) 146
Paulina, 129
Paulinus, Venetus, 5–7
Paxaea, 130
Perez, Antonio, 153
Pericles, 144

Perrenot, Antoine (bishop of Granvella), 117, 215 n.82
Perrot d'Ablancourt, Nicholas, 157
Peter of Blois, 5, 174 n.11
Peter the Deacon, 5, 11
Petillius Cerialis, Quintus, 120
Petrarch, 5–6, 16, 19, 21, 28, 175 n.18, 176 n.23, 187 n.23, 216 n.96
Petronius Arbiter, 14, 184 n.45
Petrus Episcopus of Cracow, 209 n.2
Peutinger, Conrad, 43, 189 n.35
Phaethon, 44–45
Philinus, 86
Philip II (king of Spain), 152–53
Philip III (king of Spain), 153
Philip V (king of Spain), 167
Philip the Handsome (archduke of Austria), 31
Philip of Macedon, 76
Pibrac, Guy de, 123
Piccolomini, Enea Silvio, 10–11, 30, 32–33, 37, 49, 185 n.4, 186–87 n.17, 194 n.26. *See also* Pius II (pope)
Pico della Mirandola, Giovanni, 54
Pictor, Fabius. *See* Fabius Pictor
Pirckheimer, Willibald, 59
Piso, Caius Calpurnius, 20, 75–76
Piso, Lucius Calpurnius, 20
Piso Licinianus, L. Calpurnius, 198 n.14
Pius II (pope), 10, 33, 107. *See also* Piccolomini, Enea Silvio
Pius V (pope), 117
Planche, Etienne de la, 15, 102, 155, 216 n.95, 225 n.52
Plantin, Christopher, 223 n.31
Plato, 145, 160, 166
Plautius Silvanus, 130
Plautus, 112
Pliny the Elder, 3, 37, 61, 81, 158, 207 n.79, 212 n.40
Pliny the Younger, 4, 14, 51, 53, 158, 174 n.8, 184 n.45, 220 n.1
Plutarch, 82–83, 108, 114, 128–30, 156, 203 n.54, 214 n.64, 216 n.96, 221 n.12
Poggio Bracciolini, Gian Francesco, 8–11, 13–14, 22–25, 66, 179 n.4, 182 nn.27 32, 183 n.41, 186 n.15, 207 n.79
Polemius, 4
Polentone, Sicco, 7–8, 26, 131
Politano, Agnolo, 85
Polybius, 82–83, 105, 107–8, 115–16, 203 n.54, 212 nn.33, 35, 36
Pompeia Paulina, 6
Pompey the Great, 23, 173 n.4, 203 n.52
Pomponius Labeo, 130
Pontano, Giovanni, 29, 110, 183 n.40, 185 n.52, 203 n.53, 211 n.20
Poppaea Sabina, 6, 19
Proximus. *See* Statius Proximus, Domitius
Prudentius, 61
Prynne, William, 164
Puteolanus, Franciscus, 14, 28, 87, 178 nn.49, 50, 184 n.45, 204 n.58

Quad, Matthias, 60
Quadrigarius, Quintus Claudius, 20
Quintilian, 105, 158
Quintius, Titus, 78–79

Rambaldi da Imola, Benvenuto, 7, 19, 21, 175 n.15, 180 n.9
Raynaldus, Abbot (Mediceus II manuscript signature), 175 n.14
Rhenanus, Beatus, 15, 32, 48–49, 61–65, 85, 87, 94, 101, 119, 133, 154, 189 n.35, 194 n.35, 195 nn.39, 40, 229 n.32
Ribadeneyra, Pedro, 150, 152, 154, 228 n.12
Richelieu, Cardinal, 156
Robortello Francesco, 105, 110, 211 n.20, 227 n.5
Romulus, 26, 148
Rubianus, Crotus, 40
Rucellai, the, 81–82
Rucellai, Bernardo, 29
Rucellai, Cosimino, 69
Rudolf of Fulda, 5
Rufus, Mutianus, 40

Saavedra Fajardo, Diego, 154
Sabellicus, Marcus, 34, 36, 107
Sabine (duchess of Württemberg), 190 n.48
Sadoleto, Jacopo, 89–90, 204 n.63
Sallust, 21, 27, 29, 87, 106–7, 118, 145, 185 n.52, 203 n.54, 211–12 n.33

Salmasius (pseudonym; pro-Stuart polemicist), 164
Salutati, Coluccio, 7, 9, 20–23, 27, 180–81 n.14, 181 n.17, 181–82 n.22, 199 n.21
Salviati, Lionardo, 141, 223 n.31
Sarpi, Paolo, 146
Sarzana, Gottardo de, 13
Savile, Henry, 16, 157–59, 229 nn.24, 29, 229–30 n.32
Saxe-Weimar, duke of, 135
Scaliger, Joseph Justus, 135, 137
Scaurus Aurelius, 36
Scaurus, Mamercus, 130
Scioppio, Gasparo, 151
Scipio Africanus, 46
Scoto, Annibale, 223 n.31
Sebaldus, Saint, 37
Sejanus, 159, 163
Selim I (the Grim), 43
Seneca, 7, 9, 19, 23, 26, 61, 97, 128–32, 138, 156, 158, 200 n.37, 203 n.55, 207 n.79, 208 n.84, 221 nn.9, 20
Severus, Sulpicius, 4, 175 n.18
Sextilia, 130
Sforza, Francesco I, 24, 182 n.35, 184 n.45
Sforza, Francesco II, 88
Sforza, Gian Galleazzo, 38
Sforza, Ludovico il Moro, 38
Sforza, Ludovico II, 89–90, 204 n.63
Sickingen, Franz von, 44, 48
Siculus, Diodorus. *See* Diodorus Siculus
Sidonius Apollinaris, 4, 174 n.7, 178 n.40
Sigismund III (king of Poland), 148
Silius Italicus, 102
Silvanus, Granius, 221 n.13
Silvanus, Gravius, 130
Sirleto, Guglielmo (cardinal), 128
Sixtus V (pope), 223 n.31
Soderini, Francesco (cardinal), 12, 82, 200 n.37
Soderini, Piero, 12, 96, 200 n.37, 202 n.46
Sol. *See* Apollo
Spalatin, George, 47, 58
Speroni, Sperone, 105, 227 n.5
Statius Proximus, 130
Stein, Eitelwolf von, 41–42
Strabo, 37, 212 n.40
Strada, Famiano, 150–51
Strada, Zanobi da. *See* Zanobi da Strada
Strafford, earl of. *See* Wentworth, Thomas
Sturm, Johannes, 195 n.37
Subrius Flavus, 164
Suetonius, 20, 114, 160, 190 n.45, 216–17 n.96, 220 n.1
Sueyro, Manuel, 16, 152–53, 155
Suleiman I (the Manificent), 62, 204 n.66
Sulla, 20–22

Tacitus, Claudius (emperor), 3, 53, 121, 127, 131, 173 n.2, 193 n.7
Tacitus, Gaius [Publius?] Cornelius (the man and his personal aspects), 18, 20, 28, 46, 53, 70, 83, 87–88, 106, 110, 118, 121, 127, 132–34, 145–46, 150–52, 155, 165–66, 168, 170–71, 173 n.4, 174 n.12, 175 n.18, 178 n.40, 179 n.7, 191–92 n.61, 203 n.58, 204 n.60, 208 n.83, 216 n.96, 220 nn.1, 3, 222 nn. 21, 23, 227 n.4, 228 n.12
Taylor, Jeremy, 165
Tertullian, 3–4, 61, 127, 138, 173 n.4, 220 n.3
Thucydides, 107, 114, 144, 171, 207 n.79, 210 n.19, 211–12 n.33
Thurzo (bishop of Olmutz), 40
Tiberius (emperor), 12, 80–81, 95–97, 118–19, 121–23, 125–26, 135, 142, 151, 159, 163, 204 n.60, 206 n.76, 219 n.125, 222 nn.21, 23
Timoleon of Corinth, 76
Titinius Capito, 174 n.8
Titus (emperor), 4, 70, 174 n.12, 175 n.18
Titus, Captain (anti-Cromwell fanatic), 164–65
Torelli of Fano, Lelio, 99
Torquatus, Manlius, 79
Trajan (emperor), 31, 53, 88, 142, 147, 161
Triaria, 6
Trilling, Lionel, 233 n.85
Trithemius, Johannes, 185 n.3
Trogus, Pompeius, 27, 29
Tuisco, 35, 41, 53–55, 189 n.35
Turnèbe, Adrien, 224 n.37

Ulpian, Domitius, 220 n.3

Ulrich (duke of Württemberg), 43, 190 n.48
Ussher, James (archbishop of Armagh), 164

Vadianus, Joachim, 40
Valentinian (emperor), 51–52, 85
Valerius Maximus, 136
Valla, Lorenzo, 14, 27, 85, 184 n.42, 216 n.96
Valois, Marguerite de. *See* Marguerite de Valois
Vannozzo, Francesco di, 179 n.2
Varchi, Benedetto, 105
Varus, 12, 36, 42, 45
Velleius Paterculus, 61, 106, 190 n.45
Venus, 7, 20, 180 n.12
Vergil, Polydore, 103–4, 107, 210 n.11
Vespasian (emperor), 8, 78, 80, 199 n.28
Vespasiano da Bisticci, 184 n.44
Vestinus Atticus, Marcus, 72
Vico, Giambattista, 165–67, 231 n.61
Vigenère, Blaise de, 15, 120, 140, 225 n.52
Villani, Filippo, 21
Villani, Giovanni, 21
Villiers, George (duke of Buckingham), 163–64
Vindelinus de Spira, 14, 28, 34, 178 n.49
Virgil, 3, 22–23, 102, 169, 173 n.1, 209 n.6
Virgilio, Marcello, 12–13, 200 n.37
Visconti, Bernabò, 21
Visconti, Filippo Maria, 22–24
Visconti, Giangaleazzo, 17–18, 21–23, 181–82 n.22
Vitellius (emperor), 68, 162
Vives, Juan Luis, 102–3, 209 n.2
Voltaire, 168
Vopiscus, Flavius. *See* Flavius Vopiscus

Wenceslaus (emperor), 21
Wentworth, Thomas (earl of Strafford), 163, 231 n.49
Widukind of Corvey, 5
Wilhelm IV (duke of Bavaria), 51, 55, 190 n.48
William of Malmesbury, 5
William of Orange, 117–18
Willichius, Iudochus, 101
Wimpfeling, Jakob, 58–59, 61, 185 n.5, 194 n.26

Xenophon, 207 n.79, 210 n.19

Zanobi da Strada, 7
Zarotus, Antonius, 14, 178 n.49
Zazius, Ulrich, 103, 202 n.48
Ziegler, Hieronymus, 55

Index of Ancient and Renaissance Citations and Quotations

Aesinus (codex), 9–11

Alamos de Barrientos, Baltasar, *Tácito Español ilustrado con aforismos* (translation of Tacitus), 16, 153

Alberti, Leon Battista, *De architectura*, 25, 183 n.36

Alciato, Andrea: *Annotationes in Cornelium Tacitum*, 65, 85, *86*, *87*, 88, 90, *91*, 93, 96, 97, *106*, 111, 112, 119, 203 n.53; *Annotationes in tres posteriores codicis libros*, 85; *Collectanea*, 85; *Contra vitam monasticam*, 90, 93; editions of Tacitus, 15, 85, 101; *Emblemata*, 90, *91*, 204 nn.64, 65, 66, 205 n.68; *Historiae encomium* (Preface to the *Annotationes in Cornelium Tacitum*, q.v.); letters, 90, 112, 202 n.47, 203 n.53, 204 n.63, 205 n.71, 213 n.54; *Oratio habita Ferrariae MDXLIII cum primum professurus illuc venit*, 89; *Rerum patriae libri*, 85

Althamer, Andreas: editions of Tacitus, 101; *Scholia in Cornelium Tacitum*, 47, 58

Alvia de Castro, *Verdadera razón de Estado*, 153

Amelot de la Houssaie, Nicolas, *La Morale de Tacite*, *157*

Ammirato, Scipione: *Discorsi sopra Cornelio Tacito*, 142, *143*, *144*, *145*, 153, 156; *History of Florence*, *144*

Annales Fuldensis, 5

Annius of Viterbo: *Auctores vetustissmi nuper in lucem editi*, 189 n.35; *Commentaria super opera diversorum auctorum de antiquitatibus*, 189 n.35

Aristotle: *Ethics*, 16; *Politics*, 16, 25

Atanagi da Cagli, Dionigi, *Ragionamento della eccelentia et perfezione de la istoria*, 105

Aventinus, Johannes, *52*; *Annales ducum Boioriae*, 52, 53, *54*, *55*, 56, 192 n.65; *Bayerische Chronik*, 52, *53*, *54*, *55*, 56, 57, 192 n.65; *Chronicle of all Germany*, 56; *Epitome* of the *Annales ducum Boioriae*, 52; *Haus-Kalendar*, *50*, *51*; "Imperatori Maximiliano Caesari Augusto," *51*, *52*, 192–93 n.4; *Ursachen des Turkenkrieges*, *56*, *57*

Bacon, Francis: *The Advancement of Learning*, 160; *Apophthegms New and Old*, *159*; *Briefe Discourse Touching the Happie Union of the Kingdoms of England and Scotland*, 159, 160, 161; *Of Colors of Good and Evil*, 230 n.35; *De augmentis scientiarum*, 160; *De sapientia vetorum*, 160; *Essays*, 160, 230 n.35; letters, *162*; *The Masculine Birth of Time*, *160*, 230 n.35; *The Misfortunes of Arthur*, 230 n.35; speeches, *161*

This index includes some post-Renaissance titles, but none later than 1800 A.D. Some of the titles are given in shortened form here. Check the notes for full bibliographical information. Page and note references in italics denote quotations; in such places there may *also* exist citations.

Bandino d'Arezzo, Domenico, *Fons memorabilium universi,* 19, *20,* 180–81 n.14

Baudouin, Francois, *De institutione historiae universae, 86,* 104, 203 n.54

Baudouin, Jean: translation of Scipione Ammirato's *Discorsi,* 156; translation of Tacitus, 156

Bebel, Heinrich, *De laudibus atque philosophia Germanorum,* 63, 195 n.45

Bentivoglio, Guido, *Memorie, 151*

Bernegger, Matthias, *J. Lipsii Politicorum libri ad disputandum propositi,* 155

Beroaldus, Philippus, Tacitus edition of 1515, 13, 14, 42, 69, 85, 87, *88,* 201 n.37, 207 n.79

Berosus. *See* Annius of Viterbo

Bessarion, Johannes, inventory of books, 178 n.44

Bible, 18, 57, 143, 154, 189 n.35, 219 n.125; Old Testament, 60, 192 nn.66, 72

Biondo, Flavio: *Decades de inclinatione Romani imperii,* 25, 26, 107; *Italia illustrata,* 25, 26; *Roma instaurata,* 25, 183 n.38; *Roma triumphans,* 26

Boccaccio, Giovanni: *Commento sopra la Commedia,* 7, 131; *De claris mulieribus, 6,* 7, 175 n.18; *Genealogiae deorum,* 7; letters, *6*

Boccalini, Traiano: letters, *147,* 157; *Osservazioni sopra Cornelio Tacito, 147, 148, 149; Ragguagli di Parnaso, 145, 146,* 147, 226 n.73

Bodin, Jean: *Methodus ad facilem historiarum cognitionem, 109, 110, 111, 114, 115, 116,* 119, 120, 122, 126, 127, 129, 213 n.42, 214 n.65, *220 n.3,* 221 n.12; *Oratio de instituenda in republica juventute,* 113; *Les Six Livres de la République,* 116, 120

Boece, Hector, *Scotorum historiae a prima gentis origine,* 104

Boecler, Johann Heinrich, *Bibliographia historico-politico-philologica,* 155

Boétie, Etienne de la, *Discours sur la servitude volontaire,* 120, *216–17 n.96*

Bohemus, Johannes, *Omnium gentium mores, leges et ritus,* 59

Botero, Giovanni: *Del dispregio del mundo,* 125; *Della Ragion di Stato,* 124, *125,* 126, 128, 142, 219–20 n.125; *De predicatione verbi Dei,* 125; *De regia sapientia,* 125, 126

Boucher, Jonathan, *A View of the Causes and Consequences of the Revolution,* 167, 168

Bracellus, Jacobus, *De bello Hispano,* 203 n.53

Brant, Sebastian: *Beschreibung etlicher Gelegenheit Teutscheslands,* 59; *Das Narrenschiff,* 31

Breton, Robert, *De optimo statu reipublicae liber,* 212 n.41

Briani, Girolamo, *Aggiunta ai Ragguagli di Parnaso,* 150

Bruni, Leonardo, 182 n.30; *Dialogus I,* 22; *Histories of the Florentine People,* 21, *38; Laudatio Florentinae urbis, 18,* 21, 22, 23, 69, 101, 181 n.18, 182 n.27; *On the Politeia of the Florentines,* 24

Budé, Guillaume: *Annotationes in Pandectas,* 85; *De asse et partibus eius, 220 n.1*

Caesar, Julius, 184 n.44; *De bello Gallico,* 67

Camden, William, *The Brittania,* 104

Campano, Giovanni Antonio: letters, *34,* 186 nn.11, 12; speech for Regensburg (1471), 33, 34

Canini d'Anghiari, Girolamo: edition of Tacitus, 228 n.14; translation of Alamos' *Tácito Español,* 228 n.14

Cappel, Ange, translation of Tacitus, 15

Cassiodorus, *Variae, 4*

Castiglione, Baldassare, *The Book of the Courtier,* 102, *209 n.6*

Cecil, Robert, letters, *158*

Celtis, Conrad, 101; "De nocte et oscula Hasilinae, Erotice," 187 n.25; edition of Tacitus, 34, 186 n.16; *Germania generalis,* 32, 37, 38, *39; Germania*

illustrata, 52, 56, 59; *Liber amorum*, 37, 38, *39*, 50; *Norimberga*, 37, 38, *39*, 50, 52; *Oratio in gymnasio in Ingelstadio publice recitata*, 34, *35*, *36*, *37*, 186–87 n.17
Charles I (king of England), *163*
Charron, Pierre, *Thresor de la Sagesse*, 156
Chenier, André, *167*
Cicero, Marcus Tullius, 129; *Brutus*, 106; *De amicitia*, 197 n.10; *De Oratore*, 173 n.1, *183 n.23*; *De provinciis consularibus*, 187 n.23; *Letters* (to Atticus, Brutus, and Quintus), 6, 16; *Second Oration against Catiline*, 21
Clapmarius, Arnold, *De arcanis rerum publicarum libri vi*, 65, 154, 155
Cleland, John, *Propaedia, or the Institution of a Young Nobleman*, 160, 210 n.14
Coloma, Carlos, translation of Tacitus, 153
Curione, Caelio Secondo: *De historia legenda sententia*, 106; letters, *105*, 211 n.21; translation of Guicciardini's *History of Italy*, 106

Dante: *Inferno*, 21; *Paradiso*, 175 n.14
Dati, Giorgio, translation of Tacitus, 15, 102, 140, 141, 155
Davanzati, Bernardo: translation of Tacitus, 15, *140*, 141, 142; *zibaldone*, *141*, 225 n.58
Decembrio, Pier Candido, *De laudibus Mediolanensium urbis panegyricus*, *22*
Della Casa, Giovanni: *Il Galateo*, 124; *Oration Concerning the Restitution of the City of Piacenza*, *124*, 218 n.114
Della Fonte, Bartolomeo, *Oratio in historiae laudatione*, 183 n.40
Diodorus Siculus, *Bibliotheca historiarum*, 186 n.15

Eberlin von Günzberg, Johann, translation of Tacitus, 15
Eliot, John, speech, 163
Elizabeth I (queen of England), *158*
Elyot, Thomas, *The Boke Named the Gouvernour*, 102
Epictetus, *Enchiridion*, 129
Erasmus, Desiderius: *De copia verborum*, 102; *De pueris statim ac liberaliter instituendis*, 209 n.2; *De ratione studii*, 209 n.2; *De scribendis epistolis*, 209 n.2; *Greek New Testament* (second edition), 45; *Institutio principis Christiani*, 209 n.2; letters, 48; *The Praise of Folly*, 31; *Spongia Erasmi adversus aspergines Hutteni*, 49
Estienne, Henri, *De la Préexcellence du langage françois*, 140

Fauchet, Claude: *Recueil des antiquitez gauloises et françoises*, *120*; translation of Tacitus, 15, *120*
Fazio, Bartolomeo, *De rebus gestis ab Alphonso primo Neapolitanorum rege*, 27
Ferretti, Aemilio, edition of Tacitus, 15
Flavius, Vopiscus, *Historia Augusta*, 173 n.2
Flores, moralium autoritatum (Verona manuscript), *174 n.12*
Franck, Sebastian, *Germaniae chronicon*, 58
Franklin, Benjamin, *Dogwood Papers*, 167
Freinsheim, Johannes, *Specimen paraphraseos Cornelianae*, 155
Frontinus, Sextus Julius, *De Aquaeductibus*, 207 n.79

Garimberto, Jerome: *Fatti memorabili d'alcuni Papi*, 212 n.41; *De regimenti publici de la città*, 212 n.41
Gentillet, Innocent, *Discours contre Machiavel*, 126
Giovio, Paolo: *Elogia doctorum virorum*, 178 n.41, 200 n.37; *Historiae sui temporis*, 213 n.54
Gracián, Baltasar, *Oráculo Manual*, 154, 157
Grenewey, Richard, translation of Tacitus, 16, 155, 159, *229 n.32*

Gryphius, Sebastian, edition of Tacitus, 15, 101

Guicciardini, Francesco: *Consolatoria*, 95; *Cose Fiorentine*, 97, *207 n.79*, 207–8 n.79; *Dialogo del reggimento di Firenze*, 94, 99, *124; Discorso del modo di ordinare il governo populare*, 94; *Discorso di assicurare lo stato alla casa de' Medici*, 94; *Discorso di Logrogno*, 94; *History of Italy*, *99*, 106, 107, 114; letters, *96*, 97, 206–7 n.79; *Oratio accusatoria*, 95, *97*, *127; Oratio defensoria*, 95; *Ricordi*, *95*, *96*, 97, *98*, 99, 101, 120, 121, 126, 206 nn.74, 78, 207 n.79, 208 n.83, 216 n.97; *Storie fiorentine dal 1378 al 1509*, 94

Guillomet, translation of Tacitus, 15

Harrison, William. *See* Holinshed, Raphael

Hayward, John, *First Part of the Life and Raigne of Henrie the IIII*, 158, 159, 230 n.35

Hersfeldensis (codex), 9, 10, 11, 12, 14, 28, 178 n.50

Hobbes, Thomas, *Leviathan*, 165

Holinshed, Raphael, *The Chronicles of England, Scotland, and Ireland*, 104, 210 n.17

Homer, *Iliad*, 170–71

Hotman, François, *Franco-Gallia*, 119

Hunter, Thomas, *Observations on Tacitus*, *168*

Hutten, Ulrich von, 101, 190 n.48; *Ad Caesarem Maximilianum epigrammata*, *41;* "Ad Caesarem Maximilianum ut bellum in Venetos coeptum prosequatur," 40; *Ad principes Germanos ut bellum Turcis inferant exhortatoria*, 43; *Arminius*, 12, 42, 45, *46*, 47; "De Caesare" (in the *Epigrammata*), *41;* "De magnitudine Maximiliani ad Germaniam" (in the *Epigrammata*), *41; De piscatura Venetorum*, 42; *Epistolae ad Maximilianum Caesarem Italiae fictitia*, 42; *Epistolae obscurorum virorum*, 43, 48; *Expostulatio*, 49; *Febris I*, 43; *Febris II*, 190 n.51; *In laudem reverendissimi Alberthi Archiepiscopi Moguntini panegyricus*, 42; *Inspicientes*, *44–45; Marcus*, 42; "Omnia Romae pecunia redimi," *42; Phalarismus*, 43; "Quod ab illa antiquitus Germanorum claritudine nondum degeneraverint nostrates," 189 n.34; "Quod Germania nec virtutibus nec ducibus ab primoribus de generaverit," *40*

Hyde, Edward, *History of the Rebellion and Civil Wars in England*, 165

Index of Forbidden Books, 138, 152

Irenicus, Franciscus, *Exegesis Germaniae*, 58

James I, *Basilikon Doron* or *Precepts on the Art of Governing*, 159, 160

Jerome, Saint, *Commentarii in Zachariam*, *4*

John of Salisbury: *De tyrannide*, 199 n.21; *Policraticus*, 174 n.11

Jonson, Ben, *Sejanus*, 159, 161

Jordanes, *De origine actibusque Getarum*, *5*

Krantz, Albert, *Saxonia*, *3*

Lampugnanus, Pompey (pseud.), *J. Lipsi in C. Corn. Tacitum notae cum manuscriptio cod. Mirandulano collatae*, 224 n.42

Lando, Ortensio, *La Sferza de' Scrittori*, 105, 210 n.19, 220 n.4

Linacre, Thomas, *De emendata structura latini sermonis libri sex* (*Grammar*), 102, 209 n.4

Linguet, Simon: *Annales politiques civiles et littéraires*, 168; *Histoire des révolutions de l'Empire romain*, *168*

Lipsius, Justus, *137*, *138; Admiranda, sive de magnitudine Romana*, 137; *De amphitheatro liber*, 136; *De constantia*, 136, 152; *De cruce*, 138; *Dispunctio notarum Mirandulani codicis ad Corn. Tacitum*, 224 n.42; *Diva*

Virgo Hallensis, 137; *Diva Virgo Sichemiensis,* 137; edition of Livy, book i, 136; editions of Tacitus, 15, 61, 119, 120, *135, 136,* 138, *139, 140,* 145, 152, 177 n.39; *Electorum liber primus,* 136; *Epistolica institutio,* 136; *Fax historica,* 137; letters (the *centuries*), *136, 137,* 139; *Louvanium,* 138; *Manuductio ad Stoicam philosophiam,* 137; *Monita et exempla politica libri duo, qui virtutes et vitia principum spectant, 140;* notes on Valerius Maximus, 136; *Oratio II: habita Jenae anno 1572 cum inciperet publice interpretari Cornelium Tacitum, 118, 119,* 126, 135, 223 n.30; *Physiologia Stoicorum,* 137; *Politicorum sive civilis doctrinae libri sex* (the *Politica*), 136, *137,* 138, 152, 153, *223 n.36,* 223–24 n.37; *Variae lectiones,* 117, 215 n.82

Livy, *History of Rome from Its Foundation,* 9, 203 n.52

Lottini, Gianfrancesco, *Avvedimenti civili,* 120

Lucian, *Dialogi mortuorum,* 46

Luther, Martin: *An Appeal to the Ruling Class of the German Nationality, 49; Commentary on Psalm 82, 47; Commentary on Psalm 101, 49; Against Hanswurst,* 191 n.54

Machiavelli, Niccolò: *Art of War,* 81; *Discorso sopra le cose della Magna e sopra l'Imperatore,* 66, 83; *Discourses on Florentine Affairs,* 81; *Discourses on Livy,* 12, 69, *70, 71, 72–73, 74–75, 76, 77–78, 79, 80,* 81, 83, 84, 101, 115, 119, 122, 143, 144, 191 n.60, 197 n.12, *198 n.20, 199 n.21, 199 n.27,* 200 n.36, 200–201 n.37, 201 n.43; *History of Florence, 81,* 82, 84, 115, 200 n.31, 201 nn.37, 38; letters 201 n.43, 202 n.46; *Life of Castruccio Castracani,* 81; *The Prince, 67, 68,* 69, *70,* 74, 79, 81, *84,* 101, 115, 197 n.12, 198–99 n.20, 200 n.37; *Rapporto delle cose della Magna,* 66, *67,* 83; *Ritratto delle cose della Magna,* 66, 67, 83, 192 n.2

Manelli, Giovanni Maria, translation of Tacitus, 15

Manuzio, Aldo, edition of Tacitus, 101

Marcus Aurelius, *Meditations,* 129

Mascardi, Agostino, *Arte istorica,* 151

Maximilian I, *The Dangers and Adventures of the Famous Hero and Knight Sir Teuerdank,* 51

Mayer, Martin, letters, *32*

Mediceus I (codex), 12, 13, 14, 78, 178 n.40, 200, 201 n.37, 202 n.50

Mediceus II (codex), 5, 7, 8, 9, 10, 13, 14, 18, 23, 25, 175 n.14, 176 n.25, 178 n.42, 202 n.50, 182 n.32

Medici, Alessandro de' (duke of Florence), *99*

Melanchthon, Philip: *Augsburg Confession,* 58, 135; *Ausgabe der "Germania," mit Vorwort und Beilage: Vocabula regionum enarrata et ad recentes appellationes accommodata,* 47, 192 n.68; Preface to part ii of Kaspar Hedio's *Ein auserlesene Chronik von Anfang der Welt, 58; Vocabula regionum et gentium quae recensentur in hoc libello Tacito,* 192 n.68

Micyllus, Jacobus, translation of Tacitus, 15, 102, 155

Milton, John, *231 n.57; Defense of the People of England,* 164

"Mirandulus" (codex), 224 n.42

Montaigne, Michel de, *Essays, 3, 128, 129, 130, 131, 132, 133, 134, 137,* 208 n.83, 221 nn.10, 12, 17, *20, 222 n.21, 223–24 n.37*

Montesquieu, Charles, *De l'Esprit des Lois,* 167

More, Thomas, *Utopia,* 93

Münster, Sebastian: *Cosmographia,* 59, *60,* 194 n.31; *Erklerung des newen Instruments der Sunnen, 59,* 194 n.31

Muret, Marc-Antoine, Orationes *(XIII, XIV, XV), 121, 122,*126

Naudé, Gabriel, *Bibliographia politica, 156, 228 n.19*

Niccoli, Niccolò, *Inventory*, 11

Nicodemo (friend of Cosimo de' Medici the Elder), letters, *24*

Orosius, *Historiae adversum Paganos*, 3, *173 n.4*

Otto of Freising, *The Deeds of Frederick Barbarossa*, 174 n.11

Pagnini del Ventura, Giovan Francesc(*Della Decima, e di varie altre gravezze imposte dal cumune di Firenze*, 168–69, *169*

Paschalius, Carlo, *Observations on the Annales of Tacitus*, *122*, *123*, 125, 136, 200 n.33, 223 n.31

Pastrengo, Guglielmo da, *De origine rerum*, 175 n.18

Patrizi, Francesco, *Dieci dialoghi della historia*, *107*, *108*, 109, *110*, *212 nn.35*, *36*

Paulinus Venetus: *Mappa mundi*, 5; *Satirica historia*, 6

Perrot d'Ablancourt, Nicholas, translation of Tacitus, *157*

Peter the Deacon, *Vita Sancti Severi*, 5

Petrarch: *Africa*, 19; *De gestis Cesaris*, 19, *181 nn.19*, *20;* "Italia Mia", *186 n.23*

Piccolomini, Enea Silvio: *Commentaries*, 185 n.4; *De ritu, situ, moribus et condicione Germaniae descriptio*, 32, *33*, 34, 186–87 n.17, 194 n.26; *Epitome* (of Biondo's *Decades*), 107; *Historia rerum ubique gestarum locorumque descriptio*, 185 n.4

Pirckheimer, Willibald, *Germaniae ex variis scriptoribus perbrevis explicatio*, 59

Planche, Etienne de la, translation of Tacitus, 15, 102, 155

Pliny the Elder: *Twenty Books on Germany*, 3; *Natural History*, 207 n.79

Pliny the Younger, *Letters*, 174 n.8, 184 n.45

Plutarch, 128; *Lives*, 108; *Moral Essays*, 129

Poggio Bracciolini, Gian Francesco: *Defensiuncula contra Guarinum Veronensem*, *23*, 182 n.27; *History of Florence*, 24, 207 n.79; letters, *8*, *9*, *10;* translation of Diodorus Siculus, 186 n.15

Polentone, Sicco, *Scriptorum illustrium latinae linguae libri xviii*, *8*, 26, 131

Pontano, Giovanni: *Actius*, *29*, 110, 183 n.40; *De bello Neopolitano*, 203 n.53

Puteolanus, Franciscus, editions of Tacitus, *28*, *86*, 184 nn.45, 46, *203 n.58*

Quad, *Matthias*, *Enchiridion cosmographicum*, 60

"Ragione di stato" (anonymous user of phrase, c. 1525), *124*, 218 n.113

Rambaldi da Imola, Benvenuto, *Commentum super Dantem Allegherii*, 19, *21*, *175 n.15*, *181 n.16*

Rhenanus, Beatus: edition of Tacitus, 15, *62*, *63*, *65*, 87, 101, 119; *Rerum Germanicarum libri tres*, *64*

Ribadeneyra, Pedro, *Religion and the Virtues of the Christian Prince against Machiavelli*, *152*, *228 n.12*

Robortello, Francesco, *De historia facultate*, 105

Rucellai, Bernardo, letters, *29*

Rudolf of Fulda, *Translatio Sancti Alexandri*, 5

Saavedra Fajardo, Diego, *Idea de un Principe christiano representada en cien Empresas*, 154

Sabellicus, Marcus, *Historiae rerum Venetarum ab urbe condita*, 36

Sallust, *Bellum Catilinae*, 21

"Salmasius" (pseud.), *Defense of the King*, 164

Salutati, Coluccio: *De tyranno*, 21, *22*, 181–82 n.22, 199 n.21; *Invectiva*, 181–82 n.22; letters, *20*

Salviati, Lionardo: *Discorso sopra le prime parole di Cornelio Tacito*, 225 n.54; edition of Giorgio Dati's translation of Tacitus, 141, 225 n.54

Sarzana, Gottardo de, letters, 178 n.43

Savile, Henry, translation of Tacitus, 16, 157, *158*, *229 n.24*, 229–30 n.32
Scaliger, Joseph, *De emendatione temporum*, 135
Scioppio, Gasparo, *Infamia Famiani*, 151
Scoto, Annibale, *In P.C. Taciti Annales et Historias Commentarii*, 223 n.31
Seneca, Lucius Annaeus, 128, 131; *Epistolae ad Lucillium*, 129, *203 n.55*, *208 n.84*; *Thebais*, *130*
Severus, Sulpicius, *Historiae sacrae*, 4
Sidonius Apollinaris: *Carmina*, *4*; *Epistolae*, 4
Soderini, Francesco, letters, *12*, *13*
Spalatin, George, *Von dem thewern Deudschen Fürsten Arminio*, 47
Spirensis edition of Tacitus, 34, 178 n.49
Strada, Famiano, *Prolusiones academicae*, *150–51*, *227 n.4*
Sturm, Johannes, *Beati Rhenani vita*, *61*
Suetonius, *The Twelve Caesars*, 206 n.76
Sueyro, Manuel, translation of Tacitus, 16, 152–53, 155

Tacitus, Cornelius: works in general, 3, 5, 14, 16, 20, 47, 61, 69, 87, 101, 102, 121, 141, 151, 152, 154, 165, 170, 177 n.29, 184 n.46, 208 n.79, 288 n.14; *Agricola*, 5, 9, 11, 14, 15, 16, 23, 28, 103, 104, *129*, *141*, *142*, *148*, 157, 161, 163, *168*, *169*, 174 n.10, 177 n.34, 178 nn.44, 49, 185 n.2, *187 n.24*, 203 nn.55, 57, 204 n.59, 210 n.17; *Annales*, 5, *6*, 7, 8, 12, 13, 14, 15, 16, 30, 42, 45, *46*, 52, *67*, *72*, *78*, *80*, 81, 86, *96*, 103, 104, 118, 119, 120, *122*, *123*, 129, *130*, 132, 133, *134*, 140, 141, 143, *144*, *147*, *148*, 155, 159, 164, 167, 168, 169, 173 n.5, 174 n.12, 178 n.40, *183 n.36*, 183–84 n.42, 190 n.45, 191 n.61, 199 n.24, 199–200 n.31, *200 n.34*, 200–201 n.37, 201 n.38, 202 n.52, *203 nn.52*, *55*, 57, *206 nn.76*, *79*, 207 n.79, 208 n.81, 217 n.98, *221 nn.13*, *20*, 221–22 n.21, 222 n.23, 225 n.52, 229 n.24, 233 n.91; *Dialogus de oratoribus*, 9, 11, 23, 105, 106, 128, 129, 178 n.44, 179 n.3, 185 n.52, 195 n.39, *202 n.52*, 203 n.57, *209 n.2*, 221 n.10, 229 n.32; *Germania*, 5, 9, 11, 15, 16, 30, *32*, 33, 34, *35*, *36*, *37*, 40, 42, *44*, 45, 46, 47, 49, 50, 52, *54*, *55*, 57, 58, 60, 61, *62*, 63, 64, 66, 83, 103, 104, *132*, *139*, 159, 168, 170, 171, 178 n.44, 186 n.15, 188 nn.27, *28*, *29*, *30*, *31*, 189 nn.35, *36*, 37, 189–90 n.*38*, *190 n.39*, 190–91 nn.53, 54, *55*, 56, *57*, *58*, 193 nn.9, 10, 11, 12, 203 n.57, *224 n.44*, 225 n.52; *Historiae*, 3, 4, 5, 7, 8, 13, 15, 16, *17*, *68*, 69, *70*, *71*, *73*, *77*, 79, 120, 132, 140, 143, *147*, 157, *160*, *162*, *167*, 173 n.5, 178 n.42, 179 n.7, 182 n.28, *183 n.36*, 184 n.42, 185 n.52, 198 n.14, 199 n.28, 203 n.57, 204 n.58, 208 n.1, *216 n.96*, *221 n.17*, 221–22 n.21, *234 n.91*
Taylor, Jeremy, *A Rule of Conscience*, 165
Tertullian, *Apologia*, *3*
Thucydides, *Peloponnesian War*, 144
Titus, Captain, *Killing No murder*, 164
Tuscan translator (anonymous), translation of Tacitus, 15

Ussher, James, *The Power communicated by God to the Prince, and the Obedience required by the Subject*, 164

Valla, Lorenzo: *De rebus a Ferdinando Aragoniae Rege gestis*, 27; *Disputatio ad Alphonsum*, 184 n.43; *Elegantiae linguae latinae*, 27; *Epistolae familiares*, 184 n.42; *Recriminations against Fazio*, 27, 183–84 n.42
Vannozzo, Francesco di, sonnets, *17*
Varchi, Benedetto, *Storia Fiorentina*, 105
Vergil, Polydore: *Anglica historia*, 103, 104, 107; *De inventoribus rerum*, 210 n.11
Vespasiano da Bisticci, *Lives of Illustrious Men*, *184 n.44*

Vico, Giambattista: *Autobiography, 166; Scienza Nuova,* 166
Vigenère, Blaise de: translation of Caesar's *Gallic Wars,* 120; translation of Tacitus, 15, 120, 140
Villani, Filippo, *De origine civitatis Florentiae,* 21
Villani, Giovanni, *Cronica,* 21
Vita, Henrici IV, 5
Vives, Juan Luis: *De institutione feminae Christianae,* 209 n.2; *Liber de disciplinis,* 102, 209 n.2
Voltaire, *Le Pyrrhonisme de l'Histoire, 168*

Willichius, Iudochus, edition of Tacitus, 101
Wimpfeling, Jakob: *Epitoma rerum Germanicarum usque ad nostra tempora,* 58; *Responsa et replice ad Eneam Silvium ad salutem et decorem sacrosancti imperii Romani amore patriae Germanicaeque nacionis,* 185 n.5, 194 n.26

Index of Subjects

Absolutism, 155. *See also* Tyranny
Actium, Battle of, 17, 111
Agnadello, Battle of (1509), 144
Alps, 29, 36, 125, 187 n.23
Alterati, Academy of the, 140–42, 144
America, United States of, 167–68, 170–72, 205 n.68, 234 n.91
Anabaptists, 64. *See also* Reformers
Anghiari, Battle of (1440), 24
Antiquarianism, 25–26, 87, 178 n.49, 210 n.11
Arcana imperii. *See* Secrets of state
Arminius, Cult of, 12, 47
Ars historiae, 27, 107, 202 n.51, 211 n.22. *See also* Historiography
Assassination, 21–22, 72–81, 146–47, 164–65, 199 n.21. *See also* Conspiracy
Augsburg, Diet of: of 1500, 31, 38; of 1518, 43–44; of 1530, 58, 62, 135
Avignon, 88, 90, 205 n.71. *See also* University of Avignon

Barbarians. *See* Germans (ancient)
Basel, 45, 48–49, 61, 105; Treaty of (1499), 38
Bavaria, Bavarians, 50–53, 55
Bohemia, Bohemians, 31, 35
Bologna, 17, 41, 43, 178 n.44. *See also* University of Bologna
Britons, British, 5, 103–4, 168, 187 n.24, 202 n.52
Brussels, 48; Treaty of (1516), 51

Calvinists, 113, 136–37, *See also* Reformers
Cambrai, League of. *See* War of the League of Cambrai
Campania, the, 5, 6, 71
Capponi regime (Florence), 95–96
Catholics, Catholic Church, 12, 30, 54, 56–57, 62, 64, 113, 116–17, 125, 132, 135–36, 143–44, 218 n.115, 223 n.27
Christians, Christianity, 56, 62–64, 111, 122, 124, 126, 128, 131, 137–38, 143, 222 n.25, 228 n.12; early, 3–4, 122, 126–28, 131, 173 n.1, 209 n.2, 220 nn.1, 3, 228 n.12
Ciceronianism, Ciceronians. *See* Style, Ciceronian
Classics, classical authors in general, 4, 8–9, 16, 23, 26, 40, 42, 50, 61, 64, 69, 82, 84–86, 93, 97–98, 105, 112, 119, 129, 131–32, 138, 145, 156, 159, 166, 169–70, 172, 176 n.23, 184 n.44, 189 n.35, 203 n.55, 207 n.79, 208 n.84, 210 n.19, 215 n.82, 220 n.4; discovery of, 5–6, 8–12, 16, 69, 174–75 n.13, 175 n.18, 177 n.36, 180–81 n.14, 183 n.41, 200–201 n.37; survival of, 3–5, 173 n.1
Cologne, 186 n.17. *See also* University of Cologne
Comitatus, 46
Conspiracy, sedition, 21, 72–82, 86, 160, 164, 199 n.25, 201 n.39, 211 n.32. *See also* Assassination
Constance: Council of (1414–17), 32; Diet of, (1507), 51
Constitutions, 24, 38, 92, 94, 113, 115, 120, 155, 167
Council: of Basel (1431–48), 32; of Constance (1414–17), 32; of the Hundred

(Florence), 68; of the Seventy (Florence), 68

Dacia, Dacians, 35–36
Denmark, Danes, 10, 35
Diet: of Augsburg (1500), 31, 38; of Augsburg (1518), 43; of Augsburg (1530), 62; of Constance (1507), 51; of Nuremberg (1501), 38; of Worms (1495), 31
Discretion, 98. *See also* Prudence
Dornach, Battle of, (1499), 38
Drunkenness, 44, 52, 63, 191 n.54, 192 n.72
Dutch, 136, 138, 163

Elegance. *See* Rhetoric
Eloquence. *See* Rhetoric
Emblema, emblemata, 90, 91, 204 nn.64, 66, 205 n.68
Empire: Holy Roman, 18–19, 35, 38–39, 48, 51, 56, 57, 145; Roman, 18–19, 22, 35–37, 53, 69–80, 86, 116, 120, 122, 129, 143, 158, 169–70, 179 n.7, 182 n.30. *See also* Rome, ancient
Enlightenment, the, 165–69, 217 n.96
Estates, German, 38, 51, 155, 188 n.26
Examples, exempla, 87, 106, 114, 131, 137, 140, 143

Fathers, Church, 3–4, 18, 138
Ferrara, 22, 43, 89. *See also* University of Ferrara
Five Good Emperors, 70, 76
Flavians (Flavian emperors), 70, 87. *See also* Index of Names
Florence, Florentines, 6–7, 12–13, 16–25, 51, 66, 68–69, 81–82, 92–99, 115, 120, 140–42, 145, 181–82 n.22, 182 n.30, 200 n.37, 201 n.38, 207 n.79
Formulary of June, 1562 (France), 116
Fortune (*Fortuna*), Fate, 3, 32, 57, 67, 73, 76, 83–84, 95–99, 125, 138, 142, 166, 170
France, the French, 5, 15, 31, 38, 40–42, 48, 51, 66, 69, 84–85, 87–88, 92, 103–4, 113, 115–17, 119–20, 122–23, 125, 131–32, 134, 140–41, 145, 152, 156–57, 165, 167, 169, 187 n.25, 223 n.31
French invasions of 1494, 66, 84–85, 87–88, 92

Gaul, Gauls, 35–36, 119–20, 159, 187 n.23
Geneva, 113, 135
Germans, Germany (ancient), 3, 12, 30–67, 120, 131, 139, 170–71, 187 n.23, 188 n.28, 189 nn.35, 36, 195 n.43; of the Alemanni, 62; of the Bastarnae, 35; of the Boii, 35; of the Chatti, 46; of the Chauci, 46; of the Cimbri, 41; of the Marcomanni, 35; of the Peucini, 35; of the Quadi, 35; of the Saxons, 5; of the Visigoths, 174 n.8
Germans, Germany (Renaissance), 3–5, 9–15, 25, 30–67, 82, 94, 101–4, 139, 151, 154–56, 165, 186–87 n.17, 187 n.19, 189 n.35, 190 n.48, 191 n.54, 192 n.72
Germans, Germany (modern), 169–71. *See also* Nazis
God, 18, 19, 21, 41, 53–57, 121, 125, 130, 132, 152, 166, 192 n.66, 215 n.85
Gods: Germanic, 33, 42, 55, 188 n.28; Greek and Roman, 39, 105, 132, 189 n.38. *See also* Index of Names
Golden Age, 32, 37–38, 58, 60, 70, 83, 194 n.33
Golden Sentence (of Tacitus), 72–81
Grammar, grammarians, 9, 27, 29, 86, 102, 111, 113, 151, 157
Greeks, ancient, 36, 39, 86, 144, 170, 203 n.54, 208 n.84

Handwriting, 9, 12
Heresy, heretics, 54–55, 57, 116–17, 119
Historians, 3, 13–14, 20, 22, 26, 28–29, 33, 36 42, 47–48, 50, 52, 59–60, 69–70, 86–87, 91, 93–94, 103–8, 110–11, 114–15, 138, 143, 146, 150–53, 157–59, 169–71, 173 n.4, 194 n.33, 203 nn.52, 54, 209 n.2, 210 n.16, 211 n.22, 211–12 n.33, 220 n.3, 228 n.12

Historiography, 17–18, 20–21, 25–27, 29, 38, 47–48, 52, 60–61, 65, 81, 83, 86, 88, 97, 107–10, 112, 146, 150–52, 170–71, 174 nn.8, 12, 183 n.41, 184 n.42, 189 n.35, 212 n.36, 219 n.121, 220 n.3. See also *Ars historiae*
History, histories (in general), 18, 20, 26, 29, 52, 59, 62, 69, 71–72, 84–87, 106–10, 112–14, 116, 123, 130, 133, 135, 139–40, 142, 144, 150, 153, 155–60, 163, 166–68, 174 n.8, 179 n.7, 183 n.40, 209 n.2, 211 n.28, 219 n.121, 227 n.4, 228 n.19
Humanism, humanists, 3, 9, 13, 14, 16, 18, 23, 32–33, 35, 38–40, 43, 47–48, 51, 58–60, 69, 92–93, 102–5, 113–14, 131–32, 139–40, 145, 152, 165, 179 n.6, 181 n.22, 183 n.41, 187 n.19, 189 n.35, 194 n.19, 197 n.10
Hungary, Hungarians, 31
Huns, 139

Inquisition, 118–19, 138, 152
Interdict Controversy, 146
Italy, Italians, 5, 11, 12, 14–15, 19, 25, 29, 32, 34, 37–38, 42, 44, 63, 65–66, 69–71, 73, 81, 84–85, 88, 90, 94, 96, 98–105, 115, 120, 125, 132, 140–41, 144–48, 151, 154, 165–69, 187 nn.23, 25, 205 n.71, 212 n.40, 234 n.91

Jesuits, 138, 150–52, 154
Jews, 4, 25, 29, 57, 173 n.1, 220 n.3, 229 n.24
Judgment, 106, 116, 118, 121, 127, 132–33, 137, 168, 222 n.22

Law, jurisprudence, 3, 16, 20–21, 24, 33, 53, 65, 85–86, 88, 91, 93–94, 102–6, 108–14, 116, 118, 126–29, 131, 134–35, 152, 154–55, 161, 166–68, 174 n.8, 195 n.43, 202 n.48, 203 nn.52, 54, 204 n.60, 220 n.3, 231 n.57, 232 n.61
Leipzig, 117; Debates (1519), 45
Library, librarian, 5, 131, 155–56, 172, 174 n.12, 174 nn.15, 18; of San Marco (Florence), 13, 23–25; of San Marco (Venice), 34; of the University of Louvain, 132; of the Vatican, 128. *See also* Monasteries
Lombardy, 35, 42
Louvain, 117, 135–36. *See also* University of Louvain
Low Countries, 117–19, 152. *See also* Revolt of the Netherlands Lutherans. *See* Reformers

Machiavellians, 73, 83, 123, 144, 219 nn.121, 122
Mainz, 32, 42, 48, 186 n.17. *See also* University of Mainz
Manuscripts, 3, 5–11, 13–14, 18–20, 23, 28, 34, 64, 136, 173 n.1, 174 n.12, 175 nn.14, 15, 178 nn.47, 49, 182 n.32, 200 n.37. *See also* Index of Quotations and Citations: codices Aesinus Hersfeldensis, Mediceus I, Mediceus II, ''Mirandulanus''
Maxims. *See Sententiae*
Middle Ages, medieval, 3, 14, 18, 26, 28, 90, 140, 169, 174 n.12, 188 n.28, 189 n.35
Milan, Milanese, 13, 17, 22, 24, 38, 51, 84–85, 88–89, 92–93, 96, 124–25, 153, 181 n.22, 205 n.31
''Minor Works'' of Tacitus, 9–12, 14, 23, 177 n.29. *See also* Index of Quotations and Citations: *Agricola, Dialogus, Germania*
Monarchy, 66, 68–72, 76–80, 83, 91–92, 109–11, 114–16, 119–21, 148, 163–67, 179 n.7, 181–82 n.22
Monastery: of Corvey, 12; of Fulda, 5, 11; of Hersfeld 9–10 (*see also* Hersfeldensis [codex]); of Monte Cassino, 5–7, 175 n.15; of San Marco (Florence), 13, 23–25; of Wolfenbüttel, 13
Mos: gallicus, 103, 112–14, 202 n.48; *italicus,* 202 n.48

Naples, 6–7, 14, 99, 167
Nazis, 170–71. *See also* Germans, Germany (modern)
Netherlands. *See* Low Countries
Novara, Battle of (1513), 69

Nuremberg: Diet of (1501), 38; Peace of (1532), 58

Orators, 20, 105, 107, 128. *See also* Rhetoric
Orti Oricellari, 69, 80, 142

Padua, 40, 181 n.22. *See also* University of Padua
Papacy, 3, 10, 11, 18–19, 26, 30–34, 37, 41, 43, 48, 55, 63, 118, 120, 126, 135, 138, 145–46, 163, 213 n.54
Paris, 125–26. *See also* University of Paris
Parlement: of Paris, 113, 116, 198 n.20; of Toulouse, 113
Parliament (English), 159, 161–65; Long, 164
Patria, patriae, 21, 73, 74, 76–77. *See also* Republics
Patriotism, 30, 32, 41, 48, 50, 52, 57, 59, 61, 63, 146, 189 n.35
Pavia, 41; Battle of (1525), 88. *See also* University of Pavia
Philology, philologian, 14–15, 21, 27, 34, 60–61, 65, 85, 88, 93, 101, 105, 112, 121, 135–39, 215 n.82, 224 n.44
Philosophy, philosopher, 12, 16, 86, 103, 105, 107–8, 110, 113, 115–16, 119, 121, 123–24, 129–32, 144–45 147, 151, 155, 157–58, 163, 165–66, 169, 179 n.7, 195 n.43, 208 n.84, 222 n.25, 229 n.32, 231 n.47
Piacenza, 124
Pisa, 17, 124. *See also* University of Pisa
Poet, poetry, 9, 29, 32, 43, 50–51, 63, 90, 107, 142, 187 n.19, 188 n.27
Poland, Poles, 31, 35
Pozzuoli (Puteoli), 5, 7, 27, 184 n.42
Princes, 31–32, 34, 38, 40, 46, 48, 62, 64–65, 67, 72–78, 87, 89–91, 100, 106, 108, 111, 114, 119, 121–22, 125, 137, 144–48, 152, 154–58, 160, 208 n.83
Printing, 14–16, 28, 34, 41, 45, 106, 186–87 n.17, 213 n.54, 223 n.31, 224 n.37, 226 n.73
Protestants. *See* Reformers
Prudence, 65, 88, 106, 121, 123, 154–56, 199 n.21, 223 n.36. *See also* Discretion
Puritans, English, 163–65
Pyrrhonism, 131–32

Race, racism, 39, 170–71, 188 nn.28, 29
Ragion di stato (reason of state), 65, 111, 124–26, 142–44, 152, 156, 166, 218 n.114, 219 nn.121, 125
Reformers, Reformation, 3, 11, 12, 30, 45–46, 55–59, 62–64, 105, 113, 117, 132, 135–36
Reichsregiment, 38
Republic: of Florence, 66, 68, 81–82; of Rome, 18–19, 21, 69, 76, 78–79, 86, 91, 143, 148, 179 n.7; Soderini, 25, 66, 200 n.37, 205 n.72; of Venice, 14, 17, 19, 24, 34, 40–42, 51, 99–100, 107–8, 115, 145–47, 149, 178 n.44, 212 n.36, 215 n.80, 226 n.73
Republics, republicanism, 13–14, 16–20, 23–24, 69–74, 76–80, 82–83, 87, 91–93, 100–101, 108–10, 115–16, 119, 122, 148, 166–69, 181–82 n.22, 199 n.25, 218 n.104
Restoration (Stuart), 164–65
Revolt of the Netherlands, 117–19, 136–38, 163, 215 n.82. *See also* Low Countries
Revolution, 38, 82, 87–88, 92, 98, 120, 153, 158, 164, 167–69, 171, 181 n.22, 199 n.28, 215 n.82; Glorious, 165
Rhetoric, 17, 20, 23, 26–28, 38, 85–87, 102, 105–6, 111, 128–29, 150–51, 158, 183 n.40, 202–3 n.52, 212 n.33, 221 n.10
Rome, Romans (ancient), 12, 16, 17, 25–26, 36–37, 52, 70–73, 76–81, 86, 96, 98, 112, 116, 120, 123, 125, 129, 137, 142, 148–49, 164, 170–72, 182 n.22, 203 nn.52, 54, 209 n.2, 216 n.96. *See also* Empire, Roman; Republic of Rome
Rome, Romans (Renaissance), 10, 11–14, 25–26, 40, 42, 48, 120–21, 128, 146, 151–52. *See also* Sack of Rome
Rucellai Gardens. *See* Orti Oricellari

Sack of Rome (1527), 64
Sarmatia, Sarmatians, 35–36, 188 n.29
Savoy, 3, 43, 55
Schlettstadt, 48, 61
Schmalkaldic League, 58
Scholarship, 25–26, 58–60, 88, 135–40, 169–70, 202 n.38
Scholastics, 16, 28, 54, 98
Secrets of state, 109, 114, 122, 146, 148, 150
Senate, Roman, 13, 27, 87, 111, 115, 159, 201 n.38, 222 n.21
Sententia, sententiae, 120, 123, 133, 151–57, 160, 166, 184 n.49, 217 n.101, 223 n.36
Simulation, dissimulation. *See* Prudence
Sodalities, 39
Soderini Republic. *See* Republic, Soderini
Spain, Spanish, 16, 68, 96, 102, 115, 117, 118, 123, 138, 143, 146, 147, 149, 152, 163, 187 n.25
Stoicism, Stoics, 122, 128–32, 137–38, 152, 156, 203 n.55, 222 n.25
Style, 16, 20, 29, 86, 107, 116, 145, 188 n.27, 209 n.2, 221 nn.9, 11, 223 n.31, 229 n.24; Ciceronian, 26–29, 87, 102–3, 105–7, 110–12, 117, 128, 141, 151, 213 n.53, 215 n.82, 229 n.32; Tacitan, 12, 26–29, 87, 91, 102, 105, 111–12, 118, 122, 128–29, 140, 151, 158, 160, 183 n.41, 203 n.53

Tacitism, Tacitists, 150–51, 165–66, 219 nn.121, 122
Theology, 43, 45, 55, 58, 64, 105, 113, 127, 138, 146, 166
Toulouse. *See* Parlement of Toulouse; University of Toulouse
Turks, 26, 31, 33, 38, 40, 43, 56–57, 62, 65, 90, 194 n.19
Tyranny, 16–18, 21–22, 38, 68, 74–77, 87–88, 95–98, 118–19, 120–21, 126, 141, 146–47, 148–49, 156, 158, 164, 167, 169, 171, 181–82 n.22, 199 n.21, 206 n.78, 208 nn.83, 84, 217 n.96, 228 n.17; Eleven Years', 164, 231 n.49

University: of Aberdeen, 103; of Altdorf, 64; of Avignon, 90, 202 n.48, 204 n.63; of Bologna, 85, 204 n.63; of Bourges, 90, 204 n.63; of Cambridge, 163; of Cologne, 43; of Cracow, 50; of Ferrara, 89; of Ingolstadt, 34–35, 55, 187 n.19; of Jena, 117, 135, 136; of Louvain, 135, 136, 137; of Mainz, 42; of Padua, 107, 151; of Paris, 50, 54, 103; of Pavia, 85, 90, 99; of Pisa, 208 n.88; of Rome, 121, 128, 133, 150, 151; of Strassburg, 155; of Toulouse, 112–13, 129; of Vienna, 32–50
Urbino, 69
Usury, 39

Venice. *See* Republic
Ventoux, Mount, 16
Verona, 51
Vesuvius, Mount, 29
Vienna, 39, 40, 56, 57, 90; Siege of (1529), 56, 57, 90. *See also* University of Vienna
Virtue, 19, 26, 28, 40, 48, 71, 76, 79, 84, 85, 142, 147, 156, 209 n.2

War: Civil (English), 164–65; of the League of Cambrai, 40–43; of the League of Cognac, 95–98; Peasants', 64; of Religion (France), 129 (*see also* Revolt of the Netherlands); Thirty Years', 155

Zwinglians, 105. *See also* Reformers